Religions in Movement

There has long been a debate about implications of globalisation for the survival of the world of sovereign nation-states, and the role of nationalism as both an agent of and a response to globalisation. In contrast, until recently there has been much less debate about the fate of religion. "Globalisation" has been viewed as part of the rationalization process, which has already relegated religion to the dustbin of history, just as it threatens the nation, as the world moves toward a cosmopolitan ethics and politics. The chapters in this book, however, make the case for the salience and resilience of religion, often in conjunction with nationalism, in the contemporary world in several ways.

This book highlights the diverse ways in which religions first and foremost make use of the traditional power and communication channels available to them, like strategies of conversion, the preservation of traditional value systems, and the intertwining of religious and political power. Nevertheless, challenged by a more culturally and religiously diversified societies and by the growth of new religious sects, contemporary religions are also forced to let go of these well-known strategies of preservation and formulate new ways of establishing their position in local contexts. This collection of essays by established and emerging scholars brings together theory-driven and empirically based research and case studies about the global and bottom-up strategies of religions and religious traditions in Europe and beyond to rethink their positions in their local communities and in the world.

Robert W. Hefner is Professor of Anthropology and Director of the Institute on Culture, Religion, and World Affairs (CURA) at Boston University, USA.

John Hutchinson is a Reader in Nationalism in the Department of Government at the London School of Economics, UK.

Christiane Timmerman is Director of Academic Affairs at UCSIA, Belgium.

Sara Mels is Project Coordinator at UCSIA, Belgium.

Routledge Studies in Religion

1 **Judaism and Collective Life**
Self and Community in the Religious Kibbutz
Aryei Fishman

2 **Foucault, Christianity and Interfaith Dialogue**
Henrique Pinto

3 **Religious Conversion and Identity**
The Semiotic Analysis of Texts
Massimo Leone

4 **Language, Desire, and Theology**
A Genealogy of the Will to Speak
Noëlle Vahanian

5 **Metaphysics and Transcendence**
Arthur Gibson

6 **Sufism and Deconstruction**
A Comparative Study of Derrida and Ibn 'Arabi
Ian Almond

7 **Christianity, Tolerance and Pluralism**
A Theological Engagement with Isaiah Berlin's Social Theory
Michael Jinkins

8 **Negative Theology and Modern French Philosophy**
Arthur Bradley

9 **Law and Religion**
Edited by Peter Radan, Denise Meyerson and Rosalind F. Atherton

10 **Religion, Language, and Power**
Edited by Nile Green and Mary Searle-Chatterjee

11 **Shared Idioms, Sacred Symbols, and the Articulation of Identities in South Asia**
Edited by Kelly Pemberton & Michael Nijhawan

12 **Theology, Creation, and Environmental Ethics**
From Creatio Ex Nihilo to Terra Nullius
Whitney Bauman

13 **Material Religion and Popular Culture**
E. Frances King

14 **Adam Smith as Theologian**
Edited by Paul Oslington

15 **The Entangled God**
Divine Relationality and Quantum Physics
Kirk Wegter-McNelly

16 **Aquinas and Radical Orthodoxy**
A Critical Inquiry
Paul J. DeHart

17 **Animal Ethics and Theology**
The Lens of the Good Samaritan
Daniel K. Miller

18 **The Origin of Heresy**
A History of Discourse in Second Temple Judaism and Early Christianity
Robert M. Royalty, Jr.

19 **Buddhism and Violence**
Militarism and Buddhism in
Modern Asia
*Edited by Vladimir Tikhonov and
Torkel Brekke*

20 **Popular Music in Evangelical
Youth Culture**
Stella Sai-Chun Lau

21 **Theology and the Science of
Moral Action**
Virtue Ethics, Exemplarity, and
Cognitive Neuroscience
*Edited by James A. Van Slyke,
Gregory R. Peterson, Kevin S.
Reimer, Michael L. Spezio and
Warren S. Brown*

22 **Abrogation in the Qur'an and
Islamic Law**
Louay Fatoohi

23 **A New Science of Religion**
*Edited by Gregory W. Dawes and
James Maclaurin*

24 **Making Sense of the Secular**
Critical Perspectives from Europe
to Asia
Edited by Ranjan Ghosh

25 **The Rise of Modern Jewish
Politics**
Extraordinary Movement
C. S. Monaco

26 **Gender and Power in
Contemporary Spirituality**
Ethnographic Approaches
Anna Fedele and Kim E. Knibbe

27 **Religions in Movement**
The Local and the Global in
Contemporary Faith Traditions
*Edited by Robert W. Hefner,
John Hutchinson, Sara Mels and
Christiane Timmerman*

Religions in Movement
The Local and the Global in Contemporary
Faith Traditions

**Edited by Robert W. Hefner,
John Hutchinson, Sara Mels &
Christiane Timmerman**

NEW YORK AND LONDON

First published 2013
by Routledge
711 Third Avenue, New York, NY 10017

Simultaneously published in the UK
by Routledge
2 Park Square, Milton Park, Abingdon, Oxfordshire OX14 4RN

First issued in paperback 2015

*Routledge is an imprint of the Taylor & Francis Group,
an informa business*

© 2013 Taylor & Francis

The right of the editors to be identified as the authors of the editorial material, and of the authors for their individual chapters, has been asserted in accordance with sections 77 and 78 of the Copyright, Designs and Patents Act 1988.

All rights reserved. No part of this book may be reprinted or reproduced or utilised in any form or by any electronic, mechanical, or other means, now known or hereafter invented, including photocopying and recording, or in any information storage or retrieval system, without permission in writing from the publishers.

Trademark Notice: Product or corporate names may be trademarks or registered trademarks, and are used only for identification and explanation without intent to infringe.

Library of Congress Cataloging-in-Publication Data

Religions in movement : the local and the global in contemporary faith
    traditions / edited by Robert W. Hefner . . . [et al].
        p. cm. — (Routledge studies in religion ; 27)
    Includes bibliographical references (p.) and index.
    1. Religions—History—21st century. 2. Globalization—Religious aspects. I. Hefner, Robert W., 1952–
    BL98.R423 2012
    200.9′051—dc23
    2012035923

ISBN 13: 978-1-138-92284-6 (pbk)
ISBN 13: 978-0-415-81875-9 (hbk)

Typeset in Sabon
by Apex CoVantage, LLC

Contents

List of Figures ix

General Introduction 1
SARA MELS & CHRISTIANE TIMMERMAN

PART I
Global Perspectives on Religion, Nationalism and Politics

1 Introduction: Global Perspectives on Religion, Nationalism
  and Politics 9
  JOHN HUTCHINSON

2 Islam, Politics and Globalisation: What Are the Issues
  and Outcomes? 19
  JEFFREY HAYNES

3 The Paradox of Globalisation: Quakers, Religious NGOs
  and the United Nations 37
  JEREMY CARRETTE

4 European Secularity and Religious Modernity in Russia
  and Eastern Europe: Focus on Orthodox Christianity 57
  INNA NALETOVA

5 The Orthodox Tradition in a Globalising World: The Case
  of the Romanian Orthodox Church 79
  SUNA GÜLFER IHLAMUR-ÖNER

6 Good Muslims, Good Chinese: State Modernisation Policies,
  Globalisation of Religious Networks and the Changing
  Hui Ethno-Religious Identifications 98
  MAJA VESELIČ

viii *Contents*

7 Where National Histories and Colonial Myths Meet: 'Histoire Croisée' and Memory of the Moroccan-Berber Cultural Movement in the Netherlands   114
NORAH KARROUCHE

8 Self-Sacrifice and Martyrdom in Terrorism: Political and Religious Motives   132
FRANCESCO MARONE

PART II
Varieties of Religious Globalisation

9 Varieties of Religious Globalisation   149
ROBERT W. HEFNER

10 Religion in the Contemporary Globalised World: Construction, Migration, Challenge, Diversity   159
PETER BEYER

11 Voluntarism: Niche Markets Created by a Fissile Transnational Faith   180
DAVID MARTIN

12 Women Perform ʾIjtihād: Hybridity as Creative Space for Interpretations of Islam   196
ELS VANDERWAEREN

13 Processes of Localised and Globalised Islam among Young Muslims in Berlin   211
SYNNØVE BENDIXSEN

14 Towards Cultural Translation: Rethinking the Dynamics of Religious Pluralism and Globalisation through the Sathya Sai Movement   230
TULASI SRINIVAS

15 Ghanaian Films and Chiefs as Indicators of Religious Change among the Akan in Kumasi and Its Migrants in Southeast Amsterdam   246
LOUISE MÜLLER

Contributors   267
Bibliography   269
Index   309

Figures

4.1	Wrapping paper for bread sold in a Moscow supermarket.	63
4.2	A picture of the monastery of St. Seraphim of Sarov at a bus station in Nizhnii Novgorod.	64
4.3	Self-advertisement of the Moscow Fire Department.	66
4.4	A front window of a bus exhibiting, among other things, the image of Christ placed next to the national Russian three-coloured flag (on the left).	67
4.5	Announcement for a national Russian chess competition.	68
4.6	Religious self-assessment in Eastern (Central) Europe.	69
4.7	Churches are competent in dealing with moral problems.	70
4.8	Churches are competent in dealing with family problems.	71
4.9	Agreement and disagreement with the statement 'God should have been mentioned in the European Constitution'.	72
15.1	'I am the shining light of the world'; photo taken by the author.	247
15.2	An aesthetic representation of a traditional priest in the indigenous religious Akan Ghallywood film (3a) *Wedlock of the Gods*.	262
15.3	An aesthetic representation of a pastor in the Christian Akan Ghallywood film (1a) *Nyame ne Nyame*.	263
15.4	An aesthetic representation of an Imam in the indigenous Islamic Akan Ghallywood film (2a) *Dipantiche*.	263

General Introduction

Sara Mels & Christiane Timmerman

With the fall of the Berlin Wall and the end of the Cold War in 1989, a new optimism arose and people believed it would be the beginning of a new, prosperous and peaceful period in world history. This optimism soon disappeared, and it became clear that contrary to popular belief, the world had become more complex than ever before. Problems that were once in the background of political consciousness were now right at the fore: for example, rivalry among neighbouring countries, regional wars and migration. Although contemporary problems are many and diverse, it seems that these current problems are increasingly framed in cultural and religious terms. With the events of 9/11 this new division has been further intensified, and the prospect of 'clashing civilisations' becomes more likely.

While globalisation can be understood as a long historical process that can be traced back to the 1500s, the speed, density and international impact of globalisation expanded after 1989 (Haynes 2007, 66–68). With globalisation touching all aspects of our lives, religion(s) and culture(s) are also subjected to its influence. The way religion, culture and society relate to one another, as well as their interconnectedness, is therefore crucial for understanding the world today. At the same time, global society offers an opportunity to rethink and rework old strategies and customs. To better understand this dynamic interplay of change and influence, it behoves us to look at the macro- and micro-social developments within 'traditional' religion as well as new religious movements in the contemporary world and the way in which these interactions provoke both dynamic religious innovation as well as conservative resistance. Drawing on a variety of historical and ethnographic case studies from around the world, the chapters in this book attempt just such a comparison.

SECULARITY AND GLOBALISATION

The structure, role and importance of religion around the world are constantly changing. Most discussed in regard to this is the secularisation theory and the extent to which it is just a European historical process or an all-encompassing theory for the whole world. Currently, many theorists argue that secularisation has many levels, but they diverge on how or indeed if these levels are interrelated (Gorski & Altinordu 2008, 57). Karel Dobbelaere (2007), for instance, proposed to distinguish between macro, meso- and micro-levels of analysis. According to José Casanova we can distinguish three different connotations: the decline in religious beliefs and practices, the privatisation of religion and the differentiation of the secular spheres (Casanova 1994). Casanova further argues that while the decline and privatisation theses have undergone numerous critiques and revisions in the last 15 years (Casanova 1994; Davie 1994;), only the understanding of secularisation as a process of functional differentiation of the various institutional spheres of modern societies remains relatively uncontested. Nevertheless, opposing voices like Steve Bruce continue to affirm the strong link between modernisation and secularisation (Gorski & Altinordu 2008, 59). In spite of these different opinions, some basic findings can be confirmed: 'The progressive decline of institutional Christian religion in Europe is an undeniable social fact' (Casanova 2006). 'Anyone familiar with European societies will be aware of the drastic decline of organized religion' (Bruce 2006). That no such decline is taking place in many parts of the global South seems equally apparent.

So, where early sociologists thought that through modernisation societies would turn away from religion and become thoroughly secularised, global history uncovered another picture with the rise of conflicts issuing from concerns over religious instances influencing state politics, society and ethics and the struggle of multicultural societies to address religious and cultural minority issues (Haynes 2010, 126–127). News reports and political discussions in Western as well as non-Western countries demonstrate that the way in which secularisation constructs citizenship and everyday modern life in nonreligious terms is under pressure, and that religious people and institutions try to reframe and reconstruct (other) aspects of their social life in religious terms (again). This does not mean, however, that secularism has lost its relevance and importance. Rather, pressured by the continuing pluralisation of a society in which highly secularised citizens as well as religious groups try to live together, states and societal associations have to take up the task to develop measures of a shared citizenship.

When it comes to religion, there is no global rule. All world religions are being radically transformed today by processes of modernisation and globalisation, but they are being transformed in diverse and manifold ways. World religions do not only draw upon their own traditions for this but also increasingly upon one another (Casanova 2006, 17). Diverse religious movements—Islamic, Hindu, Christian—are being regrouped within societies, and this has implications for the established secular structures; for ideologies of secularism and, by implication, for liberal democracy (Gorski & Altinordu 2008, 68). Furthermore, inter-civilisational encounters, cultural imitations and borrowings, diasporic circulation, and hybridity are all part and parcel of the global present (Casanova 2006, 17).

RELIGION AND MIGRATION

Through globalisation, the world becomes more and more interconnected. Communication happens almost instantaneously, and the migration of people, values and religious traditions around the world intensifies. In this respect, culture and religion are no longer encapsulated within local communities with their various boundaries rooted in different historic, cultural and religious components. This does not mean that world society is a global and unified society; it is in fact made up of social groups that differ in their practices, beliefs and institutions. In this a paradox arises between a growing global cultural homogeneity and the ongoing creation of new cultural diversity. Rather than creating massive cultural homogeneity on a global scale, the world system is replacing local diversity by global diversity. The process of globalisation also has repercussions on traditional belief systems. The collapse of ways of looking at religion that were once taken for granted and the rise of new religious authorities (e.g., the global religious market) has given rise to new actors and new discourses on religion.

The introduction of 'new' religious traditions or practices may lead to a pluralisation or fragmentation of the local religious landscape; it changes the position of religion in society and forces it to rethink its role. For instance, through the experience of living as minority groups in Western societies, Muslim religiosity changes; it '[. . .] placed Islam within the three interrelated paradigms of secularisation, individualisation and privatisation, which have until recently been distinctive characteristics of Western societies' (Cesari 2003, 260). As a result, a more globalised and individualised Islam is created decoupled from particular national cultures (Cesari 2006; Peter 2006; Roy 2004). Moreover, this individualisation also leads to an ongoing fragmentation of authority structures, where the 'classical' Islamic institutions (mosques, imams, etc.) are losing their influence and are giving way to 'new' types of religious authority, like Muslim intellectuals and *conférenciers* (Peter 2006, 107, 111).

Within Christian traditions, too, we witness changes influenced by the processes brought about by migration. 'New' Christian denominations seem to have a definite appeal to recently established immigrant groups within the Western world. In interaction with the other religious denominations that surround them in globalised cities, we see the emergence of new dynamics, authorities and religious practices within Christian communities.

Religious actors may perceive these changing contexts as opportunities as well as threats. The religious response to this change can be considered defensive when actors prefer to maintain the religious status quo. However, the response may be innovative and transformative, too, opening up new opportunities for participation by once-marginalised individuals and groups. For example, the pluralisation of the traditional religious landscapes may at once open up pathways for newcomers as well as religious minorities to gain authority and strengthen their positions in local societies (Hui in China, Muslims in Europe), but it may also provoke a conservative/reactionary reflex as it undermines the power and role of the majority religions and religious leaders (ROC in Romania). The introduction of new secular and religious value systems may empower people in the margin to stand up for their rights (Muslim women, secular Moroccans), but it may also prompt (religious) conservatism and violence (terrorist attacks, ROC). In this regard, religious revivals may be less a matter of numbers of believers/worshippers, or of the (de-)institutionalisation of religion's (political) influence, and more about the effect that the reconfiguration of the position in local and global society that religion has in the world and how new strategies and religious appearances change local and global religious landscapes.

The selection of essays in this volume offers a valuable contribution to the academic field of religious studies as it underscores the (continuing) importance of religions in very different settings, and in relation to greatly varied political and cultural dynamics.

ABOUT THE UCSIA SUMMER SCHOOL

Since the establishment of its summer schools in 2003, UCSIA's ambition has been to examine key issues in the contemporary reconfiguration of religion in the world. Our programme has examined the challenge of dialogue among religions; the ambivalence of faith-based radicalism (social action, terrorism etc.); religious currents and gender relations; religion and nationalism and, most generally, the relationship between globalisation and religious renewal.

This book highlights the diverse ways in which religions on the one hand take up the challenges posed by the international global society in becoming a global political, moral and social actor and, on the other hand, try to reinvent their position and role in familiar and less familiar local contexts. Religions first and foremost make use of the traditional power and communication channels available to them, like strategies of conversion, the preservation of traditional value systems, the intertwining of religious and political power. Nevertheless, challenged by more culturally and religiously diversified societies, by the incredible growth of new religious sects and by the continuing decline of church involvement in Western European countries, they are also forced to let go of these well-known strategies of preservation and reformulate new ways of establishing their roles and their position in local contexts.

This collection of essays brings together theory-driven and empirically based research and case studies dealing with both the global and bottom-up strategies of religions and religious traditions in Europe and beyond in reviving and rethinking their positions in the world and in their local communities. The papers were presented at the UCSIA summer school on religion, culture and society (2003, 2005, 2007, 2008, 2009 and 2010). Each year, established scholars join the school to discuss the topic of religion, culture and society and to help young scholars in the development of their doctoral research. Their plenary presentations were alternated with workshop sessions in which the alumni researchers were able to present the results of their doctoral research. The articles in this book are therefore a mix of essays written by well-established scholars as well as young up-and-coming academic researchers, encompassing different disciplinary fields but all written from a sociocultural perspective.

Part I

Global Perspectives on Religion, Nationalism and Politics

1 Introduction
Global Perspectives on Religion, Nationalism and Politics

John Hutchinson

Many scholars of globalisation consider that revolutions in technology and communications have ushered in a new period of human history (Albrow 1996; Castells 1996; Giddens 1990). Such is the scale, speed and intensity of interactions that the world's populations are being united into a single time and space, giving rise to a global consciousness as they face common problems that require planetary-wide solutions, such as nuclear proliferation, international terrorism, long-distance economic migrations and refugee flows, and climate change. Scholars may disagree about when this new era emerged, but there is rough agreement about its distinctive institutions: a global liberal economy, world political and legal organisations such as the United Nations (UN), a global civil society of transnational nongovernmental agencies putting forward a human rights agenda, diaspora communities as economic and ideological actors, a world language (English) and transnational media organisations promoting a universal popular culture.

There has been a vigorous debate about the implications of globalisation for the survival of the world of sovereign nation-states, and the role of nationalism as both an agent of and a response to globalisation (Halikiopoulou & Vasilopoulou 2011). There is broad agreement that there is a general weakening of the relationship between nation and the territorial state; that to attain national objects, political elites now have to operate increasingly at the transnational level; that national minorities use democratic norms to achieve greater autonomy; and that mass migration has made nations into plural communities, some of which maintain diasporic identifications with homelands outside their host state (Guibernau 2001).

In contrast, until recently, there has been much less debate about the fate of religion. 'Globalisation' has been viewed through Enlightenment spectacles as part of the rationalisation process that has already relegated religion to the dustbin of history, just as it threatens the nation-state and as we move to a more cosmopolitan ethics and politics.

The following chapters, however, make the case for the salience and resilience of religion, often in conjunction with nationalism, in the contemporary world in several ways. First, religions can be viewed not just as reacting to globalisation, but as active agents in its making, in global fora, and in their use of new forms of economic and communication systems to advance the diffusion of religious ideas. The contributions by Jeffrey Haynes—'Islam, Politics and Globalisation: What Are the Issues and Outcomes?' and Jeremy Carrette—'The Paradox of Globalisation: Quakers, Religious NGOs and the United Nations' examine the interaction of religious communities and organisations with global processes and institutions, assessing how far they offer coherent responses to continuously changing environments.

Second, a dominant assumption is that the rise of the modern state results in a privatisation of religion, whereas we now witness the re-infusion of religion into the public sphere in many regions, including Europe. This is explored with reference to Eastern Orthodox Churches, by Inna Naletova— 'European Secularity and Religious Modernity in Russia and Eastern Europe: Focus on Orthodox Christianity', and Suna Gülfer Ihlamur-Öner—'The Orthodox Tradition in a Globalising World: The Case of the Romanian Orthodox Church'.

Third, global religious networks have contributed to the crystallisation and politicisation of ethno-religious minorities, which elites in nation-states can find a security threat. Maja Veselič in 'Good Muslims, Good Chinese: State Modernisation Policies, Globalisation of Religious Networks and the Changing Hui Ethno-Religious Identifications' explores a case where, by contrast, a minority combines a loyalty to Islamic values as well as the Chinese nation-state, and the state encourages the religious networks of the Hui to advance its own developmental goals. On the other hand, an ethnic revivalism can also lead to fissures in migrant populations largely defined by transnational religious attachments that are reinforced by the secular, assimilationist pressures of contemporary European states. This is explored by Norah Karrouche in 'Where National Histories and Colonial Myths Meet: 'Histoire Croisée' and Memory of the Moroccan-Berber Cultural Movement in the Netherlands' in examining the case of the Moroccan Berber population in the Netherlands.

Fourth, religious beliefs, symbols and practices in their transnational reach can provide a powerful new repertoire for insurgent popular movements against 'alien' states. Francesco Marone addresses this in 'Self-Sacrifice and Martyrdom in Terrorist Violence: Political and Religious Motives'.

In these chapters, we see 'religion' entwined with 'globalisation' in many different ways, in considering things such as the likelihood of religio-civilisational political blocs, the capacity of religious actors to affect 'global governance', the impact of a world of religious pluralism, the relationship of specific religions to contemporary modernity, the role of ethno-religious networks in world trade, long-range migration patterns and new community formation, and the transmission of innovative repertoires of political violence.

RELIGIONS AS GLOBAL ACTORS

Religious political activism has often been presented as a reactionary response (captured in the term 'fundamentalism') of backward regions to the acceleration of globalisation after the collapse of the USSR (Union of

Soviet Socialist Republics). One of the canonical analyses in this mode was Samuel Huntington's *The Clash of Civilisations* (1997), which warned of a likely backlash against the imposition of a unipolar Western concept of the world after the Soviet collapse that would take the form of oppositional cultural blocs, in many cases defined by religion. Many outside the West have taken Huntington's claims to heart in viewing 'globalisation' as a form of covert Western neo-imperialism (Juergensmeyer 2008). Nonetheless, the chapter by Jeffrey Haynes makes clear that to understand contemporary religious activism in this way is misleading on at least three grounds.

First of all, Haynes observes correctly that globalisation is not just a contemporary phenomenon but has a long historical lineage, takes many different forms, is episodic, and that religious actors have used it to their advantage. Although global processes can be perceived by some traditionalists as neo-imperialist in promoting Western principles and institutions, the great religions have also exploited opportunities to use improvements in communications, wealth, educational provision and diaspora networks to diffuse their messages to believers (Bayly 2002, 2004). Such religious engagement, then, often seeks to reconstruct the world on its own terms. While this can be interpreted as a reaction to earlier (Western-imperial) global encroachments, it is, however, more intelligible to perceive the relationship between religions and global processes as dynamic and interactive.

Second, the current wave of activism long predates the Cold War. Haynes offers a useful periodisation of the various phases of Islamic engagement with 'modernity'. This, of course, raises the question of whether we can speak of contemporary religious politics as a 'resurgence' or whether we are witnessing a shift in how religious understandings of the world and institutional practices can be applied to current problems. Certainly, we can argue that religious forces have been midwives of epochal global change: in conjunction with major geopolitical actors, such as a revitalised United States, they have played a significant role in the downfall of the Soviet Union that has enabled the triumph of Western neoliberalism. Jeffrey Haynes notes the importance of the election of a Polish pope in 1978 that emboldened a political as well as spiritual resistance to Soviet rule well beyond Catholic Poland and Lithuania. Another factor was the defeat of the Soviet army in Afghanistan by the Mujahidin assisted by the United States. Mujahidin resistance drew crucial support from surrounding Muslim states and from recruits from across the Muslim world. Many of these had been radicalised by the Shi'ite Iranian revolution of 1979, itself of global significance in establishing a state based on Islamic principles that in the process had humiliated the United States. These two events in Iran and Afghanistan became an inspiration for disaffected Muslims, Sunni and as well as Shi'a, throughout the Middle East and Asia, fretting at the long subservience of their societies to Western and Soviet power. They appeared to offer an alternative model of development as well as restoring Muslim pride. Today, competing conceptions of the global, secular and religious are at play.

Third, as Haynes remarks of Islam, it is simplistic to view religions in their vision of the world as in outright hostility to modernisation. Although there are strong neotraditionalist tendencies, notably in Iran and Saudi Arabia, there are also reformist and modernist groups that do not regard Islam as antagonistic to liberalism or democracy. It is too early to say what the fruits of the Arab spring will be, but in Indonesia, religious parties have been prominent in the establishment after Suharto of democratic institutions. To explain outcomes, we must also look at a range of other variables, including the degree to which political systems are hierarchical, the strength or otherwise of civil societies and so forth. One can make similar points about other religions, which take diverse stances often linked to the social origins of their personnel. Although much of the Catholic hierarchy, recruited from upper social strata, collaborated with militarist dictatorships in Argentine and Peru, sections of the lower clergy (generally closer to the peasantry) were attracted to a Marxian liberation theology, which gave legitimacy to the Nicaraguan revolution. In the Philippines, the Catholic Church was central to the overthrow of the Marcos regime and the establishment of democracy.

Why are religious belief systems so socially and politically resonant in many parts of the world? A few generations ago, the intellectuals of non-Western countries were drawn instead to secular nationalist ideologies, often informed by socialism, because religion seemed to offer no capacity to resist European imperialism. As Haynes suggests, part of the answer lies in the failures of the *soi-disant* nation-states after independence to realise the dreams of liberating their populations from poverty and dependence. Their state capacities were too weak to regulate global economic, cultural and military processes where the rules of the game continued to be made by Western powers. This is, of course, only part of the answer as it may suggest reductively that religion is simply a vehicle of an oppositional politics, whereas, as the following chapters reveal, it also offers an alternative moral vision of how political life should be ordered, defining the role of families, gender relations, and social justice.

Jeremy Carrette's chapter examines the United Nations as one of those institutions responsible for 'global governance' and investigates the extent to which religious actors can make a difference. He defines global governance as a myriad of global, regional and transnational systems of authoritative rule making and implementation that is intrinsically coupled with (contemporary) globalisation. He is pessimistic about the prospects for such actors. As he states, the United Nations, particularly the UN Secretariat, attempts to work to a universalist agenda, but as an organisation of 192 member states, it is constrained by an internationalist framework, in which strong (nation-)states offering formal adherence to agreed rules are dominant. Faced with these constraints, successive Secretary-Generals have looked for support to NGOs, as embodiments of an emerging global civil society, to advance the causes of peace and development. Religious organisations such as the Quakers have (like the Holy See and the Bahá'ís) been influential through their knowledge of UN procedures and their commitment to long-term goals in many policy areas, and, working outside the state framework, have been valued neutral mediators in conflict-torn situations. He examines in some detail the record of the Quakers in their support of antidiscrimination campaigns, arms reduction and the rights of nongovernmental organisations (NGOs) to contribute to international affairs.

However, in contributing to the proliferation of non-state actors and while participating in the UN, the Quakers get caught up in what he calls 'the paradox of globalisation'. A key aspect of global governance is that there is no single system but rather a mass of interacting networks and institutions. As the processes of global governance have become ever more complex with the expansion of the numbers of non-state, regional and transnational actors of all kinds, the UN itself is now a site of many and competing systems (including the Security Council, the General Assembly, the UN Secretariat) at the centre, as well as a diverse set of practices, operations and structures at country and regional levels. He argues there is a danger of dilution and absorption as religious organisations seek to participate in a bewilderingly complex global geography. If the number of religious NGOs has increased, so too secular equivalents have multiplied. From one perspective, this might be seen as a widening of democratic voices at the transnational level. In reality, state interests in UN fora dominate and inequalities of power remain: in contrast to the case of the Quakers, new religious NGOs from the 'two-thirds world' find it increasingly difficult to gain access to power because of a lack of knowledge of processes and resources. Moreover, NGOs, as mostly single-interest causes, fail to exercise an overview of an enormously complicated policy-making environment. Not least, as unelected bodies, their claims to represent global democratic agenda are problematic. They represent a form of 'courtier politics' parasitic on the ready-made agenda of international institutions.

THE RE-INFUSION OF RELIGION INTO THE PUBLIC SPHERE

Some Islamists may envision a millenarian overthrow of the system of nation-states, but most radicals have worked towards a religious transformation of their existing state. The animus of the Hindutva in India, religious Zionists in Israel, and Hamas in Gaza is directed against the enemies within—secularists who have imposed an alien Western ideology on the people and religious minorities. Where their targets are external, they are primarily threatening neighbours. These struggles may actually re-enforce identification with a national territorial state (unless the radicals belong to a religious minority). Nonetheless, they highlight the fragility of secularism when it is unable to deliver development, justice and security, as well as the embedded character of religion in the life of populations outside the West.

To this story of the religious 're-enchantment' of public life, Europe has been characterised as the great exception, notably in enforcing a separation of church and state. Adopting a 'multiple modernities' perspective, Inna Naletova argues this is not so, at least in Eastern and Central Europe where, after the fall of Communism, a nonsecular vision is being advanced by means of the creative insertion of religious symbols and practices into public life. Using a combination of qualitative and quantitative evidence, she maintains this is particularly visible in the Orthodox countries of Russia, Bulgaria, Ukraine, Romania, Serbia and Moldova and, to a lesser extent, in Catholic countries such as Poland. This is not explicable as a conservative resistance to a western secularist individualism to which these populations are newly exposed. Instead, she suggests Orthodox populations as much as clergy are engaged in a determined and innovative effort to redefine their societies, at local, national and global level after the Communist 'hiatus'. We are speaking then of a popular rather than an elite-led process in which a spirituality is taking place outside a formal church setting, taking the form of religious practices and insertions in the workplace, leisure pursuits, schools and the market place. Orthodox churches are responding to the expectations of their populations, who exhibit an optimism about the future of religion, supporting the Church's initiatives across a broad spectrum of public life, in education, health, justice and the media. Religious icons stand in the public sphere next to symbols of (nation-) state, thereby redefining a sense of political belonging.

Naletova offers plausible explanations for the popular vitality of Orthodoxy. Orthodoxy played a historic role as definer of national identity so that religious affiliation is not just a matter of individual choice. Whereas modernisation in Western Europe was linked with individual freedom and pluralism, in Eastern Europe it was imposed by an atheist Communist dictatorship so that the allegiances to Orthodoxy (expressed, for example, in icon worship) were bound up with the defence of the traditional nation. Finally, the concept of 'symphonia' historically justifies an alliance of Church and State, which after Communism was then revived as the natural 'model' of the good society.

Suna Gülfer Ihlamur-Öner is largely in accord with this depiction of Orthodox efflorescence in a study that focuses on Romania, where religious practice is highest of all the post-Communist countries. Like Naletova, she emphasises the close links between national identity and Orthodoxy and the role of the latter in redefining, after the failed socialist experiment, social doctrines in health and welfare. As in Russia, claims of an intimate connection between religion and nation are used to justify 'protection' against 'foreign' religious missions, in spite of an avowed support for religious pluralism. But, as Ihlamur-Öner shows, the Romanian Church is also drawn into transnational commitments by a sense of responsibility to a growing Romanian migrant diaspora in Europe, arising out of Romania's insertion into European and global networks. She cites one Orthodox prelate who proclaimed the responsibility of the Church to 'make out of globalisation the world of God'.

Both authors thus reject Max Weber's conceptualisation of Orthodoxy as outside of Western modernity, arguing that it is in a critical engagement with it. Their analyses pertain particularly to Orthodoxy, but they remind us of the limits of a secularised conception of the rise of nations (too often explained by reference only to the development of centralising states, industrialisation or enlightenment ideologies). As Adrian Hastings (1997) argued, the Christian religion was central to the formation of many national communities—in the translations of the Bible into vernaculars that contributed to the formation of national languages, the dissemination of monarchical as well as covenantal political models, in conceptions of being a 'chosen people' and public liturgies and symbols, all of which continue to have resonance even in apparently secular nation-states.

ETHNIC MINORITIES, RELIGIOUS NETWORKS AND THE NATION-STATE

Francis Robinson has claimed of Muslim minorities that there is a clear relationship between maintaining a Muslim community and political separatism (Robinson 1979). Recent unrest among the Uyghurs in Western China seems to confirm the truth of his observation. Maja Veselič, however, in her chapter suggests that the largest Chinese Muslim minority, the Hui, diverges from this picture. Although there is a self-conscious Islamic revival, notably among the educated young, as a result of intensified long distance contacts with the Middle East, she argues that the Hui see no contradiction between an identification with the Chinese nation and pride in membership of a global Muslim community. Moreover, the state has used the religious contacts of this ethnic minority in order to support China's rise as a global economic power.

The history of the Hui in China is complex. Descended from Muslim traders, soldiers and officials who settled in China from the 7th to the 14th century, the Hui are a territorially dispersed and differentiated minority, who for centuries have intermarried with Han communities. Modernist Islamic movements inspired from abroad in the late nineteenth century worked to mould the Hui into a united community, loyal both to Islam and to the Chinese nation. Nonetheless, the Hui suffered repression, which triggered periodic revolts under the Empire and successor regimes, including during Mao's Cultural Revolution. At the same time, designation as a nation with an autonomous province (Ningxia) under Chinese nationality policies solidified their ethnic identity. After Mao, the Chinese state has tolerated their Muslim faith and actively encouraged contacts between them and Islamic countries in the Middle East. In turn, the proliferation of educational and religious institutions and student exchanges funded by foreign sources in China has exposed the Hui to the wider currents in Islam.

Veselič explains China's acceptance of these developments by the state's perception that religion can be a factor for social stability and that affiliations with oil-rich Arab states served its developmental goals. Concerns about the exposure of Chinese citizens to foreign ideologies were mitigated by a sense that they shared a common anti-western imperialist discourse. She suggests her interviews with Hui students in Yemen show that a heightened sense of their Muslim identity has gone hand-in-hand with a pride in their Chinese nationality as they compare their habits of thrift, cleanliness and modesty with those of their hosts. This indicates that individuals can sustain multiple identities and a consequence is that while the Hui view themselves as Chinese, they frame the problems facing their society in religious terms. Illuminating though this is, further research is needed to ascertain how representative the attitudes of her interviewees are, given the history of Hui-Chinese tensions. A second issue is the stability of this identity balance if the attitudes of the Chinese state to Islam penetration shifts as a result of further disturbances amongst their ethno-religious minorities.

Whereas the Hui are a long-established minority, nationalised in part by state policies, the Muslim Berber population in the Netherlands, studied by Norah Karrouche, are a product of contemporary migrations from northern Morocco. Karrouche highlights an issue of pressing importance—the degree to which relatively recent Muslim populations can be 'naturalised' as European in a period of global religio-political tensions. Hers is an intricate exploration of Dutch-Berber identity politics as a community caught between Dutch assimilationist policies, discourses that have viewed Moroccan youth as Muslims and Moroccan colonial and postcolonial politics. Her focus is on the rise of an ethnic revivalist *Amazigh* identity that, rejecting both assimilation and Islamism, differentiates the Berbers from Arab Muslims as a democratic 'European' people deriving from a pre-Islamic past. This is itself a product of (French) European colonialist policies that sought to set Berbers against a threatening Arab-Moroccan Muslim nationalism. One consequence was that the postcolonial Moroccan state engaged in a repression of the Berbers that from the 1960s provoked three decades of conflict and a large-scale migration from the Rif regions of northern Morocco to the Netherlands and other European destinations. The emerging migrant associations were religious in character and addressed issues in their countries of origins and the practical problems of a migrant group. Later, they established hubs of social life around mosques. The rise of *Amazigh* associations in the Netherlands, secular and even Marxist in stance, came late during the 1990s, aided by a shift in Moroccan monarchical policies that now favoured Berberism in the homeland as a shield against radical Islam. Nonetheless, while these associations, heavily oriented to homeland issues, have accumulated support amongst an emerging intelligentsia, they lack a popular base, as Islamic organisations provide a more meaningful focus of identity amongst diaspora-born Berbers oriented to local issues. In this case we see a migrant population whose capacity for independent political action is undercut by ethnic and religious cleavages.

RELIGION AND THE REPERTOIRES OF RESISTANCE

To what extent does the introduction of religion into political disputes intensify violence? Mark Juergensmeyer (1993; 2008) has written of the role of religion in transforming disputes into instances of a cosmic war, in which there can be no compromise with the enemy. The use of suicide bombings in the Middle East and Caucasus appears to confirm that religious radicals have introduced a new repertoire of violence into many contemporary conflicts.

Francesco Marone shows that, historically, martyrdom was used by many modern ideological movements to mobilise adherents into a community of solidarity. He analyses different kinds of martyrdom—*passive*, which exemplifies the will to die without at the same time killing (e.g. through hunger strikes), and *active*, in which the subject is willing to die in order to kill. Most secular revolutionary nationalists are willing to die and to kill, but, as the author says, not simultaneously. The idea of *active* martyrdom, exemplified in the suicide bomber, seems to arise in the 1980s, in order to achieve either ethno-nationalist goals (e.g. Hamas's campaigns against Israel) or religious objectives on a transnational scale. Some secular nationalist organisations have engaged in this practice, e.g. the Tamil Tigers and sections of the Palestine Liberation Organization (PLO), and it can be viewed as an effective tactic of the weak against a powerful military opponent. But amongst secular nationalists they are the exceptions and in the latter case may be explained as attempts to outbid their religious nationalist competitors.

The question then arises how far the recent emergence of suicide bombing is explained by religious revivalism? This is a complicated matter. Religion can be an intensifier. Nationalists themselves have often 'borrowed' religious imagery in order to inspire sacrifice after overwhelming defeat or when they are faced with overwhelming odds. Poles spoke of their nation as crucified after its division between three empires and the Catholic Irish of their martyred nation after the English Protestant conquest. But, as Marone argues, *suicide* is prohibited in most religious traditions. He suggests that the recent fusion of suicide killing with concepts of martyrdom is heterodox, arising out of the military crisis of the Iranian regime in its war with Iraq. The practice of suicide killings can be undertaken, he suggests, only with the support of a community of reference who will celebrate this practice through acts of remembrance, although in the case of transnational projects such as al-Qaeda, this may be a 'virtual' community constructed by institutions such as the internet.

This has several implications. The practice of suicide bombing, especially if it has terrorist intent, might be seen as an act of desperation and sanctioned by communities such as those in Chechnya shattered by war. Given the horror of terrorism exhibited by the state system, one might argue that it is likely to be at best a transitional tactic by nationalists seeking legitimacy, although it will continue to have appeal to those with millenarian objectives.

CONCLUDING REMARKS

The academic discourse of 'globalisation' owes much to the earlier theorisations of 'modernisation'. A generation ago, scholars of China concluded that viewing the nineteenth and twentieth centuries through the application of this latter framework (as in 'China confronts modernity') was deeply Eurocentric. It implied that the experiences of non-Western societies were to be understood primarily as attempts (which were graded) to answer questions that the West (perceived as 'modernity') had posed. Historians such as Paul Cohen (1985) argued that the Chinese had their own problems and questions, construed through their history and culture, which shaped how they understood and dealt with the wider world. This is in accord with current 'multiple modernities' approaches.

We might ask whether much of existing scholarship has similarly skewed the relationship between the great religions and globalisation, in which the heightened visibility in the public sphere of the former is characterised as a response to the latter, as in the term 'religious resurgence'. For in much of the world religions have never gone away, and these chapters reveal that far from being a gigantic homogenising steamroller, 'globalisation' is better understood an umbrella term that covers very disparate, inchoate and even contradictory processes (Hutchinson 2011). In other words, religion in many contexts has a profound historical weight and all the momentum that comes with this. To get a grip on contemporary religious politicisation we need to *start* with the horizons of believers and with the great baggage of traditions of thought that over many centuries have evolved creative responses to the secular world. By examining the conceptual maps and repertoires of behaviour available to believers we will allow greater agency to individuals and collectivities as they engage with the world into which they are thrown.

2 Islam, Politics and Globalisation
What Are the Issues and Outcomes?
Jeffrey Haynes

How does globalisation change our understanding of the involvement of religion in politics beyond the general idea that the core of globalisation implies increasing interdependence between states and peoples, with what happens in one part of the world affecting what happens elsewhere and which may have political ramifications? One approach is to see the issue in relation to a Western-directed 'globalisation', seen as a thoroughly malign and comprehensive Westernising process. This form of globalisation is judged to be *inherently* undesirable, a process whereby Western—especially American—capitalism and culture seek to dominate the globe, sweeping aside non-Western cultures. A second aspect of this view is that, in general, the Western world is made rich at the expense of the poverty of many non-Western parts of the world: areas which are compelled to bear the brunt of an unjust and unequal globalising process. This is possible, it is asserted, because Western capitalist interests determine trading terms, interest rates and dominance of highly mechanised production, via control of important international institutions, such as the World Trade Organization.

An alternative view emphasises that globalisation offers enhanced opportunities for international cooperation in relation to various issues, including social development and improved human rights, as well as conflict resolution and peace building. In this way of looking at things, globalisation processes are believed to enhance chances of international cooperation to resolve a range of economic, developmental, social, political, environmental, gender, and human rights concerns and injustices. In particular, the end of the Cold War in the late 1980s was seen to offer unprecedented opportunity for collective efforts involving both states and non-state actors—including religious entities—to tackle a range of pressing global concerns. Progress is measured in terms of bottom-up contributions from local groups and grassroots organisations around the world, including various religious organisations and movements. In sum, globalisation in both views is a multifaceted process of change, universally affecting states, industrial companies, local communities and individuals. Religious organisations and movements are not exempt from its influence; and, as a result, like other social agents, such religious entities participate in, and are affected by, globalisation. This chapter looks at the extent to which religion is affected by globalisation, especially in relation to political developments, with the main focus on Islam in the Middle East and Africa.

RELIGION AND GLOBALISATION: WHAT ARE THE INTERACTIONS AND OUTCOMES?

There are numerous definitions of globalisation. Many focus on the idea that globalisation is a continuing process by means of which the world is increasingly characterised by common activity, emphasising in particular how many highly important aspects of life—including politics, culture, economics, trade, wars and crime are becoming more and more interrelated. This implies that globalisation is also a matter of a change in consciousness, with people from various spheres, including politics, religion, culture, business, sport, and many other activities, thinking and acting in the context of an increasingly 'globalised' world. One result is that 'territoriality'—a term signifying a close connection or limitation with reference to a particular geographic area or country—now has less significance than it once did. Thus, globalisation suggests greatly increased interdependence, involving both states and non-states: what happens in one part of the world affects others. Overall, then, globalisation encompasses the idea that humankind is currently experiencing a 'historically unique *increase of scale* to a global interdependency among people and nations'. It is characterised by (1) rapid integration of the world economy, (2) innovations and growth in international electronic communications, and (3) increasing 'political and cultural awareness of the global interdependency of humanity' (Warburg 2001: 1).

Globalisation has deep historical roots, beginning in the 1500s and encompassing three interrelated political, economic and technological processes (Clark 1997). While it is appropriate to perceive globalisation as a continuous, historically based, multifaceted process, it is important to note that there have been periods when it has been especially speedy. For example, its pace increased from around 1870 until the start of World War I in 1914. This was partly because during those four decades, 'all parts of the world began to feel the impact of the international economy, and for the first time in history it was possible to have instant long-distance communication (telegraph, radio) between people' (Warburg 2001: 2). After World War II, the speed, density and international impact of globalisation expanded again—as it did once more after the Cold War came to an end in 1989 (Haynes 2007: 65–95). According to Keohane, the overall impact of these processes of globalisation resulted in an end state that he calls 'globalism'. For Keohane, globalism is 'a state of the world involving networks of interdependence at multicontinental distances, linked through flows of capital and goods, information and ideas, people and force, as well as environmentally and biologically relevant substances' (Keohane 2002: 31). Thus, *globalism* refers to the reality of being interconnected, while *globalisation* denotes the speed at which these connections grow—or diminish. Overall, the concept of globalism 'seeks to [. . .] understand all the inter-connections of the modern world—and to highlight patterns that underlie (and explain) them' (Nye 2002: 2). In short, globalisation can usefully be thought of as a continuing, multidimensional process with historical roots, involving intensification of global interconnectedness between both states and non-state actors. It also suggests reduction of the significance of territorial boundaries and of state-directed political and economic structures and processes.

While globalisation names a process that is still unfolding, there has been no shortage of attempts to define it. Is it possible to understand the impact of globalisation as an objective process that simply involves mapping the relevant facts in order to assess key global trends in relation to social, political, and economic organisation? Because analysis of globalisation is almost always cast in wider normative and ideological contexts, with value judgements to the fore, many would answer 'no'. Reflecting such concerns, two schools of thought are polarised in their interpretation of the impact of globalisation upon the politics and economies of countries. I shall refer to the first as the 'positive globalisation' (PG) view, and the second as the 'negative globalisation' (NG) approach.

In the PG view, the end of the Cold War clearly demonstrated the superiority of Western values and belief systems over its Communist rival. Now, it was believed, we would see not only the final achievement of capitalism's global expansion but also the universal extension of liberal democracy. The outcome would be a peaceful and prosperous new world order, a modern golden age. Globalisation would help advance the well-being of millions of people around the world, through the liberating impact of the spread of markets, democracy and enhanced human rights. To further these developments, international organisations and global institutions would be strengthened and better focussed in addressing pressing global problems. In addition, informal cross-border structures would develop further, involving interaction of local groups and grassroots organisations from all parts of the world.

The notion of 'positive globalisation' comes with a powerful cluster of liberal assumptions. Globalisation is said not only to be irresistible but also to be welcomed, with overwhelmingly beneficial consequences, including (1) more effective global and regional institutions; (2) greater economic efficiency, via the spread of markets; (3) better mechanisms for problem solving; and (4) more political choice and openness as a result of the spread of democracy (Haynes 2005: 8–14).

Negative globalisation (NG) critics of the PG view point to what they see as two main problems in this interpretation: (1) in practice, as opposed to theory, the benefits of marketisation misrepresent the past, exaggerating state economic failures in, inter alia, the Middle East and North Africa (MENA), a region that has long had state-dominated economies; and (2) to remove, or even drastically scale down, the state's economic role is problematic—not least because it may remove social measures designed to protect the weak in society from market failures and the (over-)exercise of political power by autocratic leaders. In addition, in the NG view, economic liberalisation, an integral aspect of globalisation, has been hijacked by a market liberalism which puts the mechanisms of the market before the well-being of communities. In short, the NG view sees globalisation as negatively affecting the well-being of millions of people around the world, including the countries of the MENA. The NG critique also rejects the consensual acceptance of market capitalism and argues that capitalist globalisation leads to a grossly unfair system, structured mainly to improve the position of already powerful vested interests. Overall, the NG view is that it is erroneous to accept the claims of the PG school at face value: globalisation is a highly *politicised* process, based on specific conditions that create both winners *and* losers. In this context, democratisation per se is not the panacea that proponents of the PG approach claim it to be, as the structural conditions accompanying globalisation serve significantly to undermine the possibility that democracy per se can improve the lot of the disadvantaged (Haynes 2005: 141–143).

ORIENTALISM

While these two views of globalisation clearly see the world differently, both would agree that globalisation leads to an expansion of channels, pressures and agents via which various norms are diffused and interact. For example, many people regard globalisation after the Cold War as involving more interaction between previously geographically fragmented anti-Western Islamist movements. This perception has led some to conclude that we are witnessing a widespread, even worldwide, 'resurgence of Islam' (Zemni 2002: 158), involving Huntington's (1996) notorious 'clash of civilisations'. This alleged resurgence of Islam is said to fuel growing anti-Islam sentiments in many European countries. Over the last few years, an unfinished debate has ensued, whose roots are in the recent historical period of Western political and economic domination of Islam, an intrinsic aspect of a more general, Western-led globalisation. This involved what are claimed to be core Western values and norms: pluralism, liberal democracy, relativism and radical individualism, coming into contact with different values allegedly held by many Muslims.

Various critics, notably Edward Said (1978, 1993) and Bryan Turner (1978, 1994), have challenged this notion—Said called it 'Orientalism'—on various (empirical, theoretical and methodological) grounds. He challenged the self-proclaimed objectivity of Orientalist accounts of the Middle East—and of Muslims generally—by deconstructing the assumptions and dominant themes of that discourse. The concept of Orientalism captures the idea that Islam is an inherently atavistic body of religious and social thought, fundamentally at odds with Western thought and culture. Said (1978: 2) defines Orientalism as a style of thought based upon an ontological and epistemological distinction made between 'the Orient' and (most of the time) the 'Occident'. For Said, while many Western politicians and academics have sought to essentialise both Muslims and Islam into unchanging categories, these assumptions were problematically rooted in historical generalisations—with little or no empirical foundation. His critique was damning: Orientalist thinking, built on depictions of the region as inherently backwards and barbarous as a result of supposedly inescapable characteristics of Islam, served the political prerogatives of colonialism well, because such intellectual discourse allowed the legitimisation of discrimination and exploitation (Said 1993: 96). Said quotes Lord Cromer, the British governor of Egypt from 1882 to 1907. According to Cromer, the Oriental generally acts, speaks and thinks in a manner exactly opposite to the European. While the European employs close reasoning and is a natural logician, the Oriental is singularly deficient in the logical faculty (Said 1978: 39).

Cromer was not an isolated example, an aberration; rather, he was representative of a wider trend, carrying ideas that were dominant for long periods and show no signs of dying out a century later. As Heristchi (2006) notes, Orientalism monopolised the discourse on the Middle East, from history, culture and politics, to artistic expression. Lord Cromer was, of course, a product of his times, but his prejudiced views are certainly not extinct at the end of the first decade of the 21st century. We can note the continued use of Orientalist ideas and thinking in relation to the problematic use of the term 'Islam', to imply a unifying conceptual category predicating social and political order, with related political biases. In this view, the Muslim world still is often seen as a monolithic, unchanging, underdeveloped, violent, anti-democratic space: a direct result of the perceived fundamental characteristics of Islam. Thus, one of today's most contentious issues—the nature of the relationship between politics and Islam in Europe—may be a relatively new concern in Europe, but it has long been central to political development in several parts of the world, including the Middle East, North Africa and parts of sub-Saharan Africa. In these cases, Islam has long been a central focus of political science analysis, often with an Orientalist bias.

Samuel Huntington's egregious clash of civilisations thesis is an example of what might be called *nouveau* Orientalism. Huntington first presented his argument in a 1993 article, followed by a book three years later. Huntington claimed that following the end of the Cold War, there was a new global clash underway, replacing four decades of secular conflict between liberal Democracy/Capitalism and Communism. Now there was a new clash between the (Christian) West and the (mostly Arab, mostly Muslim) East. The core of Huntington's argument was that after the Cold War, the Christian, democratic West found itself in conflict with Islamic fundamentalism, a key threat to international stability. So-called Western values—strongly informed by Protestant and Catholic versions of Christianity—were said by Huntington to be conducive to the spread of liberal democracy. For evidence of his claims, he noted the collapse of dictatorships in Christian countries in Southern Europe (Greece, Portugal, Spain) and throughout Latin America in the 1970s and 1980s, followed by the development of liberal democratic political systems and norms (rule of law, free elections, political rights and civil liberties). For Huntington, such democratisation was conclusive proof of the synergy between Christianity and liberal democracy, key foundations of a normatively desirable global order built on these (Western) liberal values. In addition, around the same time, the U.S. neoconservative Francis Fukuyama argued that Islam is inherently undemocratic or even antidemocratic, while Islamic fundamentalism has a more than superficial resemblance to European fascism (Fukuyama 1992: 236).

Nouveau Orientalism was not restricted to a few U.S. academics, however notable. It was also influential among some American and European politicians, collectively articulating the view that Islam is the undesirable Other. For example, soon after 9/11, U.S. Democratic Congressman Tom Lantos asserted that 'Unfortunately we have no option but to take on barbarism which is hell-bent on destroying civilization [. . .]. You don't compromise with these people. This is not a bridge game. International terrorists have put themselves outside the bonds of protocols' (Interview with Tom Lantos, BBC Radio 4, *Today* programme, 20 November 2001). Similar, albeit more restrained, comments were made by a former French president, Valéry Giscard d'Estaing. Critics of such claims noted, however, that it is one thing to argue that *some* Muslims have qualitatively different perspectives on liberal democracy than *some* Christians, but that it is quite another to claim that *all* Muslims are engaged in serious conflict with the (Christian) West because of their differing political and social values. They pointed out that there are, in fact, many Islams, and only the malevolent or misinformed would associate *all* Muslims and their political articulations, whether in the United States, Europe or elsewhere, with an undifferentiated and simplistic idea of an anti-Western Islamic fundamentalism.

The idea of religious/cultural/civilisational conflict is also problematic for another reason: it is impossible to identify and articulate clear territorial boundaries between different civilisations/cultures/religions, and thus unfeasible to perceive them as acting as coherent units. Huntington's image of clashing civilisations focuses on an essentially undifferentiated category—a civilisation—and places insufficient emphasis on the various trends, competitions, conflicts and disagreements that take place within *all such traditions*, whether Islam, various Christianities (Protestantism, Catholicism, Orthodoxy), Confucianism, Buddhism, Hinduism, Sikhism, Judaism, and so on. In short, it is not useful to view civilisations/cultures/religions as closed systems of essentialist values and analytically unhelpful to perceive the world as comprising a strictly limited number of civilisations/cultures/religions, each with their own unique core sets of beliefs which necessarily contrast with others.

Finally, Huntington's image of clashing civilisations problematically ignores the fact that many radical Islamist groups—such as al-Qaeda or the perpetrators of the 2008 Mumbai bombings, Pakistan's Lashkar-e-Taiba ('Soldiers of the Pure')—primarily target not the West per se but their own unrepresentative, corrupt and illegitimate—in short, un-Islamic—governments. Arguably, anti-Westernism is a by-product of this focus, not its central dynamic. Most radical Islamist groups emerged in the 1980s and 1990s following serious domestic political and economic governmental failures, regimes that for the most part were supported by the U.S. government, the European Union and/or individual European governments. This latter factor provides much of the context for the anti-Western tendencies of radical Islamist groups.

Overall, the arguments of Said and Huntington underline that there is a deep-rooted tradition in Western thought of seeing the Orient—that is, for our purposes, the Arab/Muslim world of the MENA—as distinct and distinctive compared to the Christian West. This is not, as already noted, a novel issue. During the centuries of Western imperialism, there were frequent debates about what rights non-Christian and non-European peoples should be allowed to enjoy. The specific conflicts between Christianity and Islam were moulded dualistically by notions both of holy war—suggesting a special kind of conflict undertaken effectively outside any framework of shared rules and norms—and just war, one carried out for the vindication of rights within a shared framework of values. The result was a strand of Western thought suggesting that, because of their nature, some forms of political power—such as states and/or ideologies—cannot realistically be dealt with in normal terms of engagement, that is, by accepted rules between civilised actors in international relations. Indeed, such international rules, norms and practices legitimately can be set aside when confronting and trying to deal with those perceived as non-civilised international entities. And this is not something of historical interest only. We have already noted, following 9/11, that similar ideas were expressed (see the remarks of U.S. Democratic Congressman Tom Lantos above). Earlier, during the 1980s, the Reagan administration in the United States averred that there was a basic lack of give-and-take available when dealing with Communist governments; consequently, if necessary it was appropriate to set aside basic notions of international law when dealing with them.

GLOBALISATION: CHALLENGES AND OPPORTUNITIES FOR RELIGION

Academic discussions of religion and globalisation with Roland Robertson (1995), Peter Beyer (1994, 2006) and James Spickard (2001, 2003)—all important voices—mainly concentrate on the trends towards cultural pluralism and how religions' organisations respond to this development. Some react positively, by accepting or even endorsing pluralism, such as 'some Christian ecumenical movements or the Bahá'ís. Other groups emphasise the differences and confront the non-believers in an attempt to preserve their particular values from being eroded by globalisation. So-called fundamentalist Christian, Muslim, and Jewish movements are well-known examples' (Warburg 2001). In sum, there is growing awareness of the importance of religion as a transnational actor in the context of globalisation, but little agreement as to whether the insertion of religion into international relations leads to better or worse outcomes.

Overall, the relationship between religion and globalisation is characterised, on the one hand, by tension between forces that lead to *integration* in globalisation; and, on the other hand, by *resistance* to it. In this context 'integration' refers to religious processes that both promote and follow from processes of globalisation. The concept of 'resistance' implies the opposite trend: explicit or implicit criticism of, and mobilisation against, some or all processes of global change manifested in globalisation. Both integration and resistance can be seen in relation to religious resources that generally represent various expressions of soft power. Several authors have noted religion's soft power in relation to contemporary international relations. For Ferguson (2003), it is important not to underestimate 'the power of ideology and religion—which certainly has proved more enduring than the power of the Red Army. Indeed, there are those who would say that, after Mikhail Gorbachev and Ronald Reagan, no one did more to bring down Communism in Eastern Europe than John Paul II. Faith, then, is perhaps as important a component of power as material resources'.

According to Reychler (1997), the growing impact of religious discourses on international relations is a response to a 'world where many governments and international organizations are suffering from a legitimacy deficit. [. . .] Religion is a major source of soft power. It will, to a greater extent, be used or misused by religions and governmental organizations to pursue their interests. It is therefore important to develop a more profound understanding of the basic assumption underlying the different religions and the ways in which people adhering to them see their interests. It would also be very useful to identify elements of communality between the major religions'.

Also emphasising the idea that religious organisations and movements often enjoy more legitimacy than some governments and international organisations, Juergensmeyer contends that in particular, 'radical religious ideologies have become the vehicles for a variety of rebellions against authority that are linked with myriad social, cultural, and political grievances' (Juergensmeyer 2005).

It is possible to highlight three—not necessarily discrete—areas that not only generally emphasise the significance of religion in the context of contemporary globalisation but also point to the actual or potential soft power of religious organisations in influencing outcomes in the directions and ways they prefer. They are ideas, experiences, and practices.

IDEAS

Most religions traditionally comprise the ideas, beliefs and practices of a particular community. That is, religions have provided what Peter Berger (1969) calls a 'sacred canopy', enabling followers to make sense of their world. There were once many individual and different societies around the world, each with its own set of practices, some of which today we would call religious. As a result, religious ideas can be seen as 'the major organizing principles for explaining the world and defining ethical life' (Kurtz 1995: 3). Today, however, the circumstances of globalisation dramatically undermine the notion that all members of a religious community must necessarily hold the same ideas, because globalisation encourages the free(r) circulation of ideas. At the present time, many religions compete for the attention of individuals, and there is what is known as a 'global marketplace of religion' (Bruce 2003). The consequence is that the spread of various, sometimes competing, religious ideas leads to a situation where the once relatively autonomous sacred canopy is increasingly regarded as an artefact of the past. This process may be met with resistance, 'countered by the revival of more localised practices in the form of religious fundamentalist and other protest movements' (Kurtz 1995: 99).

EXPERIENCES

There is a dynamic and dialectic connection between globalisation and religion. Globalisation may lead individuals and groups to increased self-reflection, as a result of the experiences they encounter following two simultaneous developments. On the one hand, cultural, religious and social differences between people have sometimes become increasingly visible as a result of globalisation. On the other hand, many people also experience direct or indirect pressure towards increased homogenisation and 'free' religious competition. This creates a field of tension where the value of religious belonging as identity forming becomes more important while at the same time it is rapidly changing. This is because globalisation facilitates the transmission of both material and nonmaterial factors, such as ideas, information and beliefs. Many religious actors seek to use any available opportunity to disseminate their religious ideas in various ways. Second, what religions do within a country is affected by social, political and economic experiences—and these in turn may well be affected by globalisation. As Berger notes, in some cases—for example, in relation to manifestations of Islamism (or 'Islamic fundamentalism')—this is a challenge that is seen to emanate from attempts to impose 'an emerging global culture, most of it of Western and indeed American provenance, penetrating the rest of the world on both elite and popular levels. The response from the target societies is then seen as occurring on a scale between acceptance and rejection, with in-between positions of coexistence and synthesis' (Berger 2002: 1).

PRACTICES

Religious ideas and traditions are often connected intimately to specific cultures, but this is not to imply that they are static. On the contrary, religious traditions are generally dynamic, changing as they encounter each other. As a result, there are no 'pure', unadulterated religious traditions preserved intact over long periods of time until now (Kurtz 1995: 98). This implies that religious practices differ, even within the same religious traditions. Thus, there may be various—associated but different—versions of the same religious tradition encompassing different groups, for example, dissimilar social groups and classes (Haynes 1996). Put another way, the 'sacred canopy' has generally not been uniform, and religious practices vary from place to place and culture to culture, even among those ostensibly following the same religious tradition. As with ideas and experiences, the impact of globalisation is likely to make religious practice even more diverse.

GLOBALISATION, POLITICS AND ISLAM: PLUS ÇA CHANGE, PLUS C'EST LA MÊME CHOSE?

Political change in the 'Islamic world', especially among the Arab countries of the Middle East and North Africa, is a defining theme of several recent books.[1] Implicitly or explicitly, each works from a key premise: there is nothing 'inherent' in Islam that means that Muslim countries will 'inevitably' be unable to change their extant political arrangements.

On the one hand, however, it is widely asserted not only that many Muslim countries have few structural characteristics conducive to democratisation, but also that things have been that way for a long time. This situation did not widely change among the Muslim countries during the two decades of the 'third wave of democracy', from the mid-1970s to the mid-1990s, a development stimulated by deepening globalisation (Huntington 1991). On the other hand, Muslim-majority countries around the world—of which there are more than 40, from Morocco in the West to Indonesia in the East, collectively home to over a billion people—do not comprise an unchanging, undemocratic monolith. This is also a key research theme in the topic of democracy in the Muslim world, in the context of current globalisation, a focus that also stresses that to understand why some countries in the Muslim world have democratised while others have not, we need to look for explanations in both internal and external factors, including globalisation.

In the Middle East and North Africa, the region often associated with theory and practice of 'Muslim government' or 'government by Muslims', we can note three periods, together accounting for around 120 years of often profound political changes: the 1860s–1930s, the late 1950s–early 1960s; and the 1970s—1990s. Each of these periods were also individually notable for being periods of deepening globalisation: the 1860s–1930s, characterised by the global spread of nationalism, including in the Middle East following the collapse of the Ottoman Empire; the deepening of the Cold War and the subsequent battle of ideologies that took global form in the 1950s and 1960s; and, from the 1970s, the gradual demise of the Soviet bloc and the accompanying ideology of Communism, with worldwide ramifications. Now, at the beginning of the second decade of the 21st century, the Arab/Muslim countries of the Middle East and North Africa are undergoing a fourth round of political changes. Although the phenomenon of the 'Arab Spring' is by no means played out at the time of this writing, the issue of what it amounts to in terms of political outcomes for the MENA is addressed below.

The first phase was characterised by regional political changes as Ottoman (Turkish) colonial rule began to ebb away. Between the 1860s and the 1930s, national assemblies were created in a number of countries in the Middle East and North Africa. Ottoman rule collapsed immediately after World War I. Parliamentary regimes were created under mandated British or French rule, reflecting the aegis of a newly formed global body, the League of Nations, in a number of regional countries, including Egypt (1924–1958), Iraq (1936–1958), and Lebanon (1946–1975). Second, during the late 1950s and early 1960s, there was a further period of significant political amendments in the region. Within the space of a few years, radical, often junior, army officers overthrew conservative governments in four key regional countries: Egypt, Iraq, Libya, and Syria. Influenced by the Soviet Union's impressive anticolonial and anti-Western credentials, a common goal was to oust what they regarded as unacceptably unrepresentative governments, widely regarded as unforgivably subservient to Western countries, especially the governments of Britain and the United States. However, over time, it became clear that the new rulers had no intention of democratising their political systems along lines familiar to Western governments and voters. Instead, they installed authoritarian or totalitarian regimes, with the political role of the armed forces well to the fore, and sometimes modelled on the Communist governments of the Soviet bloc. Despite their differing political characteristics, they were all regimes with few, if any, conventional attributes of democracy, beyond regular, albeit heavily controlled, elections.

Third, while the third wave of democracy (from the mid-1970s until the mid-1990s) was not generally a time of profound political changes in the Muslim and Arab world, some Muslim countries, notably Turkey (98% Muslim) and Indonesia (88% Muslim), did emerge from authoritarian rule to establish democratic systems during this time. With the reelection to power of the Justice and Development Party in the June 2011 elections, it is clear that Turkey is a 'functioning democracy' with an increasingly strong case for membership of the European Union (Haynes 2011). Indonesia emerged in 1998 from three decades of personalistic rule under General Suharto, and since then the country has gradually developed a flawed yet recognisably democratic system.[2] Other Muslim countries in the MENA that are also embarking, albeit tentatively, upon a process of political liberalisation (which may lead to democratisation) include: Kuwait (85% Muslim), Jordan (92%), and, perhaps, Algeria (99%) and Tunisia (98%). Collectively, these countries have begun a process of as yet unfinished political liberalisation that appears to denote real—if somewhat tentative—moves towards more democratic political systems.

However, despite signs of political liberalisation/democratisation among a small but not insignificant group of Muslim-majority countries, much conventional wisdom would continue to insist that the great majority of Muslim countries should be characterised in two general ways: their governments (1) resist meaningful democratisation, and (2) exhibit little respect for the human rights of their citizens. However, while various kinds of authoritarian regimes are still the norm in the MENA, it can be argued that this situation is linked to a number of historical and structural characteristics, which collectively contour the political arrangements of the Arab/Muslim countries of the MENA (Cavatorta 2010; Haynes 2010). These include:

- *Political systems headed by personalistic leaders.* Typically, in the Muslim world such rulers preside over very hierarchical, centralised states. In many cases, the extant political system depends on top-down power, and as a result rulers are most unwilling to devolve any real power to other political institutions—if they meaningfully exist in the first place, which is often not the case.
- *Politically significant militaries.* Military men quite rightly see it as their job to protect the state from attack from within and without. Among Muslim polities, there are significant examples of armies that exist primarily to thwart challenges for political control from groups wishing to change the political status quo via rebellion or revolution.
- *Weak and fragmented civil societies.* Civil societies in Muslim countries are often weak and fragmented; as a result, they do not present a challenge to incumbent governments to encourage them to amend undemocratic behaviour.
- *Cultural and religious hegemony of Islam.* Islam is often said to be a religious system that is not beneficial to democratisation. In the Middle East, the regional ubiquity and sociopolitical significance of Islam—the dominant religion in all regional countries with the clear exception of Israel and debateable exemption of Lebanon—is said to help explain not only the authoritarian nature of most governing regimes in the region but also significantly to account for political cultures of repression and passivity that are antithetical to democratic citizenship.

Karl (1995: 79) asserts that the consequence is that most Muslim countries—in the Middle East and elsewhere—are characterised by 'a culture of repression and passivity that is antithetical to democratic citizenship'. In a similar vein, Fattah (2006: 1) avers that '[t]here is no question that Muslim countries are disproportionately autocratic [. . .] no single Muslim country qualifies today as a consolidated democracy [. . .]'. On the other hand, we can note that potentially significant political changes are now taking place in some parts of the Muslim world, including the Middle East region. Political elites in various regional countries—including, Turkey, Kuwait and Jordan—are now to varying degrees engaged in processes of political liberalisation or democratisation.

Fundamental political change in the Arab/Muslim countries of the MENA is a core concern of the 'Arab Spring'. The implicit starting point is that there is nothing inherent in Islam that means that the mainly Muslim countries of the MENA will inevitably lack the capacity to change their political arrangements in a pro-democracy direction.

The Arab world is undergoing a series of uprisings and rebellions which began in Tunisia in January 2011 and led to the fall of the country's government. Soon after, the government of Egypt also collapsed. Since the beginning of 2011, there have also been major, continuing political upheavals in Libya, Syria, Bahrain and Yemen; and smaller, although still notable, expressions of political dissent in Algeria and Morocco. These concerns took a new twist with the killing of Osama bin Laden in May 2011, the ramifications of which for Western security are not yet clear.

The British prime minister, David Cameron, was sufficiently concerned, however, to announce in May 2011 the UK's major financial support for the democratisation and improved social welfare demands of the proponents of the Arab Spring. The UK announced that £110 million would be siphoned off from the existing Department for International Development budget, to be focussed upon encouraging the Arab Spring. In addition, the Foreign and Commonwealth Office stated that up to £40 million would be spent over the 2011–2015 period to try to improve three democratic cornerstones in the Arab Spring countries: increased political participation, improved rule of law and greater freedom of the press. Finally, the UK would donate a further £70 million, focused generally on economic reform and specifically on aiming to boost youth employment, strengthen anticorruption measures and promote private sector investment. In sum, the UK government was committing extensive funds to the democratisation and improved social policy of the Arab Spring countries in a bid not only to spread democratic values but also to undermine religious extremism in the MENA ('UK calls for G8 financial aid for "Arab Spring"').

However, a word of caution is necessary. For three main reasons, the region is not about to jump from authoritarianism to democracy à la Central and Eastern Europe circa 1989–1991: the rise in sectarianism which threatens democratisation, serious economic problems, and foreign policy meddling by Saudi Arabia and Iran. Firstly, despite the coming together of people from all faiths in the protests that brought down their governments, both Egypt and Tunisia have recently experienced sectarian tensions and conflict, while Syria may be embarking on the same path. Egypt was the scene of a bloody attack against a Coptic church in Alexandria in December 2010, followed by a clash in the Imbaba district of Cairo which killed at least 15, both Copts and Muslims. Tunisia saw the murder of a Polish-born Catholic priest, Father Marek Rybinski, killed on the premises of an interdenominational school in Tunis, while Islamist protesters gathered together outside the Great Synagogue of Tunis, and a chapel was burned near Gabes. In Bahrain, the political violence pitted Shias against Sunnis. In Syria the Assad-led Alawite minority government seeks to exploit the country's latent sectarian divisions by stirring up trouble in order to proclaim *après moi le déluge* (Guitton 2011).

Second, the region is undergoing a frightful economic slide. Gross domestic product (GDP) is down and social welfare declining, and all this in the context of some of the fastest growing populations in the world. Egypt is a good example of what is happening. Arguably, much of the cause of the uprising which led to the overthrow of the Mubarak government in early 2011 was the result of economic frustration, especially among the young, those in the forefront of the rebellion. Egypt's economy contracted by 7 per cent in the first three months of 2011. Tourism revenue, the mainstay of the economy and the biggest single element in GDP, fell by 80 per cent, the stock market plummeted, and the IMF revised its growth estimate to a mere 1 per cent following 5.1 per cent growth in 2010 (Fraser & Crossland 2011).

Third, both Saudi Arabia and Iran are deadly rivals in the MENA. Saudi Arabia has had to deal with the loss of its closest ally, the Mubarak government. Iran is contemplating the fall of its ally, the Assad regime. The government of Bahrain is bolstered—but for how long?—by the injection of Saudi troops, while Iran seeks to exploit the growing anarchy in Yemen in order to destabilise its Saudi arch enemy (Ghannoushi 2011).

In sum, the prospects for a clear and linear path to democracy in the region are poor, and the likely outcome is a slide into entrenched and long-term political instability culminating in some cases in state failure and regional instability.

In the events of the Arab Spring so far, the Islamists have been notable by their relative absence. However, as events unfold, especially in Egypt and Tunisia, which have scheduled elections, it is very likely that they will emerge as key components of political developments. According to Fattah (2006: 4), three predominant worldviews influence issues of religion and governance within the Muslim world: 'traditionalist Islamists', 'modernist Islamists', and 'secularists'. Traditionalist Islamists believe that they are the keepers of the Islamic traditions. It should be noted, however, that there are various kinds of traditionalist Islamists. Some propose (and/or practise) armed struggle to wrest power from governments that are seen to be ruling in un-Islamic ways, such as al Qaeda; some believe in incremental change through the ballot box, such as the Islamic Salvation Front (FIS) in Algeria in the early 1990s or Hamas in the Gaza Strip today; some seek to achieve their goals by way of a combination of extra-parliamentary struggle, societal proselytisation and governmental lobbying, including the Muslim Brotherhoods in Egypt, Jordan and other Middle Eastern countries. But despite differences in strategy and tactics, such entities have two beliefs in common: (1) politics and religion are inseparable, and (2) *sharia* law should ideally be applied to all Muslims. Traditionalist Islamists agree that for something to be authentically 'Islamic', it must be acceptable both in terms of *sharia* and among the *ulama* (Muslim clerics); in such views, democracy is anti- or un-Islamic. Many also share a third concern: Muslims as a group are the focal point of a global conspiracy, bringing together Zionists and Western imperialists who collectively aim, for both political and economic purposes, to take over Muslim-owned lands and oil resources via globalisation. This impression is bolstered by the sight of (mainly U.S.) transnational corporations' control over Arab oil, as well as by Israel's implacable denial, supported by the American government, of political and civil rights for its (largely Muslim) Palestinian constituency.

The second category, 'modernist Islamists', believe that 'Muslims can learn about anything they believe is good for themselves and society regardless of its origins' (Fattah 2006: 17). In other words, unlike traditionalist Islamists, modernist Islamists do not necessarily reject democracy. This is because they do not find either ethical or religious problems with the adoption of democratic mechanisms—as long as they are generally appropriate to Muslim beliefs. They base their acceptance on two factors: first, when appropriate and necessary, early Muslims adopted non-Islamic innovations and; second, democracy is not a Western invention, and as a consequence it can be authentically islamised. In sum, for modernist Islamists, for something to be Islamic it must not contradict *sharia*; democracy is potentially Islamic or at least 'islamisable'.

Third, there are the (Muslim or Islamic) secularists who start from two assumptions. First, Islam does not offer a *concrete* guide for governance; that is, Muslim holy texts do not tell Muslims explicitly how to run their societies, especially in the 21st century, a period marked by profound and continuing economic, cultural and social changes, many of which are traceable to globalisation. Secularists believe that holy texts, notably the Qu'ran, are valuable sources of ethics and morality, yet they do not offer that much practical assistance in providing guidance in running today's political and economic systems. The second assumption of secularists is that Muslims need to follow what the most successful societies have done in order to eventually outdo them. This is said to be exactly what the West did in the past by learning from Muslims and other non-Western peoples. In sum, for secularist Muslims, for something to be Islamic it should be in the interest of society quite regardless of holy texts. In addition, democracy is widely regarded among secularists as necessary in order to provide representative, legitimate and authoritative governments in Muslim countries.

CONCLUSION

Interest in religion as a political actor has increased in recent years, notably since Iran's Islamic revolution of 1978–1979. The revolution was an emblematic event, as it was diametrically opposed to current conventional wisdom: all societies would *invariably* secularise as they modernise, urbanise and industrialise. And, as a consequence, religion would lose both its social and political importance.

In addition, it was widely believed that developing countries—emerging in great numbers from colonial status in Africa and Asia in the 1950s and 1960s—would invariably follow the secularisation path taken earlier by the economically developed countries of North America and Europe. In both of these regions, it was surmised, religion would lose nearly all of its earlier public significance and clout. Instead, it would be 'privatised', that is, relegated to the personal sphere of belief, without an institutionalized public role.

Such views, of course, turned out to be mistaken: the evidence is now clear that societies do not necessarily secularise as they modernise; some do, and some do not. How then to account for what is widely understood as a growing political and social role for religion in many—or most—parts of the world? In fact, there is no simple reason for this turn of events, no single theoretical explanation to cover all extant examples. On the other hand, it seems relatively clear that, around the world, processes of modernisation—including, urbanisation, industrialisation and the impact of swift technological changes—conjoined with a second development. This was many people's loss of faith in (1) secular ideologies of progressive change—such as Socialism and Communism, even perhaps the notion of secular democracy itself and, in some cases; and (2) the state's ability to deliver on proclaimed developmental goals.

The latter disappointment was often instrumental in producing in many people feelings of loss rather than achievement. Thus, in this process, modernisation not only undermined traditional value systems but also tended to allocate opportunities to people in highly unequal ways—both within and between nations. It also stimulated in many people a renewed search for a feeling of identity, something to give their lives meaning and purpose at a time of historically unprecedented, diverse and massive changes.

Changes linked to modernisation cannot be seen in isolation from another important—and related—trend: globalisation. It is widely agreed that the 1980s and 1990s were filled with fundamental political, social and economic changes that affected not only individual countries but also international relations more generally. Reflecting this, a neologism, globalisation, was coined to account for the importance of multifaceted processes at the international level. A rubric for varied phenomena, the concept of globalisation seeks to interrelate multiple levels of analysis and can be defined as the myriad linkages and interconnections between geographically fragmented states and societies. During the last two decades of the 20th century, not only was there a consolidation of a truly global economy and, some would argue, the gradual emergence of an Americanised 'global culture', but also fundamental political developments, notably the steady, if uneven, advance of democracy to many previously undemocratic countries and regions. Finally, there were, as already noted, many examples of religion's political involvement both within and between countries.

The 'return' of religion to political agendas was facilitated by processes of globalisation and encouraged by the communications revolution. The consequence is that we now inhabit a 'globalising' social reality, where previously effective barriers to communication no longer exist. The development of both international and transnational religious communities was, inter alia, encouraged and facilitated by easy interpersonal and intergroup communications. This not only helped to spread religious messages, but also enabled like-minded individuals and groups to link up across state boundaries.

The political connotations of what has been called the 'unsecularization of the world' were, of course, highlighted by the events of September 11, 2001 ('9/11') and its aftermath, including the U.S.-led invasions of Afghanistan (2001) and Iraq (2003). These events directed attention not only to the nature and substance of cross-border interactions between religious actors and their global networks but also highlighted more generally a renewed importance for religion in politics and international relations.

To what extent has democratisation made progress in the Muslim countries of the Middle East and North Africa as a result of globalisation? Some observers, such as Diamond (1999: 270), believe that 'culturally and historically, [the Muslim Middle East] has been the most difficult terrain in the world for political freedom and democracy' and by implication globalisation has not done a great deal to change things in this regard. Attempts to explain why this should be the case are often linked to the political importance of Islam—its immovability and resilience in the face of often determined external efforts to change its core norms and values. Islam is also routinely linked to strong, centralised states, often led by personalistic leaders, mainly bequeathed by colonialism or imperialism, and to strongly politicised militaries anxious to maintain the political status quo. In these contexts, democratisation struggles to make progress, even when encouraged by an international *zeitgeist* led by the West that seeks to normalise democracy as a natural end state for human kind.

This is not to suggest that Islam is inherently antidemocratic, just that Western-orientated political systems based on pluralism do not necessarily find fertile ground in countries with different cultural and historical traditions. While some kinds of political Islam have qualitatively different perspectives on (Western-style, liberal) democracy than, for example, some types of Christianity, this does not imply that political Islam *necessarily* denigrates democracy per se. The current struggles of political struggles of Islamists are primarily directed against their own typically undemocratic rulers and political systems—precisely because they are undemocratic and, in many cases, egregiously corrupt. This fits in with a key historic characteristic of politics in the Muslim world, especially in what many would see as its heartland: the Arab countries of the Middle East.

In the events of the Arab Spring so far, the Islamists have been notable by their relative absence. However, as events unfold, especially in Egypt and Tunisia, which have scheduled elections, it is very likely that they will emerge as key components of political developments.

NOTES

1. See, for example, M.J. Akbar, *The Shade of Swords. Jihad and the Conflict between Islam & Christianity*, London: Routledge, 2002; Larry Diamond, Marc F. Plattner and Daniel Brumberg (eds.), *Islam and Democracy in the Middle East*, Baltimore: The Johns Hopkins University Press, 2003; Graham E. Fuller, *The Future of Political Islam*, New York: Palgrave, 2003; Jennifer Noyon, *Islam, Politics and Pluralism. Theory and Practice in Turkey, Jordan, Tunisia and Algeria*, London: Royal Institute of International Affairs, 2003; M.A. Muqtedar Khan (ed.), *Islamic Democratic Discourse. Theories, Debates and Philosophical Perspectives*, Lanham: Rowman & Littlefield, 2006; Moataz A. Fattah, *Democratic Values in the Muslim World*, Boulder, CO: Lynne Rienner, 2006.
2. See, for example, Aris Ananta, Evi Nurvidya Arifin and Leo Suryadinata, *Emerging Democracy in Indonesia*, Singapore: Institute of Southeast Asian Studies, 2005; Mikaela Nyman, *Democratizing Indonesia: The Challenges of Civil Society in the Era of Reformasi*, Copenhagen: NIAS Press, 2006.

3 The Paradox of Globalisation
Quakers, Religious NGOs and the United Nations

Jeremy Carrette

> Times of transformation can be times of confusion.
>
> Kofi Annan,
> 'The Quiet Revolution' (1998:127)

In 1998, the then-UN General Secretary Kofi Annan wrote a paper entitled 'The Quiet Revolution' in which he mapped out the implications for a new United Nations in a post-Cold War era of globalisation. The paper outlines the 'fundamental forces' shaping social organisation and discussed the 'era of realignment' within a global world. He recognised that 'globalization poses numerous policy challenges' as it 'erodes the efficacy of the policy instruments' previously used in the industrialised world. As well as recognising the importance of information technology and related global flows of information, Kofi Annan (1998: 129) underlined how new international actors, the 'expanding transnational network of nongovernmental organizations (NGOs)', were now transforming the institutional context. He noted that these NGOs encompass 'virtually every sector of public concern' and included 'virtually every level of social organization, from villages on up to global summits'. Hidden inside this summary spectrum of social organisation were the hundreds of religious and faith-based organisations with all their normative engagements and concerns about international politics and policy. The absent presence of religion in the subsets of social organisations reveals important features about religion inside the global context of international institutions. We can see such a situation in the UN-commissioned report on the UN and civil society led by Fernando Henrique Cardoso (UN General Assembly 2004). In this report, we find only one mention of religion, which is found in a footnote acknowledging that the consultation process engaged 'religion NGOs'. Although religion is never a formal classification within the Economic and Social Council (ECOSOC)—which registers NGOs at the UN—the presence of religion is nonetheless evident. As an example of religious groups involved in a global network, NGOs in the UN provide a useful case study for thinking about some of the theoretical and empirical problems of religion and globalisation. It enables us to explore some of the key tensions within globalisation theory and establish a stronger empirical basis for understanding religion in global processes.

In this chapter, I want to show how the international institutional context of the UN, and the place of religious NGOs within it, reveal what I will call the paradox of globalisation. I will seek to draw out the tensions of the category of globalisation by locating the theoretical abstractions of such an idea inside the empirical test case of the UN: holding the word 'globalisation' as an explanatory category of the global connections and the related global compression of social and political worlds. I will illustrate the paradox of globalisation by taking the case of Quakers (the Friends World Consultation Committee) at the UN, examining the key shift of activities in the post-1990s era from their founding presence at the UN in 1945. I will then reveal the way in which religious groups, such as Quakers, have adapted to the changes within global civil society and show how the expansion of civil society does not necessarily lead to greater representation: the paradox of hegemony and plurality. My overall aim is to reveal the tensions in the construction of the category of globalisation by examining the link between religious groups and global institutions. It will reveal the unique and dynamic processes through which religious groups, operating as registered NGOs at the UN, have adapted to changes within global civil society and have become partners in global politics.

My analysis is located within a broad interdisciplinary literature on globalisation, governmentality and studies of religious NGOs at the UN and grounded in extensive empirical research during a three-year (December 2009—November 2012) project on religious NGOs at the UN in Geneva and New York. In order to support my claim about the paradox of globalisation, I will follow a series of steps of argumentation. First I will outline some of the current empirical findings about religious NGOs at the UN and briefly map the history of Quaker involvement in the UN, particularly after the post-1990s expansion of civil society. I will then locate this within a theoretical discussion by answering three questions. First, I ask how is globalisation a paradox?; second, why are global governance institutions a key empirical register for assessing the dynamics of religion in a global world?; third, and finally, how are Quakers and religious NGOs caught up in the paradox of globalisation? I will conclude by showing how this context of religious NGOs and the UN reveals how the reality of global governance institutions redefines religion and how it changes the way we think about religion in a global world.

THE UN AND THE EXPANSION OF RELIGIOUS NGOS

It has been noted by the Religion Counts Report on 'Religion and Public Policy at the UN' (Religion Counts 2002), and subsequently by scholars such as Julia Berger (2003) and Evelyn Bush (2007), that there has been an increase in self-named 'religious' NGOs; although recent research from a University of Kent survey (2009–2012) suggests that a more nuanced rendering of 'religious' NGOs is required as the category is superseded by the language of 'faith-based' and the resistance of some groups to the assigning of their activities to the category 'religious' because of funding and negative attitudes and perceptions from both civil society and state actors.[1] However, 'religious' identification among NGOs can clearly be seen from the establishment, in 1972, of the Committee of Religious NGOs, with its annual *Survey of Activities of Religious NGOs at the United Nations*.[2] The complexity of taxonomy becomes clear when the latter committee includes any group that defines its work as 'religious, spiritual, or ethical'. This obviously raises the difficult problem of distinction between so-called religious NGOs and non-religious NGOs.[3] According to the Religion Counts Report, the 'religious identity of a group is not easy to determine' (Religion Counts 2002: 17), and scholars like Julia Berger (2003: 21) used 'self-identity rather than an independent measure'. Evelyn Bush (2007: 1646) used data from the official UN sources, the *Yearbook of International Organisations* and the *Human Rights Directory*. Groups identified as religious have been working with the UN from its inception, with 15 groups in the first 4 years (Religion Counts 2002: 13). The report noted that in the year 2000, there were 180 religious NGOs out of 2000, a mere 9 per cent of the total. Within this group of 180, 61 per cent were Christian; 15 per cent were Islamic; 7 per cent Jewish; 9 per cent other, 8 per cent interfaith. The Christian groups were made up of 51 per cent Catholic, 41 per cent Protestant and 8 per cent other (Religion Counts 2002: 17). In Berger's 2003 sample, of the 3,000 NGOs linked to the ECOSOC and DPI (Department of Public Information), 263 were 'identified as religious NGOs' (Berger 2003: 21).[4]

The proliferation of groups declared as religious NGOs reflects part of the wider process of extending the public policy forum under the UN Charter Article 71, outlining the consultative links of the (ESOSOC) to NGOs. In a seminal study of NGOs, *The Conscience of the World: The Influence of NGOs in the UN System*, edited by Peter Willetts, we see how, after the Cold War concern with QUANGOs,[5] there was a renewal and expansion of NGOs in the 1990s and an enhancement of their political importance (Willetts 1996). As Peter Willetts (1996: 3) argues in the introduction of this work, 'Almost all intergovernmental organizations now accept, as a norm of world politics, that they must have working relationships with NGOs.' The significance and importance of NGOs is underlined in Boutros Boutros-Ghali's address to NGOs in 1994, when he stated: 'I, for my part, am convinced that NGOs have an important role to play in the achievement of the ideal established by the Charter of the United Nations: the maintenance and establishment of peace' (Willetts 1996: 312). In his 1996 foreword to Weiss and Gordenker's (1996) study of NGOs, Boutros Boutros-Ghali gave further evidence of the importance of NGOs by showing how NGO engagement with 'international organizations' was evidence of 'a basic form of popular participation' (Weiss & Gordenker 1996: 7). Although Weiss and Gordenker do not pick up the aspects of religious NGOs, so-called religious NGOs have been increasing their own presence.

On a slightly different front, Kille (2007: 16) and others have assessed the impact of religion within the UN by examining the influence of different 'religious' backgrounds on the various UN Secretary Generals, something that has only been fully appreciated previously with Dag Hammarskjöld's Lutheran background and, perhaps, more recently, Kofi Annan's Anglicanism. The importance of religious NGOs now features as a key part of International Relations theory, with the work of Scott Thomas (2005) and Fox and Sandler (2006) among others, although these works are not without serious theoretical problems.[6]

In all the studies of religious NGOs, there is always some brief mention of the historical importance of Quakers, who were not only present at the San Francisco founding conference of the UN, but have been highlighted as a respected group with significant political influence, not least because of the award of the 1947 Nobel Peace Prize given to the Quakers (the Friends Service Committee in London and the American Friends Service Committee in Philadelphia) for their humanitarian and peace work during the Second World War (Berger 2003: 20; Thomas 2005: 101). Indeed, the Religion Counts report in 2002 takes the Quaker United Nations Office as a case example. The report highlights their various political strategies, including their 'high regard in UN circles', their UN briefing papers on various issues, their annual 'State of the UN' report and their informal diplomatic meetings in the Quaker centres at New York and Geneva (Religion Counts 2002: 30).

INSTITUTIONAL KNOWLEDGE IS POWER: QUAKERS IN INTERNATIONAL RELATIONS

The Quakers have a long history of intervention in international relations—from their emergence during the English Civil War in the 1650s, when George Fox and William Penn established the Quaker colony in Pennsylvania, to the contemporary engagements in the UN. Penn's *An Essay Towards the Present and Future Peace of Europe* in 1693 reflected not only his political vision for an American colonial state but an interstate relation and a long history of justice, peace and liberty in government. In Robert Byrd's 1960 defining work, *Quaker Ways in Foreign Policy*, he identifies six phases in Quaker international relations, which 'mark differences in emphasis in the Quaker relationship to foreign policy' across their 300 years of history, and which reflect the history of their emergence and difference to protection and particularity in political moral issues (Byrd 1960: 109).

The postwar interventions have been covered effectively by Mike Yarrow (1978) in his *Quaker Experience in International Conciliation*, which outlines activities between 1968 and 1973, and Sydney Bailey's (1985) article 'Non-Official Mediation in Disputes: Reflections on Quaker Experience'. These studies show how Quakers in the post-1945 period became closely linked with UN diplomacy and peace work. Yarrow's work reveals significant Quaker diplomatic involvement in postwar Germany, the Middle East, the India-Pakistan war of 1965 and Nigerian Civil war of 1968–1969; the latter was examined by Cynthia Sampson (1994), who argued that the Quaker team was 'the sole third party that won the complete trust of both parties in the conflict' (Sampson 1994: 110–111). The key aspects of these interventions, as Nancy Gallagher's study of Quaker activity in the Israeli-Palestinian conflict shows (2007: 8), is that during and after the Second World War, Quakers worked outside the 'Westphalian system of established states'. They used methods of conciliation, witness and advocacy (Gallagher 2007: 10) and, according to Bailey (1985: 212), have 'organised more than a hundred conferences for diplomats and other national decision-makers since 1952'. The historical respect that Quakers received resulted in specific requests by the UN for diplomatic representation, even though this resulted in some complex alliances and in certain cases errors for Quaker political engagement (Bailey 1985: 205–206).

Although acknowledging that assessing the effectiveness of Quaker involvement is almost impossible in many international situations—especially when they are part of a complex tapestry of events—Yarrow (1978: 298–300) suggested the 'usefulness' of Quakers could be seen by their 'continuing access to top leadership over a considerable period of time'. The specific diplomatic interventions were also part of the integrated approach with related NGO groups to bring about political change in relation to landmines and world debt, as with the Jubilee movement. Overviewing the interventions of Quakers in the spectrum of wider UN activity, Gallagher (2007:17) writes: 'The Quakers, along with other secular and religious NGOs, successfully lobbied for the inclusion in the charter of the new organization, to be called the United Nations, of provisions against discrimination by race, creed, or colour; for arms reduction; for NGOs to gain consultative status in the UN; and for NGOs to have the right to play a role in international relations'.

Quakers at least show the historical force of religious non-state actors. This has been supported in related studies, such as Berger (2003), and is a part of what Fred Halliday called 'the romance of non-state actors' (Thomas 2005: 95). This 'romance', however, requires a context and appreciation in relation to Quaker activity, with its 'multi-faceted approach' at different periods of history (Waugh 2001: 77). There are, for example, shifts in Quaker work from its pre-Second World War work, its postwar interventions and its reconfigurations in a post-1990s UN. It is significant that much of the value of Quaker involvement in the international arena comes from its 'engagement over a long period' (Brett 2008: 11). These historical perspectives raise questions as to how contemporary Quaker work at the UN is changing given the saturation of activity of other NGOs and the wider proliferation of global media and new Internet responses to their work, such as the controversial, radical right wing attempts in the United States to portray the AFSC [the Quaker American Friend's Service Committee] as

Communists and anti-American (see Lamb 2003). The continuous shifts of Quaker political engagement returns us to Scott Thomas's (2005: 95) wider question about NGOs: 'How should we understand the meaning and influence of these religious non-state actors or nongovernmental organisations (NGOs) in international relations today'?

In the Religion Counts report on religious NGOs, five principles of effectiveness for religious groups in the complex system of the UN were established. The first two were built on reputation by being 'indispensable to the work of the UN' through information and resources and holding 'integrity and reliability'. The third was rising above 'self-serving or narrow goals'. According to the report, other than the unique status of the Holy See, Quakers and the Bahá'ís 'stood above the rest' as they held ideals consistent with the UN on peace and operate as 'facilitators rather than partisan advocates' (Religion Counts 2002: 37). The significance of the Quaker movement, however, can be seen in the final two principles, which reflect something of the hard reality of the UN as a global political institution: knowing the 'procedures and mechanisms' of the UN and, finally, having the 'virtues of patience and perseverance'. Understanding the structural apparatus of international institutions is vital for the effectiveness of any global actor. As the Quaker-UN representative John Patterson expressed in the Religion Counts report, the key focus is on 'process'.[7] He argues that the real issue is 'strengthening the capacity of the institution to resolve the kinds of problems that need to be resolved if the world community is to be a community' (Religion Counts 2002: 37). Here, at the heart of Quaker interventions, we see how knowledge of global institutions is central to religious engagement with political systems. The question is whether those who know the system can influence the institutional structures of the UN or the World Bank and whether they can sufficiently evaluate those aspects of institutions that deliberately thwart activist groups. As Barkin (2006: 28) argues in his study of international organisations: 'Understanding the bureaucratic structure of an IO [international organisation] is similarly important in understanding what the organisation can and cannot do'. He also recognises that given the size of the UN, it is entirely possible that different parts are trying to do 'incompatible things' (Barkin 2006: 35).

Given the institutional complexity of the UN and other global organisations, the problem of the effectiveness of humanitarian groups like the Quakers comes back to the question of understanding 'process' and structure. Indeed, Byrd (1960: 203), in his own reading of Quakers in international relations, recognises that the insights they brought, despite any idealist visions, were 'an awareness of the existence of the international community and the necessity for strengthening and structuring that community'. He later underlined the importance of the international community for Quaker action: 'Thus do Friends urge the development and strengthening of the international community, international organization and international trade in goods, and the reduction of military force to the proportions required to maintain peace and order under a commonly accepted law' (Byrd 1960: 205).

Understanding the complexity of a global world also means understanding how the power to influence it is deployed through global institutions and networks. According to Barkin's reading of Hedley Bull's seminal modelling of types of international relations, the UN attempts to work according to a 'universalist' model, but is constrained by the reality of the 'internationalist model'.[8] The tension is between inclusive 'universalist' models, which incorporate NGO actors, and more 'realist' or 'internationalists' models that are shaped by the domination of state actors. This dynamic of international relations can be seen in the historical example of Quaker relations with state power during the Cold War period of the 1950s and the sharply critical response from theologian Reinhold Niebuhr (1955). It was from the vantage point of the League of Nations (the UN's historical prototype) that Niebuhr launched his critique of the Quaker document *Speak Truth to Power* (American Friends Service Committee 1955).[9] As Niebuhr had previously made clear in 1932: 'Perhaps the best that can be expected of nations is that they should justify their hypocrisies by a slight measure of real international achievement, and learn how to do justice to wider interests than their own, while they pursue their own' (Niebuhr [1932] 1960: 71).

Niebuhr questioned what he saw as the naïve engagement of Quakers in the international political order. He doubted the moral virtues of collective structures and the realism of civil society. This dilemma brings us back to the interplay of complex and paradoxical forces, which, as Thomas (2005: 210) indicates in relation to civil society, 'choke the working of the institutional representative democracy'. It becomes even more poignant after the 1990s expansion of civil society which led to Quakers working alongside a wider range of NGO actors. It is this post-1990s expansion of civil society in the global system of governance, and the paradoxical features resulting from it, which makes the Quaker-UN example such a key indicator of both the theoretical and empirical realities of religion in a global world. Following discussion of some wider theoretical perspectives on religion and globalisation, I will unfold the implications of the paradox of civil society expansion and decreasing 'third sector'[10] influence.

THE PARADOX OF GLOBALISATION

It is my contention that we can only make sense of religious NGOs at the UN, their increase and complex interaction, by returning to what I have called the paradox underlying the theory of globalisation. My argument is that the idea of globalisation is caught inside a set of inherent paradoxes and that analysing religion and any empirical claim to globalisation—within the UN system or elsewhere—faces the same set of paradoxes in its engagement with the institutions of the global order.[11] As Ulrich Beck (2005: 20) rightly indicates, there exists a tension between the '"theory only" route' of globalisation and empirical realities, such that some research indicators of globalisation still pertain to national-international frameworks of reference rather than global flows or transnational engagements. The problem here, as I have stated elsewhere, is that globalisation is both a normative concept and an empirical claim caught inside a political rationale (Carrette 2012). It is an example of how the empirical is already theoretical and how both theory and empiricism are always held within relationships of power. This tension is but one example of the complexity of territory, or 'supraterritoriality', as Scholte (2000) suggests is the key to the concept of globalisation. This crossing of boundaries is part of the paradox and tension, such that it is not just periods of transition that create confusion, as Kofi Annan suggested, but the shift in the time-space categories and our ability to think about complex social realities. Furthermore, it has been my contention that the category of globalisation is caught in a tautology. It undermines its own field of application, the singular object of globalisation, in its attempts to capture the pluralistic world (Carrette 2012).

To think about the categories of religion and globalisation requires us to continuously use and extend social science categories from national, industrial and colonial models of thinking (see Carrette 2007). We have yet to find a sufficient and adequate language to discuss the notion of globalisation from an interdisciplinary and novel spatial dimension, because globalisation as a concept pivots around different orders of reality, and social science is still largely embedded within its industrial, 1890s epistemic roots. It is for this reason that the language of paradox is so prevalent in the literature, insofar as it continually speaks about two worlds and carries previous expansion frames of industrial-colonial analysis to which the concept of globalisation adds a new and very different layer of spatio-territorial analysis. In order to show how and why the Quaker NGO engagements with the UN reflect the fundamental paradox of the category globalisation, I will explore three questions that will help orientate my theoretical claims about the nature of the paradox of globalisation, the empirical importance of global institutions and the new global dynamic facing Quakers, and other religious NGOs, when civil society expanded in the 1990s. These orientating excursions are important because of the poverty of theoretical-empirical discussion about the notion of globalisation. It will show the macro- and micro-social processes that link religious groups to global institutions.

HOW IS THE IDEA OF GLOBALISATION A PARADOX?

There is widespread agreement in the texts on globalisation that it is a contested category at all levels of its analysis. As Manfred Steger (2009: 47) points out: 'Academics remain divided on the validity of available empirical evidence and for the existence and extent of globalization, not to mention its normative and ideological implications'. The intellectual debate is also coupled with a deeper set of epistemological tensions at every level of the discussion of globalisation. Paul James (2006: 5) recognises the 'contradictory processes' involved in globalisation and maps the abstract and embodied orders, Robertson (1992) develops the tautology of 'glocalization', Giddens (2002) talks of the paradoxes and tensions of the 'runaway world' and Beck (2005) refers to the 'paradoxical alliances' between states and NGOs, to mention but a few examples within the social scientific literature. We might add that the idea of 'civil society' is also seen as a paradox, a normative ideal and empirical claim (see Foley & Edwards 1996; Trentmann 2000). However, to conclude the paradoxes with reference to religion, we may note that Peter Beyer ([1994] 2000: 227), in his incisive study of globalisation and religion, concludes his work with the following assessment: 'We live in a conflicted and contested social world where appeal to holism is itself partisan. That paradox alone is enough to maintain the religious enterprise, even if with more risk and less self-evidence'. This sentence contains much that can be unpacked, because it suggestively leaves open the idea that it is precisely inside the paradoxical that religion finds its own space in globalisation. I will develop and extend this idea of paradox throughout the chapter, drawing out the specific aspects of religious NGOs at the UN.

Summary of the Paradoxical Tensions within Globalisation

Local-global
States-Non-State actors
Sovereignty-Non-Sovereignty
Government-governance
Embodied-abstract
Embedded-disembedded
Certain-uncertain

I have already hinted that the paradox of globalisation has arisen because of a change in the knowledge paradigm and what Giddens (1990: 64) called the 'problematic of time-space distanciation'. One attempt to overcome these problems can be seen in John Urry's (2003) study *Global Complexity*. He attempts to transfer models from complexity theory from the physical world to the social world in order to capture the new social order. Networks and systems are different, overlapping, layered and interconnecting in ways that makes any simple theorising and empirical mapping extremely difficult. Urry (2003: 12, 39) argues that the idea of globalisation has been 'insufficiently theorized' and that many assessments of such a thing called globalisation remains limited in their inability to deal with the '*complex* character of emergent global relations'. As Urry (2003: 138) concludes: 'Relations across the world are complex, rich and non-linear, involving multiple negative and, more significantly, positive feedback loops. [. . .] They do not exhibit and sustain unchanging structural stability. Complexity elaborates how there is order and disorder within all physical and social systems'.

It is this complexity that brings us to the paradox within the theory and empirical analysis of the notion of globalisation. In understanding the categories of religion and globalisation in the global institutional context of the UN, we can witness these facts in greater detail and ground them in a living context. Following on from Beyer's part-whole paradox, we can add the dimension of power and representation (see Goverde, Cerny, Haugaard & Lenter 2000). The 'religion enterprise' is caught in a paradox of appearance and disappearance, the paradox of the term 'globalisation' bringing greater inclusion through a dominant system. It is the paradox of all-powerful institutions allowing greater representation or what I will call the paradox of hegemony and plurality, something that characterises religious NGOs in the post-1990s period.[12] Religion emerges inside the hegemony-plurality paradox of globalisation theory and is transformed inside this relationship. In order to appreciate the key empirical value of the UN as a site for examining these issues of globalisation theory, I would now like to focus on the wider importance of institutions for an analysis of those processes we may claim as representative of globalisation. This excursion is necessary because most research on 'globalisation' fails to provide adequate justification for its empirical field of analysis, assuming the object is transparent within the abstract concept.

WHY ARE GLOBAL GOVERNANCE INSTITUTIONS A KEY EMPIRICAL REGISTER FOR ASSESSING THE DYNAMICS OF RELIGION IN A GLOBAL WORLD?

One of the key claims in globalisation theory is the shift from a world order dominated by sovereign states to one that is shaped by new global non-state actors (Bickerton, Cunliffe & Gourevitch 2007). The idea of globalisation is therefore always, at some point or other, coupled with ideas of 'global governance', and indeed the latter arises at the same time as globalisation (Rosenau 2002: 224). As Patricia Kennett (2008: 12) makes clear, globalisation and global governance are 'interrelated processes'. We can therefore gain greater insight into globalisation—both as concept and as empirical reality—through the processes of governance and vice versa. Governance, as the UN Commission on Global Governance (1995: 2) indicates, is 'the many ways individuals and institutions, public and private, manage their common affairs'. It encompasses therefore, importantly, not just the actions of state-centred governments, but wider 'social functions and processes' (Rosenau 2002: 225). Global governance is the myriad of 'global, regional or transnational systems of authoritative rule-making and implementation' (Held & McGrew 2002: 9). It does not mean the end of state-government, but rather that governments are now 'supplemented by other actors, private and third sector—in a more complex geography' (Keohane & Nye 2000: 12, 36). The complex geography of global governance creates, as Ngaire Woods (2002: 26) acknowledges, 'an international arena for lobbying and the representation of vested interests'.

The key part of global governance is that there is 'no single system' (Duffield 2001: 44; Wilkinson 2005: 27), and that it is sustained by the global interaction of institutions and networks. This interdependence of power relations has modified realist positions within international relations, as can be seen in the 'neoliberal institutional' model of political theorists such as Keohane and his followers (Keohane 1984; Milner & Moravcsik 2009). The model argues for four primary aspects within international relations: (1) an emphasis on non-state actors, including those within international institutions; (2) new forms of power outside of military assertion; (3) interdependence within the international system; and (4) cooperation within international politics (Milner & Moravcsik 2009: 4ff). Institutions like the UN system are key parts—albeit not the only parts—in the new complex geography, and it allows us to see how networks and primary institutional structures interact in global governance. In this respect, the so-called network institutionalists provide a greater understanding of institutions as rules of behaviour. When the networks are 'stable or recurrent', it can be seen as an institution or rule of behaviour (Ansell 2006: 75). In this sense we can modify any overemphasis by Giddens (1990: 21ff) on 'disembedding' within modernity because there is always a resultant re-embedding as networks transform and new rules emerge; something we will see in relation to Quakers at the UN after the 1990s expansion of civil society. Inside global processes, institutions become more dynamic as overlapping networks shape and move across and within more established institutions structures. It is precisely in this sense that to speak of the UN is, as Barkin (2006: 53) underlines, 'misleading'. It can refer to a very diverse set of practices, operations and structures, from regional and country level to UN headquarters level. The UN system, within its varied subsystems and committees, is an example of an evolving global governance structure with 192 member states, its founding charter, its principal organs (including the General Assembly, the Security Council, the Secretariat, the International Court of Justice, the ECOSOC and the UN's various subsidiary agencies and committees). The UN system is caught in the paradoxical twists and turns of overlapping networks and the complexity of market-style exchanges.

To frame globalisation within an institutional context such as the UN is to understand the intensification of relations within the global order. Duffield (2001: 45–46) is right in this sense to identify different types of networked relations or linkages, including 'discrete' and 'innovative' networks, and right also to see how networks result in 'strategic complexes' which link state and non-state actors (Duffield 2001: 12). It requires, according to Duffield (2001: 10), a systems-approach to understanding global politics, a consideration of 'interconnections', that is, 'integrated wholes that cannot be reduced to their separate parts'. Thinking about religion in a global world is to think about religion within complex systems and to realise that it will be redefined inside the new sets of relations.

It is also important to note that in such a world, we cannot think about governance institutions without considering other kinds of institutions. When networks become complex, there will be an overlapping of institutional types and forms, and the classification of the types and forms of institution will also become difficult. The connections between institutions can be seen clearly when we move to consider economics, the dominant trope of globalisation theory, and seek to understand why economic globalisation requires integration into other forms of global institutional networks. As the Korean economist Ha-Joon Chang (2003: 51) argues: 'The institutionalist view, in contrast, does not believe in the institutional primacy of the market. It believes that the market is only one of the many economic institutions and not necessarily the primary one'.

The neoliberal emphasis on the market hides the interconnections with other forms of institution. The implications of Chang's institutional model and the history of economics reveals the importance of interconnections between types of international organisations, such the World Bank, WTO, the United Nations and religious institutions, in their various NGO forms, such as the World Council of Churches or the Vatican with its own affiliated and unaffiliated NGOs. It is these international organisations that place the greatest weight on contemporary social networks and shape the nature of thinking about the idea of globalisation. If we take these networks of institutions seriously, globalisation can be seen as the complexity of relations between institutions and not as an abstract process occurring outside the actions and behaviours of actors within those institutions. The question remains as to how the paradox and the international institutional context shape Quaker involvement in the post-1990 era of civil society expansion.

HOW ARE QUAKERS AND RELIGIOUS NGOS CAUGHT IN THE PARADOX OF GLOBALISATION?

If the central paradox of globalisation is that between hegemony and plurality and international institutions are the primary arena for understanding such processes, then it remains to show how Quaker activity is caught in the paradox. The problem was captured succinctly in a 1908 essay, 'Group Expansion and Development of the Individual' by Georg Simmel. In this essay discussing the relation of the individual and the group, Simmel (1908: 256–257) draws out the insightful relation of the opposites of groups and their emergence in wider domains: 'The nonindividuation of elements in the narrower circle and their differentiation in the wider one are phenomena that are found, synchronically, among coexistent groups and group elements, just as they appear, diachronically, in the sequence of stages through which a single group develops'.

As he continues: 'The narrower the circle to which we commit ourselves, the less freedom of individuality we possess [. . .] Correspondingly, if the circle in which we are active and in which our interests hold sway enlarges, there is more room in it for the development of our individuality; but *as parts of this whole*, we have less uniqueness: the larger whole is less individual as a social group'.

If I read this correctly—and the meaning is indeed obscure—Simmel recognises that as the circle of a group expands, there is a paradox that the social differentiation is related to a tendency to nondifferentiation. This analysis of social groups and the effects of the widening of the social circle are—intriguingly—related by Simmel to the social order of Quakers (the Religious Society of Friends) as it relates to tensions within identity across the individual and social. This becomes even more poignant when the social circle expands to the global context.

Simmel's proposition occurs within the context of industrial and colonial models and is therefore, as I have underlined, lacking the conceptual geography of sophistication that occurs in complex networks and a global circle. However, if we transpose this rule to the UN and religious NGOs, and take Quakers as a paradigm group as I have done, we can see some key issues of the paradox of the concept of globalisation. We can see something of the problem of global extension of the social group within the context of global institutions: the reduced effectiveness of multiple small groups inside a dominant system.

Furthermore, Simmel's proposition can be related and updated by linking it to the Austrian economist Friedrich Hayek, who was the economist behind the neoliberal ideology of Reagan and Thatcher and arguably the inspiration behind the deregulation of the world market that led to the full force of economic globalisation. Hayek's (1948) work is neoliberal insofar as he bases societal freedom on the market and not the state apparatus. In his attempt to overcome the problems of both fascist and Communist ideology, he believed the free movement of a deregulated market would protect against the ideals of oppressive government. While his thinking clearly attempted to respond to a situation of tyranny, his blind spot was not to see how the new sets of institutions, such as competitive market-states, could create different forms of oppression, particularly when they had global outreach. The very attempt to decrease state power by reducing state institutions only creates a new power regime of non-state institutions. The same dynamic, somewhat disturbingly, plays out in the very attempt to resist hegemonic power, because of what Hayek (1973, 1976, 1979) calls 'knowledge catallaxy' (exchanges in the self-regulating and decentralised market), which create an artificial playing field for knowledge and thus resistance.

I want to place this idea of 'knowledge catallaxy' alongside Simmel's proposition of nondifferentiation of the social group in a wider circle. When the social circle is expanded and there is a free play of social groups in a market-driven society, the resulting 'catallaxy'[13] hides the dominant social structures that persist in the new world of apparent pluralism. The concept of globalisation hides an implicit paradox in its abstract application and political normative paradigm.

The apparent increase in free expression of civil society, that is, increased differentiation, results in nondifferentiated organisational power, built on the illusion of differentiation. What I am arguing is that the global institutional environment undermines agency and action in the name of freedom and democracy. It is the paradox of allowing self-defined groups freedom of expression without altering the central institutions (in this case states, international institutions and corporations) that control such freedom of expression. It relates to what Marcussen & Kaspersen (2007: 184) call 'institutional competitiveness': 'The concept of institutional competitiveness concerns the intentional and unintentional outcomes of the attempts of people to optimize their institutions in innovative ways with a view to performing in the wake of globalisation'.

Quaker engagement in the UN is changing in this new competitive environment. In the post-1990s social catallaxy of NGOs at the UN, Quakers have modified their action. As we have seen, their distinctiveness has shifted within the wider field of NGO actors through different forms of collaboration, but it is also worth giving a few additional examples. First, in a competing environment, the Quaker-UN office in Geneva decided to allow other NGOs to carry out work on the review of the Human Rights Council in 2011, so it could focus its resources on other campaigns.[14] In an environment of social catallaxy, there is scope for a different kind of resource management. Second, as Sophie-Hélène Trigeaud has shown,[15] the follow-on work from the 1989 Convention on the Rights of the Child led to a number of interconnected implementation activities from religious groups of which the Quaker campaign against child soldiers was a part, albeit an important one, that resulted in 2000 in the UN-adopted Optional Protocol on the involvement of children in armed conflict.[16] Quakers have always been embedded in a complex civil society apparatus, but after the 1990s there is—to echo Giddens (1990: 21ff)—a new 'embedding' in the social catallaxy of civil society, a weaving together of substrands of campaign work.

The social catallaxy of NGOs at the UN can also be seen in the different competitive levels of funding and knowledge of the UN system. In contrast to Quakers, new religious NGOs from the South, or the two-thirds world, find it increasingly difficult to gain access, to shape representations, have meetings with diplomats or even put forward UN statements, because knowledge and experience of the 'processes' and networks of association is power.[17] Quakers may lose distinctiveness in the extension of civil society processes, but they still hold a unique historical reputation as a valuable currency within the system of exchanges, such as their 'off-the-record' meetings (Quaker United Nations Office 2010). The crucial issue of blending civil society actors inside the UN system is also part of the UN enculturation or adaptation of NGO actors (Martens 2005). This raises the important question of the effectiveness of NGOs in their attempts to influence global state actors.

STATE POWER, RELIGIOUS NGOS AND COURTIER POLITICS

My argument is that the proliferation of NGOs in the 1990s reflects a new social catallaxy of neoliberalism and that within this catallatic environment of religious NGOs, we face the paradox of hegemony and plurality. The increased differentiation of NGOs and self-identified 'religious' NGOs as part of this expansion is not, as it may appear, a widening of voices within democracy, but rather the ineffective catallaxy of small social units in a wider circle. The category of a 'religious' NGO is therefore not a continuation of the Westphalian state apparatus marking out new forms of power, but a part of an extended and accelerated global *differentiation* beyond state borders—a *differentiation* that is a political mechanism. The reintegration of 'religion' into International Relations theory, in Thomas and others, is therefore also a paradoxical move because the 'integration' is simultaneously a modernist differentiation, as Thomas is partly aware of (Thomas 2005: 69). Religion is brought into politics and made distinct from politics in the same move, something that is more entangled in a premodern era.

The problem of differentiation and effectiveness can be seen from wider research into NGOs—as distinct from religious NGOs—at the UN. Clark, Friedman & Hochstetler (2005) studied NGO participation in three UN conferences, which intermittently addressed single-issue topics. They examined NGO participation at the 1991 Conference on Environment and Development in Rio de Janeiro, the 1993 World Conference on Human Rights in Vienna and the 1995 Fourth World Conference on Women held in Beijing. The striking result they found was that it is 'unclear' whether the increase in NGOs 'can be equated with an emerging global civil society' and that although the events had 'meaning for the participants', NGOs 'do not necessarily affect states' positions' (Clark et al. 2005: 293). What emerged was that the plurality of NGO representation did not change the hegemonic power of states. As they concluded: 'State sovereignty sets the limits of global civil society'.

The study of the NGOs at the various UN conferences finds support in David Chandler's (2007) insightful assessment of the political model of civil society. He speculates that despite the term 'civil society', there is a resistance to the social in the global—another paradox—in that they are 'rejecting the institutionally grounded responsibility and accountability that is intrinsic to politics itself' (Chandler 2007: 152). Chandler's essay appears in a collection which critiques international relations and the assumption that state-defined boundaries have been transgressed in globalisation: the state-sovereignty global paradox. He sees the global as negative in its refusal of the political logic of the state, because in the global sphere civil society actors are an 'unelected form of representation', a form of 'courtier politics', which becomes parasitic on the 'ready-made agenda provided by international institutions' (Chandler 2007: 161–162). He believes that the result is an undermining of the social order of politics and democratic ideals in what becomes a series of ethical 'postures' rather than political change. In a way that echoes my reading of social catallaxy, he underlines the problem: '[T]he rejection of social engagement is more likely to lead to a further shrinking of the political sphere, reducing it to a small circle of increasingly unaccountable elites'. The pluralist expansion of religious NGOs becomes restricted by the elite gestures of states and international institutions serving their interests.

The elements of social catallaxy are evident again here, and it underlines how civil society, as Jan Aart Scholte (2005: 323) reveals in his own assessment of NGOs, can both 'detract from as well as add to democracy'. Such an assessment was recognised earlier by the political theorist Iris Marion Young (2000: 156) who showed that injustice covers both 'domination and oppression', the former restricting 'self-determination' and the latter denying 'self-development'. As Young insightfully points out, the plurality and associational links of civil society, inside the complex and uncoordinated systems we have already noted, can create the positive value of self-determination. However, it cannot promote the required need for self-development. 'Because', as Young (2000: 156) rightly argues, 'many of the structural injustices that produce oppression have their source in economic processes, state institutions are necessary to undermine such oppression and promote self-development'. Here we see the paradox of the idea of globalisation, the paradox of plurality and hegemony. The problem is one of power and inclusion in complex global systems.

Religion within globalisation exists inside this paradox of inclusion and the centralized systems that structure the inclusion, but part of this inclusion rests on the ability of groups, including religious groups, to be strategic; and in this sense we are witnessing a new phenomenon in the study of religion: *religion as a strategic category inside the paradox of global politics*. Religion can be seen as 'strategic' in terms of Foucault's ([1976] 1990: 102) strategic model of power, where power is 'a multiple and mobile field of force relations', something 'never completely stable', as it is not legal or sovereign power, but something 'exercised from innumerable points, in the interplay of nonegalitarian and mobile relations' (Foucault [1976] 1990: 94). In the context of the multiple and mobile sets of force relationships within international institutions like the United Nations, 'religion' is deployed as a discourse to produce a certain rearrangement of relationships, it facilitates and closes access and engagement between states, between states and NGOs, and between NGOs themselves, inside the global network of international institutions.

CONCLUSION: RELIGION WITHIN THE PARADOX OF GLOBALISATION

Kofi Anan's (1998: 129) key understanding of the relation of the idea of globalisation to the 'transnational network of nongovernmental organizations (NGOs)' provides a unique framework for theoretical and empirical analysis. It raises critical questions about the role of religion in social-state power relationships. In particular, the example of religious NGOs in the UN, as exemplified by Quakers, enables us to tease out the issues of religion and globalisation by locating the question in the context of international institutions. It allows us to see the nature of how groups compete and exchange to gain influence inside the systems of global governance. When we contextualise globalisation and cease to reify it, that is, make it into a thing that autonomously happens to the world, we return it to the social processes that create the new global order. We return globalisation to the specific social struggles of groups and institutions that structure human life, albeit within a new horizon. As Justin Rosenberg's (1994: 172) critique of realist theory in international relations makes clear, if we want to understand international relations we must understand the 'distinctive configuration of social relations [. . .] and see its object for what it is: a set of social relations between people'. Indeed, Niebuhr ([1932] 1960: 11) much earlier held the same suspicion of 'the creeds and institutions of democracy', which he believed can never be 'fully divorced from the special interests of the commercial classes who conceived and developed them'. We do not, however, have to embrace entirely Rosenberg's Marxist analysis to accept how specific social forces, and the values behind such orders, shape global processes through very specific institutional systems.

The problem of the category of globalisation is to understand the complexity of the networks and interactions inside the new geography of relations. The global domain makes systems complex, but the complexity should not hide the specific logic masked by technology, connections and reduced distance. Reading the new global logic is central to how we understand the myriad relations that shape the world. These relations inevitably produce paradoxes because of a clash of different registers, a return to industrial and colonial models and a resistance to complexity theory. However, as I have tried to show, it is precisely within the tensions and paradoxes that we see something vital about religion in the new conditions of a global world.

When the category of religion moves from a state-colonial to a state-global context, knowledge and norms enter the space of social catallaxy, leading to unpredictable and competing exchanges creating ever more complex networks. The complexity of this situation results in NGOs seeking to negotiate multilayered structures. In response, as we have seen with Quakers, they form new alliances with each other, they become embroiled in multiple side meetings and draft UN statements together to be heard for one minute on the General Assembly floor, or even become relegated to written statements with no public enactment.[18] The plurality is evident, but so indeed is the hegemony of a state-led system. As a result, NGOs deploy ever-new tactics and forms of representation.[19] Inside this new economy of relations, religion as a category becomes part of the confusing game of being heard and represented. In this atmosphere, religion becomes a strategic category; it will appear and disappear according to its effectiveness to bring about exchanges. Religion, like globalisation, is not a thing but a category, manifesting and disappearing according to its usefulness to the sociopolitical context.[20]

The reason religion exists in the paradox of the idea of globalisation is because it is no longer what it used to be, or rather, it is redefined in the new forms of relation that emerge out of social catallaxy—the market mentality of our political world. Religion is thus reshaped in the complexity of networks, exchanges and systems of representation that create so many paradoxes: it is local and global, it is abstract and embodied, it is bounded by states and linked to the international institutions, it is embedded and disembedded. Religion as a social order now exists across and within these domains and in consequence is transformed by them.

If we understand the globalisation of religion as the intensification of social relations in a new neoliberal catallaxy, as I have sought to argue, then religion will play all sorts of new roles inside international institutions, of which the emergence of religious NGOs at the UN are but one new manifestation. This chapter has sought to demonstrate one key reality of the impact of global processes on religious groups through the UN context. It shows how religious groups respond to the challenges of operating at the highest levels of global civil society. The catallatic exchanges will, however, mean that the boundaries and borders between religion and other forms of social relation will become increasingly difficult to ascertain. In the end we may not even recognise religion as a distinct social actor. It will, however, always continue to exist in the paradoxes of a new global configuration of power, located and dislocated between the forces of plurality and hegemony.

NOTES

The research for this paper forms part of a three-year project at the University of Kent, UK, on 'Religious NGOs at the UN' funded by the 'Religion and Society' programme of the AHRC/ESRC funding councils in the UK and directed by Linda Woodhead. I wish to thank my research team of colleagues, Hugh Miall, Evelyn Bush, Sophie-Hélène Trigeaud and Verena Beittinger-Lee for discussions on many aspects of religious NGOs at the UN. The ideas of this paper are part of my wider theoretical reflections for the research project, based on initial findings from the fieldwork.

 1. *Religion, NGOs and the UN* edited by Jeremy Carrette, together with Verena Beittinger-Lee, Evelyn Bush, Hugh Miall and Sophie-Hélène Trigeaud, forthcoming (AHRC/ESRC Research Project).

The Paradox of Globalisation   55

2. As we have underlined in our own research this committee is not a formal UN group, but an external support group informally linked to the UN in New York and not all its members have ECOSOC status. I am grateful to Verena Beittinger-Lee for this finding, drawn from her fieldwork at the UN in New York.
3. The University of Kent AHRC/ESRC project on religious NGOs at the UN has responded to this issue by dividing the category of 'religion' in a more complex set of subdivisions for a questionnaire sent to NGOs with ECOSOC status, the results of which are forthcoming.
4. The University of Kent AHRC/ESRC findings in 2010 reflect similar overall proportions, but with a spectrum model of 'religious' identity.
5. Quasi-nongovernmental organisations.
6. See Timothy Fitzgerald, *Religion and Politics in International Relations: The Modern Myth* (London: Continuum, 2011). He develops a critique of the category of religion within various texts from international relations, including the work of Scott Thomas.
7. I am grateful to Sophie-Hélène Trigeaud for her fieldwork research for our University of Kent AHRC/ESRC project on religious NGOs at the UN in Geneva. She discovered many examples of the problems of NGO groups seeking to know the complex system and processes of the UN, something specifically supported by the NGO Mandat International.
8. Samuel Barkin's study (2006) of international organisations draws out Hedley Bull's three traditions of the international order from his 1977 *The Anarchical Society*. The first, the 'realist' tradition, holding to a strong state model; the second position is the 'internationalist', where strong states are held within international rules; and, finally, the 'universalist' tradition, which is a non-state global structure.
9. Niebuhr responded to this Quaker document in 1955, 'Is There Another Way', in *The Progressive* (October 1955); cited in Byrd (1960: 197).
10. Civil society is known as the 'third sector' alongside the state and market sectors.
11. The French ethnologist Marc Augé picks up the idea of paradox in the wider political landscape in a recent article in *Le Monde*, 'Les incertitudes du monde contemporain', Saturday 10 July 2010, p. 19.
12. In a different way, Beeson & Bell (2009) draw out the same problematic of hegemony and collectivism in relation to the G-20.
13. Catallatics (the science of exchanges) was first discussed by English theologian Richard Whately in his 1831 Oxford lectures *Introduction to the Science of Political Economy* (at a time when political economy was still part of theology) and picked up in Hayek (1973, 1976, 1979). For Hayek, catallaxy was the 'the order brought about by the mutual adjustment of many individual economies in a market'; see Levy (1999). I seek to deploy the word to show how wider social exchanges within complex networks are shaped by a market logic.
14. I am grateful to Rachel Brett (Quaker UN Office, Geneva) for some initial reflections on this matter in 2010 and 2011.
15. See her forthcoming work on religious NGOs and international law for the University of Kent AHRC/ESRC project on *Religious NGOs and Civil Society*, edited by Jeremy Carrette and Sophie-Hélène Trigeaud, with Verena Beittinger-Lee (forthcoming).
16. I am grateful to Sophie-Hélène Trigeaud for her fieldwork in Geneva on the Convention on the Rights of the Child as part of the University of Kent AHRC/ESRC project on Religious NGOs and the UN.
17. This is supported by my earlier examination of Quakers in international relations and their commitment to institutional building (see Waugh 2001). The

importance of 'process' has been confirmed in our University of Kent's Religious NGOs research project (see note 1).
18. I am grateful to Sophie-Hélène Trigeaud's research for the University of Kent project on religious NGOs at the UN in Geneva for making this point clear to me from her fieldwork, which will be forthcoming in the Religious NGOs and UN project materials for the Religion and Society programme.
19. Initial findings from the Religious NGOs and the UN project at the University of Kent, UK, has established that classification of religious NGOs is undermined by complex forces that lead to a rejection of the classification 'religion' and bridge religious groups and none in order to fight for specific political issues.
20. Religion is now one of many classificatory terms that allow for different networks in the social catallaxy of NGO relations, standing alongside other classificatory terms such as faith-based, spiritual and ethnic-cultural. The University of Kent's Religious NGOs and the UN project is presently gathering information on ECOSOC-registered NGOs to assess the classification and influence of groups in the UN.

4 European Secularity and Religious Modernity in Russia and Eastern Europe
Focus on Orthodox Christianity

Inna Naletova

ORTHODOXY AND ASPECTS OF MODERNITY IN EASTERN EUROPE AND RUSSIA

After the fall of the Berlin Wall and the dismantling of the Iron Curtain, which led to a closer reacquaintance with Eastern Europe and Russia in political and cultural terms, Western Europe came face to face with a different vision of religion in modern society. This vision is rooted in a specifically Eastern European and Russian experience of modernisation and social change, unparalleled in the West. It is also embedded in the ethos or spirit of Orthodox Christianity supportive of the development of different models from the Western European forms of mentality and institutional organisations.[1] Following Max Weber, some scholars assume that traditional Orthodox values are unfavourable to the advancement of capitalism and Western rationalism and, as such, would be likely to lead to further inner-European cultural clashes caused by the increasing migration and globalisation. Other scholars disagree with these negative prognoses and assume that Orthodox cultures are not 'immune' to the secularising influences of the West and that the post-Communist interest of people in religion is simply a matter of short-lived fashion. There is also a third position, however, where modernity is viewed as a multiple construct in which various manifestations coexist without either melting into a single globalised trend or necessarily clashing with each other as incompatible civilisations. In this chapter I will look at Orthodoxy in Russia and Eastern Europe from the third perspective, namely, the perspective of multiple modernities, and will reflect on the forms and features of Orthodox religiosity as they appear in different domains of public life.

It is a matter of continuous discussions in academic literature whether Max Weber was right in placing Orthodox civilisation outside of the realm of Western modernity (Buss 2003). It is also a matter of ongoing academic interest to establish how (and whether) Orthodox churches in European countries contribute to a common European identity while being, at the same time, critical of the Western European values and ways of life. Indeed, during recent decades, Orthodox communities have shown signs of both conservative resistance to Western modernity and creative engagement with modern institutions. In this chapter, I will look at how contemporary Orthodox communities and believers use the possibilities offered by the modern world to strengthen their voices in the pluralistic public setting and to interpret modernity in their own terms. In order to do that, I will at first indicate a few historical aspects that characterise the uneasy relations of Orthodox churches with Western modernity, leading to what I would call a religion-friendly Orthodox-oriented non-Western model of modernity.

A central feature distinguishing Western and Eastern models of modernity is located in different forms of church-state relations. The Eastern approach to church-state relations has been branded (in the West) with the pejorative term 'caesaro-papism' and viewed as incompatible with the Western, highly differentiated forms of social organisation. More recently, however, the idea of a rigid church-state separation has been reconsidered even in Western societies as religious communities began to act on the borderlines of established social domains, exploring new ways of connecting the spheres of the spiritual and the temporal. At the same time, traditional Western churches became more cautious in expressing their beliefs, symbols and rituals in public, especially in France, where religion has been virtually expelled from shared life. This Western development is in marked contrast to the developments in the Eastern, traditionally Orthodox part of Europe, where connection rather than separation between the sacred and profane has been appreciated and supported. Inherited from Byzantium, the Eastern ideal of relations between church and state has been called 'symphonic', in which the notion 'symphony' signifies a harmonious coexistence of two powers, without either separating or merging in one another. We know, however, that in reality this ideal has been more often violated than followed (Dragon 2003). For instance, the authoritarian regimes in Russia and Eastern Europe tried to obliterate any possibility of a symphonic cooperation of churches with the state and, as a result, churches became marginal and subservient to the state. Yet, in recent years, the idea of symphony regained its popularity as it suggested a 'natural'—'authentically' Orthodox—way for the national churches to express their relations with the state and to justify a way to enter not only local but also global politics ('Patriarch Kirill Reminded' 2009). Thus, the Byzantine tendency toward a unity of the two spheres has been revived as an alternative to the Western ideal of separation.

In order to understand Eastern European/Russian (Orthodox) modernity, it is helpful to place religion in the context of the development of the modern scientific and capitalist economy. While in the West, in the middle and late 19th century, the rationalisation and bureaucratisation of social spheres had already reached its full flow, being seen as an 'iron cage', the modern scientific and capitalist economy has only just began to make an impact on the predominantly agrarian societies of Eastern Europe and Russia. Eastern European cultures, being on the periphery of the Western modernity, preserved a spirit of religious tradition. The spirit of Orthodoxy—magical, ritualistic and resistant to rational systematisation and fragmentation—has been, up until the turn of the 20th century (in Russia, up until the mid-1920s) a source of public morality and social conduct that was taken for granted. These premodern cultures had been idealised by leading thinkers of the 19th and early 20th centuries as an alternative to Western civilization. This sounded convincing because Orthodox cultures were Christian but, at the same time, non-Western, and, therefore (supposedly) able to interact with the West and, at the same time, demonstrate the errors and shortcomings of Western developments.

National consciousness is also an important element in the formation of a non-Western modernity. The rise of national consciousness in Eastern Europe and Russia falls approximately in the second half of the 19th century.[2] This was the period when religion began to act as a counter-modernising and anti-Western power, with churches and monasteries passionately opposing Western influences, viewing the West as incompatible with the traditional way of life.[3] As guardians of specific national cultures, Orthodox churches began to use a specific language for liturgical services and to advance specific territorial claims to emphasise the idea that certain people with their religion constitute a nation. The Western, Enlightenment-inspired ideology, centred on an autonomous individual as a carrier of ultimate values, has been perceived as incompatible with Orthodox values focused on a community. Not an individual, according to this perspective, but a social group—family, local community (*obshina*), the Church, the motherland, holy Russia or holy Serbia—would be a true object for ultimate concern for the group's members. This way of thinking continues to manifest itself in contemporary political and religious discussions.[4]

Modernisation of Eastern Europe and Russia was inseparable from inter-ethnic conflicts caused by the geopolitical position of their societies on the border area between Europe and Asia. Located between East and West, Orthodox Christianity has been, and continues to be, a powerful source for constructing national and cross-national unities, but also for drawing lines of separation between ethnic groups, local political orientations and whole cultural areas. The link between Orthodoxy and Russianness, Serbianness, Bulgarianness or Romanianness has been strengthened by the close ties that churches maintain with the local ethnic cultures in which Orthodoxy appears as a distinctive marker of ethnic identities. This fundamental link between religion and ethnicity was difficult to obliterate in the memory and imagination of the people, even for the most cruel atheist regimes (Ramet 1984). Imbibed at birth or through cultural upbringing, or revitalised as the result of acute social experiences, such as the post-Communist social change, post-Communist migration and encounters with the West, Orthodox Christianity continues to provide contemporary Eastern Europeans with a sense of belonging to their specific ethnic groups, thus challenging the Western view of religion as, primarily, a matter of personal choice.

Another characteristic aspect of specific Eastern European modernity is caused by the dramatic developments of the 20th century, namely, a period of state-imposed secularisation, or, to use the term of Paul M. Zulehner, 'atheisation' from above. Different in terms of the length and degree of a state's hostility toward religion, the Communist secularisation was successful in some countries but failed in others. Today, the countries of a traditional Orthodox orientation, particularly Romania, Ukraine, and Serbia, have a more religious population than their neighbours, such as Slovenia, Hungary and the Czech Republic. Eastern Europe in general continues to be—and remarkably so—more religious then Western Europe (Zulehner, Tomka & Naletova 2008). As David Martin observed, atheist persecutions were 'gut for religion' as they helped religious traditions and institutions to regain their strength and to resist the all-European tendency toward secularisation and the privatisation of religion (Martin 2008: 2).

There are also important theological and spiritual features of Orthodox Christianity that shed light on the formation of a non-Western modernity and help us to see how Orthodox cultures succeed in preserving their religious traditions by resisting unfavourable political circumstances. Here, I would like to mention a substantial layer of popular piety and the emphasis on mysticism and ritual that helps Orthodox religiosity to survive and even flourish underground, in semi- and noninstitutional forms. Today, the popular expressions of Orthodox faith, such as the veneration of icons and the belief in the healing power of holy water, continue to help religious people to pave their way through the modern secular environment and to create religiously charged public spaces outside of the church's institutional structures. Orthodoxy's historical ties with a patriotic ideology and with popular culture have also had a negative (secularising) effect on religion. This happened particularly when religious practices, performed in nonreligious settings, became endorsed with secular meanings.

In the following pages, I will try to convey to the reader a sense of Orthodox Europe as being, on the one hand, a part of a united Europe, yet, on the other, remaining the European 'Other', challenging the current political attempts at constructing a common European identity along the lines of a Western European (secularised) vision of modernity.[5] After presenting some visual material found in Russia during my recent field studies, I will proceed to present the data of the public surveys with the purpose of giving a broader perspective on the Orthodox religious situation in Europe and to compare the religious data of the European East with the European West. Then, I will turn to sociological theories of religion to review their explanatory power as applied to the Orthodox area of modern Europe. I will conclude by outlining the most characteristic aspects of a religion-friendly Orthodox-oriented non-Western modernity as it emerges in the respective parts of Eastern Europe and Russia.

RELIGION IN THE PUBLIC SPHERE

A Western visitor to contemporary Russia, Ukraine, Bulgaria or Romania is likely to be surprised when seeing the abundance of religion present in public areas in various visual, auditory and tactile forms, all linked to Orthodox tradition and customs. Quite often religious objects, such as icons and crosses, are placed in areas open to public view, such as the bulletin boards of public schools, public libraries, ordinary grocery shops, in city buses and conference halls. Pictures of the onion-shaped church domes and abbreviations of prayers may also be seen on placards and advertisements carrying both religious and nonreligious meanings. It is equally quite common for local priests to be invited to offices, factories, public celebrations or simply to fields to perform the ritual of blessing or to conduct a public prayer. The popularity of religious practices, such as pilgrimages, bathing in holy springs and fasting, reaches far beyond churches. They are broadly utilised as part of work environments and in leisure culture. They found their use in business and academic communities, as well as in schools and public offices, as these ritualistic elements affirm a sense of belonging to a community. Through religious practices, symbols and objects, society is presented as an essential reality or, as one scholar put it, a 'paramount value which englobes the empirical individuals' (Buss 2003: xiv).

To illustrate, I will to mention fasting practice, for example. In recent years it began to enjoy a great popularity inside and outside of churches. Compared to the similar tradition in the Roman Catholic Church, Orthodox fasting is very demanding in terms of time, detailed rules and specific food regulations. Nevertheless, the periods of fasting are reported in the TV news and are observed, in one way or another, in practically all social settings. The fasting menus offered in the Kremlin are made known to the public; fasting dishes are available in the kitchens of many public schools; fasting products are typically present in ordinary grocery shops, and it is quite usual for a restaurant to be able to satisfy customers' need for fasting or to offer a menu with special fasting options. In response to social or natural calamities, specific 'extra fasting' may be requested. This happened, for instance, in Russia in August 2010, when an unusual heat wave struck the European parts of the country, causing an immense loss of harvest, various technical breakdowns, as well as illnesses and deaths of people. In response to the suffering, Orthodox clergy and laity wrote a letter to Patriarch Kirill asking him to announce an extra three-day fast and national repentance. In their letter, the need for the nationwide fasting was justified by the following words: 'prayer services and private repentance is certainly a necessary remedy for healing the existing situation, but it is not enough. We think we need a *national repentance* as here the *whole nation* is guilty of apostasy rather than one person's guilt. We are not going to run into temptation and blame someone as we are also sinful people, but we insist on our request' ('Clergy and Laity' 2010, my italics). In this example—and in the examples that will follow—one can sense a need for the presence of religion in the very centre of shared life to affirm a common sense of national, cultural and religious belonging.

The data of public surveys show that the majority of the population in the traditionally Orthodox parts of Eastern Europe and Russia would like the Church to be present in the public sphere and expect religious institutions to be competent in responding to the needs of modern society. Studies show that between 41% and 59% of respondents in the traditionally Orthodox countries, such as Romania, Moldova, Ukraine, Serbia and Bulgaria, asked a priest to perform the ritual of blessing. In the traditionally Catholic Poland, Slovenia, Lithuania, and Hungary the number of individuals seeking blessings is between 30% and 36%, and in the former East Germany and Czech Republic, it is less than 15%. Similar differences are seen in the responses to questions about possessing religious objects such as icons. Between 85% and 90% of the respondents in Moldavia, Romania, Ukraine, Belarus, Serbia, and Bulgaria stated that they have icons as compared to less than 50% of those in Hungary, Lithuania, and Slovenia; about 30% in Czech Republic; and less than 15% in East Germany (Zulehner & Tomka 2008: 187–196; Naletova 2009). The Orthodox in Eastern Europe are also more inclined than other groups of respondents to have holy water and blessed objects. Certainly, having an icon, holy water or asking a priest for a blessing do not necessarily mean having strong religious convictions. Yet such a broad popularity of the traditional religious practices and the spread of traditional religious objects show a degree of acquaintance with the religious tradition and indicate their sense of belonging to the religious culture, at least, through sharing in its symbols and practices.

Snapshot 1. A Sense of Religious Belonging

Icons are certainly the most common religious objects appearing in various contexts in public life. Here I would like to draw attention to an abbreviation 'ХВ', which in Church Slavonic means the Easter greeting: 'Christ is Risen'(Христос Воскресе)! This abbreviation can be seen—sometimes quite unexpectedly—on the advertisements of various culinary products and household things. It may appear on paper used to wrap blessed bread and cakes on bottles of spring water, oil or wine, on packages containing baby food and other things offered in ordinary supermarkets (see Figure 4.1). This abbreviation is supposed to help customers to locate the specifically 'Orthodox products' on the market shelf, that is, the products blessed by the church, produced in a local monastery or a parish, or made in a church-run bakery or farm. In recent years, the 'ХВ' (Христос Воскресе) abbreviation has appeared on a greater variety of products—a fact indicating that, on the one hand, there is a need for religion's presence in a secular market and, on the other hand, that churches, monasteries and religious communities have learnt to utilise religion as a marketing resource. In other words, religious communities have learnt to act as entrepreneurs.

To explain the success of the 'Orthodox products' on the market, it would be insufficient to refer to their quality and prices for in many cases the price and quality of these products are simply comparable with that of their secular equivalents. What allows the blessed products to survive the challenges of

European Secularity and Religious Modernity in Russia   63

Figure 4.1 Wrapping paper for bread sold in a Moscow supermarket. The paper has a symbolic representation of the Easter greeting 'ХВ' (Christ is Risen) and a note explaining that this bread was baked in the Trinity Lavra of St. Sergius.

the market economy is their 'religious value', the ability to respond to the needs of a number of customers to have religious rituals and symbols outside of a specifically religious setting, in the supermarket, at home, at the workplace and on the street. By preferring religiously branded products to secular equivalents, these customers, in my view, support the church-run enterprises and, in exchange, bring home 'something religious', thus becoming involved, at least indirectly, in the life of the greater community, the Church. Grace Davie, using Western materials, coined this religious expression with the term 'vicarious religion', meaning specific forms of religious beliefs and practices in which a personal participation in religious life is substituted by an indirect support of religious activities or by an approval of religion's presence in public domains (Davie 2007: 21–36). The Orthodox forms of vicarious religion, as I see them in Russia and Eastern Europe, are more active, more personal and more expressive then the Western forms. After all, what do the customers demonstrate by buying the 'Orthodox products'? Not a mere approval of religion but a degree of engagement in it by taking part in the market, since one has to make a choice of products, buy them, bring them home, and share them at a dinner table with friends and family—all of which offers a more practical and concrete, though still indirect, religious participation.

Snapshot 2. A Sense of Cultural Belonging

Visitors to Russia are likely to notice that the meanings of religious symbols present in public areas are not fixed and stable but flexible and adjusted to the needs of individuals and institutions. Many of these symbols are loaded with local and national cultural references (see Figure 4.2).

In the summer of 2004, dozens of pictures, similar to the one presented above, could be seen all around Nizhnii Novgorod, showing an ongoing cultural cooperation between the local monastery of St. Seraphim of Sarov and the city administration of Nizhnii Novgorod. On the one hand, these pictures helped the monastery to invite pilgrims to its annual celebrations. On the other, they provided a sense of belonging to a common culture in any person for whom the prayer words appeared meaningful. The ending

Figure 4.2 A picture of the monastery of St. Seraphim of Sarov at a bus station in Nizhnii Novgorod. On the upper right corner there is a portrait of the local Saint Seraphim of Sarov, at the bottom the words of a prayer: 'Holy Father Seraphim, pray to God for us!'

of the prayer 'for us!' referred to a vaguely defined social group: it could mean the pilgrims, Orthodox Christians in general, Russians and any other people, not necessarily Orthodox and not even practicing believers. The prayer words were both all inclusive and specific as they appeal to the history of the region rather than the personal religiosity of the viewer, for it is there, in the land of Nizhnii Novgorod, that the great Russian saint lived, worked and advised his numerous visitors. He is still 'present' through his images affirming the distinct cultural and religious identity of the region (Naletova 2010).

Snapshot 3. A Sense of Professional Belonging

Many professional groups are willing to use Orthodox symbols to advertise their business and to demonstrate their orientation in relation to (what they understand as) Orthodox values. These can be insurance groups, travel agencies, real estate enterprises, artists, clubs, cafes, and even police departments (see Figure 4.3).

Even at first glance, this advertisement does not appear to be simply warning the viewers about the danger of fire or informing them about the emergency number 01. Using the icon, the Fire Department communicates to the viewers something else; namely, its own professional image as a respectable, reliable and ancient service. Moreover, by using the imperative form: 'venerate the Virgin of the Burning Bush!' it points to the fire fighters' (divine-like?) ability to save and protect people at moments of danger. One might think that this protection is offered not just to any endangered individual but only (and how much so!) to the faithful. But who are these faithful? The professional image of the Fire Department creates an impression that their service is given only to a specific community, excluding those who do not view the fire fighters' duties in these religious terms. The poster was designed in all likelihood to evoke in the viewers respect for religion as the foundation of the social order, which echoes the easily recognisable references to the anti-immigration policy of the Moscow administration: danger, order, and protection. By fostering an image of Moscow as an 'Orthodox city', the Moscow authorities discourage newcomers from settling in the city and impose harsh restrictions on any newcomers from Asia and the Caucasus. Religious symbols, in the case of the Fire Department's advertisement, reflect the anti-immigrants policy of the city administration.

Snapshot 4. A Sense of Political Belonging

The Red Square marked by the onion-domed roofs of St. Basil's Cathedral and the pointy roofs of the state buildings is one of the most recognisable images illustrating the Orthodox ideal of traditional relations between church and state, in which the religious and secular institutions seem to be harmoniously sharing the same physical space. A variety of other representations of

66 *Inna Naletova*

Figure 4.3 Self-advertisement of the Moscow Fire Department placed on the second floor of a building, while the information about the department's current events and activities is presented on the first floor. The image of the Virgin of the Burning Bush is accompanied by the statement written in a white Slavonic ligature: 'Venerate the "Virgin of the Burning Bush" and the Fire Department 01!' A group of fire fighters is depicted as working under the heavenly protection of the Virgin. The statement on the bottom in red 'Save and Protect!' refers (presumably) to both the Virgin and the Fire Department.

this idea can be seen in public domains, as individuals and institutions use religious and state symbols by placing them in close proximity to each other. The state symbols, such as flags, images of the Kremlin or portraits of the presidents, are often placed next to religious symbols, such as icons, crosses or pictures of religious architecture, the first having an equal size or being slightly higher or bigger than the second (see Figures 4.4 and 4.5).

The abundance and variety of Orthodox religious images in the public sphere give evidence of a great openness in Russian public life to traditional

Figure 4.4 A front window of a bus exhibiting, among other things, the image of Christ placed next to the national Russian three-coloured flag (on the left).

religion. It reflects the need of religious communities and individuals for being visible in public life and the need of local authorities to use religion for political and cultural purposes. The use of religious symbols is not subjected to state control as the monasteries and religious communities act independently or in cooperation with a city government, professional groups and leisure activities associations, and private individuals. After the breakdown of the atheist regime, religious symbols reemerged as the means to articulate religious and nonreligious messages, to draw lines, to include and exclude others; and to address national, cultural and professional ideas and sentiments.

An important issue in this religion-saturated context concerns the amount of freedom available there for secular and non-Orthodox sectors of society. At this point, it seems to me, no clear-cut social tendency toward religious exclusion or religious inclusion can be identified as religious images have both inclusive and exclusive meanings. What religion does in this context is primarily present itself to the public. Grace Davie's concept of 'vicarious religion' helps to understand this function of religion in modern society. It is that religion spreads outside of a church setting and involves participants with and without church affiliations. It calls attention to itself. It invites people to get involved in thinking about the world religiously. It confronts

68 *Inna Naletova*

Figure 4.5 Announcement for a national Russian chess competition. The symbols of the state (the pointy roofs of the Kremlin) and the Church (St. Basil's Cathedral with its trademark coloured roofs) are depicted as chess figures.

secular institutions with religious meanings. In Western Europe and Great Britain, according to Davie, vicarious religion is normally *invisible* as it only clearly manifests itself at moments of social trouble, when Europeans and the British (suddenly) become aware of the Christian roots of their culture, as happened, for instance, during the shocking death of Princess Diana. In contrast to the Western situation, in the Orthodox context, vicarious religion is publicly *visible*. It is an all-pervasive and dominant phenomenon that is often taken for granted as it exists in a great variety of practices and symbols, some of which I have illustrated above.

This thesis about a specifically Eastern European kind of vicarious religion that is widespread in Eastern Europe will lead me to the next step in my argument in which I will show that in Eastern (Orthodox) Europe, traditional religion remains a rich source of construction of *modern* institutions, not

European Secularity and Religious Modernity in Russia 69

only in 'vicarious' (evasive, noninstitutionalised or quasi-religious) forms, but also in the forms as measured by standard sociological methods.

RELIGION IN EUROPE: EAST VS. WEST

I will now turn to quantitative data concerning the state of religion in the European (Orthodox) East and the European West.

While in the West, and particularly in the countries with a historically Protestant profile, traditional religious forms have been in decline since the 1960s–1970s, but in most parts of Eastern Europe, approximately since the late 1980s, religion has been increasing or stabilising on a comparatively high level. According to the results of the Religion Monitor 2008, individuals defining themselves as no-religious constitute a majority in Germany, Great Britain, France, Austria, and Switzerland. Sweden and Spain can also be added to the list of countries with a predominantly nonreligious population if the data of the World Value Survey 2005–2007 are taken into account. Nonreligious people also constitute a very high portion of the population (40%) in Finland and about the same in the Netherlands. Even

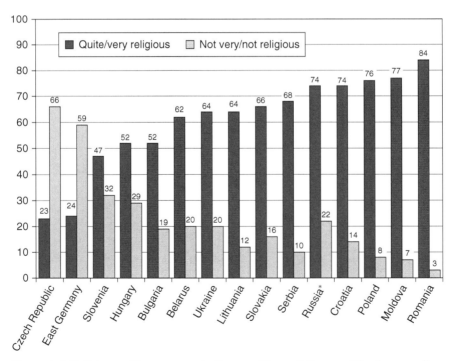

Figure 4.6 Religious self-assessment in Eastern (Central) Europe. The data on all countries except Russia are taken from the survey Aufbruch 2007. The data on Russia is taken from the World Value Survey 2006.

in Italy the proportion of self-defined nonreligious people has reached a level as high as that of religious people, namely 44% vs. 45% (Bertelsmann 2009). In contrast, the Eastern European landscape is dominated by a religious population with only two exceptions: former East Germany and the Czech Republic.

Figure 4.6 shows the results of the survey *Aufbruch* (from German 'Departure') conducted in 2007 in 14 countries of Eastern (Central) Europe and based on a representative number of respondents (1,000–2,000) interviewed in each country (Zulehner, Tomka & Naletova 2008; Zulehner & Naletova 2009).

While in Western Europe, with the exception of Italy, traditional churches have a hard time preserving their authority in matters of family life and in questions of moral, social and spiritual concern, in Eastern Europe, and particularly in the Orthodox area, the majority consider churches as competent institutions.

The proportion of people in each country viewing churches as competent institutions are illustrated in Figure 4.7 and Figure 4.8, for which I used the data from the Aufbruch 2007 and World Value Studies (WVS surveys) of 2005–2007.[6] The Orthodox countries are placed as a group on the left

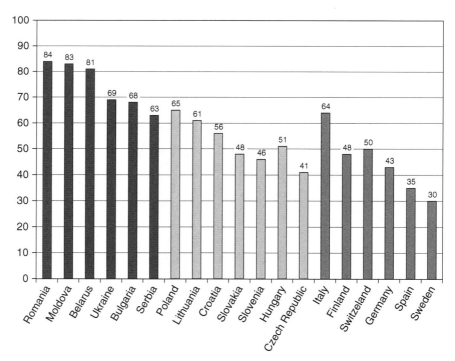

Figure 4.7 Churches are competent in dealing with moral problems*.
70.5% of Russians view churches as competent in moral issues (WVS 1999).

European Secularity and Religious Modernity in Russia 71

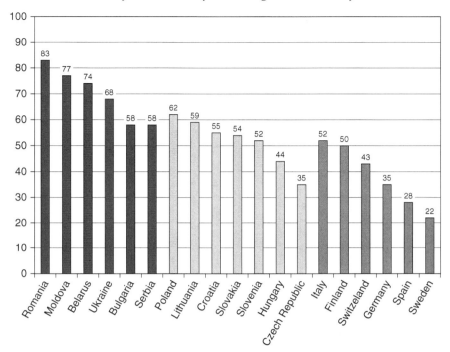

Figure 4.8 Churches are competent in dealing with family problems*.
**55% of Russians view churches as capable of dealing with family problems (WVS 1999).*

side of the figure. The groups of Catholic and religiously mixed countries of Eastern Europe are in the middle, and Western European countries are on the right. Orthodox countries view the churches' ability to deal with moral problems more positively than do the countries in other parts of Europe.

The questions about the competency of churches to provide answers to spiritual needs of people and to respond to contemporary social problems reveal the same dynamic in their answers: Orthodox countries are more inclined to consider the churches as competent institutions compared to people in the rest of Europe. The aforementioned Western European countries, with the exception of Italy, are quite sceptical about the competence of churches in spiritual, moral or social matters.

According to the survey of Aufbruch 2007, Orthodox countries are characterised by a certain 'religious optimism', this term coined by Paul M. Zulehner to point out the belief that in the future, religion will be more important. The Orthodox countries in Eastern Europe are more optimistic about the future of religion than their Catholic neighbours or countries with a religiously mixed profile (Zulehner, Tomka & Naletova 2008: 146). Another important characteristic of Orthodox Europe is related to the fact that their populations almost unanimously (up to 94% of the respondents) approve the engagement of churches in various social initiatives, such as

72 *Inna Naletova*

establishing church-based schools, hospitals, and kindergartens, trade unions and even media organisations. The fact that the churches are expected to be involved in building basic social institutions is a remarkable characteristic of the Orthodox part of Europe.

As the Orthodox-oriented countries are joining, or seeking to join, the EU as fully-fledged members, political recognition of Christianity, primarily Roman Catholicism, as a foundation of European integration is gaining new importance. New tensions are emerging between religious traditions and secular states. Ironically, the idea of God being mentioned in the European Constitution receives greater support from countries with an Orthodox orientation than from countries with a traditionally Catholic orientation. Figure 4.9 shows per cents of respondents in different countries who agreed and disagreed with the statement 'God should have been mentioned in the European Constitution'.

More than a decade after the political changes, Eastern Europe continues to present the European community with social developments that are distinctly religious. Social expectations from the churches; views about the moral, spiritual or social competence of churches and the general visibility of religion in public life are significantly higher in Eastern Europe (and

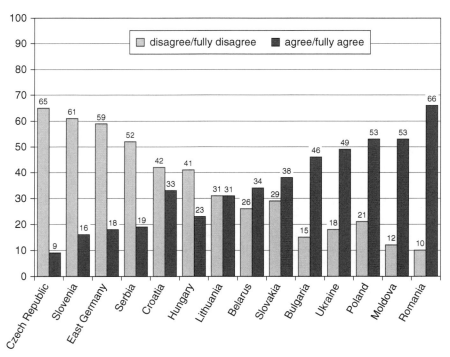

Figure 4.9 Agreement and disagreement with the statement: 'God should have been mentioned in the European Constitution'. Per cent per country. Survey Aufbruch 2007.

specifically in the Orthodox part of it) than in Western Europe, where the social demand for the public presence of religion is weaker or virtually non-existent and where churches, losing vitality and active members, are searching for a way out of the crisis (Zulehner 2010). From the material presented above, one could conclude that the Western idea of a 'religion-neutral' public life does not fully fit into the Eastern European perception of 'common space', where traditional religion—with its symbols, beliefs, and practices—is having (and is expected to have) a strong voice in the shared life.

RELIGION AND MODERNITY: SEARCHING FOR A PROPER THEORETICAL FRAMEWORK

In this section, I would like to return to the question stated at the beginning of the paper, namely, whether religion has a role to play in the modern world, and if yes, in which form(s) and under which conditions? In the academic literature, arguments are usually formulated along the lines of one of the three main paradigms: secularisation, privatisation or rational choice paradigms (Hellemans 2005). Based on the data from Western Europe, Great Britain or North America, these paradigms are often misleading when used to explain religious life outside of the Western context. As a Romanian sociologist Dan Dungaciu pointed out, these theories focus scholarly attention on the empirical elements that are supportive of a theory while encouraging them to underestimate other important elements of religious life (Dungaciu 2006).

SECULARISATION THESIS

According to the classical secularisation paradigm, religion in modern society is becoming progressively more marginal due to the continuous process of social differentiation and rationalisation, leading to what Max Weber called the 'disenchantment' of the world (Brown 2001; Wallis & Bruce 1992). In recent years this paradigm has been criticised for its Eurocentrism: the assumption that the secularisation process, as it is known in Western Europe, is the paramount model applicable to the rest of the world (Hervieu-Léger 2001; Martin 1978). 'The world today', to refer to an oft-quoted statement of Peter L. Berger, 'is massively religious, as anything but the secularized world that had been predicted by so many analysis of modernity' (Berger 1999:10).

With only a few exceptions, a majority of scholars would agree that secularisation cannot explain the state of religion in most parts of the world, but it does still explain the decline of religious life in Western Europe, which remains exceptionally secular (Berger, Davie & Focas 2008). Many scholars agree that in Western Europe the large Christian churches find themselves in deepening crisis with the number of registered members declining and the remaining members hardly conforming to the traditional norms of religious ethics and piety (Müller & Pollack 2009).[7]

As mentioned at the beginning of the chapter, some scholars predict a further spread of Western European secularisation from the West to the East as they expect that the people in Eastern European countries, while acquainting themselves with the Western way of life, become more distant from their religious institutions, receiving secularisation as a 'package' together with Western democracy, market economy and individualism (Berger 2005). This development, indeed, can be seen in some Eastern European countries, particularly those historically influenced by Protestantism, such as East Germany and the Czech Republic. In some Catholic countries, such as Poland and Slovenia, a decline in the importance of religion in the private life of individuals has also been observed. This development reflects a stabilisation of the political situation in the region (the prominent position of the Catholic Church in Poland in the recent past, during the Solidarnost movement, should be noted) and a crisis-like situation of Roman Catholicism generally in Europe.[8] Yet no comparable decline of religion in the Orthodox countries has been observed so far. On the contrary, a steady growth of church-oriented religiosity has been recorded. In Russia, for instance, the interest of people in religious ceremonies is increasing, and there is a growing demand for Orthodoxy's 'official' presence in various sectors of public life (Lokosov & Synelina 2008). The results of the recent studies of religion in Orthodox areas of Eastern Europe put into question the assumption that modernisation would inevitably lead to secularisation and that modernity causes dramatic distortions and a decline of church-based religiosity.

PRIVATISATION OF RELIGION THESIS

Another influential approach to religion and modernity is associated with the privatisation of religion thesis, initially formulated by sociologist Thomas Luckmann (1990, 1991). Religion from this perspective appears as drastically transformed by modern conditions, as individualised, marginalised, and unable to keep its importance beyond the sphere of the individuals' private life. This approach has also been criticised, however, primarily for underestimating the involvement of churches in matters of civil society; interreligious concerns; and, recently, in the discussions about the role of Islam in Europe. Despite the fact that the numbers of churchgoers are indeed declining, people continue to be involved—though indirectly and nonregularly—in the various public initiatives of the churches.

In criticising the privatisation of religion thesis, scholars emphasised the ability of religion to be transformed and adjusted to modern conditions (Först 2006; Hellemans 2001; Polak 2006; Zulehner 2005). Grace Davie, as already mentioned, has pointed out the existence of vicarious religion, and Daniele Hervieu-Leger has looked at religion as a being a part of society's 'chain of memory'. Paul Heelas and Linda Woodhead (2005) viewed spirituality as a modern expression of religion. Based on the material taken from Western Europe, Britain and the United States, Woodhead (2010) showed interactions between holistic spirituality and specific public issues, such as human rights, ideas of personal health, ecology, and new media, thus claiming that a certain global tectonic shift is on the way: the shift from the traditional community-based religiosity to translocal and transnational religious forms, which are, according to Woodhead, more suited to the conditions of (Western) modernity. In the same spirit, some scholars went as far as to see modernity as a new axial age characterised by a new religiosity emerging as a substitute for traditional church-oriented religion (Yves 1999).

The religious situation in Eastern (Orthodox) Europe does not fit within the framework of these discussions because in that part of Europe, private spirituality has not been disconnected from the church- and community-based religion. Traditional Eastern (Orthodox) religiosity remains to a large extent church based as churches continue to serve public needs as competent institutions, both spiritually, morally and socially.

RATIONAL CHOICE APPROACH

While the secularisation and privatisation paradigms characterise the religious situation in Western Europe very adequately, the rational choice approach, developed in North America, is most applicable to that region. The rational choice paradigm connects religious participation directly to the degree of freedom on the religious 'market' and views religious beliefs as the outcome of an individual's calculation of the 'costs' and 'benefits' involved in their religious affiliation.[9] Within the framework of the rational choice approach, one would have considerable difficulties in explaining the vitality of religious life in those countries in which a (quasi-) monopoly by a traditional church has been established for a long period of time and continues to exist today. Although the rational choice framework may bring valuable insights in understanding the ways religion functions in a Western society, it is difficult to apply the idea of a rational choice to an environment where the idea of 'shopping' (rational decision or calculation) is entirely alien in matters of religion and where the majority of the population does not consider any particular religion as a choice but simply accepts traditional religion unquestionably as a part of their cultural identity. In other words, religion for a great number of people in Russia and Eastern Europe is not a matter of choice but rather a marker of ethnic/cultural belonging. In such contexts, religious affiliations are regulated not by market forces but by historical and national factors.

In sum, one can conclude that none of the available paradigms is able to adequately grasp the religious situation in Eastern (Orthodox) Europe nor able to put traditional religion—as it manifests itself in that part of

Europe—in the framework of Western modernity. The return of churches and church-oriented public religion challenge the available theories of religion and encourage scholars to redefine the very concept of 'modernity' as a secular formation.

IS A RELIGION-FRIENDLY MODEL OF MODERNITY POSSIBLE IN ORTHODOX EUROPE?

Is it possible that modernity in Eastern (Orthodox) Europe and Western Europe will develop differently? Is Orthodoxy able to resist the supposedly pan-European process toward secularisation and privatisation? If so, what makes the Orthodox cultures exceptions to this general European development? What are the sources of their 'resistance'?

This chapter, written from the perspective that Orthodox symbols, practices and ideas saturate all possible aspects of public life, started with an overview of the relations between Orthodoxy and Western modernity. Several reasons were given to explain the prominent position of religion and of churches in matters of spiritual, moral and social concern. The reasons for the all-pervasive preeminence of churches in the Eastern European (Orthodox) area are manifold. Partly, they are related to the experience of state-imposed atheism. As I pointed out earlier, Eastern Europe experienced secularisation from above and resisted the atheist ideology from below. Other reasons for religious resilience can be found in the history and theology of Orthodox Christianity. The traditional Orthodox ideal of 'symphonic' relations between church and state, brought to Eastern Europe and Russia from Byzantium, is useful for explaining the 'natural' engagement of churches with political institutions and authorities. A positive association between religion and nation is also an important source of rebuilding for the post-Communist societies. In most areas of Orthodox Europe, the link between religion and nation/ethnicity strengthens the public voice of churches and helps them to establish themselves in the very centre of the new institution building. The significant role that traditional religion plays in the region depends on their ability to express the national identities of the people, and this role is unlikely to be challenged in the near future.

Taking the liberty of summarising by means of a rough and simplified East-West comparison of modernisation processes, I would argue that in Western Europe, modernisation originated in the ideas and ideals of the Enlightenment which went hand-in-hand with pluralisation and the individualisation of the public sphere, progressively deepening the separation of religion from other social spheres. This process weakened the churches and led to a decline of traditional religion in general. In Eastern (Orthodox) Europe, modernisation was linked *not* to individualisation and pluralisation, but to the rise of national (ethnic) identities and the establishment of what David Martin calls an 'organic collectivism', an 'unproblematic and undifferentiated' connection between religion, national, and local cultures (Martin 2008: 16). After the breakdown of the state-imposed antireligious ideology, this triple link between religion, nation and culture automatically pushed the churches to the forefront of public life, strengthening the value of traditional religion for modern society. By exploring the distinctive features of this Eastern European (Orthodox) pattern of modernity—which this chapter has sought to do—one can come to understand the meaning and the roots of Orthodox resistance to assimilation into Western European secularised modernity—the kind of modernity which is viewed by the churches (and by a great portion of the populations) as incompatible with the traditional (Orthodox) set of values.

This encourages me to make a sociological prediction: as long as Orthodoxy is able to support the formation of national identities in the region, and as long as Orthodoxy maintains its close link to culture, it is likely that churches will keep their prominent positions vis-à-vis the political and public domains and will serve as carriers of a religion-friendly and church-oriented modernity. The high degree of religious optimism observed among the Orthodox population, as well as the highly expressive presence of traditional religion in the public sphere, are but two of the signs proving the possibility of such a scenario.

NOTES

1. From the approximately 226 million Orthodox living in the world, 209 million live in Europe, of which 75 million live in Russia, 27 million in the Ukraine, 19 million in Romania, 7 million in Bulgaria, 6 million in Serbia, 6 million in Belarus and 3 million in Moldova (Alfeyev 2004: 18).
2. This corresponds to the period of state building and the establishment of independent national churches, when the structures of religious institutions began to reflect the structures of the state. Important dates of this period were the establishment of the autocephalous Orthodox Church of Serbia (1879) which immediately followed the recognition of Serbia as an independent state; the unification of the Metropolis of Moldavia and Wallachia to form the Romanian Orthodox Church (1972); and the recognition by the Patriarch of Constantinople of the independent Metropolis of Romania (1885) which later (1920) become a Patriarchate, and the election of the first Bulgarian Exarch (1872) with the subsequent establishment of the Bulgarian Orthodox Church as the religion of the Bulgarian nation (1895).
3. Not only Western modernisation, but also the Soviet/atheist variant of it was for obvious reasons unacceptable for the churches. Furthermore, most recently, the document called 'Bases of the Social Concept of the Russian Orthodox Church' presented the 'modern time' and 'modern world' as inseparable from the loss of Christian tradition, distorted consciousness, ecological crisis, 'sin and vices', and other 'passions and addictions (such) as drinking, drug addiction, fornication and adultery' (Department for External Church Relations of the Moscow Patriarchate (2010)).
4. Articles of the Metropolitan Kirill (currently Patriarch of Moscow and All Russia) could be seen as the first attempts on the part of the Orthodox hierarchs

to formulate a non-Western vision of modernity after the fall of Communism (Kirill 1999, 2000, 2001). For a review of these publications, see Naletova 2012.
5. This research was made possible through a project supported by the Austrian Research Society in 2010, for which I am very grateful.
6. 70.5% of Russians view churches as competent in moral issues (WVS, 1999). 55% of Russians view churches as capable of dealing with family problems (WVS 1999).
7. Scholars point out that among traditionally Catholic countries in Western Europe, those with the highest degree of modernisation are those where church involvement is the lowest (Pickel & Müller 2009: 153).
8. Irena Borowik (2010), studying the Catholic Church in Poland, has observed a decline in beliefs and practices in the Catholic Church, down from the high level of religiosity established in the 1990s. This decline, however, cannot be compared with the religious crisis in Western European countries, such as the Netherlands and France, since the Polish data show that religion remains comparatively important.
9. Here I refer to the numerous writings of Rodney Stark, Roger Finke, William S. Bainbridge and Laurence R. Iannaccone. For instance, Rodney Stark & William Sims Bainbridge (1996). *A Theory of Religion*. New Brunswick, New Jersey: Rutgers University Press (first published in 1987 by Peter Lang).

5 The Orthodox Tradition in a Globalising World
The Case of the Romanian Orthodox Church

Suna Gülfer Ihlamur-Öner

INTRODUCTION

Religion is constitutive of, and constituted by, the world we are living in. It is a 'historical product' (Berger 1990: vi) as both society and religion are embedded in the same human activity (Ibid: 47–48). The very modernity that eroded traditional societies and the basis that religions stood on, also create the need and room for religious activism (Davie 1999: 80). Globalisation, together with the crisis of the nation-state and the ongoing construction of a global civil society, further provides the ground for religious activism in the public sphere and reinforces the role that religious institutions play as transnational actors (Casanova 1994: 225–227). Religion, which resists against its containment in and by the nation-state, plays a significant role in connecting the global and the local and reordering social borders in line with global forces (Levitt 2006: 393). New religious movements contribute to the spread of different forms of global consciousness (Beckford 2004: 207). In short, religion functions both as a 'world-maintaining' and 'world-shaking' force (Berger 1990: 100) in the globalising world and needs to be studied within this context as it poses challenges to the scientific study of religion by bringing the issue of the nature of religion to the fore (Turner 2006: 439).

However, religion receives only limited scholarly attention in globalisation studies (Beckford 2004: 206), and those that take religion into consideration define the relation between religion and globalisation in rather negative terms, pitting religion against the forces of globalisation (Beyer 2007: 167) or representing it as an 'outside' force (Beyer & Beaman 2007: 1) or as an obstacle, enemy or victim of modernity. It is true that religion is one of the means of resisting or questioning globalisation, since modernisation, globalisation and commodification put religious traditions to the test by challenging their communal and social foundations and force them to transform themselves (della Cava 2001: 536; Turner 2006: 440). Moreover, the ethno-religious resurgence of the global age is a sign of this 'vibrant contestation and localization' (Hefner 2000: 3), since globalisation does not only lead to homogeneity and harmony, but also proceeds through conflict and difference (Roudometof 2001: 2).

Because the relationship between globalisation and religion is not straightforward but rather complex, it is necessary to place religion in a historical context in order to study it. The global religious system, which is in itself a historical construct (Beyer 2006: 9), provides us with the framework to study religions in the global era. The global religious system is constituted by different religious traditions that evolve in constant interaction with each other as well as with local, transnational and global social processes, and religions have become part of the global religious system through compliance as well as resistance. Orthodox Christianity,[1] which endured the Communist rule, started experiencing the transformative power of globalisation to the full amount with the end of the Cold War. While the Orthodox Churches are in communion with each other, their encounter with globalisation is very much intertwined with national factors and follows different courses. The Romanian Orthodox Church (ROC), as the only Orthodox Church with a neo-Latin language and tradition (Introvigne, Zoccatelli, Macrina & Roldàn 2001: 112; Pacini 2000: 59), faces the challenge of transformations brought through globalisation, coupled with Romania's accession to the EU and transnational migration in the post-Cold War era. This chapter describes and evaluates the dialogue between globalisation and the Orthodox world in general and the ROC in particular. After a discussion of the global religious system in the first section, the second part seeks to evaluate the encounter between globalisation and Orthodox Christianity and the ROC by focusing on ethics and values in a globalised world, social justice and assistance issues, religious pluralism and the agency of the Orthodox Churches in a diaspora.

THE GLOBAL RELIGIOUS SYSTEM

Religion is an 'eminently collective thing' (Durkheim 1915: 47). It is part of social processes, is shaped by the transformations that societies go through and takes particular forms in particular settings (Beyer 2006: 255). Therefore, rather than substantive definitions that treat religion as transcendent or try to come up with a universal theory of religion, which is true for all times and places, a functional definition of religion that explains what it does and serves (Ibid: 4) suffices for the purposes of social research. If society is understood as the 'interconnectedness of communication' (Ibid: 35), religion could be defined as a social phenomenon that constructs itself as communication (Ibid: 10), taking new forms in different periods and proceeding through continuities as well as discontinuities.

Communication was gradually organised in the form of institutions to serve certain specified functions and with the emergence of modern societies religion, which had played a very important and extensive role in social organisation throughout history, had to redefine itself as a function system. While modernisation represents the emergence of functional differentiation in social organisation (Beyer 2006: 42), globalisation entails the spread as well as evolution of the function systems through the universalisation of particular social forms and the particularisation of universalisms (Ibid: 56).[2] Globalisation, which can be thought of as 'the process of increasing interconnectedness between societies' (Baylis & Smith 2001: 7) or 'as a process (or set of processes) which embodies a transformation of the spatial organization of social relations and transactions' (Held, McGres, Goldblatt & Perraton 1999: 16) creates, redefines or structures the institutions, channels and media of communication. This has important implications for global society as composed of different function systems (Beyer 2006: 3) and religion as a communicative function system.

In the global era, the global religious system as an institutional domain emerges as an important sociostructural component of world society (Beyer 2006: 14). A religious system functioning through organisations, movements, networks and interactions on a global scale becomes the arena for opposing trends, such as harmony and contention, collaboration and resistance, all of which are intrinsic to the functioning of the global religious system. The global religious system is contingent (Ibid: 12) and in its current global form religion is both invented and real, a Western imposition and a rejection of it, in conflict with globalisation and constitutive of it, a continuation of the past and a radically new form (Ibid: 115).

The construction of the global religious system, rather than the creation of something new, is a 'reordering' of religious and cultural resources (Beyer 2006: 82). The formation of the global religious system was embedded, rather than isolated, in complex social transformations that paved the way for the dominance of the function systems in the organisation of social life in the modern era. Religion is a precondition and contributor to the emergence of the modern age, just like the nation-state or capitalism (Ben-Rafael & Sternberg 2005: 15; Beyer 2006: 301; Beyer & Beaman 2007: 5). Even though the religious sphere is different from nonreligious spheres such as the economy, politics or education, these different spheres emerged and developed in parallel to each other (Beyer 2007: 170). The global religious system which is based on 'selective modelling', is constructed through the inclusion of different world religions. Within the system, different religions can serve as models depending on the time and circumstances. Christianity, particularly its Protestant and Catholic variants, linked with the supremacy of European power in world politics and influence in globalisation, emerged and served as the most prominent model in the formation of the global religious system (Beyer 2006: 120; Beyer & Beaman 2007: 4). The presence of the 'Christian model' (Beyer 2006: 117), however, does not prevent any particular religion from refusing to conform to the model or challenging or adapting the model to its own needs (Beyer 2007: 183). Therefore, in the globalised religious domain, rather than one model dominating over the others, different religions participate and contribute through their particular characteristics, since it was not only the Christian model that has been in a process of formation, but also other religious and secular spheres and actors that influenced and were influenced by the forces of modernisation and globalisation (Ibid: 174). Moreover, the Christian experience does not present itself through a single, unvarying model. While it is debatable whether political factors and conceptions of society, rather than the dogmatic differences, create the main difference and division between different Christian Churches (Gillet 1995: 360), it is certain that Catholicism, Protestantism and Orthodoxy followed different courses in constructing and becoming part of the global religious system.

Composed of 'world religions', the global religious system is intrinsically pluralistic. Religions face the challenge of being 'one religion among many' and coexist and compete with others. Religions also have to uphold the religious dogma, tradition and worldview, while trying to reach out to people and become more socially engaged (Hefner 1998: 98–99). Moreover, as individuals gain the freedom and capability to integrate themselves into systems of 'subjective significance', and as religious institutions fail to be monopolistic and coercive, religious freedom and pluralism are institutionalised, and public institutions do not feel the need to maintain a religious worldview (Casanova 1994: 37 and 47). Therefore, religions embedded in the global system take centre stage in the tension between pluralism and homogeneity.

Organisations[3] play a vital role in all global social function systems, since communication flows through the organisational channels (Beyer 2006: 51). Religion is unthinkable without the religious institutions—the most common being the ecclesiastical institutions—since religious institutions give religion its 'generalized form' in order for it to prevail (Moberg 1962: 6). While religious tradition is kept alive by the community that lives, practices and reproduces it through ritual practices (Kurtz 1995: 9), the religious institutions ensure continuity, regularity and reproduction of the religious tradition and shape the organisation of religious life (Ibid: 82–83). Organisations give religions their current form and their span from local to global. The main differences between different religions also manifest themselves in organisational form (Beyer 2007: 173). Hence, religious pluralism is, in fact, organisational pluralism (Ibid: 109); and the global religious organisations, rather than following a centre-periphery model, work through multiple centres and particularisations of a central authority. Through organisations, religions can formulate responses to globalisation by blending local elements with universal aspirations. Therefore, adaptive capacity is crucial for religious institutions to survive and remain relevant in a globalising world.

ORTHODOX CHRISTIANITY AND GLOBALISATION

The Eastern Orthodox world's encounter with, and responses to, globalisation have been shaped and influenced by two main factors: 'the legacy of communism' and the 'institutional culture' of Orthodoxy (Agadjanian &

Roudometof 2005: 9). The Eastern Orthodox world faced a very serious challenge with the establishment of Communist regimes in the Soviet Union and Eastern Europe. It was in the Soviet Union that religions suffered the harshest treatment. In Eastern Europe, the restrictions on religious institutions took different forms, but overall restrictions on religion were serious, and it had to retreat to the private sphere (Pacini 2003: 165). Communism disturbed the balance of *symphonia*[4] in the Orthodox Church-state relationship, and the state outweighed the Orthodox Churches, which had grown together with their states (Stan & Turcescu 2007: 7). Communism also restrained the missionary activity within and outside of the Orthodox heartland. Even though religious persecution came to an end with the fall of the Communist regimes in the early 1990s, as Agadjanian and Roudometof (2005: 12) argue, 'Eastern Orthodoxy came out of the communist ghetto with a circumscribed ability to respond to rapid restructuring' and found itself surrounded with new challenges.

As regards institutional culture, the current organisation of the Eastern Orthodox Church is shaped both by ancient traditions and the Ecumenical Councils as well as by modern conditions. The organisational trend in the Orthodox world has been 'centrifugal' and towards the formation of churches on a regional or national basis (Confino 2005: 351). The dissolution of the Byzantine Empire and the process of nationalisation of the Orthodox Churches have altered the universalistic orientation of the Churches (Makrides 2007: 557). The emergence of new autocephalous churches attendant on the birth of new nation-states in the Balkans and Eastern Europe[5] served to reorganise the region along national lines, while Orthodoxy became an integral part of people's national identity (Roudometof 2001: 16). Therefore, the Orthodox world does not have one unitary church that is organised and administered from one centre or by a pope (Volkov 2005: 226). The Ecumenical Patriarchate in Istanbul has the honorary distinction of being *primus inter pares*, and it has certain rights and duties in terms of coordinating the collaboration of the Orthodox Churches; however, it cannot interfere in the internal affairs of the independent churches. The autocephalous churches[6] have the authority to decide about all the internal matters regarding the church and faith. They elect their own patriarchs, bishops, priests and deacons. The autonomous churches[7] are under the jurisdiction of the autocephalous churches. When an autonomous church seeks independence, it is up to the Mother Church to recognise its independence (Meyendorff 1996: 10). However, this leads to fragmentation at the expense of Orthodox ecumenicity (Payne 2007: 834) and creates the problem of overlapping jurisdictions in the Orthodox heartland. Moreover, in the post-Cold War era, Orthodoxy as a 'source of national ideology and collective legitimization' has become an important element of geopolitics in the region (Thual 1993: 122), turning claims for autocephaly from a primarily religious issue into a political one (Borowik 2006: 274) and leading to further divisions within the Orthodox world.[8] These divisions are also reproduced in the new contexts through the extension of the Orthodox diaspora and the transnationalisation of the 'canonical territory' (Payne 2007: 841). Further fragmentation and conflicts weaken the Orthodox solidarity in developing common responses to the global challenges.

As an autocephalous Orthodox Church that went through the communist experience, the ROC presents an interesting case in evaluating the dialogue between Orthodoxy and globalisation. Since its inception, the ROC went through different transformative processes and had to work under different rulers and regimes until it took its current form. The ROC declared its autocephalous status in 1865 following the unification of the Romanian principalities. It was recognised in 1885 by the Ecumenical Patriarchate (Tappe 1977: 288) and became a patriarchate itself in 1925 (Bria 1995: 12). With the rise of the Romanian nation-state, the Orthodox Church became part of the institutional set-up of the state (Leustean 2009: 18). The ROC was under Fascist rule during the interwar years, and by 1948 it came under Communist control. The ROC's experience under Communism was rather different from that of the other Orthodox Churches in Eastern Europe. The Romanian Communist regime allowed the ROC to continue its religious activities to the extent that it served its interests in terms of controlling society (Ibid: 19, 192). Following the fall of Ceausescu, it emerged as one of the most powerful and trusted institutions in Romania (Ibid: 22). Today, it is a church revered by 87% of the population,[9] which makes the ROC second after the Russian Orthodox Church in terms of adherents (Stan & Turcescu 2007: 1467). Within the entire Orthodox world, post-Communist Romania occupies first place in terms of a high level of religious practice and commitment.[10] The ROC is also extending its reach beyond the borders of Romania through transnational Romanian migration and the European integration.

In the post-Communist era, the ROC became an important actor in the transformation of Romanian society and succeeded in reconquering the political, religious and sociocultural spheres of life. Religious freedom after 40 years of repression, the freedom of the ROC to be more active in social life and public space and its striving to be the moral guide of the people in Romania through its clergy in churches, schools, the army, prisons and other public institutions[11] paved the way for the ROC's growing importance. By associating itself with Romanian national identity and using a nationalist discourse, the ROC could maintain its influence over society after the Communist rule ended (Leustean 2009: 190). Church building with the support of the Romanian state emerged as an important means for the ROC to increase its power, role and visibility in the public sphere (Andreescu 2007: 456). While Romanian-ness and Orthodoxy are inseparable for the ROC, it does not have a constitutional status as the 'national church' of Romania. Therefore, in the post-Communist era, the ROC defines itself as the 'representative institution' and the 'translator' of the 'will of the majority' (Conovici 2006: 8).

Orthodox Christianity's and the ROC's dialogue with globalisation is evaluated in more detail in the following four sections. Each section sheds light on a different aspect of this dialogue and discusses both the challenges and opportunities posed to the Orthodox world in general, and the ROC in particular, by the factors and forces of globalisation.

ETHICS AND VALUES IN A GLOBALISED WORLD

The Orthodox Tradition sets the main norms of Orthodox life, which has evolved throughout history to reach to current generations of Orthodox Christians (Kirill 2001). However, as Burawoy and Verdery argue (1999: 2), the 'post-socialist moment means constant change' and parameters of action, laws, norms and interests keep shifting in a short span of time obliging the actors to work with short-term strategies and live with uncertainty (Ibid: 7). This requires the Orthodox Churches to be proactive to maintain and reproduce the 'unbroken tradition' (Ramet 2006: vii) in a globalising world. The collapse of the Communist regimes in Eastern Europe also led to a transition to a new political system and the creation of a new institutional structure. Weak welfare state regulations, uncontrolled consumerism, the process of secularisation coupled with globalisation within the post-Communist societies, all challenge the tradition by weakening people's commitment to it and require the Orthodox Churches to develop an urgent response (Binns 2002: 235; Sztompka 2005: 541).

While trying to preserve the Orthodox Tradition, the Orthodox Churches seem to adopt a sceptical approach towards Western values and globalisation, which leads them to be placed within the anti-globalist camp. Ramet (2006: xi) defines the Romanian and Russian Orthodox Churches as conservative forces working against secularisation, Westernisation and globalisation. The challenge posed by globalisation to the national character of the Orthodox Churches[12] and the secularising trends that globalisation brings forth are among the most negative consequences stated by different hierarchs of the Orthodox Churches (Makrides 2007: 558). It is true that the Orthodox Churches have put more emphasis on tradition and communitarian values (Makrides 2005: 183–184), and this respect for the tradition might turn into 'stiff and formal traditionalism' (Erickson 1999: 27). Moreover, even though the Orthodox Tradition is part of European culture and heritage, the Orthodox world does not want its total absorption by what it calls 'the Western civilisation'. While attributing to Orthodoxy a higher spirituality (Bogomilova 2004: 3–4), it is sceptical about liberal values and modernity (Pacini 2000: 21). However, this sceptical and ambiguous stance does not mean the Orthodox world is not in dialogue with globalisation.

Globalisation is a multifaceted process that could be analysed at different levels and through different units of analysis. Globalisation from above, or neoliberal globalisation, is based on 'the collaboration between leading states and the main agents of capital formation' such as transnational corporations and political elites (Falk 1993: 39). It is facilitated by the growing integration of the world economy and intensifying interconnectedness of economic actors through the diffusion of new technology and expansion of capitalist markets (Giddens 2009: 131–133). Globalisation from above is contested by globalisation from below, which is constituted through the alliance or collaboration of transnational social movements, forces and processes of different sorts, all acting and interacting with various concerns ranging from human rights issues to environmental issues to eradication of poverty or oppression (Falk 1993: 39). In other words, globalisation from below resists the homogenising forces and processes of globalisation from above through constructing a global civil society and trying to establish a democracy that goes beyond the borders of the nation-state (Ibid: 40). The Orthodox world's perception of globalisation fits well with the globalisation from above and below dichotomy and, while challenging the unrestrained globalisation from above, it defines itself among the forces that constitute globalisation from below.

The economic aspects of globalisation are one of the main concerns of the Church hierarchs of different Orthodox Churches. The main question for Metropolitan Paul Yazigi of Aleppo is whether it will serve to distribute benefits or to further exploitation. He believes that the Orthodox world has a responsibility to guide the globalisation process and to 'make out of globalization the world of God' (Yazigi n.d.). However, the Orthodox Churches do not disregard the material needs of human beings or the importance of economic growth. Referring to the Greek origins of the word economy, which means building or construction, Metropolitan (currently the Patriarch) Kirill argues that economics guided solely by material interests will eventually lead to destruction rather than construction. Therefore, he expresses the need for economics guided by ethical principles, which can be both efficient and just; and he is critical of the global economy, which falls short of being sociably responsible and observant of moral principles (Fantini 2008). Similarly, the Ecumenical Patriarch Bartholomew I (2008: 155) states that the concern for the 'life of the world,' that is, the 'divine economy', is at the heart of the Orthodox spirituality. The Russian Orthodox Church while recognising the 'inevitability' of globalisation argues for taking control of unrestrained market forces and the 'recognition of the legality of religious worldview as a basis for socially significant action'.[13]

In the post-Cold War era, before fully recovering from the injuries incurred during the Communist period and without proper preparation, the ROC had to confront rapid social transformations, the growing influence of mass media on society and the change in social values (Bria 1995: 44). These drastic transformations required the ROC to adopt a new stance so it could embrace the new era. Stoica (2007: 206) criticises the conservative stance within Orthodoxy, which makes the Church fall behind global developments. He emphasises the need for 'awakening' to the new realities and therefore 'awareness and metanoia', which he describes as a 'fundamental change in thinking' (Ibid: 194). Flora and Szilagyi (2005: 138) argue that the ROC needs to go through a process of institutional restructuring and revise its way of relating to the people and of communicating its message. Similarly, Bria (1995: 47) argues for the need to reform the parish system and redefine the mission of the Church. Patriarch Daniel Ciobotea of the ROC argues that the ROC, rather than focusing on the advantages of globalisation, needs to discover what role spirituality and morality would play within the context of globalisation and develop a response accordingly (Ciobotea 2003: 328).

SOCIAL JUSTICE AND ASSISTANCE

Given the Orthodox world's criticism of globalisation from above, its emphasis on social justice and fair distribution is noteworthy. The Orthodox Churches failed to develop a 'modern social doctrine' (Enev 2001: 159) due to the lack of resources and autonomy to do so until the very end of the Cold War (Agourides 1964: 219). Moreover, the Orthodox Churches' involvement in social assistance was seen as a sign of secularisation and increasing Western influence over the Orthodox world (Ibid: 211). However, the issue cannot be postponed any further, as the encounter with globalisation requires a new perspective and a new activism in this field, according to Patriarch Bartholomew I ('Activitatea Sectorului Biserica și Societatea' 2002: 162). The new era requires the Orthodox Churches to take more responsibility in the social sphere in terms of training its priests for social work and assistance. Orthodox theology also needs to address social issues to guide those churches working in different cultural and sociopolitical contexts. Therefore, it should go through a form of reorientation in order to formulate a vision for the future (Binns 2002: 235). Only by getting closely involved, developing solutions for social problems and using their theological and material resources for innovation, can the Orthodox Churches provide guidance and remain relevant.

Even though the Orthodox world is far from developing a social doctrine as of yet, it is aware of the need for change, as Patriarch Bartholomew I's words clearly reveal: 'the Church is called not to conform to but to transform this world' (Bartholomew I 2008: 232). He states that akathist,[14] meaning 'standing' (Ibid: 234), staying alert and aware is the way to deal with the world's problems (Ibid: 235). He also argues that the involvement of the Orthodox Churches in the lives of human societies and their capacity to mobilise people into action (Ibid: 145) can, in turn, lead to a transformation and awakening within the Churches to social problems and injustice (Ibid: 151). This transformation allows the Orthodox Churches to act upon their responsibilities (Ibid: 155) in terms of ensuring social justice and acting as a balancing force in a globalising world (Ibid: 145). The eagerness of the

Ecumenical Patriarchate to be more involved in this sphere could also be seen as a sign of its search for transforming itself from a transnational religious institution of (mainly) ethnic Greeks into a global actor (Roudometof 2008: 77). In a similar line, the Archbishop Anastasios of Tirana and All Albania, in his opening sermon delivered at the World Council of Churches in Porto Alegre, urged the participants 'not to be spectators of divine interventions and actions' but to take the initiative and become coworkers with God (Jacobse & Johannes 2009). Therefore, despite its critical stance towards the West and modernity, it would not be wrong to define Orthodoxy as part and parcel of it and *as one of the religioscapes constantly shaped by (premodern and modern) globalisation* (Roudometof 2008:70). Through its 'living tradition', Orthodoxy is able to adapt and accommodate to new situations as it has done throughout history (Erickson 1999: 27–28).

In the post-Communist era, social issues pose an immediate challenge to the ROC. The failure of the Romanian state to tackle social problems right after the fall of the Ceausescu regime was indicative of the need for civil society's involvement (Muntean 2005: 96) and provided a new sphere of activism for the religious institutions in Romania. This required the Romanian religious institutions to revitalise their ability to provide the social assistance that was curbed by communism and 'modernise' and reorganise their pastoral work (Lakatos 1998b: 18). When compared to the Catholic and Protestant Churches, the Orthodox Church in Romania has been less active in the social realm and has tended to see the delivery of services as the state's responsibility (Féltoronyi 1992, cited in Lakatos 1998b: 5). Unlike the Catholic and Protestant Churches that follow the Western model of social work and get assistance from the churches in Europe and the United States, social work is not performed through an institutionally autonomous and separate structure in the case of the ROC.[15]

Following the collapse of Communism, the ROC has reactivated many associations and foundations for charitable work and established some new ones. The main area of charitable activity of the ROC is health care and abandoned children (Flora & Szilagyi 2005: 136). The church is helping abandoned children, trying to prevent school dropouts and assisting youth's socioprofessional reintegration ('Activitatea Sectorului Biserica şi Societatea' 2002: 672–673). The enormous social problems of Romania, due to economic crises, high unemployment, inadequacy of health care and psychological support services, as well as 'moral decay' have led the ROC, in collaboration with the state, to create new departments within the faculties of theology that train students for social assistance (Ciobotea 2003: 326). As the social problems became more complex and other denominations became very active in social work, the Holy Synod of the ROC adopted a regulation for the organisation and functioning of a social assistance system of the Church in 1997, which made philanthropic activity and social assistance one of the priorities of the ROC ('Activitatea Sectorului IV al Administratitei Patriarhale' 1998: 374).[16] However, despite all these improvements in social services, the ROC still expresses the need for a strategy and for unified action ('Temei nr. 3806/2006' 2006: 33). Preda argues that an Orthodox social theology, rather than leading to secularisation of theology, would show that the Church is taking the developments in the world seriously, focusing its efforts on social issues and following closely how social policies are formulated (Preda 2006, cited in Lobonț 2009: 55–56).

RELIGIOUS PLURALISM

As a constitutive element of the global religious system, one main issue that the Orthodox world has to cope with is religious pluralism. In the post-Communist era, religious pluralism has become a global phenomenon with repercussions at the institutional and individual level of consciousness (Berger 2005: 439) such as the competition among religious institutions and subjective religiosities, something that is worrisome for the Orthodox Churches that have always been the church of the majority in their countries. Being an inseparable part of the national identity that strengthened the anti-individualist doctrine of the Orthodox Church makes its relationship with pluralism a problematic one (Enev 2001: 160). Payne (2007: 831) argues that the main obstacle in the way of religious pluralism in Eastern Europe is the association of the Orthodox Churches with nationalism, the state and cultural identity. Furthermore, while the reemergence of the Greek-Catholic Churches was already a cause of concern for the Orthodox Churches, many missionaries have arrived from the United States and Western Europe with the belief that the region's exposure to the communist-atheist propaganda requires its re-evangelisation (Ramet 1998: 200). The 'proselytism of the foreign sects' (Clément 2005: 28–29; Merdjanova 2000: 253), in a region where social and economic problems make people more 'vulnerable' to the conversion efforts of the missionaries with resources, has alarmed the Orthodox Churches.[17] Despite this tension, one should not underestimate the efforts of the Orthodox Churches in furthering the ecumenical dialogue with other churches and different religious traditions within and outside of the Orthodox heartland.

The fall of the Communist regime meant change not just for the ROC, but also for all the other religious denominations in Romania. Soon after the fall of the Ceausescu regime, the Decree Law No.1 of December 1989 reestablished the Greek-Catholic Church, which was united with the ROC under the Communist rule, and with Decree Law No. 126 of April 1990, the Church was recognised and the rules for property restitution were specified (Stan & Turcescu 2007: 95).[18] The transition to liberal democracy and the prospects for joining European institutions led to legislative initiatives[19] for further democratisation, which had important implications for religious institutions in Romania, particularly for the ROC. European integration also challenges the ROC to become more accommodating of religious pluralism and new institutional frameworks.[20] Under increasing pressure from the EU, Romania adopted a new law regulating the church-state relations and its religious landscape on 27 December 2006 (Legea nr. 489/2006). Stan and Turcescu (2007: 28) call the current Romanian system of church-state relations 'managed quasi-pluralism'; it is managed because the denominations have to register and get recognition from the state to work freely in Romania, and it is quasi-pluralistic, since the ROC has primacy among 18 denominations recognised by the Romanian state. The criticisms against the new law on religious denominations reveal that Romania will have to do more in terms of harmonising its system with that of the EU.[21] Nevertheless, with this new law the Romanian religious space is reorganised so as to be more accommodating of religious pluralism.

Besides legislative changes and the EU accession process, there are other factors inducing religious pluralism in Romania. The Patriarchate's official website states that the biggest challenge for the ROC in the post-Communist era is religious pluralism.[22] The ROC started facing competition from the other churches that became free to act in Romania with a crucial amount of foreign support and pressure on the Romanian governments. The emergence and religious activities of 'foreign' evangelical groups and the missionary movements are seen as 'proselytism' by the ROC (Bria 1995: viii; Muntean 2005: 88). The conversion strategies, such as free English courses and assisting migration to Western countries, are worrisome for the Church. The ROC strongly opposes certain denominations or 'sects'[23] and seeks states' support in impeding their work on Romanian territory, such as the Jehovah's witnesses or the Pentecostals. The number of converts to conservative Protestantism in Eastern Europe is significant, particularly in Romania (Martin 1999: 37). The Pentecostal and Adventist Churches found a base among the lower classes, particularly the Roma population (Lakatos 1998a: 30), which has been marginalised and is less affected by ethno-nationalist rhetoric.[24] The fact that traditional churches employ ethno-nationalist strategies associating religious identity with an ethnic one and make alliances with different secular forces to monopolise the religious landscape, do not create favourable conditions for religious competition (Ibid: 89). Therefore, free religious market theory cannot be applied to Romania, as the conditions for free competition of religions are not mature enough (Ibid: 88), and mutual interdenominational acceptance and collaboration are not very well established.[25]

Despite its scepticism towards the new religious movements and neo-Protestant Churches, the ROC is aware of the need to present a very authentic Christian message to the world and reveal the universal character of the Orthodox Church, which has led to the intensification of contacts and relations with sister Orthodox Churches ('Activitatea Sectorului Relaţii Externe Bisericeşti' 2001: 487). Theological and ecumenical dialogue with the other Christian Churches continues at the national and international level and the involvement of the Church in the lives of the Romanian Orthodox diaspora is emphasised (Ibid: 488). Collaboration with the other churches is also growing due to Romania's European accession, which has led to the 'reconfiguration of [the ROC's] role in the European context' (Carp 2007: 18). The ROC represents the highest number of Orthodox people in the EU. Moreover, Katzenstein (2006: 4) foresees an important role for Orthodoxy, which, in closer contact with Catholicism, is challenging the EU's secular impact on Christian values.[26] The EU accession and the growing number of ROCs in Europe motivated the Church to open a representative bureau in Brussels in 2007. The ROC is thus becoming a transnational actor within the EU; however, to what extent the ROC will embrace the EU agenda and use Romania's EU membership to heighten its status as transnational agent remains to be seen.

DIASPORA

The emergence of the Orthodox Churches in the diaspora that maintain a network of social, cultural and religious relations with the homeland has turned Orthodoxy into a global religion (Berzano & Cassinasco 1999: 14). The term 'diaspora'[27] within the Orthodox world is used to refer to 'the dispersion in time and space of the Orthodox communities, which settle in regions different from where their Mother Churches are located, keeping with them the ultimate canonical dependence relation or spiritual ties, but progressively searching to organize themselves in an autonomous way' (Bobrinskoy 2003: 303). The dispersion of the Orthodox faithful across the world took place in waves linked with political and economic developments throughout history.[28] The extension of the Orthodox Churches outside of their traditional homeland to Europe, the United States and other parts of the world, gives the Churches the possibility to express the universality of the Orthodox Tradition and to state that they are not 'religious foreigners' in the West (Kesich 1961: 193), while bringing the Orthodox world into contact with globalisation, transnationalism and other social processes in different contexts. The interaction between the Orthodox heartlands and diasporas is crucial, since the 'Orthodox diasporas are usually more tuned to global perspectives and develop corresponding strategies that can benefit the homelands' (Makrides 2007: 559). This also gives the Orthodox diaspora in the host societies the chance to introduce their responses to global challenges and issues (Clément 2005: 139). Ware (1997: 186) argues that the dispersal is a *kairos*[29] for the Orthodox world, a moment of opportunity. However, to seize this opportunity, it has to overcome its own divisions both within and outside of the Orthodox heartland.

Even though it is possible to talk about the presence of a sizable Romanian Orthodox diaspora in the United States from the 19th century onwards, the Romanian Orthodox diaspora grew rapidly and spread to different parts of the world through mass migration after 1989. The growth and spread of the

Romanian diaspora radically changed the ROC's perception of its jurisdiction. While under Communist rule the jurisdiction of the Church was delimited by territory,[30] marked by the boundaries of Romania, after the fall of the Communist regime it was the nation—the Romanian Orthodox people living within and outside of Romania—[31] that became the defining factor for the definition of the Church's jurisdiction.[32] Since the official figures fail to present the actual size and scope of migration flows, it is hard to estimate the exact size and extent of the Romanian diaspora (Pehoiu & Costache 2010: 608). Yet, the president of Romania, Traian Băsescu, estimates it to be around 8 million people.[33]

It is post-1989 Romanian migration that brought the ROC into Europe, which is still the main destination for Romanian immigrants. The ROC has responded to the rapid growth of this diaspora by forming a well-structured and connected network of churches in a very short span of time, though with limited resources. For the first generation, the local parish in the diaspora is the main link with Romania and a social space where the national language and traditions are reproduced. This maintains the role of the Church in the diaspora as a symbol of belonging and a point of reference. The transplantation of the ROC in new settings provides the ROC with a new area of agency and transnational actor status. While requiring the ROC to develop responses to the local and global issues in settings other than the Romanian Orthodoxy's heartland, this influences the role of the ROC and religious life within Romania. According to Father Valdman, the priest of the ROC in Milan for more than 30 years, the Romanian Orthodox Patriarchate is the 'trunk', growing stronger as its 'branches' develop in the diaspora, and both the trunk and branch gain from this interaction (Valdman, personal interview, 18 July 2007).

CONCLUSION

The relationship between globalisation and religion is a complex one and cannot be defined solely in conflictual terms. While religion challenges or resists the homogenising trends of globalisation in certain respects, it is itself a globalising force acting at the local, transnational and global levels. The emergence of the religious function system and its transformation into a global one is therefore embedded in the sociostructural transformations that paved the way for the construction of the global society. The global religious system, which is historically contingent, is composed of different world religions and their variants. Orthodox Christianity, which went through different political, economic and social transformations that set it apart from Catholicism and Protestantism, is experiencing the forces of globalisation in the post-Cold War era at every level.

Today, the Orthodox Churches and populations are facing a rapidly changing and globalising world. While issues such as the Communist legacy, unresolved jurisdiction issues among the Churches, a wary attitude towards religious pluralism and Western values and a lack of experience within the social realm, all pose challenges to the Orthodox world, the flexible institutional organisation of the Orthodox Churches that can coordinate diversity, the rich Orthodox Tradition, and the growing agency of the Orthodox Churches within and outside of their heartlands are the means that the Orthodox world deploys to cope with the challenges of globalisation.

The ROC, which has shown a great adaptive capacity to survive regime changes in Romania, from Fascist rule to a Communist one, and now to a democratic regime and European integration (Gillet 1995: 359–360), has indulged in vigorous reconstruction activity inside Romania, while simultaneously having to cope with serious social problems exacerbated by a long process of transition towards democracy and a global market economy. The accession of Romania to the EU also creates challenges for the ROC while making the ROC an actor within Europe. Finally, while transnational migration is extending the reach of the ROC to different destinations, it presents the Church with new forms of local and global forces in different settings. The Orthodox Churches in general and the ROC in particular are embedded in the global religious system, and their dialogue with globalisation is ongoing. As they develop new responses to globalisation by drawing inspiration from the Orthodox Tradition, as well as historical and current experiences inside and outside their heartland, their terms of involvement with the global processes becomes clearer, and the scale and extent of their agency at the local and global level are upgraded.

NOTES

1. Orthodox Christianity has a very rich tradition consisting of Greek, Arabic, Slavic and Latin elements. Orthodoxy can be differentiated into the Eastern Orthodox Churches and the Oriental Orthodox Churches (Non-Chalcedonian, those whom refused to acknowledge the fourth Ecumenical Council of Chalcedon in the mid-fifth century). In this chapter we will be looking into the Eastern Orthodoxy's encounter with globalisation as the Romanian Orthodox Church (ROC) is an Eastern Orthodox Church, and the majority of the Orthodox population in the world belongs to the Eastern Orthodox Church and lives mainly in Eastern Europe and Russia (Pacini 2000: 22–23; Pacini 2003: 168).
2. Roudometof, who underscores the 'historicity of globalization' (2001: 4) and defines it 'as a world-historical process' (2008: 68), argues that the emergence and intensification of particularistic trends such as nationalism have played, and still do, an important role in the creation of a global international society (Mayall 1990 cited in Roudometof 2001: 8). Nationalism, rather than being a force clashing with globalisation, should be seen as part of it (Robertson 2001: xiii). Moreover, it is globalisation itself that contributes to the generation of national differences, rivalries and conflicts (Ibid: 2).
3. Apart from organised religion, religions take different forms. Thus, one can have social movement religion, which is episodic and lacks central organisation

and is only part of societal function systems through the politicisation of religion; or social network religion, which is unformed religion taking place through interactions (Beyer 2006: 108). 'Network religion' is organised through flexible and mobile ties extending beyond national boundaries and denominational loyalties (Agadjanian & Roudometof 2005: 5). However, the global influence of New Age religiosities is limited, since they spread through networks that are limited in scope and are not intrinsic for the functioning of the system (Beyer 2006: 284) the way religious organisations are.

4. *Symphonia* means that the power of the state and the power of the Church have to balance each other and work in harmony. The ideal of *symphonia* is 'a bipolar structure' (Clément 2005: 15), which necessitates the coexistence and complementarity of these two powers.

5. As Robertson argues (2001: xiii), nationalism, rather than being a force clashing with globalisation, is part and parcel of globalization. He further states that the rise and spread of nationalism within the Orthodox heartland was directly linked with the effects of the second phase of globalisation processes in the region.

6. There are 13 Patriarchates in the Orthodox world. Four of them are ancient churches: Istanbul, Alexandria, Antioch and Jerusalem; and 9 of them are national patriarchates: Russian, Serbian, Romanian, Bulgarian, Georgian, Greek, Albanian, Polish, and Cypriot (Macar 2003: 23–24; Ware 1997: 6).

7. The Mount Sinai Autonomous Church is under the jurisdiction of the Patriarchate of Jerusalem, while the Finnish and Estonian Churches are under the authority of the Patriarchate of Istanbul, and the Japanese and Chinese Orthodox Churches are under the jurisdiction of the Patriarchate of Moscow (Pacini 2000: 35–37). The autocephalous status of the Orthodox Church in America is not recognised by all the Orthodox churches. The Autonomous Orthodox Church of Macedonia, which is seeking independence from the Serbian Orthodox Church, did not achieve recognition yet (Binns 2002: 27).

8. The status of the Orthodox Churches in Ukraine and Estonia led to conflicts between the Moscow Patriarchate and the Ecumenical Patriarchate, while the status of the Orthodox Church in Moldova created problems between the Russian and Romanian Orthodox Patriarchates.

9. The final data of the 2011 census carried out across Romania has not been released yet. According to the census data conducted on 18–27 March 2002, the population of Romania is 21,680,974; and Orthodoxy is the religion revered by the majority of the population (18,817,975, 86.8%). There are other churches and religions within the Romanian religious landscape. The number of Roman Catholics is 1,026,429, which is 4.7% of the population, and they are mainly of Hungarian or German origin, while the number of Greek Catholics is 195,481 and represents 0.9% of the Romanian population. The reformed church members reach up to 701,077 or 3.2% of the population. There are different Protestant churches revered by 5–6% of the population. There is also a small Muslim community composed of Turks and Tartars, which makes up 0.3% of the population. Those of other religions are 0.4%, without any religion 0.1%, atheists under 0.1% and those that do not declare their religious denomination is 0.1%. Retrieved 28 January 2012 from http://www.insse.ro/cms/files/RPL2002INS/vol1/tabele/t50a.pdf and http://www.insse.ro/cms/files/RPL2002INS/vol1/tabele/t51.pdf

10. According to the pooled World Values Survey data collected in five waves from 1981 to 2001, Poland, Romania and Bosnia-Herzegovina emerge as the more religious of the post-Communist countries, while Eastern Germany, Estonia and Montenegro tend to be less religious (Norris & Inglehart 2004:

The Orthodox Tradition in a Globalising World   95

121). According to different surveys conducted in 2000, Romania emerged as one of the most religious countries in the region (Voicu 2007: 13).
11. The ROC's presence and activism in public institutions is not matched by any other denomination in Romania (Andreescu 2007: 462).
12. 'This recognition of the right of nations to their own way of life, to the preservation of their religious and cultural identity, should become an integral part of the standard offered to us as a universal uniting principle. Only in this case will integration not turn into depersonalizing unification' (Kirill 2001). The Ecumenical Patriarch Bartholomew I (2008: 163) argues that it is not economic progress and growing welfare and collaboration through globalisation that the Orthodox Church is against. Rather the homogenising trends that challenge the distinctiveness of the Orthodox Church concern the Orthodox world, since this form of globalisation precludes encounters between differences.
13. 'The Basis of the Social Concept' is an important document as it guides the work of Synodal institutions, dioceses, monasteries, parishes and other church institutions as well as being included in the curriculum of theological schools of the Patriarchate (The Basis of the Social Concept, n.d.).
14. The Greek word 'akathistos' means not sitting. Therefore, the *akathist* hymn can be translated as the standing hymn. During the recitation of the *akathist* hymn, which praises a saint, holy event, or one of the persons of the Holy Trinity, the congregation is expected to stand.
15. According to Article 137 of the Statute of the ROC, the system of social assistance is integrated into the administrative organisational structure of the Church. 'The Statutes for the Organisation and Functioning of the ROC General Stipulations', pp. 65–66. Retrieved 5 May 2008 from http://www.patriarhia.ro/_upload/documente/121438488425759490.pdf
16. The ROC is working actively in collaboration with some state institutions and NGOs and assuming new roles in the social sphere, such as preventing trafficking in human beings, through giving information and granting assistance to victims ('News in Brief' Jan–Mar 2003: 9); through the free distribution of medicines to social-medical settlements of the Church ('News in Brief' April-June 2003: 4–6); aiding victims of the natural disasters ('More than 500,000 euro' March 2005: 6); and combating HIV-related intolerance ('Patriarch Teoctist Urges' Jan-Feb 2004, 1: 4).
17. The Russian Orthodox Church called on the Russian state to work together against the 'pseudo-religious structures presenting a threat to the individual and society' (The Basis of the Social Concept, n.d.).
18. Following its reestablishment, the Greek Catholic Church demanded the return of the property confiscated by the communist regime. There are around 3,000 churches confiscated by the regime and given to the Orthodox Church, most of which belonged to the Greek Catholic Church, though also to Catholic and Hungarian churches (Muntean 2005: 89). However, property restitution is still an unresolved issue today.
19. Article 29 of the 1991 constitution guarantees freedom of conscience and the autonomy of religious sects, charging the state with the duty to facilitate the presence of religion within state institutions. In 2000, Law 21 of 1924 on associations and foundations has been abrogated by means of Law 26. The new law eliminated the obstacles in the registration process for religious institutions—since in Romania, in order to be officially recognised and to fulfil its functions, a religious institution need to be registered—as well as the need for the approval of the State Secretariat for Religious Denominations in order to be registered (Stan & Turcescu 2007: 128). In 2002 an amendment was made to the constitution to allow churches to establish their own

educational institutions (Ibid: 133). Moreover, the state has passed laws on two very delicate issues despite opposition from all religious denominations. The state legalised abortion in 1989. Abrogation of the Communist law that punished homosexuality proved to be more difficult, since it provoked reactions from all religious denominations (Ibid: 203).
20. The EU accession process and growing Western influence on the Romanian way of life were causes of concern for the ROC, while it considered democratisation as a challenge to the Byzantine model of church-state relations (Mungiu-Pippidi 1998; Tanasescu 2005: 62). Western Europe, where family and traditional values are 'in retreat' due to secularisation, which champions individualism and the privatisation of religion, was seen as a menace to the Orthodox Tradition and its values by many of the Church hierarchs. However, as ultra-nationalist and anti-Western tendencies lost their strength in Romanian politics and as the EU accession seemed more within reach, pro-European tendencies within the ROC grew stronger.
21. Romania was the last country in Eastern Europe to pass a new law on religious denominations in late 2006 (Stan & Turcescu 2007: 25). While the ROC was content with the promulgation of the new law, the other churches (particularly Protestant ones) accused the ROC of 'imposing its will on the text of the law'. Another criticism is that the criteria for the recognition of a religious denomination make it hard for many small religious groups to succeed. The new law stipulated that any cult has to wait 12 years before applying for recognition and introduced some restrictions on the recognition of new cults. For a denomination to be recognised by the State Secretariat it has to have members, which should consist of not less than 0.5% of the population (Ibid: 33). The bill foresaw a fine for unregistered religious activity (Ibid: 35–36). Since the denominations asking for recognition have to submit their statutes and organisational information as well as a detailed report about their dogma and doctrine to the State Secretariat, this might provide a basis for the state to interfere in the internal religious affairs of denominations (Jubilee Campaign 2003: 25). As the Orthodox Church refuses to bury any deceased belonging to a different religious denomination or to bury only in accordance with the Orthodox rite, it makes the issue more acute and complicated.
22. See: Reverend M. Pacurariu, 'Short History of the ROC': http://www.patriarhia.ro/en/roc_structure/history7.html.
23. The term 'sects' is used by the ROC in a pejorative sense.
24. Through conversions today the Pentecostalism has become the fourth religious denomination in Romania with 324,462 adherents (1.5% of the Romanian population) (Fosztó 2007: 91). The number of churches and places of worship of the Pentecostal Church in Romania doubled between 1995 and 2003 (Andreescu 2007: 460).
25. Having a cult status does not always make a denomination immune from attacks or provide it with guarantees against discrimination (Andreescu 2007: 454).
26. The ROC, in agreement with the Catholic Church in Romania, has proposed the inclusion of the phrase 'preponderant Christian' to the preamble of the Convention Treaty of the EU, therefore suggesting the phrase should be: 'The member states and the citizens of the European Union [. . .] [are] aware both of their history and of the universal indivisible values of the human dignity, liberty, equality and solidarity, as well as their preponderant Christian religious inheritance.' ('A Christian Perspective' Jan–Mar 2003: 5).
27. The classical definition of the term 'diaspora' refers to the dispersal of an ethnic population from an original homeland to new regions of the world, often

in a forced manner. The diaspora emerges through the conscious efforts of the members that reproduce the shared memory about the original homeland and maintain diasporic identity and solidarity over time and distance. As Olwig (2004: 55) argues, diaspora requires a mental state of belonging that can be extended back in history. Today, there is the tendency to define diaspora as 'communities with transnational networks' (Schwalgin 2004: 73; See also Brettell 2006: 328).
28. The dispersion of the Orthodox faithful from the Orthodox heartland started under Ottoman rule. Following World War I, new Orthodox communities emerged in Western Europe. After World War II, labour migration carried a high number of Greek, Serbian and Arab Orthodox faithful to Western Europe, Australia, and New Zealand (Lemopoulos 2000: 58–59). Following the fall of the Berlin Wall, mass migration from Eastern Europe mainly to Europe but also to the United States, Canada and Australia has led to the rise and spread of big Orthodox communities in lands with 'no Orthodox presence' (Ibid: 60).
29. It is an ancient Greek word meaning the right time, the critical or opportune moment.
30. Statutul Pentru Organizarea si Functionarea Bisericii Ortodoxe Române (1948): Art. 1. 'Biserica Ortodoxă Română cuprinde pe toţi crecincioşi de religie creştina ortodoxă din Republica Populară Română. (Ministry of Cults, 1949). Retrieved 1 February 2012 from http://www.legex.ro/Statut-Nr.4593-din-17.02.1949-198.aspx.
31. Statutul Pentru Organizarea şi Funcţionarea Bisericii Ortodoxe Române 1989(1990). Art.1. 'Biserica Ortodoxă Română cuprinde pe credincioşii de religie creştină ortodoxă din România şi diaspora ortodoxa română'. *Biserica Ortodoxa Romana* [Official Bulletin of the Romanian Orthodox Church], 108(7–10): 222.
32. Within the Romanian context, the term 'diaspora' does not refer to all the Romanian nationals living abroad and does not include ethnic Romanians living as natives in Ukraine, Serbia or Hungary. The ROC categorizes Romanian nationals living out of Romania into three groups: the Romanians living around the borders (Republic of Moldova, Hungary, Serbia and Bulgaria), the Romanian Diaspora and the Romanian settlements or communities in other foreign countries (such as in Istanbul, Jerusalem, Mount Athos, Cyprus, South Africa). Retrieved 20 August 2011 from http://www.patriarhia.ro/ro/administratia_patriarhala/sectorul_comunitati_externe.html.
33. See: http://www.presidency.ro/?lang=ro.

6 Good Muslims, Good Chinese

State Modernisation Policies, Globalisation of Religious Networks and the Changing Hui Ethno-Religious Identifications

Maja Veselič

Muslims in China are hardly ever featured in international media, except when stories of bomb explosions and riots in the Chinese Central Asian region of Xinjiang or the destiny of Uyghur Guantanamo detainees hit the headlines for a day or two. Such reporting not only presents Uyghurs as conflictual (regardless of whether the journalist is sympathetic to their cause or not), but it also obscures the existence of other Muslim groups in China, in particular the Hui. Contrary to the Uyghur who speak a Turkic language and inhabit China's Northwestern-most region, Hui are predominantly Chinese speaking (see below) and spread all over China's vast territory. With a population of approximately 10 million, they are also the most numerous Muslim ethnic group in the country and the third largest of all Chinese minorities.

The presence of Islam in China proper comes as a surprise to many, a curiosity[1] or even an anomaly, despite the fact that the first Muslim traders settled there within decades of the establishment of Islam in Arabia, some of them eventually making China their home. Moreover, the Hui's marginal position and relative isolation from the core Muslim areas as well as centuries of accommodation to Chinese society may lead some to assume religious syncretism. Nevertheless, Hui beliefs and practices 'in all points conform to the general Sunni orthodoxy and no external ingredient comes to taint their "purity"' (Allès 2000: 279).

This chapter examines the changes and continuities in Hui ethno-religious identifications in modern and contemporary China. In particular, it traces the impact of Chinese nation building, state modernisation policies and the growth of religious and economic ties with Muslim majority countries on the (self-)definitions of Hui as Chinese and/or Muslim. Non-Hui observers (including some academic ones) often presuppose that the two loyalties must be exclusive and therefore the source of an inherent contradiction (cf. Gladney 2008; Israeli 1978). I strive to move beyond the dichotomous interpretations of contemporary Hui identity as caught between assimilation/secularisation, on the one hand; and conflict/separatism, on the other. Instead, I take as my starting point a claim that the majority of Hui simultaneously perceive themselves as an inalienable, constitutive part of the

Chinese nation and a part of the global *ummah*. Here, I attempt to tease out some of the complexities of Hui positioning with reference to state, religion and economy in an increasingly transformed and globalising China.

In the recent years, several books have been published specifically focussing on the relationship between the state and religion in modern and contemporary China (Ashiwa & Wank 2009; Goossaert & Palmer 2011; Kidnopp & Harmin 2004; Overmeyer 2003; Yang 2008). Topics examined by authors include the particular historical context of the introduction and use of the concept of religion in the late imperial and Republican era, the mutual remodelling of state and religion at various phases of modern Chinese state building, the adaptations of official definitions and the management of religion by the Communist government, as well as the paradoxical consequences that the opening up of the religious field has had on power relations between state and religion in the post-Mao period. Following their insights into the constant redrawing of boundaries between the secular and religious spheres and the distinctly Chinese aspects of the separation between the public and the private, I first outline the normative state framework within which religion in general and Islam in particular operate in China today. I then briefly explain why Hui identifications should be understood in ethno-religious terms, highlighting the specific entanglement of Islam and ethnicity in the ethnic policy of the People's Republic of China (PRC). The core of the chapter is concerned with one particular aspect of state-Hui relations: the state's promotion of Hui Islamic connections for economic purposes and its (un-)intended consequences for Hui religious practices. Finally, I consider whether the globalisation of Hui religious networks leads to more localised or more globalised visions of Hui Muslim identity.

POLITICS OF RELIGION IN MODERN AND CONTEMPORARY CHINA

As argued in the recent scholarship (see above), the contemporary conception of religion in China is distinctly modern in origin. The word itself (*zongjiao*) was adopted from Japanese at the end of the 19th century, its meaning heavily influenced by Western, particularly Christian notions of religion as a 'formally constituted social organization associated with a body of written doctrine that expressed both cosmology and an ethical system' (Szonyi 2009: 317). Any existing religious practices which could not be subsumed under this definition were relegated to the category of superstition (*mixin*), also newly introduced and subject to various attacks. The discourse on religion was just one strand of the wider ideological project of transitioning China from tradition to modernity. It was therefore closely linked to the discourses of nation, science and development, which came to dominate the thoughts of Chinese elites of the time.

Where religious practices could be made to fit the new conception of religion, a process of institutionalisation was initiated. In 1912, immediately after the establishment of the Republic, the first such systematic attempts were made by creating national Daoist, Buddhist, Confucian and Muslim associations. Their purpose was to organise clerics and adherents into unified, hierarchical institutions. The former three projects largely failed, and later on Confucianism was even excluded from the list of religions. Although considered for the position of state religion at first (like *Shinto* in Japan), the need for a radical break with the imperial regime resulted in 'the abrogation of all kinds of state and ritual doctrine' (Goossaert 2008: 220). Thus, in China, the process of secularisation ran parallel to religious institutionalisation.

For Islam, institutionalisation coincided with the introduction of the Ikhwan (*yihewani*) movement (inspired by the same sources as the Muslim Brotherhood) by imam Ma Wanfu, upon his return to his native Gansu in 1895 following several years of study in Arabia. The religious reformist trends, however, were soon combined with nationalist ideas, which were promoted, first, by those Hui who studied in Japan in the beginning of the 20th century, and then, by those who were sent to Al-Azhar in Egypt in the 1920s and 1930s. Their joined struggle for the creation of nationwide Hui educational and charitable organisations resulted in the formation of an ideal of a Muslim citizen, characterised by his dual loyalty, to the nation(-state) on the one hand and to Islam on the other (Chérif-Chebbi 2004; Matsumoto 2006). The support for the modernisation and unification of Hui (in more than just religious terms) led the *yihewani* into close cooperation with the state. This not only changed the movement's nature in China from oppositional to collaborative, but also guaranteed it a strong influence over various other Muslim associations in Republican China.[2] Due to their modernist orientations and their solid infrastructure in the form of networks of mosques and schools covering certain parts of China, *yihewani* imams were given the most prominent role in the China Islamic Association that the Communists established in 1953 (Chérif-Chebbi 2004; Gladney 2008), despite the fact that in the Northwest they were closely connected to warlords who supported the Kuomintang during the civil war.

The newly established PRC built its religious policy around many of the Republic's ideological and practical formulations. It recognised five official religions—Buddhism, Daoism, Islam, Protestantism, and Catholicism and established one or more national-level patriotic associations for each of them. They were to act as intermediaries between the state and local religious communities, but their main task was and remains carrying out the Party's religious policy and gaining support for its various other ideological projects. Political and economic campaigns of the early years often targeted those practices, places of worship and clerics that were excluded from or marginalised within the institutionalised religion, like Sufi orders in the case of Islam. However, even official religions were labelled as feudal superstition (*fengjian mixin*) during the Cultural Revolution. Considered an obstacle to class struggle, they came under severe attack, since their eradication would presumably quicken the progress to Socialism. In 1975, resistance to religious repression resulted in the largest Hui-state incident in the PRC's history, a massacre of more than 1,000 villagers in Shadian (Yunnan province) by the People's Liberation Army.

Reform period leaders, however, have taken a more flexible position towards religion, recognising certain forms of religiosity again while still disapproving of or proscribing others. Both the political and economic context in post-Mao China has allowed for, or even encouraged revival of, many religious movements as well as the emergence of new ones. A document with the title *The Basic Viewpoint and Policy on the Religious Question During Our Country's Socialist Period*,[3] which was circulated as an internal Party document in 1982, but had been discussed by the Party leadership already in 1978, outlines the principles for management of religious affairs during the last three decades. Most importantly, it recognises that religion is a complex and long-lasting phenomenon, and that the excesses of the Cultural Revolution only turned people against the Party. Furthermore, it points out that religion has implications both for ethnic relations within China and for China's international relations.

This is of particular importance in the consideration of Islam. Since most Muslims belong to various religious ethnic minorities, that is, 'ethnic minorities in which nearly all the people believe in one particular religion' (MacInnis 1989: 22), Islam (like Lamaism), in certain regions at least, enjoys a special protection against Christian proselytizing, in an attempt to avoid tensions and the consequent threat to national unity (Fällman 2010: 959–960). Such alignment of ethnicity and religion also implies that religious practices can be defended as the customs (*fengsu xiguan*) of particular minorities. On the other hand, the document warns that Islam's international character can make Muslims vulnerable to foreign manipulation with the goal of destabilising China (MacInnis 1989: 23–24). Although the global discourse of the war on terrorism is now regularly instrumentalised by the Chinese government to justify religious and political repression in Xinjiang,[4] Islam is generally viewed with less suspicion than Christianity due to the anti Western-imperialist rhetoric and sentiments China shares with many Muslim majority countries as well as to the lack of Islam's political influence in more recent historical periods (cf. MacInnis 1989: 23–24).[5]

In the past few years, certain new developments could be observed in regard to the official treatment of religion. First, a level of complexity has been introduced in the discourse on religion, running from the permitted 'normal religious activities' of 'proper religions' to less dangerous forms of 'superstition' to the 'abnormal religious activities' and 'evil cults'. Also, Chinese popular religion is by and large no longer disparaged. Furthermore, the Communist Party of China (CPC) now quietly accepts religiosity in its own ranks. According to some studies, at least a third of the total 60–70 million members belong to a religious organisation. Having joined the Party for the economic and social benefits provided by membership, they perceive religion as a part of their private sphere and therefore not in conflict with the Party's declared atheism (Hornemann 2007). Finally, CCP's fears of the mobilising power of religion and the challenge it could present for its authority are increasingly weighed against the positive influence of religious individuals and organisations in the social and economic development of the country. In a speech in 2007 at the first Politbureau meeting dedicated exclusively to religious issues, Chinese President Hu Jintao stressed the contributions that religion can make in the new political goal of creating a 'harmonious society' (Hu 2007). These are exemplified in the varied provisions of education, welfare and disaster relief initiated by religious philanthropic organisations.

The changes, however, should not be considered as a challenge to the secular nature of the Chinese state. As the radically different treatment of the same religious practices among Hui and Uyghur demonstrates, the distinction between appropriate public, and hence normal, religious activities and those which are not is not based on differences in doctrine or practice. Rather it rests on the criterion of what is perceived to be a threat to social stability and the Party's ideological monopoly, which remain exclusively under the government's purview (cf. Potter 2003; Veselič 2011).

ISLAMIC REVIVAL IN THE POST-MAO PERIOD

Like other religions, Islam has been thriving in China from the outset of the political and economic reforms. According to one fairly reliable survey conducted between 2005 and 2007, 31.4 % of those aged 16 and above or about 300 million people in China—three times the official estimates, declared themselves as religious (Freedom of Religious Belief 1997; Wu 2007). As neither the census nor other countrywide surveys collect information on religious affiliation, it is impossible to determine how many consider themselves Muslim. Officially advertised numbers are based on adding up the population of the 10 ethnic groups which traditionally profess Islam, making the total approximately 20 million people, according to the 2000 Population Census.[6] This, however, excludes those believers who belong to other official ethnic groups, while including those members of the 10 Muslim groups who do not believe at all or believe in some other religion. Although Islamic activities remain constrained (more strictly so in certain parts of China than others), their scope and intensity testify to the fact that the religious renewal of the past three decades is more than a revival of the pre-PRC religious situation.

One prominent example of Islamic resurgence is the strengthening of a modern Islamist type of religiosity among Hui youth and young intellectual elite. Such religiosity is characterised by high levels of literacy, an ability to use modern information and communication technologies, an emphasis on personal responsibility in leading a pious life and the denunciation of sectarian differences for a 'purer' form of Islam. A third year undergraduate student of economics at an institution of higher education in Northwestern China, who called herself a reborn Muslim (*huigui de musilin*), explained to me: 'Before I came to the university, I didn't know anything. I just knew I was a *Huizu* [belonging to the Hui nationality]. I didn't know what it means to be Hui, what it means to be Muslim or what the difference is between the two of them'. Joining a religious study group on the campus towards the end of her freshman year, she began to learn Arabic so she could properly recite from the Qu'ran, she adopted a (Malaysian-style) headscarf, struggled to uphold the five daily prayers and participated regularly in online and offline discussion groups to further her knowledge of Islam. Like growing numbers of other newly pious Hui students who found faith or became increasingly strict in their understanding of Islamic rules during their studies at (state) universities, she was learning to distinguish between 'the customs' of her parents and the 'real' Islam.

The rise in public piety observed among young Hui at the Northwestern universities and elsewhere in China (e.g., Ma 2006) is only one aspect of a recent Islamic resurgence, although perhaps the most fascinating one, given the state's sensitivity about religious interference with the state educational system. Other phenomena include new mosque constructions, the development and rising popularity of different forms of religious and semi-religious education, the flourishing of Islamic publishing, Internet websites and forums, Islamic consumption, the growing numbers of Hui students in Muslim majority countries and Hui pilgrims to Mecca.[7] In this form, the Islamic revival in China thus closely resembles what has been observed in more central parts of the Muslim world (for example, Göle 2000; Hefner 1998). As at other moments in history, this time, too, new ideas are brought to China by those Hui who study in Islamic centres abroad and the foreign Muslims who come to China for trade, tourism, proselytizing or any combination of the three.

Yet the social and political context of Hui everyday lives differs considerably from Muslim majority countries or societies with large proportions of Muslim populations. Although they are about as numerous as Tunisians, Hui in China present a very small proportion of the country's population—less than 0.8 percent. Contrary to Muslim migrants in the West, Hui are characterised by the length of their presence in China and their historical embeddedness into Chinese society, although, they, too, face a similar challenge of how to express their religious beliefs and to practise religion in everyday life in a state that is secular, or, in the case of China, even avowedly atheistic. As the Hui student statement quoted above indicates, 'Muslim identity in China can best be understood as ethno-religious, in that history, ethnicity, and state nationality have left an indelible mark on contemporary Muslim identity' (Gladney 2008: 181). In the following section, I therefore delve into the complex interplay of the ethnic and religious dimensions of Huiness.

THE LABYRINTH OF HUI ETHNO-RELIGIOUS IDENTITY

China defines itself as a unitary multiethnic state (*duo minzu yi ti guojia*). *Huizu*, which is a short form of Hui *minzu*, is one of the 56 officially designated ethnic groups (including the majority Han) which constitutes the Chinese nation under Communist government.[8] Unlike other minorities, which traditionally reside in one or the other part of China, Hui had settled in all provinces. They are said to be descendants of linguistically and ethnically diverse Muslim merchants, soldiers and officials who came to China either over sea or land from the 7th through to the 14th centuries and became sinicised due to assimilation pressures and intermarriage with Han. While in Imperial, and to a large extent also in the Republican China (until 1949), the name Hui (*Huimin* or Hui people) denoted all Muslim inhabitants, including Turkic- and Persian-speaking populations of Chinese in Central Asia,[9] and in the PRC it came to delineate an ethnic category. The shift started to occur in the 1920s and 1930s when nationalist and anticolonialist projects in China and the Middle East led some Hui elites to increasingly define themselves as a *minzu*. This was also the period when the phonetic translation *yisilan* became used in addition to the traditional names for Islam—*Huijiao* (Hui teaching)[10] or *qingzhenjiao*[11] (pure and true teaching), for example, in the names of various cultural and philanthropic associations set up by Hui/Muslim intellectuals.

In the 1950s, following the Soviet example, the new state embarked on a project of ethnic identification, using Stalin's four characteristics of a nation—that is, shared territory, language, economic life and culture—to determine which groups deserved official recognition. Hui were granted nationality status, and *yisilan* or *yisilanjiao* were established as exclusive official terms for Islam. As Hui Marxist historian Shouyi Bai (2003: 118–123) explained: Islam is a world religion, not a religion of Hui, who are a nationality. The new category of *Huizu*, however, did not include groups in Northwest China whose languages belonged to Turkic, Mongolian or Persian language groups. *Huizu* thus became a residual category of those who spoke Chinese (more precisely, its different local dialects) or, in few cases, other languages of the localities they inhabited.[12] They were recognised as one of the minority nationalities despite their lack of at least three of Stalin's four nation-defining criteria. The Hui's foreign origin, belief in Islam and self-ascription were given as reasons (Bai 2003: 118–123).

Dru Gladney's (1991) seminal work on Hui religious revival in the early reform period has shown that Hui should not be considered as a monolithic, homogeneous group. In his book, Gladney describes how different Hui communities throughout China, the Eastern coast and Western inland areas, both urban and rural, understand being Hui in many different ways. Their interpretations of Hui-ness range from their genealogically proven descent from foreign merchants to endogamy to belonging to one of the numerous Islamic religious groupings (i.e., traditional single mosque communities,

Sufi brotherhoods, Ikhwan, Salafi). He argues, however, that despite these different expressions of Hui identity, the state-designated category of Hui nationality gained saliency for officials and ordinary people alike, mostly by way of preferential policies for minorities. According to him, this resulted in the nationwide ethnic consciousness of the Hui.

Elisabeth Allès (2000: 296), another anthropologist who conducted long-term fieldwork on the interplay of ethnic and religious dimensions of contemporary Hui identity, believes otherwise. In her comparative study of three different communities in the central province of Henan (an exclusively Hui village, a traditionally mixed Hui and Han village and a modern city), she concluded that the Hui in most places do not conceive themselves in clear ethnic terms, even if their nationality status satisfies both their need for recognition as a constitutive group of the Chinese multiethnic nation and the state's need for a common representation of all Hui communities. She describes Hui identity as a 'juxtaposition', that is, constantly emerging as a response to a particular situation of Hui-Han cohabitation. In her three settings, it is precisely Hui religious beliefs and practices that determine this interaction. My own research confirms that in Northwest China, where their communities are most numerous and of highest density, at least, for a vast majority of Hui Islam as practised tradition remains the core marker of their self-definition (and of its ascription by others). The following personal comment of an editor of a widely popular Hui/Muslim monthly newsletter from Lanzhou summarizes this well: 'As I see it, we, Hui [*Huizu*], are a now at the crossroads. We can either become a sort of *minzu* like the Han or we can be Muslims. In my opinion, without Islam there are no *Huizu*'.

What particularly complicates the issues surrounding Hui ethno-religious identity is the rigidity of *minzu* categories. By the end of the 1980s, every citizen had his/her nationality identity marked on all official documents, without possibility of changing it. The only exceptions are children of mixed marriages who can choose the *minzu* of one of the parents once they are of age.[13] The *minzu* identity then becomes conditioned purely by ascribed descent (i.e., 'I am a *Huizu* because my parents' *minzu* status is Hui'). While official categorisations certainly need not correspond to local or personal identifications, nor the latter necessarily conform to the former, a degree of overlap is required if they are to be meaningful for the state as well as the people. Most Hui I talked to believe, that if being Hui is emptied of Islam (be it as a practised religion or as an awareness of certain inherited traditions), little would remain to help distinguish Hui from Han. On the other hand, as illustrated by the student above, the increasingly orthodox interpretations of Islam among some young Hui, make the distinction between being Hui and being Muslim very relevant for them. In this sense, university students may be seen as fully accepting the state claim that *Hui minzu* is independent of Islam.

Finally, Han conversion to Islam, which seems to be relatively negligible so far, can also present a challenge for an ethnic category based on religion.

Due to the lack of survey data, it is impossible to discern the scope of this phenomenon. During my fieldwork I have heard of only a handful of Han converts, although some of my Hui interlocutors assured me that "many many" Han have become Muslims already. Gladney (1991: 58) notes that in the 1980s, he encountered no single case where conversion was not due to Hui-Han intermarriage or adoption into a Hui family. Although intermarriage remains the predominant impetus of Han conversion to Islam, popular Muslim magazines occasionally publish conversion narratives of Han Muslims who were motivated by other reasons. While in the past Han who became Muslim would after a while simply be considered as *Huimin*, that is, Hui people, now they are Han who believe in Islam. The *minzu* paradigm of ethnic and cultural incorporation into the Chinese modern nation(-state) thus resulted in rigidifying the (perceived) social boundaries of Hui communities from soft and vague to hard and clear-cut (cf. Duara 1995: 65–69).

CHINA'S ISLAMIC CONNECTION

As mentioned above, contacts with foreign Muslims and experiences of living in societies with large Muslim populations served as a source of inspiration in the current Islamic resurgence in China. As in the past, now, too, those who studied in Muslim countries are respected as figures of considerable religious authority upon their return to China. This admiration continues despite the fact that there are nowadays literally hundreds of Hui students enrolled in educational institutions in Egypt, Pakistan and Malaysia to name just the most popular destinations. At the same time, China's economic rise has attracted numerous foreign businessmen and professionals, visiting or settling down in the country, many of them Muslim. Indeed, growing numbers of Hui students abroad now envision their future careers in business, (Arab) language interpretation and cultural mediation, rather than in a religious profession.

It is also noteworthy that it was first Hong Kong in the 1980s and then the Southern business centres of Shenzhen and Guangzhou in the 1990s, which served as entry points for Islamic books, magazines and other religious materials as well as for the proselytizers. Since the religious activities of foreigners are strictly regulated, much of such work was and still is generally conducted underground. Finally, like elsewhere, new information and communication technologies continuously intensify the flow of (global) ideas circulating among Hui, strengthening both the nationwide and transnational dimension of their networks.

The process of intensification of Hui religious and economic contacts with Muslim majority countries, however, cannot be understood simply as an inevitable consequence of China's full incorporation into the global market economy or as the overflowing of global Islamic fervour onto the margins of the Muslim world. On the contrary, with the onset of reform policies it was the state itself, which actively instigated establishment of such ties. Already in 1980, a Soviet weekly commented sarcastically on China's sudden interest in Islam and its keen publicising of the well-being of its Muslim minorities:

> What is the need for this eyewash about 'the happy life of the peoples of China professing Islam'? Who is this intended for? The authorities are trying to present the position of national minorities in China in a light that suits Peking. But the main reason of the sudden 'love' for the Moslem peoples is different. The Peking strategists have started darting glances in the direction of the Near and Middle East, have started devision [sic] means of getting access to the oil-rich Moslem countries and for this reason are posing as 'protectors of Islam'. (BBC 1980)

Indeed, in the early 1980s a number of important mosques were renovated or rebuilt with state funds, and soon foreign financial aid was attracted. In 1986, Islamic Development Bank presented China with 4.06 million USD in financial assistance for the (re-)building of Islamic institutes (madrasas) in Beijing, Ningxia, Xinjiang and for an Arabic School in Tongxin (also Ningxia) (Yang 1991, Yisilanjiao fazhan 1990). In the 1990s, another 2 million USD of donations were solicited for madrasa constructions in the provincial capitals of Shenyang, Kunming, Lanzhou, Zhengzhou, as well as for a girls' middle school in Tongxin and Muslim vocational middle schools in Tianjin, Xi'an, Guangzhou and Heilongjiang (Chang 1999). These middle schools trained students in Arabic and religious subjects while also carrying out a part of the regular state curriculum. The focus on religious education reflects the major concerns reported in the Middle Eastern media with regard to the situation of Muslims in China at the beginning of China's opening up (Bagader 2009: 87). The investment projects enumerated, and many others have been handled by the China Islamic Association, which thereby gained increased influence in Chinese international affairs. Strengthening exchange and cooperation with foreign Muslim and Islamic organisations remains one of the association's central tasks.

Perhaps the most prominent example of mixing religion with business is the case of the Ningxia Hui Autonomous Region, a provincial-level administrative unit with the largest percentage of Hui inhabitants in the country. In Ningxia, Hui constitute nearly 35% of the population, accounting for almost a fifth of all Hui in China. For this reason both national and local authorities worked early on to develop trade and business links with Muslim countries as a means of developing this poor Northwest region. For example, in the years 1985–1986, the provincial government organised 32 technological fairs and receptions for diplomats and businessmen from Muslim countries, sent a delegation to Saudi Arabia, Egypt and six other Arab countries. By 1991, tens of foreign officials, religious leaders and businessmen had visited the province, and more than 10 financial consortiums or

Islamic financial institutions were active in Ningxia (Yang & Zhang 1991: 21). Nowadays Ningxia is known in Muslim countries as 'China's Muslim Province'. The main trading articles are various Muslim commodities and halal foodstuffs, the latter now taking up 80% of the entire Ningxia food industry (Tan 2010: 26).

Furthermore, as in the case of other religions, especially Buddhism, the state has been heavily promoting Muslim historical sites for the purpose of international religious tourism, for two reasons. First, tourists bring immediate revenue to local communities and second, the raised international profile helps attract foreign investment at home or ease the way for development projects abroad. Muslim cultural and religious heritage is often placed in the context of the Silk Road, thereby drawing attention not only to the spiritual bonds of Chinese Muslims with their coreligionists elsewhere, but also to the pathways of actual historical, maritime and land trading routes. The symbolism has escaped neither politicians nor journalists who now increasingly describe the deepening of Sino-Arab economic ties as the New Silk Road. With expansions of fields of cooperation to, amongst others, finance, China is being encouraged to introduce Islamic banking tools in dealings with Arab and Muslim banks (Ghazal 2010). The growing research interest among Chinese academics in Islamic finance and law observed over the past few years may well be an indication that these instruments are under serious consideration.

What about the consequences of these developments on Hui religious practice? In the past, every time the state instrumentalised Hui and other Muslims for its political and economic goals, it further opened the doors of the religious field, willingly or not. For example, when towards the end of the 1990s the Islamic Development Bank changed its funding focus from religious education to vocational training centres and regular primary schools, the promotion of Sino-Arab schools—secondary schools which combine instruction in modern Arabic with religious and general subjects, was taken up by the Hui themselves. Educational levels in Gansu, Qinghai and Ningxia are among the lowest in the country since the steep financial costs of schooling are barely affordable to many parents in these least developed provinces of China. Enabling youngsters to attend school for little or no fee and to learn religious knowledge that is considered useless by the mainstream society yet highly appreciated in local Muslim communities, quickly raised schools' popularity. Thus, many more sprung up in Western China in the following decade. They are now financially supported by Hui themselves with or without donations from abroad. Worried about this trend, the rumour was that Gansu authorities had decided to discontinue issuing permits for further schools as of 2007.[14]

Similarly, several activities of university students I observed and participated in during my doctoral fieldwork were clearly modelled after Tablighi Jama'at practice of travelling, lay missionary groups, which have been visiting China as tourists and businessmen, mostly from Pakistan, since as early as the 1980s (Metcalf 2003: 141). The movement's name was never actually brought up by students, but I later found out about at least two popular Tablighi proselytizing centres. On the other hand, all group religious activities on campus came under close scrutiny when a regular inspection from the relevant central body was announced for 2007. They were eventually banned when Muslim students and several Hui faculty members demanded a small mosque be built in the vicinity of the school's isolated new countryside campus. School authorities adopted some measures which had for years been applied to the Uyghur in Xinjiang (for example, shortening the opening hours of the halal cafeteria during Ramadan to discourage students from fasting). Still, unlike Xinjiang, individual practices such as praying alone or wearing a headscarf remained permitted. That this strictness was a part of a larger trend became clear on my subsequent visit to the region in 2010. If my participation in various religious events never raised any concerns on the part of my hosts during my fieldwork in the mid-2000s, I was now asked several times not to attend similar activities lest I (as a foreigner) drew additional attention of the security forces. There seemed to be a general agreement that at least in parts of the Northwest, conditions have worsened with respect to the practising of religion.

GLOBAL MUSLIMS? CHINESE MUSLIMS?

Is the state's uneasiness with the intensification of Hui religious activities justified or not? I was fortunate to be able to visit a group of around 30 Chinese students in Yemen, some of whom I had met during my fieldwork. I wanted to establish whether the experience of living and studying there served to reinforce or transcend ethnic and/or national boundaries. Most of the students had already finished an undergraduate degree in China, be it in sciences or humanities and some had even obtained an MA degree, but now all were enrolled in an undergraduate program in Islamic studies at one of the state universities in the capital San'a. Having arrived in two separate groups nine months apart, some having just finished their first year while others were still taking part in the intensive Arabic language courses before continuing on to their major. Moreover, while the first group obtained full financial support through different scholarships given by wealthy Muslims from Yemen and the UAE, the second group was partly self-funded. As I discussed with some of those who had been there longer whether they noticed any changes in their perceptions of Islam or their own religiosity, one of the female students answered:

> Only after coming here did I realise how little I understood about Islamic history, the rules and practices. You know that all of us here counted as very knowledgeable among students in China, but really, we knew nothing of particular reasons for certain practices. I've learned so much since

110 *Maja Veselič*

> I came here. For example, just the other day we've learned how much *zakat* one is supposed to give. [. . .] In China, people speak of *zakat*, they pay it, but I have never heard anyone explain how to calculate it and no one really gives according to the prescribed amounts. [. . .] Before, I knew what one must do, now I understand the detail of how and the logic of why.

While this student emphasized the positivistic knowledge she had obtained in her courses, for another male student the most significant change was the ease of observing everyday Islamic practices:

> I struggled to live as a good Muslim in China, but there are so many difficulties there, so many limitations, not just at the university, everywhere, especially when it comes to things like prayer or fasting. In China, fully practising a Muslim way of life could only be an ideal. Here, it has become reality—everywhere there are places to perform ablutions and pray, and during Ramadan it's so easy, because everyone is fasting, there's no school or university, all the shops have opening hours adjusted to it. So, now I feel I've obtained this ideal and it's so easy. It makes me very happy.

Other students, too, repeatedly acknowledged that much of factual knowledge about Islamic beliefs and practices they had lacked in China was considered a common understanding in Yemen. They admired how the general way of life was adjusted to the needs of a practising Muslim. This filled them with great appreciation and respect for the Yemenis.

Nevertheless, the experience of studying abroad at the same time reinforced their Chinese-ness. Students complained about the patronising, even denigrating attitude by some of their Yemeni classmates, who were insinuating that they (the Chinese) were ignorant or less good Muslims.[15] A female student, who unlike most of her Hui counterparts did not adopt black Yemeni attire but combined colourful headscarves and face veils instead, raised her voice:

> I'd like to see *them* in China. They're spoiled, they have no idea how difficult it is, how determined and strong you must be even just to wear a headscarf at the university or at work. Besides, they often think everything they do is Islamic, when sometimes things are just their customs. I admit, in general people know Islam better, this is where Islam started. But only because Arabs were the first to convert, doesn't mean people now should automatically assume to know everything.

There were other things, however, which made Hui students even more aware of cultural differences between them and the locals or the students from other countries in their Muslim-only dormitory. In particular, they singled out Chinese hard work, modesty and respect for food (both in terms of the variety of tastes as well as by not wasting it), cleanliness and their own good organisation. Although studying in Yemen clearly contributed to the process of a further 'objectification of Islam' (Eickelman 1992) and raised their fluency in the styles and contents of Islamic debates, it also resulted in the amplification of their sense of Chinese-ness.

CONCLUSION

In this chapter, I examined current Islamic resurgence among the Hui in China as a response to state-imposed modernisation and ethnic policies as well as the consequence of their intensified contact with foreign Muslims. My aim was not to provide a definite answer of how Hui ethno-religious identity should be understood in contemporary China. Rather, I sought to demonstrate the multifaceted, processual and situational nature of what it means to be Hui. The case of newly pious Muslim university students serves to illustrate this point well. When in China, the students invested great amounts of time, energy and money to learn about and promote Islam, to reflect on and attempt to emulate what they considered the ideal of a 'proper' Islamic lifestyle. Not going as far as alienating them, these processes did, however, involve a level of separation from their parents, their traditional communities and Chinese society at large. When their everyday circumstances changed upon moving to study in Yemen, the Chinese dimension of their self-identification became more pronounced. Yet this did not in any way diminish their commitment to the ideal of good Muslim life as they understood it. As Elisabeth Allès has pointed out, the perceived contradiction of being simultaneously Chinese and Muslim lies only in the eye of the beholder: 'Where the external observer would expect to find the tensions, the coexistence of disparate elements seems completely natural' (2000: 209).

Of course, one may ask if the religious oppression in Xinjiang has worked toward a stronger shared Hui-Uyghur Muslim identity, or if the recent increase in state control of Hui religious activities is a consequence of the Uyghur unrest of the past few years. I believe the answer to both questions is no. Although Hui and Uyghur share a belief in Islam, the differences in language, history and cultural background weaken the power that religion might have as a common identification point. While many Hui sympathise with Uyghur about the constrictions the Uyghur face in their religious practice, they relate to a much lesser degree, or not at all, to their other grievances. (It is important to recognise here that religious oppression is only one of the reasons for Uyghur discontent). For example, the Hui can hardly understand the Uyghur fears of language loss and assimilation. Although the Hui have, to various degrees, maintained their Islamic traditions, they are culturally much closer to Han in other respects.

The state, too, is well aware of the differences between the two groups and continues to treat their communities accordingly (including the Hui in

Xinjiang). While Uyghur turbulence is perceived as a direct threat to China's territorial unity, stronger Hui religious confidence is feared due to its potential for social instability and possible challenge to the Party's authority. Hui loyalty to the Chinese nation-state as such need not be questioned. While the Hui remain for most Chinese the 'familiar strangers' as Jonathan Lipman (1997) so eloquently put it, they firmly continue to see China as their home even as they seek more active inclusion in the global *ummah*.

NOTES

This chapter is based on ethnographic fieldwork I conducted over 14 months for my doctoral dissertation in Gansu and Qinghai provinces in Northwest China between September 2005 and March 2007, and a three-week research visit with a group of Hui students in Yemen in the summer of 2009. Doctoral research was supported by the 'Young Researcher' programme of the Slovenian Research Agency (2003–2008) and by the Chiang Ching-Kuo Foundation PhD Dissertation Fellowship (2008/2009). Fieldwork in Yemen was funded by the Chiang Ching-Kuo Foundation East European Committee Program Research Grant (2009). Finally, this paper has benefited from my inclusion into Marie Curie Actions SocAnth grant programme (2005–2010), which has also generously funded my travel to the UCSIA summer school. For helpful comments on earlier versions of this paper, I thank the participants of UCSIA summer school 2010, Martina Bofulin and the anonymous reviewer.

1. As experiences of Hui students and travellers abroad testify, this also includes many ordinary people in Muslim majority societies.
2. Disagreeing with *yihewani*'s deviation from the original reformist efforts, one group branched off in the late 1930s, calling for a purified, non-accommodationist and nonpolitical Islam, naming themselves Salafiyya (*salafeiya*) (Ma 2000: 107–111). Just as at the time of their inception, they have remained active only in certain areas of Northwest China.
3. The English translation of the document can be found in MacInnis (1989: 9–26).
4. As James Millward (2009: 348, 355–356) poignantly demonstrates, there were no reported incidents of Uyghur separatist and political violence between 1997 and 2008, nor was Islamism in any way relevant for the 5 July 2009 riots in the Xinjiang capital of Urumchi.
5. Indiscriminate anti-Western imperialism, however, sometimes resulted in very paradoxical stances on the part of my Hui interlocutors. They often showed anger and disappointment with Western treatment of Muslims worldwide, especially in relation to the Palestinian question and the wars in Afghanistan and Iraq. Yet, in discussions of conflicts in former Yugoslavia, they, with rare exception, expressed their strong sympathies with and admiration for Serbia and its former president Slobodan Milošević, not considering that the majority of the victims of his actions were actually their co-religionists.
6. At the time of writing, the 2010 census data, broken down according to particular ethnic groups, had not yet been released.
7. In 2011, some 13,700 Chinese Muslims completed hajj, a new all-time record. As in previous years, the majority of them were Hui (Li 2011).
8. *Minzu* is used as a translation for a variety of disparate concepts, such as nation, nationality (in Soviet terms) and ethnic group. In Chinese official parlance, it refers to the Chinese nation (*Zhonghua minzu*), as well as—in the

plural—to the official ethnic categorisations. The status of *minzu* therefore recognises a group's legitimate cultural and political citizenship and provides access to certain resources. *Minzu* in the plural sense used to be rendered in English as 'nationality' in official documents, but 'ethnic group' has been the preferred term for more than a decade. Here, I mostly follow the newer translation, although the Chinese concept of *minzu* differs considerably from the standard definition of an ethnic group.

9. Additional markers were added to names to make more precise distinctions according to, for example, their language or location. Nevertheless, Hui, that is, Muslims were not administratively perceived as one category, since Qing did not create a system of Muslim administration, perhaps due to the nonexistence of the concept of religion (Matsuzato & Sawae 2010: 338).
10. *Huimin* (Hui people) or *Huijiaotu* (the followers of Hui religion) was also often used to speak of Muslims worldwide. In Taiwan, *Huijiao* is still used to refer to Islam and Hui and are conceived exclusively in religious terms.
11. *Qingzhen* (literally 'pure and true') is also the most common translation for the word *halal*.
12. For discussions of Tibetan and Dai Hui in Yunnan, see McCarthy (2005); for Austronesian-speaking Hui of Hainan island, see Pang (1996).
13. There have been a few cases where communities have proven to have been mis-categorised and managed to change their *minzu* status from being members of one group to another (but no new *minzu* have been recognised since 1979). In some cases the change was even initiated by local authorities so as to boost the tourism industry (for an example, see Mu 2008).
14. I have not seen documents in support of this, but I heard it from several informants whose institutional positions would make them privy to such information.
15. Such experiences have often been reported by hajjis, both in the past and today. It was precisely the discrimination he encountered from other pilgrims that led Hu Songshan, one of the famous *yihewani* imams to become a fervent nationalist. He believed only a strong China could guarantee Hui the safety and status when abroad, while also allowing them the individual and collective freedom to practice Islam (Lipman 1997: 209–210).

7 Where National Histories and Colonial Myths Meet
'Histoire Croisée' and Memory of the Moroccan-Berber Cultural Movement in the Netherlands

Norah Karrouche

In November 2004, the murder of Theo van Gogh in the streets of Amsterdam by a young Moroccan shook national and global media and politics. Theo van Gogh had become a contested public figure in the Netherlands because he was very critical of Dutch multicultural society, both in his written work as a journalist and as a documentary and film producer. During the trial, the accused Mohammed Bouyeri admitted to ruthlessly killing van Gogh and emphasised that he had acted out of his Islamic faith.

Afterwards, journalists and politicians openly claimed that the story of Mohammed Bouyeri, a member of the radical Islamist Hofstadt group, proved that Dutch integration policies had indeed failed—the very point van Gogh had tried to make all along—especially in the country's impoverished and neglected suburbs. The murder of Theo van Gogh was seen as the ultimate expression of a young Dutch-Moroccan's radicalisation. Likewise, journalists and politicians argued that the murder was yet another consequence of 9/11, after which terrorist acts had begun to be considered as legitimate and almost fashionable by Dutch-Moroccan youths. The murder was thus considered a terrorist act, and national representatives in the Netherlands called for a debate on the rise of terrorism in the Netherlands and the reinforcement of criminal law provisions regarding terrorism and terrorist acts. On the other hand, the figure of Bouyeri spiked a wave of parliamentary debates on related issues: the threat against Dutch values and the protection of the freedom of speech in the Netherlands; the possibility of new restrictions on Dutch immigration legislation, but also the integration of second-generation Moroccan youth in general; and the problematic status of having dual citizenship and two passports—one Dutch and one Moroccan.

Although very critical of Theo van Gogh's opinions on Moroccan second-generation youth, Dutch-Moroccan associations fiercely condemned the murder. Bouyeri, some of these representatives of Moroccan associations were compelled to say, was a descendent of migrants originating from Morocco's northern Rif area, and thus first and foremost an *Amazigh*, or Berber.[1] This view was expressed by Moroccan associations which labelled themselves as democratic as well as Berber. Because they posited Bouyeri as a Berber, they excluded him from being Arab. Rather than solely seeking an explanation in radicalisation through the consultation of 'online imams', some of these representatives likewise pointed out the failure of Dutch integration policies on the one hand, and of pedagogy among the first generation of Moroccan guest workers on the other hand. Consequently, second-generation Moroccan youth had remained unaware of the constitution and meaning of a true and authentic Moroccan identity. In the aftermath of the murder, Bouyeri became paradigmatic of derailed Moroccan youth, who had lost their way in Dutch society by turning away from their true identity, family history and heritage. Such a break with his homeland and the presumed silencing of Bouyeri's parents concerning their Rifian identity, had led to his failure to take pride in a Rifian heritage and instead, led him to turn towards an 'imported' Middle Eastern Islam which is exogenous to Moroccan identity and prevented him from integrating into Dutch society.

Since the murder of Theo van Gogh, Berber associations in the Netherlands have sought to fight against the appeal of radical Islam among disadvantaged Moroccan youth on the one hand, but have also continuously warned against discrimination against Muslim populations in the Netherlands. One could say that Dutch-Berber identity politics are caught between Dutch assimilationist policies and discourses—that have primarily viewed Moroccan youth as Muslim—on the one hand, and Moroccan postcolonial politics on the other. In fact, when Morocco became independent in 1956, Arab and Islamic identities were favoured as a shared frame of identification under the nation's flag, something that discriminated against the Berbers' languages and regional interests. All over North Africa, the indigenous Berbers suffered from homogenising Arab nationalism expressed by predominantly undemocratic regimes, both during their respective battles for independence and afterwards.

In both views, the current discourse of Berber associations on local identity is reminiscent of, and rooted in, French colonial politics, which favoured Berber identity as opposed to Arab-Islamic identity. In colonial discourse, Arabs and Berbers were objectified (Hammoudi 2001: 112). The French thought the Berbers adhered to French values such as democracy and *laïcité*. Up to this day, the 'Berber' has remained a signifier (McDougall 2003) of otherness in Moroccan politics and among Moroccan migrant communities abroad. Berbers in both localities have been claiming membership of a marginalised group, both analysing the nature of their particular oppression and celebrating their uniqueness as local and ethnic groups. By objectifying the Berber as naturally democratic, regionally autonomous, and lay, identity comes to serve as the basis for the politicisation (Woodward 1997: 24) of all matters pertaining to linguistic, cultural and regional rights in Morocco and among Moroccan-Berber activist communities in host societies.

Envisioning the Berber as millennial, his presence must be authenticated through a revision of the past in order to justify the struggle for the Berber's current rights—and lack thereof—in societies and among migrant communities perceived as predominantly Arab and Islamic. A political agenda and a cultural ideal have always gone hand in hand within the Berber Cultural Movement. Moreover, precisely their will to inscribe themselves within a political modernity and to adhere to Western values (Hoffman & Gilson Miller 2010: 9), encompassing democratic values, ideas of gender equality and multicultural affinities, is tied up with cultural representations of a democratic, gender-neutral and tolerant Berber throughout North African history. As such, an intrinsic duality in its discourse has come across as conservative and progressive at the same time, building on the idea of a preexisting and separable ethnic identity and a traditional group while celebrating cultural adaptability, modernity and hybridity. At different times and places, this has resulted, not just in cultural but also political nationalisms with separatist ideals (Leersen 2006).

This chapter focuses on the *histoire croisée* (Werner & Zimmermann 2006) of colonial politics and myth making on the one hand, and Berber migration processes and the subsequent rise in associations in the Netherlands and Morocco on the other.[2] The objectification of 'the Berber' is analysed from the perspective of memory, namely *la longue durée* (Hutchinson 2008) of colonial and postcolonial power relations and formations. How do such historic ties find their expression in current Berberist discourses in Morocco and the Netherlands?[3]

The objectification of the Berber is still present in current cultural Berberist discourse. This has given rise to a particular *Amazigh* and Rifian memory politics within the global *Mouvement Culturel Amazigh*. However, the first generation of *Amazigh* activists in the Netherlands, the secular revivalists, have failed to mobilise both first-generation labour migrants and second-generation Moroccan-Dutch youth. The latter are concerned with their fate as Muslims in the Netherlands and consequently claim that the Berber activists who founded these associations are dividing and not uniting the Moroccan migrant population in the Netherlands.

HISTOIRE CROISÉE OF THE *MOUVEMENT CULTUREL AMAZIGH*: MOROCCO AND THE NETHERLANDS

The first Berber association in Morocco, the *Association Marocaine de la Recherche et de l'Echange Culturel* (AMREC) was founded by a group of Berber-speaking students in Rabat in 1967 (Kratochwil 2002). Although the name did not contain any reference to a Berberist programme, these students sought recognition for their people's language and culture in Morocco. During the early '90s, Berber associations in Morocco developed into the *Mouvement Culturel Amazigh* (MCA), clearly and openly acting as a Berber cultural umbrella association (Crawford & Hoffman 2000) during the repressive regime of former King Hassan II, when a new generation of *Amazigh* activists emerged out of *l'Union national des Etudiants du Maroc* and its Marxist-Leninist branch in particular (Pouessel 2010).

By the end of the 1960s, large segments of the Moroccan population had already started to migrate from Morocco towards European countries as a result of economic growth in Western Europe and lack of employment in Morocco.[4] A part of this migration cohort ended up in France because of previous colonial ties between Morocco and France on the one hand and Algeria and France on the other. During colonial times, in fact, many Moroccans worked as guest labourers for colons in French Algeria (De Haas 2007). Following the example of other European countries, the Dutch and Moroccan governments reached an agreement on the recruitment of Moroccans as guest workers in 1969 (Cottaar & Bouras 2009). Though intended as only temporary and rotational, the vast majority of these migrants eventually 'settled' in the Netherlands due to the oil crisis in 1973 and a lack of opportunities in Morocco (De Haas 2007). More than half of the 1969–1973 cohort originated from the northern mountainous Rif region (Fokkema & Harmsen 2009), a zone that geographically both bordered and interlinked the Maghreb and mainland Europe.

These large-scale migrations of Moroccan men, typical of the late '60s and early '70s in Morocco, coincided with the establishment of the first Berber associations in Morocco's urbanised centres, predominantly active in Rabat and Agadir. In Paris, the *Academie Berbère*, quickly renamed *Agraw Imazighen*, started out as both a venue for academic research and elite activism on Berber languages and history around the same time (Pouessel 2010). But Berber associations would remain absent in other European host societies until the early 1990s. In the Netherlands, they began to flourish especially during and after the mid-1990s. Little is known, however, about these associations' founders and activities and their potential impact on the constitution of ethnic and religious affiliations within the large and diverse body of Moroccan migrants and their offspring and consequently, their ability to mobilise these cohorts politically against both Moroccan and Dutch regimes.

Inquiry into the migration of Berber populations and the presence and popularity of the Berber Cultural Movement in the diaspora has therefore become a pressing matter (Hoffman & Gilson Miler 2010). Moreover, precisely because Berber associations are not directly linked to the period of large-scale migration, but rather to that of locally sustained migration patterns and the local history of the northern Rif region, following labour emigration in the late 1960s and early 1970s, the rise of Berber associations offers an interesting case with which to explore the interconnectedness between cultural and religious dynamics in a sending region and a migrant community abroad. Both in the Moroccan Rif and Dutch urban areas, Berber associations have focused on indigenous minority rights, pertaining to regional autonomy based on cultural, historical and linguistic particularity within Morocco, and ethnic migrant minority rights within a community that is principally labelled as Moroccan and Islamic. Both the Rif and the Dutch-Moroccan diaspora are 'border zones' and thus key areas wherein the constitution of *Amazigh* identity can be understood (Hoffman 2010: 40).

Debates on migrant activisms, in particular those associated with nationalist and ethnic projects, have been conceptualised as diaspora activisms (Brubaker 2005) precisely because flows of people and ideas transcend not just the borders of two but of multiple nation-states. Ties between multiple localities thus operate in vertical and horizontal modes. A diaspora connects multiple communities, either rooted in, or dispersed from, a homeland. Not to be misconceived analytically as bounded groups, diasporas rather relate to the idea of 'imagined communities' (Anderson 1991). What matters is that the category of diaspora is *felt* as a dispersion from a homeland towards which the members will orientate themselves. Due to this orientation towards an imagined homeland, members of diasporas and host societies will try to maintain boundaries throughout successive generations, even though in practice, boundaries often tend to fade into hybrid practices and syncretism (Brubaker 2005: 5–7). Diasporas always entail an element of cultural, political and social struggle (Sheffer 2003).

The expression of such a Berber diaspora activism is the *Congrès Mondial Amazigh* (CMA), a global network of Berber activists that was founded in 1997 (Kratochwil 1999) as 'an act, a commitment, a project which is political' (Brubaker 2005: 12). The CMA unites those networks of activists that operate within their own particular national and historical frameworks of host societies and homelands or nation-states. Often, they have acted as sources of inspiration for each other. Berber activism in the Moroccan Southern Souss region has, for instance, modelled itself after the Algerian Kabyle case (Pouessel 2010). Diasporas are thus not so much entities bounded *in* time and space, but rather projects and practices that cut *across* borders of space and time.

'THE GOOD BERBER': A TRAVELLING COLONIAL MYTH IN *LA LONGUE DURÉE*

The same observation applies to the constitution of ethnicities and identities (Brubaker &Cooper 2000), which are equally acts of framing and narrating. They are collective political and cultural projects, rhetoric and narratives, held together by a collection of 'memories' and commemorations (Brubaker 1996), called into being by actors and leaders of those 'imagined communities' and meant to provide some ontological security for those 'lost'. The case of the *Mouvement Culturel Amazigh* has in fact also proved of high interest with regard to *la longue durée* of the Arab and Berber divide prevalent in Berber activist discourse. The quest for an authentic and true Berber identity can therefore not be thought without the notion that identities are closely intertwined with the production of history and memory. Identities are in fact produced within specific 'regimes of historicity' (Lorenz 2010).

But this ethnic divide, which objectified both Arabs and Berbers, was in fact a colonial invention. France's *mythe berbère*, which consisted of an amalgam of ethnic stereotypes, was based on the canon of Berber tribes in Algeria and Morocco devised by French ethnologists (Burke 2007). This would suggest that the ethnic sentiments and ideology (Smith 2009) of the current *Mouvement Culturel Amazigh* are in fact historically rooted in French colonialism and the *mission civilisatrice*. In France, for instance, current Kabyle 'Berberist' politics elaborates the imagery of independent Algerian Berber tribes, as claimed by French ethnographers and linguists (Silverstein 2004).

The French experience in Morocco, however, took place almost a century after neighbouring Algeria became a French colony. Contrary to Algeria, Morocco was never legally conceived as a colony, although in practice, this difference between the French colony of Algeria and the French protectorate of Morocco was not outspoken. Their histories, however, differ quite considerably. Study missions that had been set up by France in Morocco, long before the country would become a protectorate in 1912, had offered a nuanced and flexible view on the ethnic composition and political sociology of the country. Relations between Arabs and Berbers were seen as 'fluid'. However, from 1904 onwards, the French resident-general Lyautey saw how an emphasis on the so-called division between a *makhzen* or urban and Arab central state power on the one hand, and a *siba* or dissident rural area inhabited by resistant and rebellious Berber populations on the other hand, could work in France's favour. This dichotomous image of Morocco (Burke 1973) as a country divided geographically and politically into such a *makhzen* and a *siba* was in reality more nuanced; it was constructed by the French because it was deemed useful for obtaining a tighter grip on more remote areas outside of Fez and Rabat. In fact, by promoting the idea of 'pacification'—the bringing of unity between these two political-geographical concepts—Lyautey considered he could gain support from the *makhzen* in his role as general and consequently win Morocco over. But by 1912, Lyautey's policy of pacification had come into question. The main problem was the resistant tribes of the Middle Atlas who refused to submit to the new coloniser. Their resistance was not only motivated by a previous distrust of the *makhzen* as a political apparatus—whether conceived as Moroccan or French—but also by a reluctance to submit to yet another system of institutions and customs.

The French feared that relations between the coloniser and colonised would escalate. In Algeria, by the 1860s, the colons had already started to oppose France's unforeseen favouring of Arab and Islamic identity and rallied in favour of civilian instead of military rule as well as a settler-dominated Algeria instead of the participation of native Arab elites (Gross & McMurray 1993). An anti-Arab and anti-Islamic campaign was organised by these colons, formulating new representations of the Berber populations, most notably of the 'good Kabyle Berber', Algeria's largest Berber-speaking population. By the time Morocco had become a protectorate, the Berber myth had lost importance in the Algerian colon's imagination because the relation between colonisers and colonised had changed. A politics and ideology of domination was preferred over the participation of any native elite, be they Arab or Berber. However, the policies based on this former distinction, remained unchanged.

Developments in Algeria combined with disturbances in the Middle Atlas forced Lyautey to reflect on a new strategy. This new politics would have to prevent a repeat of the mistakes made in Algeria, where the favouring of Arabic language and Islamic law had resulted in unexpected anti-French nationalist sentiments. The French were in fear of similar developments—a rising Moroccan nationalist opposition—that would obstruct France's attempts to gain control over Morocco. The French accordingly tried to construct an ethnic difference that would set one Arab group off against the Berber other. It was proclaimed that the Berber populations in Morocco were only superficially islamicised and that Islam and Arab culture were limited to the *makhzen*, where the central state power was located. Because of a lack of thorough knowledge of Berber society and culture in Morocco and in order to support their new political strategy, the French more or less copied the image of the 'good Berber' or 'Kabyle myth' they had created in Algeria (Goodman 2005). French experts now started to construct a set of characteristics that set the Berbers apart from the Arabs. As such, Berbers were viewed as the original inhabitants of North Africa, with probable European origins, preserved customs, rituals and superstitions of previous faiths, most notably Christianity. Their natural distrust of personal power reflected their democratic spirit. In addition, they were said to be monogamous and treat their women in a more European way than Arabs. Consequently, the Berbe was thought to assimilate more easily than the Arab.

With the Algerian experience and political developments in mind, and faced with the local Middle Atlas resistance, the French changed their strategy accordingly and asked the Berber tribes to submit to a *dawla* (state) instead of a *makhzen* and guaranteed them the continued use of their customary law or *azerf*. A first *dahir* (1914) at the time of the Middle Atlas upheavals set out the principles with respect to judicial regimes: use of *azerf* would be permitted in rural areas, while Sharia was restricted to urban areas. The so-called *Berber dahir* from 1930 specified the terms under which customary laws would be administered, and it ignited an ever-growing Arab nationalist movement, predominantly in the ancient capital of Fez. These *Fassi* elites were the ones who most severely opposed the 1930 *dahir* (Hoisington 1978).

The anticolonial sentiments of the nationalist independence movements resulted in a neglect of linguistic and cultural sensitivities altogether, as the *Istiqlal* set out to unify the colonised. Opposition in Fez gradually slid into an Arab nationalist framework, which would, in the long run, disadvantage the Berber-speaking populations (Kratochwil 2002: 67–75).

Berber identity has been reasserted as an ethnic identity coconstituting Moroccan identity in Morocco and the diaspora in cultural, artistic and scholarly work. Colonial politics underwrite and inform much of the discourse of these *Amazigh* associations, both academic and activist, blurring boundaries of what constitutes Berber 'history' and what is regarded as the Berbers' 'myth' (Silverstein 2010: 83). While Moroccan society is trying to make amends with respect to this colonial past, the Dutch are faced with the outcomes of global migration patterns that are more often than not seen as problematic.

The interconnection between colonial legacy in Morocco and Algeria and postcolonial reality in host societies remains problematic, however. Ethnological and historical knowledge of Berber populations in the Maghreb arose in a complex colonial setting. The production of such ethnological knowledge served colonial purposes (Asad 1973). The *mythe berbère*, as canonised by the French, was also rooted in a conception of history that was dependent on the spatial unit of the nation-state. 'History' coalesced with the process of nation formation. This also had consequences for the temporal perception of history. It was linear and teleological (Lorenz 2010: 70). This was also the case for the postcolonial Moroccan regime of historicity.

1956–1994: A SHORT HISTORY OF FORGETTING

In the context of Algerian migration towards France, the Berber was restored, while in Algeria he was repressed as a signifier in national politics (Silverstein 2004: 72). In Morocco, where the new King Mohamed V was confronted with the Arab nationalist *Istiqlal* party operating in urban environments, a similar Arab/Berber dichotomy served as an axis of national politics. As a reaction to the 1930 *Dahir berbère*, the programme of the *Istiqlal* party sought to incorporate the Berbers into one larger Moroccan national identity based on Arabism and Islam. Moreover, support for the Berber case was now seen as support for French colonialism. On the other hand, the allegations of collaborating with the former coloniser were mutual. The *Mouvement Populaire* encouraged the new King Mohamed V to make room for a Berber element in newly independent Morocco. However, because the latter wanted to preserve national unity in order to secure his own position, he negotiated between both parties and, as a result, proclaimed a Moroccan identity based on Islam, Arabism and Moroccanism. The concept of 'Moroccanism' solved the Berber-Arab problem, which became euphemistically called 'the rural issue' (Mezran 2001). The Moroccan Alawi dynasty, moreover, claimed descent from the Prophet, justifying the King's role as 'Commander of the Faithful'.

Demands made by Berber activists throughout the 1970s, 1980s and early 1990s, were ignored by King Hassan II. Moreover, any sign of Berber identity in public space was seen as an act undermining state authority and identity. Hassan II did loosen his tight grip towards the end of his kingship, by proclaiming a general *pardon* in 1994. Even though Morocco became an Arab-Islamic nation-state constitutionally, cultural ties with France were not fully cut off. Up to this day, French remains the primary language in business and has retained a secondary position in education after Arabic. Arabs were and still are viewed historically as 'culture makers and imprinters' (Issawi 1989), and Arab culture used as a 'high culture' (Gellner 1983): a literate, sophisticated culture to be taught formally in public education with repercussions in the domains of law, the arts and religion. In addition, in the midst of nation building, very little attention was given to peripheral areas, including the northern Rif, the homeland of the vast majority of Dutch-Berber activists.

RIFIAN MIGRATION AND THE MYTH OF SELECTIVE RECRUITMENT

As a matter of fact, the Rif had been a Spanish, and not a French protectorate. The treaty of Fez (30 March 1912) had stipulated that the northern Rif would be put under Spanish auspices. The two colonial powers thus split the country into a central zone to be governed by the French and a northern and southern peripheral Spanish zone. But whereas the French modernised the infrastructure of the urban centres, the Spanish did nothing of the kind in the Rif region. Precisely because of this difference, the Rif leader Abdelkrim El Khattabi united the local northern tribes against the Spanish coloniser (Tahtah 1999). Abdelkrim was eventually arrested and deported.[5]

The local Rifian leaders—'tribesmen'—who had previously been granted administrative positions under Spanish administration were now replaced by Moroccan administrators who had previously lived and worked in the French protectorate zone and were considered a new 'foreign' bourgeois elite. As a reaction to this neglect of local sensitivities, an uprising took place in the winter of 1958–1959, which consisted of a series of revolts locally led by Mohamed Ameziane. The banished Abdelkrim, who was now being accused of not only wanting to oust the Spanish, but also the Moroccan sultan, was living in Cairo at the time and is said to have coordinated these revolts (Aarab 2009). The Moroccan army, led by General Oufkir and then-Prince Hassan, son of Mohamed V, severely and violently suppressed the series of uprisings that later became referred to by the local population as the 'year of the helmets'. It was followed by the 'years of lead': three decades of severe repression of all political opposition, accompanied by economic neglect that eventually led to the 1984 and 1987 revolts in the areas of Al Hoceima, Nador and Imzouren.

Precisely this experience of suffering during the violent 'years of lead' in the Rif is what binds the new elite, predominantly consisting of male intellectuals, artists, poets, and journalists, who initiated Berber associations in the Netherlands during the period in which family reunification and family formation often served as the means to emigrate (Van Amersfoort & van Heelsum 2007). In fact, 55 per cent of Moroccan migrants who came to the

Netherlands during this very first period of large-scale migration towards Europe (1969–1973) originated from two central Rif provinces: Nador and Al Hoceima and the neighbouring province of Tetouan to the West (Fokkema & Harmsen 2009). Historically, the Rif had already been a sending region (De Haas 2009) prior to international migration towards the West. In the days of the protectorate, many men departed towards Algeria and the Moroccan urban areas of Tangiers and Tetouan (De Haas 2009).

Up until a few years ago, little was known about the migration history of Moroccans in the Netherlands. Most demographers (De Haas 2009) generally held that the newly independent Moroccan state intentionally selected men from the northern Rif region, known—and represented in Moroccan and European academic analyses—as an underdeveloped, rebellious mountainous area, as part of Hassan II's strategy to weaken the Rif, in view of the 1958–1959 rebellious episode. Only a decade had passed between the 1958–1959 winter uprising and the signing of the bilateral agreement. Stories about Hassan II's attempts to deliberately select Rifian men have not stopped circulating among the Moroccan community, and Berber associations in particular, and even academics in the Netherlands themselves have upheld the programme of selectivity. The 1960s and 1970s '*makhzen*-programmed' mass migrations are viewed as the punishment for resisting state authority during the 1920s and 1950s. The low number of Moroccan guest workers appearing in the official lists of companies and governments has started to debunk the 'hidden agenda myth' of selective recruitment: most migrants departed individually without government intervention. In addition, most recruitment agencies operated from the capital of Rabat (Cottaar & Bouras 2009). As most Dutch-Moroccans migrated from the northern zone of the country, it has remained the main region of emigration up to this day, even though the Dutch government has imposed restrictions (De Haas 2009).

The representation of Hassan II as a dictator who deliberately tried to eradicate Rifians, who suppressed *Amazigh* language and culture and erased the *Amazigh* contribution in Moroccan official history, was not bound to Morocco only but reached the diaspora communities. During the first decades of immigration in the Netherlands, Hassan II's *Amicales* (friendship associations) (Brand 2008) were meant to improve contacts between the consulates and families and to improve the latter's living circumstances. But they were also seen as a means of control. This in turn created a climate of fear and suspicion, while Hassan II continued to stress that the migrants 'remain Moroccan'. A cultural agreement between Morocco and the Netherlands ensured that Arabic language and culture instruction became possible in 1983.

Up until now, Morocco has tried to retain strong ties with its *Marocains résidents à l'étranger* (MRE).[6] Morocco's emigration policy (Brand 2008: 45–91) is thus still interpreted as a reinforcement of the boundaries between Moroccans living abroad and the societies they live in. A recent plan (2000–2004) affirms state sovereignty over these MREs, stressing that 'bonds are still very deep' and 'complete integration' into the host society is to be avoided. The Moroccan government thus continues to emphasise 'the strong Moroccan identity'—economic, political and cultural—of those residing abroad. The current King Mohamed VI implemented economic and agricultural reforms in order to improve living standards in the hope of reducing these traditional emigration flows (Belguendouz 2009).

Undoubtedly, local material conditions have had a strong effect on the economically weak area, which has largely been dependent on labour migration, especially after independence. The consequences of the colonial construction were also ideological. The displaced Berber myth, travelling from French Algeria towards French Morocco, remained a marker within an Arab-Islamic defined Morocco, where the Berber was 'forgotten'. In this 'regime of historicity', the colonial invention was reversed: from geopolitical and ethnic differences towards a unified national identity.

DECOLONISING NATIONAL HISTORY

By engaging in so-called memory work (Maddy-Weitzman 2007), both in Morocco and in the diaspora, and by revolting against the prestige of both French and Arab-Islamic cultures and languages deemed 'colonial', these travelling and migrating intelligentsia are the key driving forces (Smith 2009) behind the resurgence of an *Amazigh* ethno-cultural activism, and explain the rise of *Amazigh* associations in the Netherlands. However, because these associations in the Netherlands simultaneously defend both migrants' rights in host societies and 'indigenous rights' in the homeland, its praxis and discourse are located in a 'third space' (Bhabha 1994) where the national and transnational and the local and the global meet, cultural and political spheres interact, and where history and memory intertwine (Young 2001).

The idea of Rifian and *Amazigh* ethno-cultural identity is rooted in the memories of activists, their thoughts, actions and cultural productions (Brubaker 1996). The *Imazighen* and Rifians, those in Morocco as well as those living abroad, do not constitute a group as such and might not even be perceived as such by those members at all times. But in order to overcome a lack of *Amazigh-ness*, such a collective identity—always a retrospective notion—must be forged through a construction of a shared understanding of the past and the meaning that can be drawn from its representation. The past becomes a site where representations within and between nations and nationalisms, between myths of nations and collective memories of nationalists, overlap and compete with each other (Bell 2005). This is what Bhabha (1990: 1) refers to as 'a particular ambivalence that haunts the nation, the language of those who write of it and the lives of those who live it'. The memory of the Berber Cultural Movement becomes a narrative strategy (Bhabha 1990) or mnemonic strategy competing with the dominant versions of the past of both the Moroccan and Dutch nation-states. In the words of Pierre Nora (1989), these are *lieux de mémoire*, spatial or ideational 'sites', where the past can be recuperated and where people can build and maintain a direct link with the past at a time when the acceleration of history is felt as too rapid, and therefore the distance between the present and the past has grown too large. Paradoxically, memory can only exist when there is a sense that (a connection with) history has been lost.

The resurrection of memory as a category of practice and analysis occurred during the 1980s and coincided with changing perceptions of objectivity, the marker of the regime of historicity typical of the nation-state (Lorenz 2010). Memory has come to dominate so much of political discourse that we are witnessing a memory boom. It is a sign that we are preoccupied with the location of the past in our present, since it is felt to be too distant or downright lost. The location of the past in the present reflects the way individuals and 'mnemonic communities' (Zerubavel 2003) perceive themselves in a wider historical perspective (Assmann 2008) and thus situate themselves in time (Grever 2009). In fact, identity politics ultimately comes down to 'memory politics', and maintaining a dynamic balance between 'identity' and 'memory' in the public sphere (i.e., national) is a 'delicate' exercise (Frijhoff 2007).

In order to obtain and sustain a sense of self, individuals need such sites of memory to which they can meaningfully relate. They may do so individually, but memory is always socially embedded: whether in institutions, the shared experiences of specific generations, or in 'imagined' communities (Olick & Robbins 1998: 122–126). In other words, autobiographical and collective memories will equally and mutually influence each other. This is shown in the lives and both cultural and ethno-historical productions of Berber activists in the Netherlands. An analysis of the life stories of Berber activists and the cultural and historical productions of their Berber associations show how the resurgence of an *Amazigh* and Rifian 'memory' accompanies the decolonisation of Moroccan postcolonial and migration 'history'.

Mohamed Chacha, a Rifian poet, founded the first *Amazigh* association in the Netherlands, named 'Izouran', in Amsterdam in 1990 (El Aissati 2010). In Amsterdam, the association Amazigh started out just a few years later with a cultural festival. Naming practices reflect both attachment to prominent Berber associations located in the homeland and a reconnection with pre-Islamic North African history. The Hague is home to 'Tifawt' ('light') and Gouda to 'Nekour', referring to the Rifian town said to have been the centre of the eighth and ninth century 'Kingom of Nekour' which comprised nearly all of the Rif area, and named after Al Hoceima's most prominent cultural *Amazigh* association. 'Bades', an association named after the *lycée Al-Badissi* in Al Hoceima, which the associations' founders attended, and was initiated around the same time in the smaller city of Roosendaal in the province of Brabant, alongside Adrar operating from Nijmegen and two associations, Syphax and Apulleius, in Utrecht. The latter two names refer to prominent Berber historical figures from pre-Islamic times: Syphax, a third century BC Berber king and Apulleius, the writer of *Metamorphoses*, the famous Latin novel better known as *The Golden Ass*, were both born in the ancient land of Numidia, a region which is now known as Algeria. During the 1990s, *Amazigh* associations in the Netherlands bloomed, while the same activists assisted the setup of similar associations in neighbouring countries, such as Germany and Belgium. Around the same time, both Adrar and Syphax started to publish newsletters ('Adrar Newsletter' and 'Rif Bulletin') in Dutch, French, and *Tarifit*, the Rifian language, written in Arab script. But they also started to familiarise their readers with a version of the *Tifinagh* alphabet. Contributors were *Amazigh* scholars and artists from Morocco, the Netherlands and France. Each edition devoted attention to political developments, scholarly analysis on Berber linguistics and ethnology, Berber poetry, interviews with prominent activists, and reports on communications with fellow activists in the *Amazigh* associations in Belgium, Germany, France, Spain and Italy. Readers were also able to follow developments in the U.S.A. with the help of 'The *Amazigh* Voice', a newsletter published by the American *Amazigh* Cultural Association. Although attempts were made at initiating more local associations and national, overarching organisations such as ABIN,[7] few of these associations were able to develop a group of volunteers and stood the test of time. Associations are organised locally in the urban areas, with the highest concentration in the *Randstad*, the most industrialised and urbanised zone of the Netherlands. However, a core of activists from all over the Netherlands and abroad visits these festivals, language classes and lectures. These cultural festivals make up the central business of the Berber Movement that, on a local level, has also tried to take up the social function of mosques as locations where Moroccan migrants often seek information on psychological and social issues.

Activities consist mostly of cultural festivals with music, poetry readings and art exhibitions. Books, compact discs and pamphlets produced in both European countries and Morocco are sold at these events. Cultural production is related to the ethnography and history of the Berber people in North Africa and the northern Rif area, as well as poetry and music produced by Berber and Rifian poets and singers. The legacy of Abdelkrim El Khattabi was made the subject of a graphic novel *Emir of the Rif* (Nadrani 2008a). Another graphic novel deals with the subject of the 'Years of Lead' by telling the life story of a Rifian political prisoner (Nadrani 2008b).David Hart's ethnography and history 'The Aith Waryaghar of the Moroccan Rif' was translated into Dutch and has become an authoritative source for the Movement. In fact, most activists originate from the area of the *Aith Waryaghar* where the renowned anthropologist conducted his fieldwork. In addition, (Dutch-) Rifian bands regularly perform at festivals and fuse the traditional protest lyrics of Rifian song with other musical influences. Collections of poems written by Moroccan-Rifian migrants are promoted, and sometimes copublished by associations. Poems are usually rendered in the *Tarifit* dialect, written in Arabic or Latin script, and translated into Dutch or French. Ahmed Ziani published 'Song of Praise for the Groom' in 1997, with themes revolving around migration, identity and Berber culture. Ahmed Essadki's 'Battle Cry from the Earth', including the poem 'Ziyaan goes digging for his roots', was inspired by his own biography of growing up in the Rif and a family history of migration. Mohamed El Ayoubi, a Rifian-Berber linguist who was educated in Brussels, Paris and Leiden, published a collection of Berber fairy tales entitled 'Les Merveilles du Rif' in 2000. In a collective effort of activists and Dutch linguists, a Berber Library was initiated, which will start to publish a selection of Berber classics starting in the spring of 2011. Asis Aynan, a second-generation Dutch-Rifian publicist, whose collection of essays 'Battle and Other Stories' documented the struggles he faced with his *Amazigh* and Moroccan background when his father passed away, first made the appeal. One particular essay outlines a conversation with yet another activist, Abttoy, whose comics and artwork are inspired by his conviction that Berber identity may be mobilised to counter Islamist and Arab conceptions of Moroccan identity among second-generation youth.[8]

In contrast to these locally organised associations and activities, the women's association *Timazighin*, is nationally organised and devoted to the support and empowerment of *Amazigh* girls and women. Through a website and more informal meetings, the art of *izran*, Berber women's traditional oral poetry, is practised, collecting and sharing 'ancient' *izran* and building upon the songs of their mothers and grandmothers, and reconnecting with a 'millennial' agency, stressing the role of women as leaders in pre-Islamic times. Currently, the association is without a president because of internal strife about the place of Islamic religiosity in an *Amazigh* association and, since it concerns a women's association, secular and religious interpretations of feminism compete with one another. The discussion on religion and secularism within *Timazighin*, however, is indicative that the Berber Movement is present on a global scale.

Set against the history of Moroccan migration to the Netherlands, the slow rise and far smaller number of *Amazigh*-Rifian cultural associations, compared to the predominant Islamic-religious ones, is surprising. However, the historical framework of Schrover and Penninx (2001) on the rise and demise of migrant associations, explains the late arrival of this kind of migrant association.[9] During the earliest stages of the settlement of Moroccans in the Netherlands, organisations primarily attended to issues concerning their country of origin. Associations served practical purposes and offered aid with social security and working permits. This was followed by a stage where the focus on the specific needs and infrastructures for the migrants in the receiving country became more pressing. In this period, for instance, mosques began to constitute themselves as social organisations, offering communal leisure activities. As the heterogeneity of the Moroccan community grew more marked, prompted by family reunification and family formation processes, associations became more aware of the changing demands and needs of their fellow members This resulted in the growth of women's and youth organisations. All in all, the majority of Moroccan associations today remains religiously oriented (Van Heelsum 2001).

The rise of *Amazigh* associations, within the historical framework of Rifian migration, may in addition be explained by trends in Moroccan politics. First of all, the most logical reason given consists of the policy shift in Morocco, especially since Mohamed VI's ascent to the throne, towards its citizens abroad: the MRE (Brand 2008). Hassan II's *Amicales*, for instance, have been dissolved and consultative bodies were installed in order to assure participation of MRE. While still operative, the *Amicales* were opposed in several diaspora. In the Netherlands, where this opposition was more marked than in other European destination countries, the Dutch wing of Morocco's student union and the leftist *KMAN*, a committee of Moroccan labourers, were able to oppose the *Amicales*, leaving them with very little influence.[10] Nowadays, the leftist *KMAN* has retained but a small fraction of members compared to the 1970s and 1980s (Van der Valk 1996). Conversely, the democratic *SMDN* has taken up a public role as critic of Moroccan policies that might affect the *MRE* currently living in the Netherlands.[11] Today, the opposition emphasises its right to a separate identity, culture and history, aside from aiming at democratising the Moroccan regime and lessening the influence of the Moroccan state in the diaspora.

Nevertheless, Mohamed VI has generated a wave of democratisation since ascending the throne in 1999 and directed much of his attention towards the economic development of the countryside—including northern Morocco— to the modernisation of state bureaucracy, and is committed to human and women's rights (Sater 2010). The reform of the Islamic family law or *Moudawana* was finally accomplished in 2004, after more than 25 years of efforts to change it, and gained a powerful symbolic status since it proved a significant improvement for the legal status and protection of Moroccan women, including those residing abroad (Foblets 2007). Some of the Berber Movement's demands were granted by way of initiation of the *Institut Royal de la Culture Amazigh au Maroc*, a state-funded research institute devoted to Berber studies.[12] Here, researchers developed a standardised version of *Tamazight* and a new *Tifinagh* alphabet to be used in primary education. Several publications on Berber linguistics and the Berbers' history and sociology in Morocco are under way. An indemnity commission, examining detentions and disappearances under former King Hassan II's reign, has been installed (Slyomovics 2001). Yet Moroccan civil society and its elites in general, including *Amazigh* activists, not the least those in the Moroccan diaspora, remain sceptical about how progressive the king can be as well as the level of democracy. Notwithstanding the significant integration of Berber minorities in Morocco, Berber activism in Morocco has not lost its raison d'être. Claims that the *makhzen* is yet again trying to incorporate an element of opposition are frequently made. In the Netherlands, Berber associations are accused of 'divide and rule' politics, especially because of their secular ideals.

MULTIPLE *BERBERITÉS*

During the past decade, the *Mouvement Culturel Amazigh* has developed a cultural discourse with an emphasis on 'Western' secularity and historical connections with Europe, while faced with a growing interest from second-generation youth neither willing to adhere and participate in an exclusively secular ideology nor to forego their observance of Islam in order to bring about social, cultural and political change in the Netherlands and in Morocco. In fact, as culture makers, these intelligentsia function altogether as 'gatekeepers' (Hoffman & Gilson Miller 2010: 10) to what is 'acceptably *Amazigh*', by not only seeking inclusion in Western history but also by drawing on comparisons with 19th-century European Enlightenment and radical secularism, and a Marxist conception of religion in particular. The latter two ideas are contested by those born in the diaspora and explain the reluctance of Moroccan youth who wish to associate with the Movement. For them, Islam is equally constitutive of their identity and if it is not, they still would not wish to dismiss the participation of religious youth as yet another 'divide and rule' tactic because it would split up the migrant community and lessen its impact, as a grassroots movement, on Dutch and Moroccan politics. They prefer connecting with the *Amazigh* heritage as citizens of a global community, with roots that are as *Amazigh* and 'historic' as they are Islamic and thus religious, being equally at 'home' in, and belonging to, both Dutch and Moroccan society.

The embodied memory of the first Berber activists, embodied within one generation, has failed to transform itself into a disembodied and re-embodied memory that cuts across generational differences (Assmann 2008: 56), precisely because mnemonic practices differ greatly from those of the second generation who do not share the grievances against Morocco based on a shared memory in the Rif. Moreover, though the second generation is more highly educated than the first generation of guest labourers, the level of education and employment, and the number of changed life trajectories, do not merely seem to indicate a rise in ethnic attachment on the one hand, and adherence to secularist ideals on the other—on the contrary (Maliepaard, Lubbers & Gijsberts 2009). Shared memories do unite *Amazigh* activists in the Netherlands. Where in Morocco they have adapted their discourses according to local political and cultural vagaries (Silverstein 2011), will activists in the Netherlands do the same? They themselves have acknowledged the disunity of the Movement and their inability to mobilise large masses with clear political demands.

At the same time, in both Morocco and the Netherlands, *Berberité* is becoming a mainstream idea. At a time when Morocco has almost 'solved' the Berber issue, Islamist threats (Howe 2005) to the throne are on the increase. The initiation of *IRCAM*, the incorporation of Berber language in school curricula and structural regional economic reforms, seem to some *Amazigh* voices no more than an effort to incorporate a *Berberist* element in Morocco's fight against Islamism (Maddy-Weitzman 2006), which could equally pose a threat to the Moroccan monarchy. An application for funding submitted by Syphax at the IRCAM in support of a language programme in the city of Utrecht was not welcomed by all *Amazigh* sections. In the Netherlands, umbrella organisations such as SMN and SMDN have acknowledged the *Amazigh* Movement by using *Tifinagh* and *Tarifit* in addition to Arabic and Dutch in communication towards member associations and their public, and the Dutch-Moroccan Women's Association provides translation and legal advice regarding the *Moudawana* in *Tamazight*, and many translation bureaus in Dutch cities have picked up on this need and demand.

At the same time, and in view of the recent popular uprisings against undemocratic regimes in the Middle East and North Africa, the Berber Movement is searching for a new political purpose and relevance in Morocco, as it has always associated itself with other grassroots movements aimed at bringing about democratic and multicultural North African societies where human rights and freedom of religion are respected and women's rights promoted. At gatherings organised by the so-called Twenty February Movement in the Netherlands in early 2011, Berber flags were omnipresent.

Last, the parallels drawn between the European Enlightenment and North Africa's lack thereof by the *Amazigh* intelligentsia and founding members of Dutch-Berber associations, highlights their observation that 19th-century European nationalisms were secular ideologies, which acted as counterparts to religion. But even though, as an ideology, nationalism could relate to the core themes present in religious representations of origins, death, salvation and continuity, by sharing a past, present and future as an—imagined—community, it did not replace religiosity but rather extended it (Anderson 1991). For a non-Western cultural activism in a Western, postcolonial context, this seems very much to be the case too. Debates between secular and Islamic voices within the *Mouvement Culturel Amazigh* have not subsided and often revolve around the 'incompatibility' of Islamic and Berber identities precisely because of the latter's affinity with 'Western' values, culture, and history, and the Arab-Islamic lack thereof. By claiming that North Africa cannot be viewed historically and culturally as an extension of the Middle East, the Berber Movement in the Netherlands, which is exclusively made up of Moroccan-Berber migrants, states that by implication neither can the Moroccan diasporas be regarded as such.

The *histoire croisée* of Moroccan-Berber migrations and associations in the Netherlands on the one hand, and colonial politics and myth making on the other, have shown how the objectification of the Berber in current cultural *Berberist* discourse has given rise to a particular *Amazigh* and Rifian memory politics within the global *Mouvement Culturel Amazigh*. Despite efforts to 'decolonise' Moroccan history, colonial 'divide and rule' politics are present throughout the memories, narratives and cultural production of the first *Amazigh* activists in the Netherlands. What is needed, according to second-generation activists and critics, is a uniting factor and not a divisive one. Given the focus of the Dutch integration debate on 'Muslim identity', radical secularism, like radical Islam, would only work to their collective disadvantage and deny an equally important part of the second-generation's multiple 'identities' and rich heritage.

NOTES

1. 'Amazigh' (pl. 'Imazighen': 'free people') is often preferred because 'Berber' has a derogatory ('barbarous') connotation. I use both terms interchangeably.
2. 'Histoire croisée' (Werner & Zimmermann 2006) analyses connections between 'various historically constituted formations'. Closely related to the methodology of comparative and shared history; 'histoire croisée' draws on pragmatic induction: synchronic and diachronic intercrossings between objects of research, ways of looking at the object, and the intercrossing between researcher and object (reflexivity).
3. This chapter is based on qualitative research conducted between 2008 and 2011 in the Netherlands, Belgium and Morocco (Rabat). In the diaspora, I drew on the life stories of Berber activists, observations at Berber cultural festivals and debates organised by Berber associations, private and associational archival records, as well as public, cultural and historical productions of knowledge. In Morocco, my inquiry was limited to archival research and interviews with Rabat-based activists.
4. In the post-WOII-era, most Moroccan guest workers left for Germany, Belgium and the Netherlands. In France, Maghrebi migrant communities originated mostly from the Algerian Kabyle and Moroccan Souss region. See De Haas (2007) and Silverstein (2004).
5. After Abdelkrim's departure from the Rif, and when Franco launched his rebellion from Northern Morocco, a 'historical solidarity' between the Berbers and the Spanish was invoked, proclaiming a common history in Moorish Spain (Gross & McMurray 1993).
6. Hereafter referred to as 'MRE'.
7. '*Amazigh* Beweging in Nederland' or '*Amazigh* Movement in the Netherlands'.
8. See Abttoy (2008) *Cartoons van een Berber*, Amsterdam: XTRA, in particular.
9. Penninx–Schrover (2001) take the opportunity structure of the receiving society, internal dynamics, and the migration process into account.
10. 'Komitee Marokkaanse Arbeiders in Nederland' or 'Committee of Moroccan Labourers in the Netherlands'.
11. 'Stem Marokkaanse Democraten in Nederland' or 'Voice of Moroccan Democrats in the Netherlands'.
12. Royal Institute of Berber Culture in Morocco, hereafter referred to as IRCAM.

8 Self-Sacrifice and Martyrdom in Terrorism
Political and Religious Motives

Francesco Marone

Le vrai martyr attend la mort, l'enthousiaste y court
Denis Diderot,
Pensées philosophiques (1746), XXXIX

Suicide attacks have become one of the most important and emblematic forms of violence of today, particularly since 11 September 2001. These acts of self-sacrifice are often constructed as forms of religious martyrdom, and they therefore require an investigation in terms of the role of religion in world politics and, especially, in terrorism.

This chapter aims to examine the growing role of religious factors in self-sacrifice and martyrdom in modern terrorism. This evolution is out of line with a classical vision of modernity as shaped by linear processes of rationalisation and secularisation (cf. Smith 2008). By contrast, acts of self-sacrifice and martyrdom in terrorist violence represent a dramatic sign of the (complex) revival of religion in our age.

Suicide attacks are acts of organised violence in which the perpetrators deliberately sacrifice their own lives (see Moghadam 2006a). The willingness to die is combined with the willingness to kill simultaneously in the same act (Gambetta 2006a; Merari 1990): the goal is therefore 'dying to kill' (Bloom 2004). Moreover, in suicide attacks, the 'martyr's death is a necessary requisite of the mission because it is self-inflicted, frequently by means of explosive devices. Consequently, the expression *suicide* attacks is not inappropriate even if it is usually rejected by supporters of this form of violence.

Suicide attacks can be part of a strategy of terror. Despite its popularity, 'terrorism' is a notoriously elusive and controversial concept. In this chapter, I will refer to a stipulative definition of terrorism associated with a high level of abstraction: terrorism can be thought of as a strategy of underground violence employed by a sub-state organisation in order to weaken the will and resistance of a state by influencing an audience. Terrorist organisations cannot fight on the battlefield because they do not have enough capabilities and resources to sustain a military confrontation with their adversary and they cannot rely on the support of a large number of militants (see de la Calle & Sánchez-Cuenca 2011; Merari 1993). The relative weakness of terrorist organisations in terms of capabilities, resources and support leads them to adopt an indirect manoeuvre: terrorist violence is usually designed to have a deep psychological impact in order to impose high costs on the adversary and force it to agree to important concessions, without going into battle. Here the concept of terrorism refers to a strategy of violence and does not imply any judgement on the legitimacy that the perpetrators can enjoy.

Suicide terrorism is usually a powerful weapon of the weak, but it is not necessarily a weapon of last resort. Hezbollah, for example, launched its first suicide attacks soon after its foundation, before it became a significant military and political force in Lebanon (Gambetta 2006a: 260–261).

It is possible to identify some historical antecedents of contemporary suicide terrorism: the Jewish Sicarii under the Roman occupation of Judea in the first century and the radical Shi'a sect of the Assassins active in Syria and Persia from the 11th to the 13th centuries amongst others (Rapoport 1984), and a few Muslim communities in Southeast Asia in conflict with European colonial powers (Dale 1988).[1]

However, despite recurrent references to the past and a return to the 'true' fundamentals of religion, genuine suicide terrorism is a recent phenomenon which emerged only in the early 1980s during the Lebanese civil war, in a sort of point of intersection between the history of suicide violence in the Middle East and the history of modern terrorism. Suicide attacks spread to Sri Lanka in 1987, the area of the Israeli-Palestinian conflict in 1993, India in 1995, Turkey in 1996, and Chechnya in 2000. The diffusion of this method was facilitated by processes of imitation and learning, as well as by opportunities for interorganisational cooperation, for example, between Lebanese Hezbollah and Palestinian armed groups (Horowitz 2010). All these cases of ethno-nationalist violence can be associated with a local version of suicide terrorism in which the ultimate purpose of violence is the liberation of a territory from a foreign occupation.

Since the 1998 bombings against the U.S. embassies in Tanzania and Kenya, al-Qaeda has carried out several suicide attacks against targets in the Islamic world (in connection with the 'near enemy') and in the West (against the 'far enemy'). After 11 September 2001 (Holmes 2006), al-Qaeda was followed by a considerable number of Salafi-jihadi organisations and groups in many areas of the world. The al-Qaeda network is the protagonist of a new transnational version of suicide terrorism with global aims of Islamist inspiration (Moghadam 2008).

After its debut in the early 1980s in Lebanon, this extreme form of violence has witnessed a dramatic increase of instances: according to reliable estimates, more than 2,000 suicide attacks were carried out around the world from 1981 onwards (CPOST 2011); approximately a 1,000 were carried out in Iraq after the U.S.-led invasion in 2003 (see also Hafez 2007).

However the idea and the practice of self-sacrifice and martyrdom have considerable relevance in the history of modern terrorism (Silke 2006), long before the rise of suicide terrorism and the appearance of today's 'religious wave' of terrorism (Rapoport 2004).

This chapter aims to explore the role of self-sacrifice and martyrdom in modern terrorism, paying attention to the relation between political and religious motives. It compares different experiences, distant in space and time, from a historical perspective that is often neglected in the scientific literature on terrorism.[2] Nevertheless, the essay is not intended to present an accurate and detailed historical discussion: in fact, the effort is more analytical and interpretative than historiographical. The presentation is mainly based on the examination of relevant secondary sources.

The chapter is divided into four sections: the first section looks at the episodes of passive martyrdom in which the martyr is ready to die without at the same time killing. The second section examines the forms of offensive martyrdom in which the martyr is willing to die in order to kill other people. The third section focuses on the function of acts of self-sacrifice and martyrdom in modern terrorism. The fourth section explores the political and religious motivations of these deeds and links the return of martyrdom to the changes of the modern world.

PASSIVE MARTYRDOM

The phenomenon of modern terrorism arose in the 19th century in Europe and America. Anarchists and Russian revolutionaries were quick to assign great value to the notion of martyrdom.

For those groups the insurrectionist route proved almost entirely futile, leading to a combination of popular indifference or puzzlement, on the one hand, and military repression, on the other. From this position of weakness, Anarchists applied their talent to propaganda. Political violence, often in the form of spectacular assassinations against politicians, capitalists and the police, represented a strategy of 'propaganda by deed' in addition to propaganda of the word, as officially confirmed in the International Congress held in London in 1881 (Jensen 2004).

The prison was the typical stage of this performance. By the mid-19th century the ritual of the courtroom had replaced the spectacle of public physical punishment (cf. Foucault 1975). Anarchists framed the trial and especially the execution as an act of martyrdom (Gabriel 2007). For example, the executions of the supposed perpetrators of the 1886 Haymarket massacre in Chicago in 1887 (McKinley 1987) and of the Italian immigrants Nicola Sacco and Bartolomeo Vanzetti in Massachusetts in 1927 were famous and influential and carefully followed by the mass media of that time. By means of the martyrdom narrative, punishment lost its terrorising effect for Anarchists, rendering the exercise of power, to some extent, powerless. They saw their own sacrifice as hastening the coming world of justice by revealing the glory of Anarchism and the brutality of the reigning system. Moreover, the prison was viewed as a mirror of the broader hierarchical society they rejected (Gabriel 2007: 43–44). In the end, though these acts of martyrdom represented a dramatic form of testimony, their concrete political effects were modest.

Moreover, several members of the variegated galaxy of Russian terrorism, from the end of the 19th century to the beginning of the 20th century (Populists, Nihilists, Socialist-Revolutionaries and Anarchists (Ternon 2007) showed a genuine readiness to sacrifice themselves for their political cause by engaging in high-risk missions or even suicide missions (e.g., Kalyvas & Sánchez-Cuenca 2006: 221–222 and 226–227).

It is interesting to mention the figure of Ivan Kalyayev, member of the Socialist-Revolutionary Party and poet, hanged for the murder of the reactionary Grand Duke Sergei Alexandrovich in 1905, at the age of 28. Kalyayev is portrayed with sympathetic features by Albert Camus, in the play *Les Justes* (1950) and in some pages of the essay *L'Homme révolté* (1951). According to the French writer, the terrorist's readiness to die made the practice of assassination more acceptable (Camus 1950, 1951). Stephen Holmes draws on this intriguing perspective to make sense of contemporary suicide attacks (Holmes 2006: 147–148):

> One paradoxical, but interesting, line of thought on this matter is that suicide itself provides a way to overcome the norms that prohibit the killing of innocents. In *Les Justes*, Albert Camus describes such a strategy to assuaging the guilty conscience of killers. His idea, put succinctly, is that dying justifies killing. At one point, the Russian anarchist hero of the play, Ivan Kaliayev, says: *Si je ne mourais pas, c'est alors que je serais un meurtrier* [If I were not to die, I would be only a murderer]. In other words, doubts about the morality of murder can be answered by the willingness of the killer to die. Readiness for self-sacrifice established the Christ-like purity of the assassin. [. . .] In suicide attacks, at least according to Camus, the cause need not be so obviously compelling, for the willingness of killers to die by itself demonstrates their subjective belief in the righteousness of their cause. Third-party observers may disapprove of the cause, but no one can plausibly deny that terrorists themselves were convinced that the ends justify the means. For those with a moral conscience, if Camus is right, suicide terrorism is psychologically easier than hit-and-run terrorism.

In this regard we can observe that these militants show both components of suicide terrorism: willingness to die and willingness to kill, but usually not in a simultaneous act. Interestingly, Camus suggests that the former can justify the latter; in other words, the connection between the two components is psychological.

Some decades later, the idea of martyrdom was adopted by the German RAF (*Rote Armee Fraktion*, 'Red Army Faction'), a Marxist-inspired organisation, also known as the Baader-Meinhof Band (Aust 2008). The stage of these actions was once again a prison. After their arrest in 1972, the first-generation leaders of this terrorist group organised three influential collective hunger strikes between 1972 and 1975 that led to the death of two prisoners. In prison, hunger strikes were glorified through a rhetoric of sacrifice and martyrdom. This narrative enabled them to maintain the morale and the discipline of the group. Vis-à-vis the outside world the RAF leaders were able to frame self-starvation as an extreme form of 'anti-fascist' and 'anti-imperialist' resistance in a struggle against an external process of 'medicalisation' of the public debate on terrorism that tended to mystify and deny the political sense of their decision to take arms by linking it to the field of mental disturbance (Passmore 2009). Notoriously, the RAF leaders Andreas Baader and Ulrike Meinhof were said to have committed suicide in prison in 1977 and in 1976 respectively. The hunger strikes organised by the second-generation RAF in the ensuing years, in a different political and social context, had much less visibility and relevance.

Probably the most well-known cases of hunger strikes associated with terrorist organisations were carried out by Northern Ireland militants in the early 1980s. In Ireland, hunger strikes have a long history as a method of political and social confrontation, even dating back to oral codes of the pre-Christian era (Sweeney 1993: 421–422). The Catholic nationalists organised at least 50 hunger strikes in the period from 1912 to 1923 involving almost 10,000 male and female prisoners throughout the country (ibid.). After a few episodes in 1972–1974, two waves of highly influential hunger strikes were organised by Provisional IRA (Irish Republican Army) and INLA (Irish National Liberation Army) volunteers in 1980–1981 in the Maze Prison near Belfast, as the culmination of a five-year protest for recognition of the status of political prisoners. In 1980, seven prisoners participated in a two-month collective hunger strike. The second wave in 1981 represented a dramatic showdown between the prisoners and the Thatcher government leading to the death of 10 volunteers, including Bobby Sands who was elected as a member of the British Parliament before his death.[3] These hunger strikes did not gain immediate formal concessions, but they had very important consequences for the Catholic community, radicalising nationalistic politics and enabling *Sinn Féin* to become a mainstream political party (Dingley & Mollica 2007; cf. Baumann 2009).

In all these cases of self-sacrifice, we can find both the components of suicide terrorism, willingness to die and willingness to kill, in the same terrorist context, but they are not yet united in a single act: members of these terrorist organisations are willing to kill, and they are also ready to die for their cause, but they do not die to kill simultaneously.

In fact, despite an impressive growth of suicide attacks in the last years, the great majority of rebel and terrorist organisations refrain from using this method. A number of organisations can have moral or ideological constraints: they tend to see themselves as engaged in some sort of 'just war' in which some practices, such as suicide attacks, are outside acceptable bonds (no matter how objectionable these justifications may seem from the outside) or they ideologically reject individualistic actions, as most Marxist groups do. However, these normative preferences often represent soft constraints and can be easily reinterpreted, bypassed or removed (Kalyvas & Sánchez-Cuenca 2006: 213–216).

Probably more salient are constituency costs. Most rebel and terrorist organisations depend on the support not only of a hard core of those who practically assist them but also of a wider community that they claim to represent (Paul 2010). This community can disapprove of the use of suicide attacks: on the one hand, with regard to normative considerations, supporters can reject the act of homicidal suicide because they consider it as fanatical or extremist; on the other hand, in strategic terms, they can fear possibly disproportionate reprisals or an escalation of indiscriminate violence on part of the enemy, or they can be concerned about the reputation of the organisation at the international level (Kalyvas & Sánchez-Cuenca 2006: 218–219). In other words, the community of support can accept and share the ends of a campaign of terrorist violence, but not some means, particularly suicide attacks.

The experience of Northern Ireland offers some indirect evidence of these constraints: in the early 1990s, the Provisional IRA was responsible for a few 'forced' missions: it kidnapped Catholic civilians involved in work with the British security forces and coerced them to drive car bombs into British military targets without any chance of escaping (Bloom & Horgan 2008). This campaign of proxy bombs provoked widespread public revulsion and indignation, even in the Republican side, and it was soon abandoned. Interestingly, 'the nationalist community supported the self-sacrifice of the hunger strikers but rejected the notion of killing oneself deliberately or being coerced by the organization' (ibid.: 581).

Moreover, to the extent that ethno-nationalist movements (even those defined by religion) require recognition from an international community of states, often influenced by public opinion, for their ultimate success, this could create disincentives for acts of unconstrained violence. However, in some circumstances, terrorist organisations can believe that the domestic benefits of suicide missions exceed its negative international repercussions (Kalyvas & Sánchez-Cuenca 2006: 218).[4]

OFFENSIVE MARTYRDOM

The origins of contemporary suicide terrorism date back to the time of the 1979 Islamic Revolution led by Khomeini in Iran. Some Iranian religious and intellectual figures promoted an effective reinterpretation of the notion of martyrdom, crucial in the Shi'a doctrine since the death of the third Shi'a Imam Husayn in the Battle of Karbala in 680, from a religious ritual of collective sorrow and mourning to a political act of emancipation (Khosrokhavar 2002). During the Iran-Iraq war (1980–1988), thousands of young Iranian volunteers blew themselves up to clear Iraqi minefields in the service of their army; they wore a key around their neck in order to open the doors of Paradise (see Reuter 2002: chapter 3).

Combative martyrdom has a very long tradition in Islam (Cook 2007). In the Koran the word 'martyr' (*shahīd* in Arabic) refers to simple testimony (*shahāda*), as in the Christian tradition (*marturia* in ancient Greek). It was probably after the conquest of Palestine in the seventh century that this expression came to designate sacred death (Khosrokhavar 2002). The Islamic martyr became the believer who is killed in the battle against the infidels, 'on the path of God' (*fi sabīl àllah*), with the promise of everlasting rewards in the afterlife. This fight is characterised by legitimate violence and violence is bidirectional. In this sense, martyrdom is the outcome of a defeat on the battlefield. In the Sunni doctrine the concept of martyrdom is sometimes connected to the idea of *jihād* as a war against the infidels.

Clearly, sponsors and supporters of this form of violence do not accept the notion of 'suicide', in the light of a creative interpretation of the doctrine and tradition which arrives at the point of opposing common suicide (*intihār* in Arabic) as a greatly blameworthy act, prohibited by Islamic doctrine and punished with everlasting damnation, to 'self-martyrdom' (*ishtishād*) as a greatly honourable act, legitimised and encouraged by religion and rewarded with eternal salvation.

Unlike this traditional form of active martyrdom, contemporary martyrs do not usually sacrifice their life on the battlefield in order to defend their faith: in fact, they are not forced to convert. In contrast, offensive martyrdom has become a powerful weapon in a large repertoire of forms of violence at the disposal of terrorist organisations, frequently against civilian targets.

In a schematic way, three waves of offensive martyrdom for terrorist purposes can be identified.

i) *Offensive martyrdom of religious inspiration for ethno-nationalist goals*. In the early 1980s in Lebanon, an Arab country with a Shi'a majority population, the idea of voluntary martyrdom, sponsored by Iran, entered the repertoire of forms of political violence adopted by a few substate organisations, especially the Shi'a movement Hezbollah, in massive bombings against the military personnel of Israel, the South Lebanese Army (a Lebanese militia supported by Israel) and the Multinational Force (amongst others: Pape & Feldman 2010: chapter 7; Ricolfi 2006). For the first time the influential Shi'a cleric Fadlallah justified the use of suicide bombings as a form of legitimate martyrdom, opposed to common suicide, in the service of God and the fatherland (Kramer 1991). In the 1980s Lebanese suicide attacks numbered more than 30; they proved to be very effective, contributing to the

Self-Sacrifice and Martyrdom in Terrorism 139

withdrawal from the country of the Multinational Force in 1984 and the Israeli army in 1985.

This form of violence was then adopted by Hamas in 1993 and by Islamic Jihad in 1994—two Palestinian, religiously inspired organisations. From Lebanon through the Palestinian Territories, thanks to the common hostility against the State of Israel, suicide attacks entered the larger Sunni world, in combination with a radical interpretation of the concept of *jihād*. The Palestinian armed groups organised more than 150 incidents on the whole, above all during the Second Intifada (2000–2005) and mainly against civilian targets (amongst others: Hafez 2006a; Marone 2008; Ricolfi 2006).

Moreover, Chechen insurgents have been responsible for more than 40 suicide attacks against Russian targets since 2000 (Pape & Feldman 2010: chapter 9; see also Speckhard & Ahkmedova 2006).

ii) *Secular offensive martyrdom for ethno-nationalist goals*. In 1987, suicide attacks were adopted by the Liberation Tigers of Tamil Eelam [Fatherland] (LTTE), a powerful separatist organisation which sought to establish a Tamil state in Sri Lanka (Bloom 2005: chapter 3; Hopgood 2006; Pape & Feldman 2010: chapter 10). The Tamil Tigers were militarily defeated in 2009, after carrying out, according to some estimates (Gambetta 2006b: 302) almost 200 suicide attacks in the country. It is important to remark that the Tamil Tigers were secular, without any link to Islam (in fact, Tamils are mostly Hindu).

This form of violence was employed by secular organisations in the Middle East as well. The PKK (*Partîya Karkerén Kurdîstan*, 'Kurdistan Workers' Party'), a Kurdish separatist party of Marxist-Leninist inspiration, organised a short campaign of suicide attacks against Turkish targets in the late 1990s; it was responsible for approximately 15 incidents (Bloom: chapter 5; Ergil 2000; Pedahzur 2005: 86–95).

In the Palestinian Territories, suicide attacks also involved Fatah, the historic nationalistic party led by Yasser Arafat (until his death in 2004), affiliated factions (such as Tanzim) or associated armed groups (the al-Aqsa Martyrs Brigades), on the one hand; and the Popular Front for the Liberation of Palestine (PFLP), a radical Marxist-oriented group, on the other. During the Second Intifada these secular organisations decided to run after their rival factions of religious inspiration in the use of this method by pursuing a logic of outbidding in order to gain the support of the Palestinian population (Bloom 2004, 2005; Marone 2010). Despite some symbolic and rhetorical references to religion (see Frisch 2005), the aims of violence are essentially political and concern the ultimate aim of the liberation of Palestine.

iii) *Religiously motivated offensive martyrdom for ethnic and ideological goals on a transnational scale*. Al-Qaeda and other Salafi-jihadi organisations and groups have become the main perpetrators of suicide terrorism in many areas of the world (amongst others, Moghadam 2008; Pape & Feldman 2010), often against civilians, including Muslims (see Kepel 2004). In opposition to a local nationalist version of suicide terrorism exemplified by the Lebanese, Tamil, Palestinian, and Kurdish organisations, they are associated with a transnational version of suicide terrorism. This new version is not aimed at the liberation of a specific territory, but it is interested in more ambitious and elusive purposes, driven by an apparently utopian fervour, with an all-encompassing aspiration that has three components: (1) the liberation of Muslim-majority countries, 92) the reunification of those countries under an Islamic 'state' ruled on the basis of sha'ria law and 93) the reestablishment of the Caliphate and the expansion of its predominance. In Iraq the fight of the al-Qaeda network seems to be only a phase of a wider conflict; in fact, many 'martyrdom operations' were carried out by non-Iraqi Salafi-jihadi volunteers and were intended not just to remove the occupation force but also to cause the collapse of the new regime and to foster sectarian strife between Sunni and Shi'a Muslims, with an agenda beyond Iraq (Hafez 2007).

FUNCTIONS OF SELF-SACRIFICE AND MARTYRDOM IN TERRORISM

In the West, terrorist acts of self-sacrifice and martyrdom, especially suicide attacks, can provoke an immediate feeling of dismay or repugnance which does not encourage a dispassionate and accurate analysis of their motives. Sometimes they are seen as purely irrational or even crazy actions. Actually, they fulfil important functions (Marone 2008: 212–213).

In passive martyrdom, the intention is simply to die for a cause, without killing other people: the main goal is connected to testimony. Thus the primary function of the readiness to die is symbolic, concerning the communication or representation of messages. In particular, the act of self-sacrifice permits to (1) draw attention and publicise the cause; 2) reinforce the legitimacy of the cause, by expressing through this extreme choice the seriousness of the situation of perceived injustice and the relevance and genuineness of such a commitment; 3) build the solidarity of the group and of the community of support, imposing moral obligations on both on behalf of the martyrs' memory and families, sometimes by means of elaborate narratives, symbolic representations, and rituals.

Offensive martyrdom, in which perpetrators die to kill, maintains these three symbolic benefits, and adds the power of intimidation against enemies, by provoking the fear that there are no common means of deterrence against individuals willing to die for their cause. Moreover, suicide attacks show important benefits with respect to the material function of violence (the imposition of immediate physical damage). In particular, suicide attacks (1) overcome traditional security measures, hitting even highly protected targets; (2) enable one to control the time and place of the operations, increasing the chances of success and maximising the lethal nature of the attacks (see Pape 2005: (3) reduce the risks affecting the secrecy and security of the underground organisation, in particular by preventing the capture of perpetrators and organisers.

In some respects, suicide terrorism represents the translation of a symbolic performance into a reliable and innovative form of control technology (Lewis 2007, 2008): '[i]n this light, suicide bombing appears as a technological solution to a practical problem—how to make best use of available resources in order to produce a weapon system that can deliver ordnance reliably and with precision' (Lewis 2007: 224). Suicide attacks have thus become a powerful weapon at the disposal of violent substate organisations. In this regard it is important to underline that, unlike self-immolations (Biggs 2006), which are often individualistic acts, suicide attacks are usually instigated or coordinated by an organisation or group.

In sum, suicide attacks are effective in terms of benefits with respect to both the symbolic and material functions of violence; moreover, they are efficient in terms of costs because on the one hand they usually do not require particular abilities, know-how and experience from perpetrators (at least when adequately assisted by a group), or conspicuous resources, information and logistical skills from terrorist groups, on the other. This can explain the dramatic growth of suicide attacks in the last years, especially after 11 September 2001.

In offensive martyrdom, besides the symbolic value given by self-sacrifice, the connection between willingness to kill and willingness to die is tactical: in fact, the simultaneous combination of these two elements tends to maximise the benefits and minimise the costs.

POLITICAL AND RELIGIOUS MOTIVES

We can point out two main reasons that explain the relevance of the idea of martyrdom in the history of modern terrorism.

First, terrorist organisations usually rest on a deep sense of devotion to a political cause that can be perceived as more important and compelling than the terrorists' own life. As Bruce Hoffman noted, unlike the ordinary criminal, 'the terrorist is fundamentally an *altruist*; he believes that he is serving a "good" cause designed to achieve a greater good for a wider constituency—real or imagined—that the terrorist and his organisation purport to represent' (Hoffman 2006: 37, italics in the original). The loyalty to a cause is often reinforced by psychological dynamics that are typical of small underground groups. Thus, it is not surprising that under some circumstances, this altruistic attitude can turn into the acceptance or even the active pursue of self-sacrifice.

Second, by definition, terrorist organisations are in an asymmetrical position vis-à-vis the state they fight: if they had more resources, capabilities and support they could adopt other, more direct strategies, such as guerrilla warfare (see de la Calle & Sánchez-Cuenca 2011; Merari 1993). Their struggle necessarily has a strong symbolic and psychological dimension. Therefore, the resort to 'martyrdom operations', with their powerful symbolic value, is ideal in a relation of marked asymmetry, by turning a weakness into a useful resource.

The experiences mentioned in this chapter can be associated with all the 'four waves of modern terrorism' identified by David Rapoport (2004): the 'Anarchist wave' (here represented by Anarchists and Russian revolutionaries), the 'anti-colonial wave' (particularly the Lebanese, Tamil and Palestinian cases, in addition to the Northern Ireland case), the 'New Left wave' (the RAF) and in the end the 'religious wave' (al-Qaeda and other Salafi-jihadi organisations and groups). Religion has a different role and scope in each wave.

The Marxist-inspired RAF avoided any explicit reference to religion. Interestingly, in all the other terrorist organisations and groups, religion has a significant role and, looking more closely, a growing one: starting from a simple repertoire of powerful symbols, images and models of intense emotional impact, it became a factor that defined the collective identity of the groups and their community of reference and could offer a possible justification for violence, before ending as an important driving force of actions perpetrated.[5]

Anarchists and Russian revolutionaries frequently adopted a religious tone. In particular, Anarchists did not hesitate to resort to several Christian symbols and expressions in order to justify their acts of sacrifice, despite their anticlerical attitudes and their frequently atheistic beliefs. They were well aware of the symbolic and emotional power of Christian imagery, especially with respect to the themes of the sacrifice of Jesus Christ and the end of time.[6]

In the case of the Irish nationalist militants' religion, or rather religious affiliation, plays a more important role. Northern Ireland's hunger strikes were politically motivated and explicit religious references were infrequent; nevertheless Roman Catholicism was salient because it was presented as a defining characteristic of the community that the terrorist organisations claimed to represent (cf. Dingley & Kirk-Smith 2002; see Dingley & Mollica 2007).

In some respects, religion plays a similar role in the local version of suicide terrorism in which the ultimate aim of violence is territorial liberation from a foreign occupation; the driving force is essentially political (Brym 2008), even if in Lebanon and the Palestinian Territories, religion (namely Islam) exercises a pervasive public influence on society and can be evoked in order to justify violence. In particular, religious dictates can be less influential than the religious *difference* between perpetrators and victims: Muslims vs. Jews and Christians in Lebanon, Muslims vs. Jews in the Israeli-Palestinian conflict and also Muslims vs. Christians in Chechnya, Hindus vs. Buddhists in Sri Lanka and Sunni Muslims vs. Shi'a Muslims and Christians in Iraq. As Robert Pape remarked, '[r]eligion is normally more exclusive than other national differences (except for race) under the conditions of an occupation and so often becomes the principal defining boundary between an occupier and the local community' (Pape 2005: 87). In fact, religious difference reduces the room for compromise because it presents the confrontation as a zero-sum conflict and (1) enables extreme demonisation of the infidels; (2) legitimises the practice of martyrdom, bypassing the prohibition of suicide and (3) (ibid.: 89–92).

As stressed by Jeffrey Lewis, 'martyrdom is not something that simply happens—it is a constructed process'. Individuals who are willing to die are necessary but not sufficient for this process, for their deeds must be interpreted and presented if they are to become a part of public discourse. The martyrs, of course, have no control over their story after death, so, ironically, they become less important in the process of image creation than those who survive and cultivate their image. Michael Barkun calls these people martyrologists (see Barkun 2007: 119–120; cf. also DeSoucey, Pozner, Fields, Dobransky & Fine 2008; Lewis 2008: 81).

In this sense, terrorist organisations can be, and sometimes are, shrewd 'martyrologists'. Some organisations are able to promote and reinforce a sort of culture of martyrdom, shaped by a set of elements presumed to be from tradition, often of religious origin, which are revised and adapted, providing models for inspiration and emulation alongside modern techniques. As Islamist fundamentalism shows, religious tradition, symbolism and imagery are particularly suitable for the formation of a culture of martyrdom because they already include the notion of noble, legitimate self-sacrifice in the form of martyrdom.

On the other hand, the status of martyr has to be accepted and legitimised by significant sectors of the community that the terrorist organisation and the suicide attacker purport to defend. In the local version of suicide terrorism, the culture of martyrdom rests on a sort of triangular relation between the terrorist organisation, the suicide attacker and their community of reference (see Gill 2007; Hafez 2006b; Moghadam 2006b; Tosini 2009) all present in a physical area. The social dimension of suicide terrorism is crucial. Suicide attacks do not only represent a destructive tactic that is simply more effective and efficient than many others; they also have a deep collective value and significance, based on an elaborate social construction of this practice. In this view, sometimes imbued with religious themes, the suicide attacker is a martyr who, faced with the military superiority of the enemy, does not hesitate to deliberately sacrifice his/her own life in order to defend his/her community, in this way redeeming its dignity and honour. On the other hand, the community is ready to recognise this sacrifice as a form of martyrdom and revere and celebrate it through a number of collective narratives, symbolic representations, and rituals.

Suicide attackers usually present a mix of different motivations. Many candidate martyrs exhibit their religious devotion. Nevertheless, it is not easy to understand if such a claim represents a genuine motivation. Obviously the identity of suicide attackers is usually disclosed only after the achievement of their fatal missions, when, by definition, they cannot be interviewed any more. Interestingly, Jon Elster argued that 'a would-be suicide bomber might abstain from a mission if he thought it would bring about salvation without political gains or vice versa, but commit himself if both goals can be achieved'. In this perspective, 'religion is a form of consolation or a bonus rather than a motivation': 'the belief in some kind of afterlife may attenuate the psychological costs of commitment. [. . .] [R]ather than offering a positive motivation the religious and financial expectations might have the disinhibitory effect of lifting some of the normative constraints against suicide missions' (Elster 2006: 243). Elster also conjectured that in some cases, the desire to attain paradise could simply be an attitude that within the Christian tradition would essentially represent a form of simony (ibid.: 242–243).

Religion assumes a greater role in the new transnational version of suicide terrorism exemplified by al-Qaeda and several Salafi-jihadi organisations, networks, and groups around the world. Here religion and politics seem to be inextricably intertwined. On the one hand, these groups are sensitive to political cost-benefit analysis (see Sedgwick 2004); but, on the other hand, following extremist interpretations of Islam, they regard themselves as committed in a sort of 'cosmic war' (Juergensmeyer 2001: chapter 8) and reject the distinction between politics and religion, attributing the absolute sovereignty exclusively to God (*hakimiyya 'allah*). They expressly frame the conflict in religious terms.

In the new transnational version of suicide terrorism the construction of martyrdom is not linked to a sound triangular relation in a specific geographical area. Groups and militants are connected with a transnational community of support by means of modern communication systems, particularly the Internet. In their eyes this virtual community can realise the monolithic *ummah* (the community of Muslim believers) that they idealise. This lack of a direct and strong connection with the masses of a delimited territory and their concrete interests tends to reduce the constraints on forms of killing and victim selection (Kalyvas & Sánchez-Cuenca 2006: 221–223). It also contributes to an explanation of the radicalism of al-Qaeda and its associated groups.

This growing influence of religious factors is consistent with the well-known phenomenon of the revival of religion or 'desecularization of the world' (Berger 1999; see also Karpov 2010) which characterises many phenomena of our time. This complex process of de-secularisation includes a reduction of differentiation of the secular spheres from religious institutions and norms, a resurgence of religious beliefs and practices, and a return of religion to the public sphere ('de-privatisation') (see Casanova 1994). A large body of empirical evidence and arguments show that modernisation does not necessarily lead to a decline of religion, as the classical theory of secularisation assumed: Peter Berger, formerly an eminent advocate of that theory, acknowledges that the world today is 'as furiously religious as it ever was, and in some places more so than ever' (Berger 1999: 2).

The diffusion of religiously inspired suicide terrorism is connected to the rise of religious fundamentalism and is evidently part of the proliferation of religious violence around the globe (amongst others, see Juergensmeyer 2001). Several conflicts are framed more and more in religious terms: the Israeli-Palestinian confrontation is a telling example in this respect. Needless to say, faith-based radicalism represents only the 'dark side' of a wider revival of religion.

In international relations the rise of religiously inspired suicide terrorism worldwide is an important manifestation of the 'return of religion from exile' (Petito & Hatzopoulos 2003), a relevant topic overlooked until recent years (Fox 2001); in fact, the establishment of the Westphalian international order, which arose from the European wars of religion, brought about the expulsion or at least the de-politicisation of the religious element in international relations. Today we can notice a clear shift in the understanding of world politics and international conflicts, from one based on ideology (an essential pillar of the Cold War) to one more centred on identities within which religion finds a natural place (Davie 2010: 165). Huntington's controversial 'clash of civilizations' thesis (Huntington 1996: esp. 42, 47) is the most well-known reference here.

In the end, it is important to highlight that the latest development of self-sacrifice in terrorist violence, the transnational version of suicide terrorism, does not represent an anachronistic relic of the past faced with extinction, but is instead a significant part of the modern world; it implies modern processes of erosion of tradition, individualisation and global diffusion. First, despite frequent references to the doctrine and the past, Salafi-jihadi fundamentalism introduces some relevant innovations: self-inflicted martyrdom for terrorist purposes represents a substantial break with the history of Islamic martyrdom. Second, al-Qaeda style martyrdom, far from being an action rooted in a traditional Islamic community, is a deeply individualised experience: on many occasions the result of an extreme decision freely taken by an individual obsessed by the quest for authenticity in a pluralist modernity without any clear centre of gravity (see Khosrokhavar 2002). Third, terrorist organisations like al-Qaeda are active on a global scale, form transnational linkages with other like-minded movements in many areas of the world, profess an ideology that is not limited by state borders and rely on global media and communication techniques and modes to spread their messages worldwide. The role of transnational missions, migrations and diasporas is crucial. The al-Qaeda network is not interested in a specific place, but it appeals to an imagined global *ummah*, 'de-territorialised' and even 'de-culturised' to the extent that it evokes the myth of a religious purity that is constructed transcending particular cultures (see Roy 2002, 2008). In some respects, fundamentalism can be regarded as 'the religious form that is most suited to globalization, because it accepts its own de-culturation and makes it the instrument of its claim to universality' (Roy 2010: 25–26).

On the other hand, the position of al-Qaeda and other Salafi-jihadi groups is unequivocally antimodernist in the sense that it rejects and opposes the *Western* version of modernity. The phenomenon of self-sacrifice and the representation of martyrdom in terrorism illustrate this contrast very well. Today in the West, death is often seen as an event to postpone as far as possible through a hedonistic treatment of the body, an event that is more and more private, hidden, even repressed and denied (see Elias 1982). Furthermore, from a Western point of view, suicide attacks combine two types of 'bad deaths'—suicide and murder—generally deemed as 'abnormal' and socially stigmatised (Hassan 2011: 183–186). The contrast between the fascination with death and the public glorification of self-destruction for a higher cause, peculiar to 'martyrdom operations', could not be more evident.

NOTES

1. Japanese kamikaze pilots during the Second World War did not act in the context of terrorist organizations (Hill 2006).
2. For example, Ranstorp noted that terrorism studies are characterised by an inclination to focus on recent episodes, with the drawback of overlooking historical developments (Ranstorp 2009: 18, 19 and *passim*).
3. It is interesting to notice that self-starvation is an extremely demanding act of self-sacrifice, in many respects more than instantaneous self-explosion (Merari 2006: 109).
4. For example, there is a heated discussion on the international effects of suicide attacks within the Palestinian camp. In a debate on 'martyrdom operations' aired on al-Jazeera in late 2001, Hani al-Masri, a Palestinian political analyst, warned that after 11 September, international support turned against the Palestinians because of the use of suicide attacks against civilians, while Muhammad Nazzal, a member of Hamas's political bureau abroad, claimed that 'world opinion does not matter' (Hafez 2006a: 28–29).
5. However, as emphasized by Gunning and Jackson (2011), the distinction between 'religious' and 'secular' terrorism is problematic in concrete terms.
6. As historian Blaine McKinley remarked, '[C]onscious that they lived in a culture attuned to Christian language and symbols, the anarchists chose terms for their propaganda which reflected the values of the population to whom they appealed. Yet the anarchists' use of religious language was much more than a rhetorical device; it reflected a theme at the core of their thinking. Anarchists regarded history as a struggle between the polar opposites of good and evil, represented as the powers of Freedom and Authority, in which Freedom, however long submerged and defeated, must eventually triumph. The martyrs personified this conflict (McKinley 1987: 400).

Part II
Varieties of Religious Globalisation

9 Varieties of Religious Globalisation

Robert W. Hefner

During most of the 20th century, Western policy makers and social theorists confidently predicted that non-Western societies would witness the gradual privatisation and decline of their once vibrant religious traditions. The bases for this forecast were too widespread if, we now realise, erroneous assumptions: that privatisation and decline had been the fate of religion in all Western countries, and that religious modernity elsewhere was destined to replicate the secularised Western experience (cf. Davie 2001). African, Asian, and Muslim societies might be latecomers to the privatisation and decline of religion, it seemed, but they too would inevitably succumb to the secularist juggernaut (Lerner 1958).

By the time the Islamic Revolution swept Iran in 1978–1980, this forecast had begun to look *jejune*. As the late 20th century witnessed the rise of the Christian Right in the United States, a Hindu resurgence in India (Hansen 1999; van der Veer 1994), the conversion of 500 million people in the Global South to Pentecostal Christianity (Martin 2002; Robbins 2004), and, starting in the 1990s, religious revival in the People's Republic of China (Overmyer 2003), the idea that modernity and globalisation everywhere would usher in religion's decline began to appear, not just premature, but downright mistaken (Berger 1999; Casanova 1994).

The almost worldwide resurgence of religion also coincided, imprecisely but still suggestively, with the end of the Cold War and the global ascendance of market-oriented and neoliberal models of political-economic development. This coincidence raised questions as to whether there was a causal relationship between the religious resurgence and the political and economic aspects of late-modern globalisation. Some observers speculated that the religious resurgence was a societal response to the ostensible retreat of the state in the face of a globally ascendant neoliberalism. Others saw the resurgence as the welcome expression of a civil society rising in the face of a long overbearing state. Still other analysts portrayed the resurgence as a consequence of the destabilisation of once secure secular nationalisms, themselves the offspring of a secularising Western colonialism. Although no consensus emerged on the genealogy of this resurgence, analysts agreed that, contrary to earlier forecasts, globalisation was not pushing religion aside everywhere, but in many settings was actually making it stronger and more public.

The essays in the second section of this book speak to these and related questions on religion and globalisation, as seen from the perspective of varied case studies and theoretical traditions. The essays do not speak with a single voice, but together they hint at a framework for understanding religion and globalisation today.

In the first essay of this section, Peter Beyer of the University of Ottawa brings a *longue durée* perspective to bear on the question of the relationship of today's religious resurgence to foundational shifts in Western politics and religion in the early modern period. During Europe's Middle Ages, Beyer notes, Western Europe witnessed changes that set the stage for a profoundly new relationship of religion, state, and society. The changes included the establishment of semiautonomous universities, the growth of powerful urban centres and middle classes, and the expansion of church institutions and authority across most of Western Europe. The church's institutional consolidation was part and parcel of its increasing differentiation from other spheres in society. Signed in 1648 in the aftermath of Europe's religious wars, the Treaty of Westphalia might at first seem to be a countercurrent to the growing differentiation of religious and sociopolitical institutions, inasmuch as its foundational principle was that each polity should have just one religion, chosen by its ruler. As Beyer observes, however, the cultural message implicit in this arrangement was that Christian religion came to be seen as plural, and the 'possibility of a disjunction between political and religious identities continues to exist in principle and in reality'. As European models of governance were imposed on colonial possessions, the same Westphalian linkage of religion and national identity was implemented there. Beyer recognises that there were exceptions to the Westphalian model. The rise of Protestant nonconformists and free churches challenged the isomorphism of religion and state, but these and other developments never fully undermined this globalised religious arrangement.

With the worldwide spread of nationalism in the 20th century, key features of the Westphalian model were applied to countries beyond the European heartland. A Westphalian vision underpinned the rise of Zionism in the late 19th century. A similar premise informed the 20th-century emergence of Hindu nationalism, although, as Peter van der Veer and Thomas Blom Hansen have shown, this was but one stream of Indian nationalism, and a highly contested one at that (Hansen 1999; van der Veer 1994). In modern Japan and China, Beyer notes, political elites favoured a civil religious option, which, by casting religion in a negative light, came closest to breaking with the Westphalian model. Although subject to endless qualifications and localisations, the model was nonetheless 'adopted around the world'.

The pervasiveness of the Westphalian model, Beyer concludes, is what makes the present moment so distinctive. Globalisation has ushered in a post-Westphalian dynamic characterised, not by the abandonment of the

Westphalian union of religion and nation, but by its relegation to the status of one choice among several. The resurgence of religion in a post-Westphalian age, Beyer notes, has also brought about changes in religion itself. Whereas in Western Europe, religion had earlier been recast in a Westphalian mould, the new religious globalisation has created religious entities whose networks and authority stretch across multiple localities rather than being concentrated in a single homeland. Beyer cites the example of African missionaries travelling to Europe to promote Christian revival and a 'return to authentic Christianity' as a striking case in point. One could add here that, as Olivier Roy (2004) and Peter Mandaville (2001, 2007) have both shown, the Muslim world too has seen the ascendance of globalising versions of the faith whose centres of gravity are no longer linked to a neatly demarcated homeland. In these and other examples, Beyer reminds us, 'what is clearly receding is the role of individual states in disciplining' the process of religious revitalisation.

Beyer comments that another aspect of today's global religious change is the rise of more individualistic, "à la carte" attitudes toward religion. In places like Western Europe and Latin America, legal changes in the establishment of religion had to be put in place to enable this change (Chesnut 2003; Freston 2001). But the process has also been facilitated by the emergence of religious varieties that adopt an entrepreneurial approach to a liberalised religious market and compete for market share. Not surprisingly, the individualisation and liberalisation of the religious market has led growing numbers of people to distinguish personal "spirituality" from a collective and putatively coercive 'religion'. Some readers might wish to qualify somewhat this last among Beyer's generalisations. In some parts of the late-modern world, the linkage of state power to religious governance remains strong, even as religions have gone global. The linkage has actually decreased the religious options of some citizens, and channelled a hitherto heterogeneous spirituality into a more restrictively 'religionised' mould (Hefner 2011). Notwithstanding examples like these, Beyer's cogent analysis correctly observes that we are witnessing a weakening of Westphalian models and the emergence of a more varied landscape of religious governance.

Professor emeritus of the sociology of religion at the London School of Economics, and one of the most acclaimed sociologists of religion of the late 20th century, the author of the second chapter in this section, David Martin, was both a contributor to and critic of early secularisation theory. Martin's 1978 *A General Theory of Secularization* brilliantly anticipated the post-secularisation turn in the social theory of the 1990s, with its insistence that there is no single pattern of secularisation even in the West. After long years of neglect, one can note, Martin's early argument has become the foundation on which more recent research on comparative secularism is being conducted (see Calhoun et al. 2011; Casanova 2012; Warner et al. 2010). Martin's study demonstrated that the pattern of religious establishment peculiar to each of the main Western European countries reflected, not a universal process of structural differentiation (as classical secularisation theorists had argued), but country-specific, and thus path-dependent, struggles for influence and power among rival classes, political elites, and religious groupings. From the mid-1980s on, Martin devoted much of his research to what was in those years the intellectually unfashionable subject of Christian Evangelicalism. Martin went on to write two works that have become foundational references for the now booming field of Evangelical and Pentecostal studies (Martin 1990, 2002). It is the Pentecostal variety of Christianity on which Martin's present essay focuses.

Martin's concern in this chapter lies in the global expansion of Pentecostalism today. He begins by locating the phenomenon in processes similar to those highlighted by Beyer: the relative detachment of religion from state and nation, and the emergence of transnational and voluntary forms of Christianity. In its vigorous de-territorialisation and de-ethnicisation, Pentecostalism recalls the transnational voluntarism of the early Jesus movement (cf. Kee 1993). But Pentecostalism also builds on uniquely modern circumstances. In the United States, the formal separation of religious organisation from state power authorised, not only religious voluntarism, but fierce denominational competition that undermined any effort at religious establishment. Competitive denominationalism became the dominant form of religion in the United States, and its religious impulse was no more vigorously expressed than in Pentecostalism.

Martin notes that this American-born brand of populist Christianity was also distinctive in that it fused 'white' and 'black' varieties of revivalism. In so doing it generated a cultural heat that, at least during the early phases of each new church's organisation, 'melts down distinctions of colour, gender and class'—even if these have sometimes harshly reasserted themselves later, when, as with the North American Assemblies of God (see Poloma & Green 2010), once marginal communities move up the social and ethnic ladder. Even after the luminous effervescence is gone, the contours of a religiously enabled transcendence remain visible below the faith's surface, and revivalists and nonconformists may later try to restart the fire. Its rediscovery by new generations of believers helps to explain why, when Pentecostalism arrives on distant shores, it often escapes from the organisational ambitions of its official carriers, including those who hope that believers in the Global South might neatly align with North America's conservative Christians.

It was processes like these that brought Pentecostalism to Latin America, the first continent beyond the United States in which the Pentecostal movement took on society-transforming proportions. Today about 12% of Latin America's population is Protestant, and perhaps two-thirds of those are Pentecostal (Freston 2008). Pentecostalism took off in Africa a few years later, and today claims more than 100 million followers (Meyer 2004). Pentecostalism has displaced African Independent Churches as the primary institutional rival to mainline Christianity. Since the 1990s, varieties of Pentecostal Christianity have also gathered momentum in mainland China, although the more populist varieties often borrow from indigenous Chinese spiritualities based on healing and mediums (Bays 2003; Chen 2003).

In the end, what does the Pentecostal surge say about religion and globalisation? In the early years of the Pentecostal boom, some observers argued that the faith's diffusion was primarily a by-product of North-American hegemony. As with their Evangelical cousins, some in the Pentecostal community do benefit from ties to American sponsors, and in everything from hymnals and dress styles to Southern accents and savvy media skills, one can still see North-American influences today. However, the culturally porous and hybrid aspects that have marked Pentecostalism from the beginning have not disappeared, and even as it creates a new global ecumenical Pentecostalism—indeed, even in its Prosperity theology, which scholars have shown to be more varied than earlier thought (see Coleman 1995; Maxwell 1998)—they take on strikingly local hues. These qualities are amplified by Pentecostalism's emphasis on reading the whole Bible, not just the New Testament, and in emphasizing gifts of the Holy Spirit for healing, speaking, and making oneself new.

Pentecostalism's hybridity is also reinforced by the fact that, as Martin puts it, 'Pentecostalism is about being moved, body and soul, and being ready to move'. Although it has comfortable middle-class devotees in Singapore and Lagos, the faith takes root especially widely among migrants and the aspiring poor of the Global South's mega cities—people in need of islands of dignity and civility in the midst of a raging social storm. Notwithstanding the lip service most Pentecostals pay to the patriarchal family, Pentecostalism also thrives for reasons of gender. As Bernice Martin and Elizabeth Brusco have both observed, the politics of the family in many Pentecostal communities works on the basis of a bold patriarchal bargain: wives acknowledge their husbands as the head of the household, but the husband is enjoined to stop drinking and carousing so as to spend time with his wife and children. By providing scope for female spirituality in religious studies and healing (but only rarely in church leadership), the church also offers believing women an expanded, if not formally equal, role (Brusco 1995, 2010; B. Martin 2001).

As Martin points out, the Pentecostal appeal only resonates where 'a world of spiritual animation remains intact', which is to say, where much of the populace addresses moral and existential needs by way of religious imaginaries. Once thought the precursor for all of religious modernity, but now recognised as a special-case-in-itself, Western European societies have largely preempted this style of appeal, except among immigrants and marginalised minorities. For Europe's older Christian denominations, ties to the state and the bureaucratisation of church administration created an enduring social hegemony, but one which has proved incapable of competing with the secularist ideologies of left, right, and consumerist romanticism (Campbell 1987).

The next two chapters in section II of this volume assess the situation of Muslim immigrants in Europe. Their situation presents a striking contrast with the Christian globalisation at the heart of Martin's essay. Unlike mainline

Christianity, the Sunni variety of Islam to which some 85% of the world's Muslims adhere has neither a formal ecclesiastical structure (a 'church') nor a centrally appointed clerical hierarchy. The lack of a centralised authority has meant that Muslim communities have often been marked by a significant interpretative heterogeneity on matters of religion, not least being those that concern the boundaries between religion and local culture. However, like Judaism, Islam places great emphasis on scholarly religious learning. Religious scholars and the madrassas in which they pass down traditions of knowledge provide an intellectual and organisational skeleton for the Muslim community, even in the absence of an institutionalised clergy (Berkey 1992; Hefner 2009; Hefner & Zaman 2007). In premodern times, these scholarly networks, and the scripturally oriented variety of Islam to which they gave rise, were particularly influential among the lettered middle and lower-middle classes. At the social and geographic margins of the Muslim community, and among tribal people and the illiterate poor, Sufism and less scripturally based varieties of Islam have thrived, including those that have incorporated local spirits into popular observance (Bowen 1993; Hefner 2010). The great social transformations of the late 20th century brought Muslim lands significantly higher rates of literacy; beginning in the late 1960s, the changes also ushered in new and more popular varieties of religious revitalisation. Although the pattern varied from country to country, and although they did not preclude popular interest in updated forms of Sufi mysticism (see van Bruinessen & Howell 2007), these developments also greatly increased the Muslim public's interest in scripturally based piety and Islamic law.

The recent emergence of newly globalised Islam has complicated this story considerably. Today, almost 40% of the world's Muslims live in societies that have a non-Muslim majority. In Western Europe, where most of today's Muslim citizens are either immigrants or second- or third-generation offspring of immigrants, the challenge of religious learning has been compounded by two facts. First, although a network of mosque-based congregational leaders (imam) has been put in place over the past two generations, a system of Islamic schools, whether madrassas or some more hybridic variety, has yet to be put in place in most countries (the UK being a notable exception), at least on a scale commensurate with the needs in the general Muslim population. As Martin van Bruinessen (2011) has recently observed, in the absence of a settled educational establishment, debates have raged over what type of Islamic learning is appropriate for Western European Muslims. A second difficulty is that, as John Bowen and Peter Mandaville have both noted (Bowen 2009; Mandaville 2007, 121–32), across much of Europe a generation gap as regards religious matters has emerged. The gap pits older immigrant parents, who practice their faith in a manner consistent with their remembered place of birth, against a new generation of European-raised youth who see the Islam of their elders as ill-informed and out of date, and thus ready for replacement by Islam beyond ethnicity and local space. Combined with the higher rates of education and expanded social horizons of European Muslim youth, as well as European protections for freedom of religion, these circumstances have created a fiercely competitive religious marketplace among European Muslims.

It is just such a pluralised environment on which Synnøve Bendixsen trains her attention in her chapter on localised and globalised Islam among young Muslim women in Berlin. With some four million Muslim citizens, Germany has the second largest Muslim population in Western Europe (after France). As elsewhere in Europe, in Berlin different Muslim groups claim to represent Islam, and local professions of the faith draw on complex mixes of urban, national, and global religiosity. Nowhere is this competition more apparent than in associations organised to recruit Muslim youth. Many among the young faithful explore their faith independently of the mosque leaders (imams) and associations at the centre of the established Muslim community. Young people also rely on the German language as well as European associational models to organise their meetings and conduct public debates. Well-educated and upwardly mobile, the young are eager to discuss how to be religiously observant in a European setting 'without embracing all aspects of the secular environment'. Many young women also use their piety to declare a measure of independence from their tradition-bound parents. But they also find that their parents are more likely to grant them that freedom when they adopt the headscarf.

Young women's use of Islamic websites adds to this self-selected but networked religiosity. The women are familiar with the more famous among the new Islamic transnational authorities, including established figures like Yusuf al-Qaradawi and bold reformers like Tariq Ramadan. But they are often drawn to less famous figures, especially those who address 'urgent issues that the youth experience in their everyday life'. The vision of modernity that results from this rich social mix, Bendixsen concludes, is one that combines Western commitments to education and career fulfilment with visions 'dissimilar to [. . .] Western models' in their emphasis on 'deep religiosity'. The contrast Bendixsen so vividly highlights would perhaps be less striking in the United States, where immigrants and residents are almost equally likely to be religious.

Els Vanderwaeren's study of Muslim women of Moroccan origin in Flanders provides a fitting complement to Bendixsen's chapter. In Flanders, too, young Muslims encounter a dizzying variety of forms of Islamic observance. For many believers, this poses a problem. For those aspiring to piety one has to determine 'which aspects of Islam are contextual and negotiable [. . .] and which are essential and universal'. As with Bendixsen's Berliners, many Muslims in Flanders 'have come to realize that they can no longer rely solely on the established religious authorities to understand and explain their religion', not least on matters relating to women and piety.

Among Muslim youth in Flanders as well, it seems, 'More people are claiming the right to interpret the religious resources personally'. However, Vanderwaeren shows that the individualisation of religious interpretation is counteracted by the widespread conviction that Islam has what are supposed to be universal and divine normative ideals (see Cook 2000). The challenge is to devise and agree on methods for identifying them. This responsibility cannot be fully individualised, many people believe, lest it lose all authenticity. Young women thus come to explore their faith collectively. But they do so, not in the established confines of the mosque or older religious associations, but in informal home settings, 'outside the direct scope of the androcentric orthodoxy'. In seeking out religious rulings on matters important to their lives, many women also prefer to 'choose from [. . .] different outcomes [. . .] one that corresponds with their hearts'. Vanderwaeren's case study highlights a mode of religious individualisation still intimately bound to a perceived need for collective and scriptural moorings.

The last two essays in this section take aim at different religious traditions and different aspects of religious globalisation. Tulasi Srinivas uses the concept of cultural translation to examine the way in which the well-known neo-Hindu movement known as the Sathya Sai has managed to appeal to followers in diverse national settings. The movement has created a form of multicultural cosmopolitanism different from that of Western liberalism, but still cosmopolitan. One key to this success has been Sai Baba's willingness to draw from religious traditions as diverse as Sufism, Vaishnavite and Shaivite Hinduism, and Christianity. 'Sai Baba has created a divine persona that is nomadic in spite of [. . .] the fact that traditional Hinduism [. . .] has no proselytisation mechanism'.

The movement's spiritual exuberance can only be saved from being perceived as incoherent by the believers subscribing to one additional premise: the idea that Sai Baba is himself divine. Without this confidence, the embarrassment of spiritual riches and the lack of a systematic theology make the movement's cosmopolitan pretensions absurd. In all this, there is what Srinivas calls a 'strategic ambiguity' that 'allows for a polysemic symbol and a multiple interpretation of any image or event'. But the polysemy of meaning resonates with believers only inasmuch as they are convinced that the riot of meanings borrowed from diverse religious traditions is in reality a spiritual garden of Sai Baba delights.

Louise Müller offers a final variation on part II's themes of religion and globalisation. Müller looks at Ghanaian films to assess changing attitudes toward religious pluralism among an ethnic group known as the Akan, a fair number of whom have today emigrated to the Netherlands (cf. Meyer 1999). Ghana's population of 16 million is made up of some 70 ethno-linguistic groups, but Akan dominate the country's film industry. Many Ghanaian films treat spiritual themes, notwithstanding the fact that, in addition to ethnicity, the population is divided along Christian, Islamic, and indigenous religious lines. Each religious community has its own filmmakers. But there is a striking contrast in the ways in which religious communities consume these religiously themed films in Ghana as opposed to in the Netherlands.

In their native Ghana, Akan audiences tend to take in all types of films, including those dealing with faith traditions other than their own. This cinematic pluralism reflects the fact that tribal chiefs still enjoy considerable authority in Akan society, and the chiefs emphasize religions' commonalities rather than its differences. Here, in other words, is a tradition- and chief-leveraged model of West African pluralism. In contrast to this native Ghanaian multiculturalism, Akan immigrants to the Netherlands show no such inclusiveness with respect to cinematic taste. They avoid films oriented towards a religious community other than their own. Indeed, in general in the Netherlands, the immigrants interact less extensively with Ghanaians from other religious communities than is the case in their ancestral homeland.

Part of the reason for this difference in religious sociability, Müller explains, is that the institutions of chiefly authority have lost their influence among Netherlands-based Akan. By contrast, globalised religious institutions, particularly those of a Pentecostal Christian variety, have gained influence. The churches offer 'an alternative sense of belonging than that of being part of an ethnic African minority', one that works to integrate African immigrants into 'a global Christian community that includes Caucasian Europeans'. Indeed, Christian and Muslim Akan 'form separate religious groups whose Akan members interact more with other Muslims and Christians than with other Akan people'. Social life in the Netherlands, it seems, has undermined an earlier, indigenous Akan pluralism. The cultural shift has left immigrant Akan more integrated with their Dutch fellows, but also more religiously apart from Africans of other faiths.

What can we conclude from the parade of religious differences we see in these essays? The first and most obvious conclusion is that, contrary to the forecasts of an earlier secularisation theory, modern forms of migration, communications, and economic integration have not led all late-modern societies down the slippery slope to religion's privatisation and decline. In all but Western Europe's tired Christian communities (Davie 2000), religious citizens have discovered the will and the way to reshape themselves in the new global macrocosm. To take the term 'resurgence' too literally in describing this phenomenon would be misleading. In most cases, it is not a question of old religions feeling fresh and alive once again, but of new religious actors taking advantage of late-modern modes of communications, association, and self-identification to make something new. Young Muslims in Berlin and Flanders find the village-based Islam of their elders ill-informed and out of date. Pentecostal Christians in Latin America profess their allegiance to an authentic Christianity, but in doing so they make an end-run around established church hierarchies. So too with Srinivas's Sai Baba: although an offshoot of devotional Hinduism, this movement circumvents established masters and temples to open its ranks to people from all faith backgrounds. Neither a simple resurgence nor revival, all these are examples of late-modern religions' reimagination and reorganisation.

A second point follows from this first. It is that the most successful of today's religious currents are those that put aside the pattern of established religion, with its learned virtuosos and done deals with rulers, and open the religious field to a wider public. Although sometimes understood as religion's 'democratisation', this shift can be ambiguous in its political and ethical effects. As religion has 'gone public', the process has fragmented religious authority and given once marginal believers access to new forms of spiritual authority. But not all new religious publics tolerate religious minorities or dissenters. No less important, many among the new religious traditions push aside established hierarchies to reassert exclusions of their own.

A third and final point follows from all this. It is that, notwithstanding the errors of classical secularisation theory, secularisation is a real social phenomenon, and research on its genealogy and locations should remain an important part of our understanding of religious globalisation (see Calhoun et al. 2011). All around the modern world, religious discourses have been repositioned or recast in fields like biomedicine, engineering, military training, and mass communications. In these technical fields, modern Muslims, Hindus, and Christians have embraced practices and discourses the internal logic of which is predominantly secular. If, by secularisation, we mean the reorganisation of a once-religious field without direct reference to religious authorities or meanings, then secularisation has indeed taken place in many modern social fields, even in societies otherwise in the throes of religious resurgence. In fact, over the long term, one of the most vexing challenges to citizenship and public culture will be how to facilitate civil coexistence across organisations and arenas animated by divergent ideas on religion and secularity (see Bowen 2003, 253–238; Rosenblum 2000; Wuthnow 2004, 12–17).

To be analytically useful, however, the concept of secularisation has to be separated once and for all from modernization teleologies that assume that the decline of religion is uniform and inevitable. Secularisation can and does occur, but not usually as a tsunami-like force that sweeps evenly across the social landscape. Rather, as David Martin (1978) recognised a generation ago, secularisation and religionisation often proceed simultaneously and unevenly, reflecting the contingent accommodations reached by different social groupings in diverse social fields (cf. Casanova 1994; Gorski 2003; McLeod 2003). Classical secularisation theory's tendency to see secularisation as a unitary and society-wide force was based on the confidence that a growing differentiation of structures, roles, and meanings is intrinsic to modern social life. Social differentiation generates cultural and cognitive pluralisation, and this pluralisation undermines shared belief systems while favouring the autonomy of the individual. "Unless we can imagine a reversal of the increasing cultural autonomy of the individual, secularization must be seen as irreversible" (Bruce 2001:262).

When religion and modernity are viewed from a global perspective, however, it is easy to find many examples of such reversals. As the case studies in section II of this book have illustrated, modern social differentiation unleashes, not just individualisation, but vigorous contests to create new publics, new fields of socialisation, and new terms of admissions to and exclusions from religious communities. There is no imminent end to religion's history. Religious re-figurations of this sort will remain at the heart of global modernity for some time to come.

10 Religion in the Contemporary Globalised World
Construction, Migration, Challenge, Diversity

Peter Beyer

RELIGION RESURGENT AND PROBLEMATIC IN THE EARLY 21ST CENTURY

Over the past few decades, we have witnessed a change of attitude with regard to the category of religion, not just in the academic circles dominated by Western observers, but also in much public discourse in countries as diverse as the United States, South Korea, France, Russia, India, and Canada. Restricting myself for the moment to the academic manifestations, in many disciplines, such as political science, sociology, and international relations, religion has for the first time in a long time ceased to be completely ignored and become a topic that is actually deemed worthy of study over the last couple of decades. In disciplines whose specific purview has always been religion, notably religious studies and the sociology of religion, there has been an important shift in the basic reigning assumptions about religion. Where the former used to treat religion as a domain that was *sui generis*, if somewhat isolated and set apart from and to some extent at odds with the (modern) social world in which it occurred, there has since the 1980s emerged a strong trend in the discipline emphasizing the embedded and even dependent character of religion in its social, economic, political, and cultural contexts. Critique, if anything, has moved from society to religion itself, even to the point of seeking to deconstruct the category completely and dissolve it into the generally social, cultural, and political (see, e.g., Fitzgerald 2000; McCutcheon 1997). The sociology of religion, in comparison, has deliberately sought to move itself more into the centre of the overall discipline and has in the process abandoned in almost wholesale fashion the secularisation paradigm which once directly or indirectly informed most of its endeavours (cf. Berger 2001; Stark & Finke 2000). Now exceedingly few talk about the inevitable weakening or disappearance of religion, and places like Europe, where institutional religion is quite weak, are the exception (Davie 2003), the rest of the world being comparatively religious.

A number of concepts have arisen in various disciplines to lend expression to the new understandings. We are, for instance, witnessing 'religious resurgence' (e.g., Westerlund 1996; Zeidan 2003), 'desecularisation'(Berger

1999), 'resacralisation' (Shimazono 2008), a 'spiritual revolution' (Heelas 2002), even the 'revenge of God' (Kepel 1994). Or we are said to be living in a 'post-secular' age (Habermas 2010) that includes the rise of 'post-materialist' religion (Inglehart 1997). Perhaps the most widespread expression of this reassessment is contained in the idea of 'fundamentalism' (Marty & Appleby 1991–1995), a word that better than most combines within itself the idea of a 'religious comeback' with an implicit nostalgia for the former 'secular age' (cf. Hammond 1985). Indeed, fundamentalism seems to designate the kind of religion that the observer feels is somehow 'out of its place' or 'out of its time'. Consonant with this meaning, almost all the other concepts take the form of negative designations: through the prefixes 're-', 'de-', or 'post-', they define themselves more in terms of what they are not than in terms of what they are. The notable exception is the idea of the 'spiritual' replacing the 'religious'.

The fact that the meanings of these concepts that are currently dominant have risen in popularity in various disciplines only over the past three decades immediately raises the suspicion that they correlate with specific historical events which have led people to question their previous assumptions about religion. And indeed, such seminal events are not difficult to isolate. Virtually none of this debate happened before the very late 1970s, a time when three semantic and one set of religious events took place. The latter includes, in the first instance, the Islamic Revolution in Iran, and the rise of the (New) Christian Right in the United States; but also, at the same time, or the decade thereafter, a string of others, such as the Nicaraguan Revolution, the sharply increased prominence of religious Zionism in Israel after 1977, and the Khalistan movement in Punjab. With a small bit of hindsight, we can also locate in this period the beginnings of the rise of Hindu nationalism, with the founding of the Indian Bharatiya Janata Party (BJP) in 1980. The year 1979 also marked the Soviet invasion of Afghanistan, which, as we now know, set off a chain of events that led to the rise of the Taliban in the 1990s. On the semantic side, the late 1970s marked the beginning of the solid emergence of the concept of *globalisation*, the rise to prominence of the word *fundamentalism* applied globally to many religious tendencies outside the American conservative Protestant fold, and the popularisation of the notion that we are living in a *postmodern* era or that there existed an increasingly important postmodern condition (Lyotard 1984).

In terms of historical events, however, there is also another side to these positive demonstrations of religious muscle. If terms like 'postmodernism' and 'fundamentalism' already exploded as descriptive terms in the 1980s, globalisation had to await the 1990s for this to happen. Without question, the intervening set of events that paved the way for globalisation in its move from a technical term in business, political science, and sociological literature to an everyday mantra on virtually everyone's lips was the almost complete disappearance of the avowedly atheist and secular Socialist world after the fall of the Berlin Wall in 1989. In a few years, the Soviet Union also disappeared, its surrogates in Eastern Europe crumbled, and the 'capitalist roaders' in the People's Republic of China carried the day. In the absence of a credible rival, global (neoliberal) capitalism—essentially the most widespread meaning of the word, 'globalisation'—appeared to have become the 'only game in town'. The antireligious Socialist alternative lost credibility as a defining identity for a great many leftist political parties and for oppositional nationalist and subnationalist movements in most parts of the world.

In the subsequent two decades, most of the former militantly atheist countries witnessed a noticeable return of religion, but this was of such modest proportions that, by itself, it would probably not have brought about talk of a de-secularised or post-secular world order. Two kinds of development were undoubtedly more influential. First of all, there was the continued and even increased prominence of 'fundamentalist' tendencies in many parts of the world during this time. To a certain degree, they filled the vacuum in terms of what could replace the 'other' of the liberal democratic state and global capitalism (see e.g., Juergensmeyer 1993). Second, however, there was the post-World War II transnational migration. From about the mid-1950s, and increasingly over the remaining decades of the 20th century, most of the rich countries in the world (eventually including the oil-rich countries of the Middle East) accepted significant numbers of long-term migrants both temporary and permanent, from other parts of the world, sometimes as refugees but especially as economic migrants. While some of these countries, notably the colonial settler countries of North America and Australasia, had a long history of immigration, the difference even here was that the sources of migration were now predominantly from non-European regions. Among the effects was the introduction into all these countries of the much greater presence of what almost everyone perceived as cultural and religious 'others'. A prevalent question that has arisen in consequence is how these various countries are to respond to the novel presence of these minorities. Their presence and growth has come to be seen as something ranging from an 'opportunity' and a 'challenge' to a 'problem' and even a 'threat'. Hence, the often controversial questions of 'multiculturalism' and 'religious diversity'. Moreover, the two developments, fundamentalisms and religious diversity as the result of migration, have inevitably been connected in the minds of many observers, especially in the sense that both have tended to be embodied by Islam much more than any other religion.

A number of aspects need to be emphasised in this context of shifting observations. First, there is the simultaneity of semantic, institutional, and concrete historical developments. The former seek to make sense of the world in the context of the latter. Another is that the primary social unit of observation in all this has necessarily come to be the globe or global society, rather than, or in addition to, a territorially delimited state or national society. And finally, while religious events are not the only ones that signal a transformed state of affairs, religion is nonetheless seen as a key domain for understanding the transformation, and more often than not as a problematic

162 *Peter Beyer*

one. Together, these aspects point to certain assumptions and even self-evidences that inform the prevailing observation. These obviously include assumptions about the core categories involved, especially religion, state, and society; but also about the relations among these categories, relations informed by other categories which appear in the compound terms beginning with post-, for example, 'secular' and 'modern'. It is to the assumptions embedded in these words that I want to turn, not in an entirely abstract way, but rather through constructing a historical narrative parallel to the one I have just outlined for the last 30 years.

RELIGION, STATE, WESTPHALIA, AND GLOBALISATION

The story is a portion of, and a variation on, a very well-known one: (Western) European society, from somewhere after the beginning of the ninth century Christian Era, gradually emerges from its Dark Ages and undergoes what is often called a renaissance. This story of rebirth is multidimensional, including political, artistic, religious, economic, technological, and intellectual aspects, among others. Institutionally and semantically, a number of related yet also independent developments were happening in tandem. Important among these are the emergence of a plurality of political state units rather than another empire, the foundation and growth of universities as somewhat independent intellectual centres, the increasing power and independence of cities as economic centres, the development of law, and the solidification and increasing power of a Roman Christian Church that is more and more effective in all parts of Western Europe. This last dimension is critical: during this long period, the renaissance is being carried by this peculiar religious institution as well as in others that are increasingly developing in a, by comparison, nonreligious direction. Often, renditions of the narrative document the increasing power of this church in these other secular domains. Here, I want to emphasise how this religious institution was also able to exert a greater and greater say over what exactly was going to count as religion, and to foster those peculiar institutional forms of religion that it sought to control (see, e.g., Délumeau 1983; McGuire 2008; Nelson, 1969). This differentiation of religion, as something institutionally and semantically distinct and selective, is just as important for the story as the way the Church exercised its influence in state, law, university, and city. These other institutions, in turn, can be seen as engaging in a parallel activity of self-definition and self-aggrandisement just like the Church. Moreover, the interrelations of these various institutional dimensions manifest themselves in a significant degree of mutual institutional modelling. Just as state/secular law develops in parallel and in competition with ecclesiastical law (Berman 1983), just as the Church felt the need to construct itself also as a state, so did science within the universities bear a similar relation to theology, and art developed its more and more independent forms in large part under the sponsorship of the Church which, in turn, saw this art as a necessary form of its own expression. To be sure, all these developments had various antecedents in older semantic understandings and institutional forms, such as in the Roman Empire and Roman law, Greek philosophy, Christian theology and Episcopal and monastic ecclesiastical structures. Discontinuity can only happen on the basis of continuity. What was different in the period under discussion is the degree to which this functional differentiation became dominant in European society, and the level of power that the resulting institutions eventually afforded their carriers.

In the current context, the key chapter of the narrative begins with the Protestant Reformation. To a large extent, the aim of the main reformers was the purification of religion and the reform of the ecclesiastical institution. The Roman Catholic reform later in the 16th century had much the same aim, only in a different way. From this perspective, therefore, the Reformation was all about the further differentiation of religion, understood as Christian religion. The mutuality of differentiated institutional development, however, assured that this complex religious event would become implicated in other, notably political, transformations as well. The (absolutist) rulers of various states related to the Reformation movements in various ways: some seeking thereby to assert their independence of the Roman Church, others to consolidate their authority over their realms by taking sides, yet others to further power rivalries among their royal houses. The question that could not easily be answered, however, was what would be the more precise relation between religion and state? How would their differentiation be expressed both politically and religiously? The unintended outcome was a series of protracted and violent conflicts, most notably the 16th-century French Wars of Religion and the 17th-century Thirty Years War. The latter ended in the Peace of Westphalia of 1648, a set of treaties that expressed the development of a model answer to this question.

The famous formula of Westphalia, *cuius regio, eius religio*, is both revealing and deceptive. On the one hand, it seems to enjoin that a realm or political territory should have one religion: that all the people in a state should have the same religion. It also states that the ruler, to whom the realm is deemed to belong, is the one to determine that religious identity. The 'secular' (in political terms, 'sovereign') power trumps the 'religious' power. Indeed, political science has seen solidification of the idea of state 'sovereignty' as the central and most important legacy of the Westphalian treaties (see, e.g., Tilly 1992). On the other hand, the formula implicitly contains, if not a contradiction, then certainly a permanent ambiguity. If the ruler is to determine the religion of the realm, then that implies that there is a *choice of religions*. The formula therefore assumes that religious and political identity can be something different and therefore that there exists a plurality of religions alongside the plurality of realms or states. The Westphalian formula, in other words, carries the implicit assumption that religion is its own differentiated domain, and just as importantly that religion comes in the plural—religions (cf. Despland 1979; Harrison 1990). And it tries to resolve this ambiguity by giving to political power the task to reconcile the matter, to contingently and locally dictate a degree of de-differentiation through the regulation of religion. Nonetheless, if religion does come in plural units, if people within the same political unit *can* have different religions, then the possibility of a disjunction between political and religious identity continues to exist in principle and in reality, no matter what the ruler decides. This, in turn, leads to the creation of another consequential idea, namely, that of a religious minority, the dissenters and nonconformists, the religious others within the realm who in this context become a problem which one has to address, especially through forms and degrees of toleration.

Another implicit assumption in this scenario runs as follows: if, in addition to why religion should be conceived as a plurality of distinct units, one asks why a plurality of religions should be problematic for these Europeans, then the immediate answer is that religion had become a prime source of violent conflict, and something had to be done about that. Yet there is a deeper assumption that lies behind the conflicts; religion as understood by these Europeans is clearly something very foundational. It is, as later 20th-century formulations will put it, a matter of ultimate concern, the source and condition of social cohesion. Religion is a way of life that self-defines as having no limits to its jurisdiction. On this understanding, the only way to have more than one religion peacefully coexisting is to limit them in some other way that is not religious, meaning secular almost by definition. The Westphalian formula inserts the territorially delimited and sovereign state, specifically the ruler of the state, in this role as the secular regulator of religion; doing so, however, encourages the conditions in which religions will structure themselves as somehow analogous to states. That is a consequence of the partial de-differentiation implied in the formula. This confluence of understandings was going to have consequences in subsequent centuries, especially as Europeans began to extend their power and influence to eventually cover the entire globe.

If all these developments had remained restricted to European society, the narrative would probably be of relatively little interest for my concerns here. Quite the opposite was the case, however. As already indicated, the shift within European society to a sociostructural domination of these functionally differentiated institutional domains (Luhmann 1997) allowed the Europeans to develop modalities of economic, political, scientific, technological, and indeed religious power which both motivated them to a correspondingly multidimensional expansion of their presence and influence around the world, and provided them with important conditions for succeeding at these enterprises. They engaged in this expansion equipped with their peculiar and often newly developed cultural understandings, including their idea of religion. They had come to understand religion as a differentiated domain and as something that occurred as religions in the plural; they further saw different religions as associated with different peoples or social groups, an older tendency very much reinforced by the Westphalian formula and its implicit understandings. Accordingly, as they expanded their power beyond the European subcontinent, they sought to understand the people that they encountered in terms of these understandings. They looked for and in many cases 'discovered' not only peoples, but also the religions of these peoples (Masuzawa 2005); they also tried to expand their own religion, something that by this time they actually called Christianity (Smith 1991).

A further conceptual development, especially as of the 18th century, was a gradual shift in the European understanding of the state. Whereas at the time of the treaties in the mid17th century, this word still referred by default to territory ruled by, and as an expression of, single, usually absolutist, rulers, over the next two centuries one witnesses a fateful change toward the idea that states are, and should be, the instruments of collectivities, of peoples, of nations. The American and French Revolutions famously sought to put this idea into force, but so did, in a slightly different way, the Glorious Revolution in England and then the many nationalist movements from Eastern Europe to Latin America in the 19th century. The invention of the idea of the nation-state has a number of consequences, one of which is that, in tune with Westphalian logic, it is the people who will determine the religion or religions of the state. A second is that a nation requires a state for its expression just as a state is the expression of its nation. In other words, Europeans came to assume that the cultural idea that the world is divided into distinct cultural units called nations or peoples correlates with the division of the world into political units called states. In this context, religious identity and nation-state identity came to be seen as self-evidently related, even if the precise nature of this relation was not thereby also already determined. Moreover, the continued understanding that religion is in its essence foundational, that, to borrow from Durkheim and Simmel, it was critical for social solidarity or making social order possible (see Durkheim 1965; Simmel 1971), encouraged the institutionalisation of another Westphalian assumption: a state needed something foundational to hold it together, to integrate its society. Whatever that was would be an identified and institutional religion, or something religious in the sense of being observable as such without thereby being considered an actual religion. Out of this confluence of understandings, quite a number of variants developed in different states. There were state or established religions that were defined as the religions of nations and therefore of their states. England, Russia, and the Scandinavian countries, as examples, had these. There were national religions, meaning the religion deemed to be inherent to the identity of the nation, whether these were established as state religions or not. This was one of the main contending ideas in 19th century-France and eventually in Italy after unification. There was, however, also another possibility, namely, what Rousseau in *Du contrat social* originally called civil religion, a kind of national ideology whose role was to provide the necessary foundational cohesion even if the members of the nation were in fact allowed, or already had, diverse religions. The United States and the 'other' France embodied this idea. Admittedly, few observers actually called this option religion; and in some instances, especially France, the name given it was eventually what appeared as the opposite of religion, namely, secularism, here *laïcité*. On the Westphalian model's logic, however, it worked like religion and had many of the symbolic and ritual accoutrements of, as Rousseau put it, a 'religion of the heart' (Rousseau 1977). Its deemed necessity was Westphalian and, like state and national institutional religions, it also created the conditions for the identification of excluded 'minorities' and national 'others'. Another way of understanding this variant is to note that established religion could be replaced by established secularism, but that such secularism, being the reverse image of religion, not only depended on the existence of religion for its meaning, but also, as a foundational 'way of life', necessarily took on some of the apparent characteristics of religion (cf. esp. Asad 2003).

What sometimes ended up operating in a religious way under the Westphalian logic was therefore not always institutional and differentiated religion. This varied from state to state and within states over time. Conversely, the institutionalised state churches also did not subsume all that religion became within European society and its coloniser societies of the Americas and Australasia. The Westphalian solution does not undo the differentiation of the political state and religion; it is more a case of the differentiated rationales of state and religion conditioning one another in the way that each operates. This is in part what I mean by modelling. Accordingly, just as the state is institutionally far more than its relation to religion, so does religion construct itself as far more than what might come under the heading of state or national religion. In particular, the Roman Catholic Church maintained and enhanced its transnational profile, continuing as a quasi-state-centred and complex organisation, seeking and gaining recognition as a minority religion where it could not be the national or state religion, expanding itself beyond the confines of European states through its extensive missionary efforts, and acting as host institution in social domains such as education and health. By the 19th century, many of the state Protestant and Orthodox churches had joined in the missionary initiatives. At least as important as the established or national religions were the numerous Protestant dissenting or free churches, as well as other movements that dated from the Reformation era, such as the various Anabaptist movements. That these were in many cases variations on the state or established church model is evidenced in their characteristic structure of incorporating their members, as it were, in their religious entirety: church membership and national citizenship were in important ways quite analogous. Their status as variants is also manifest in their typical fate when they managed to become dominant or co-dominant in the coloniser states of North America and Australasia. Here, either there never was a state church or attempts at establishing a state church did not properly succeed. One of the most consistent outcomes was that these countries created what one might call denominational, 'shadow', or mainline establishments consisting of Protestant or Protestant and Catholic churches (for Canada and the United States, see Clark 1948; Herberg 1960). Here as well, there were more central and more marginalised groupings, with the latter being disadvantaged to various degrees, just as minorities or dissenters were in European states. Although the Westphalian principle in its strict sense was thus significantly modified, the underlying logic held: these were also all 'Christian nations' within the boundaries of their territorial states, and the religions within them were structured in key ways like subnational groups.

The fate of the one non-Christian religion that was significantly present in European countries further completes the picture. This is Judaism. Jews had been more or less marginalised in all countries throughout these centuries. With the development of the differentiated institutional structures and their semantic correlates, Jews and Judaism could rather straightforwardly fit into the model of a people and its religion. In fact, not much had to change with regard to the understanding of Jews when compared with pre-Westphalian centuries in Europe. The Westphalian logic, however, manifested itself with peculiar clarity in 19th- and 20th-century Zionism, a movement that resulted in the founding of the correspondingly Westphalian state of Israel. It is notable that the case of Israel reproduced all the inherent ambiguities of this model, including the question of religious minorities and their toleration, the way that nation and religion were inextricably linked but also in certain ways at odds, and the generation of a contested 'civil religion' (Liebman & Don-Yehiya 1983) founded as a variant of secularism.

The complex case of Jews, Zionism, and Israel points to the question of the globalisation of this model over the last two centuries. Israel is in one way a typical European nation-state, and yet it is not geographically in Europe. In the light of the contested nature of Israel, one could see it as evidence of the difficulty of applying the Westphalian logic outside of Europe and its settler societies. I would suggest, however, that the opposite is the case: the conflict surrounding the state of Israel is so intractable precisely because the Westphalian logic has been appropriated and institutionalised in the formation of sovereign states all around the world since the 19th century, albeit not without very important variations. Opponents of Israel assert that the realm, the 'regio', does not belong to the Jewish people with its religion, but rather to another people, the Palestinians with their religion or religions. And the two-state solution advocated by many is simply the creation of two states on the Westphalian model. A look at some other examples, especially in Asia, will make clear that this is not an isolated case.

The term 'Hinduism' was invented by Western orientalist scholars in India after the late 18th century (Chatterjee 1995). It was, however, local Indian elites during the 19th and 20th centuries that took up this idea and attempted to reconstruct and reimagine the complex South Asian religious culture as containing a number of religions, including Hinduism, Jainism, and, eventually, Sikhism (Oberoi 1994). These historical reconstructive efforts have remained only partially successful, but the existence of these religions is now institutionalised in a number of ways, including in the political and legal structures of independent India. Historically, the construction of the religion of Hinduism by Indians was also congruent with the rise of both Indian and Hindu nationalism (Joshi 2002). A key debate during this rise was very explicitly about the relation between religion and nation, with Hindu nationalists arguing that there existed an isomorphism between being Hindu and being Indian; while the dominant forces in the nationalist Congress movement sought to style this option as destructive 'communalism', substituting their own multireligious 'secularism' as the only viable option (Pandey 1992). Their direction can be seen as the equivalent of seeking to develop a civil religious version. Parallel Muslim movements, however, were never convinced, insisting that the Indian state would always be a Hindu state by virtue of the Hindu majority, making Muslims an inevitable minority. Both Muslim League and Hindu Mahasabha took the Westphalian logic for granted. Partition in 1947 institutionalised the Westphalian model in Pakistan (and then also Bangladesh) almost by definition. Sikh nationalism sought to repeat the process for Punjab and Sikhism. India has inherited the model with all its ambiguities. These were to some extent held at bay during the Nehru years but came back thereafter, especially with the new ascendancy of Hindu nationalism in the late 20th century (Jaffrelot 1996).

The cases of China and Japan are quite different, but not as much as might appear at first sight. Aside from the aborted effort to develop Confucianism as a state religion around the time of the 1911 revolution (Hsiao 1975), modernising Chinese elites generally favoured what amounts to a civil religious option, on a Confucian or a Communist model for example (Jensen 1997). The Maoist era represented the temporary victory of the latter option, and a version of this is still the official ideology of today (Beyer 2006). Like French *laïcité*, this Chinese model continues to relate to institutionalised religion negatively, although in China, all institutional religion consists de facto of 'religious minorities' and disadvantaged ones at that (MacInnnis 1989). Japan's trajectory, by comparison, is rather more overtly Westphalian. Here, beginning in the late 19th century, modernising elites promulgated State Shinto as the national religion, but insisted that this was not an institutional religion, that, like all civil religions, adherence to its tenets and practices was a matter of patriotism and not religion (Thal 2002), and that those entities that were recognised as religions were relegated to effective minority status. Similar to the Chinese case, Japan accepted the originally Western category of religion while considering it as something suspect, not foundational, and inherently corrosive of social solidarity if not kept in check through a state civil religion. In this context, it is important to underline that a state is following a Westphalian model if it establishes a national or state religion on the basis of the identity of this religion with the people of the nation. It is also doing so, only in mirror image, if it sets up a civil religion and defines this in opposition to institutional religions. One of the prime symptoms of this latter option is that the state sees it as being of vital importance to insist on its own secularity and *therefore*, somewhat paradoxically in the circumstances, on the need to control religion specifically in its institutionalised and differentiated forms.

The case of Indonesia in the post-World War II era gives us yet another variation on the Westphalian model. The establishment, under Sukarno but especially under Suharto from the early 1960s on, of the Pancasila ideology as the official state ideology is in many ways a construction that parallels what had happened in Maoist China and Imperial Japan. Pancasila has been an explicitly state and nationalist ideology that distinguishes itself from institutional religion while recognising and seeking to control religions. The difference from the Chinese and Japanese cases lies in the civil, religious 'reference' religion: not (reconstructed) Confucianism or Shinto, but quite straightforwardly Islam, with an echo of Christianity. In addition, Indonesia is very positive about religion and its foundational quality for social order, for the state, and for the nation. Under this ideology, everyone must have a religion (until relatively recently, one of five), failing which one is deemed suspect as a citizen. This is the reverse of the Imperial Japanese situation but with a strictly analogous logic.

Other examples could be given, but these should be enough to demonstrate the varied ways the Westphalian model has been adopted around the world. A number of qualifiers are nonetheless necessary. The first is the clearly contingent and even arbitrary nature of many of these arrangements, whether in Europe or elsewhere. That contingency is demonstrated in the fact that, in most cases, the relations between religions, nations, and states have not remained the same over time, something that the various European cases, like those of Britain or France in the 19th century or that of Japan in the 20th-century post-World War II could amply illustrate. A second qualifier is that the very existence of minorities or dissenters points to the perpetual need for the model to, as it were, encompass what it cannot properly encompass, to include the excluded in ways that seek to have them adopt a form analogous to the dominant ones as a condition for being tolerated. This is the ambiguity I have been stressing. A third problem flows from the second one: much that could be recognised and enacted as religion in all these countries largely escapes, or is only marginally included in, the differentiated religious system as constructed and incorporated into the Westphalian arrangements. Words like 'superstition'; 'cult'; 'esotericism'; and perhaps most significantly, the currently popular meaning of 'spirituality' point to such phenomena. In other words, no matter how one constructs religion more precisely as a differentiated system, such a construction is always going to be contingent, open to the possibility of doing it differently; and some of that contingency is going to be reflected in the seemingly troubling existence of a range of phenomena that look like religion but are not quite counted as religion. All these qualifiers together, of course, mean that the Westphalian model for constructing religion in relation to the parallel construction of political states is by no means set in stone. It can change, it has in various respects been changing historically and around the world for quite some time—one might even say already from 1648 onwards—and it may be that the era we are living in at this moment is evidencing changes that would justify us in beginning to speak explicitly of post-Westphalianism or, to paraphrase Lyotard (1984), of a post-Westphalian condition. That said, the complex changes over time might also convince us to locate such a post-Westphalianism well before the current time, much as the process to which the neologism globalisation refers can be seen to be both a very recent development and one that has been going on for a long time. That possibility aside, in what follows, I want to concentrate on post-Westphalianism as a more recent phenomenon, signalled, for instance, by the changing observation of religion that I discussed at the outset.

A POST-WESTPHALIAN CONDITION AND A POST-WESTPHALIAN STRUCTURING OF RELIGION

What Post-Westphalian Does Not Mean

Post-Westphalianism in this context does not mean that the Westphalian arrangements are being superseded by a revolutionary and new set of arrangements. The relation between Westphalian and post-Westphalian is a little like the relation between the neologism of globalisation and the older idea of modernisation: more a matter of the reconsideration of the latter term than a question of substituting the former for the latter. Globalisation implies the end of a single modernisation and instead yields talk of multiple modernities (see, e.g., Eisenstadt 2002), such that the old modernisation becomes at best one option among several. Thus, a post-Westphalian condition will only negate the seeming necessity of the Westphalian structuring of religion, leaving open the possibility of the continuation of Westphalian arrangements as a contingent or reflexive choice only, one that will appear as particular, without a claim to universality. A second caveat is that we cannot at the moment have any real idea of what the positive characteristics of post-Westphalianism may eventually be. The language of 'post' already says this. Therefore, instead of talking about characteristics of a post-Westphalian condition, I only want to talk about intimations. A final denial is in some ways the most important. Post-Westphalian is not the same as post-secular or desecularisation. If anything, it may be pointing in the opposite direction, namely, that the post-Westphalian condition, in providing for a de-linking of state and religion in a much more radical way, marks a further secularisation of state and society, provided that we do not think of secularisation as the necessary weakening or disappearance of religion and that we include civil religion within our observations.

The Post-Westphalian and the Post-Secular

A good way to begin is to compare the idea of a post-Westphalian condition to the idea that we are entering a post-secular age. The main difference in the two terms is, of course, the word secular. If we are in a post-secular age, then we must at one time have been in a secular one—that is, meaning non-religious by definition. Conversely, a post-secular condition must be *comparatively* more religious, or at least religion has to have a more prominent place. The idea of post-Westphalian distinguishes itself in that it focuses, not on which sphere, the secular or the religious, is stronger or strengthening, but on the relation between the secular and the religious, on the ways that the secular—here, in the first instance, the state and the nation—and the religious are constructed in relation to one another.

A more concrete outline can begin with the sort of events that I discussed at the beginning and that seem to be instrumental in generating talk of a 'post' situation. I put aside the religio-political movements dubbed 'fundamentalisms', and concentrate instead on those developments dependent on transnational migration and the resultant greater religious diversity in a number of, mainly rich, Western, states. The increasing presence of religious others within the bounds of the nation-state introduces new forms that end up challenging Westphalian assumptions. The United States and several Western European countries can serve as examples. The former, of course, has a long history of incorporating and structuring religious plurality, including the religions of those newly migrated, along what have been called congregational, denominational, and organised lines. There is strong evidence to suggest that this tradition is continuing with the current increase in religious diversity brought by the 'new immigrants' (see Warner 1993; Yang & Ebaugh 2001). What is, however, intriguing in the current context is the apparent movement in the United States to alter an aspect of American civil religion, namely, to expand the religious identities through which one can be American—hitherto, to cite Herberg, Protestant-Catholic-Jew (1960)—to include all 'Abrahamic faiths', most specifically Islam (cp. Haddad & Esposito 1998). This is a way of saying that the dominant religion of the American nation in the Westphalian sense is being recast as an Abrahamic one. If the process continues, it will amount to including in the religious majority something that is or was one of the religious minorities, and this in turn begs the question of the limits of such majoritisation. Will Hindus be included (cf. Kurien 2007)? What about Buddhists, Sikhs, Wiccans, and Scientologists? Projected forward, I suggest, this development is an 'intimation of a Post-Westphalian condition', one in which the critical distinction between majority/national religion and tolerated national or religious minority loses its cogency and above all its self-evidence. In that sense, it decouples religion and nation/state within the peculiarly American variant of the Westphalian model. The implication is that, as the process continues, one can increasingly be American without being of a particular religion and, above all, without being particularly religious.

Perhaps the most striking aspect of Western Europe's response to the new religious diversity introduced through postwar immigration is the prevalence of Islam in the equation. It is not at all going too far to say that when many Europeans say 'religious diversity', they mean Islam; and when they say Islam, they see a problem. To some extent that is the case in all Western countries, but it is especially so in Western and Central Europe. If one then asks what is so problematic about Islam in Europe and, through Islam, about religious diversity, then the much-discussed idea of a European Islam is probably indicative. Embedded in this discussion are a number of assumptions. These include, first, that Islam isn't already European[1]—by itself an idea with strong Westphalian resonance. Conversely, there is the often implicit assumption that for Islam to be or become European, it has to restructure itself more along the lines of the established Christianities that, even if vicariously or as a chain of memory (Davie 2000; Hervieu-Léger 1993), currently dominate in European countries. In these countries, on a Westphalian basis, the secular is also deemed to trump the religious. A third assumption, therefore, is that Islam supposedly does not accept this Westphalian subordination and also does not accept being a minority religion; that is why it has to develop a European identity and structure that allows both. An intimation of post-Westphalianism would in this case be that this insistence on Islam becoming European will appear highly contingent, not at all self-evident, and that Islam will successfully resist the pressure to conform.

The third set of events, namely, the fall of avowedly atheist but nonetheless civil religious Socialism/Communism points in a parallel direction. The iconic dismantling of the Berlin Wall as harbinger of the virtual elimination of the Socialist option represents, among other things, the removal of a strong set of staunchly secularist Westphalian variants. In its wake, Westphalian logic has immediately asked, what will take its place? Will it be secular or religious nationalisms? Will it be Islam? Will it be Huntington-style (Huntington 1996) imagined civilisations? A post-Westphalian intimation would be to ask, why do we need a replacement? A post-Westphalian stand would not be post-secular so much as it would be post-secular/religious. If there are post-Westphalian intimations in the European and the post-Socialist cases, then these would be twofold. First, that in a few cases a Westphalian solution does not even appear on the horizon, cases like China or Great Britain; second and much more importantly that the several attempted Westphalian solutions appear anodyne, controversial, or downright oppressive. Countries as varied as Russia, France, the Netherlands, Germany, and India would fall under this latter heading. They distinguish themselves in how careful they feel that they have to be in reasserting a Westphalian order. Thus, the Russian Orthodox Church has a renewed special place, but one is careful not to give it any real privilege and at least to pretend not to 'minoritise' other religions. Muslims in countries like Germany, the Netherlands and France are no longer told openly that they are simply foreigners or excluded minorities (as Turks in Germany were in principle and practice not so long ago), but that they have to integrate or to adopt local values. And when the Swiss ban minarets or the French pass laws against Islamic women's clothing, they do not exactly meet with understanding and approval from other countries or from all quarters of their own populations. The intimation of post-Westphalianism is therefore the relatively greater difficulty one has in self-evidently continuing to pursue the Westphalian model, including in the name of the nation, and in defence of a civil religion.

The Post-Westphalian Remodelling of Religion

Post-Westphalian intimations from the side of the secular, from the side of the state, are only one part of the thesis. Just as important are developments on the side of religion. These include some of what has already been discussed, like religious changes attendant upon intensified transnational migration or the rise of 'fundamentalisms'; but these are, from the perspective of religion, not so much the main events as developments that make a greater number of observers aware of religion and the changes happening in this domain. The more consequential transformations would be ones that have more to do with the form of religion—with its remodelling—than with the way religion impinges upon nonreligious domains.

We can begin an analysis of these changes in form by looking at other aspects of the religious developments just discussed. Here I mean in particular the degree to which they demonstrate how religions are crossing and even ignoring state and other boundaries in multiple and more intensified ways. Although religion transcending political boundaries is far from new in human history, the Westphalian model *is* relatively new. The religions are themselves to a large degree the product of construction and reconstruction over the modern centuries—and this to an extent, but certainly not entirely, following a Westphalian logic. Their reconstruction has, in that context, also been transnational and increasingly global. With the increasing globalisation of communication and thus of connectivity around the world over the past century, and especially since the end of the Second World War, religions have more and more extended themselves globally such that their centres of recognised authenticity and even authority now lie in multiple places, and not just or not necessarily in their historic 'heartlands' (Beyer 1998). One can certainly see this process happening in the case of Christianity and its many subvariants, as, for instance, when Ugandan and American Episcopalians struggle internally over the direction that the Church of England is to take; when African missionaries go to the European Christian heartlands to 'return authentic Christianity' to those who sent them the message in the first place (Adogame 2000); or, when a worldwide Pentecostal movement grows rapidly, has no recognisable centre, and yet is by its own narrative and activity single and global. It is possible today to make a cogent case for Christianity precisely shifting its predominant centre of gravity away from the historic heartlands in the Global North to the Global South (Jenkins 2007), and that includes the still quite centralised Roman Catholic Church which is now arguably moving to the sort of transnational stance that it had before the Westphalian era (Casanova 2001). The case of Islam, while very different in the details, is analogous. The centres of authenticity for this religion are not just in Saudi Arabia, at al-Azhar in Cairo, in Pakistan, or in some other country. They are, on the one hand, in a great many countries and in no country (cf. Beyer 2007). It is legitimate to talk about a very convergent and clearly defined global Islam whose centre is everywhere and nowhere, including in cyberspace (cf. Roy 2004). Similar cases can be made for Buddhism and to a lesser extent for Hinduism, Sikhism, Jainism, and Judaism. Yet this de-centring of religions does not also mean their effective de-construction as single social institutions. Each one of them still has an enacted unity that is carried by their adherents, albeit not a unity founded on centralised orthodoxy or even any uniform orthodoxy at all (Beyer 2003). And in all these developments, what is clearly receding is the role of particular states in disciplining, let alone regulating this process. The states in this process are, and probably have been for some time, fading, but *only* in this Westphalian sense (cp. Rudolph 1997); as institutionalised and systematised modalities of power, they are as strong as ever, if not stronger, unless one insists that this is to be measured by their 'Westphalian' role.

Consonant with this process of de-centring and globalising, there appears to be another sort of development which, again, has probably been happening for some time, but which has also accelerated significantly since about the middle of the last century. This is a tendency in many, though not all quarters, to individualise the practising of religion, to, for instance, practise 'religion à la carte', to engage in a Luckmannian 'bricolage' (Luckmann 1967), what Ingelhart calls 'post-materialist religion', what Troeltsch already called 'mysticism'(Troeltsch 1931), and what is reflected in the current focus of some scholars on 'lived religion' (Hall 1997; McGuire 2008) or 'popular religion' (Parker 1996). The relatively recent rise of the word 'spirituality' (Flanagan & Jupp 2007) to express religion that is individual, experiential, nonauthoritative, and even nonnormative—and this in explicit contrast to collective, dogmatic, and authoritative 'religion—would be another manifestation of this development. Just as remarkable, however, is that this change does not necessarily negate or replace the institutionalised religions; a great deal of this process of individualisation is happening 'within the religions', as people, who otherwise have no trouble identifying themselves and being identified as adherents of one of the religions, participate in and reproduce these religions selectively, in many cases intensively, very often only occasionally and often not exclusively. If one were to look at this process only from the perspective of the individuals, then one could well regard it as a shift of religion from the collective to the individual. From the perspective of the religions, it might appear worrying for some authorities but would not really constitute much of a threat to the regular reproduction of that institutionalised religion. If coming to church, mosque, or temple to engage in ritual activity is not all that some individual may do to express their spiritual selves, they nonetheless do help reproduce the institutional religion by that activity. If they do it only once or twice a year, the result is the same because many others are doing the same thing. To be sure, there are still around the world a great many exclusivists, people who not only identify with only one religion, but make sure their religious practices, their spirituality, is exclusively carried out within the operative boundaries of that religion. These are the people that probably still attract the attention of most observers. But even here, the process of individualisation is happening for a great many.

Considering these various phenomena together, what is most important in the present context is the degree to which they question the self-evidence of the Westphalian assumption that religions, states, and national identities—'peoples and their religions'—'naturally' overlap to a high degree. What this suggests is that religion as an institutional domain may be modelling itself less than under the Westphalian regime on the state and, conversely, that the state will be modelling itself less on religion as the institution responsible for the foundational unity and identity of the state-centred society. If this mutual modelling is lessening, what alternative sorts of modelling might be taking place?

State and religion are not the only strongly differentiated institutional systems that dominate in contemporary global society, just as the mutual modelling that I have been describing under the heading of the Westphalian model is not the only relation between systems that has been important. Religion, for instance, has also modelled itself on science, styling itself at times very explicitly as a kind of scientific knowledge with different sources. That has been going on as long as and longer than the Westphalian relation between state and religion. Analogous long-standing relations of modelling have existed between religion and art, medicine, and education. What may be comparatively new and thus a stronger intimation of a post-Westphalian condition developing is religious modelling on the basis of economics and mass media, two systems that are in the popular and much scholarly imagination most closely associated with globalisation.

Current sociological observation of religion is a good place to start with respect to the possibility that religion may be modelling itself more on economics and less on the state. A type of theory of religion that has risen to strength only in the last 30 years is the religious economy or rational choice theory such as that championed by Rodney Stark and Roger Finke, among others (see, e.g., Stark & Finke 2000). In this theory, religion behaves like an economy, consisting of suppliers and consumers, products which are marketed, religious firms, competition, monopolies, capital, cost-benefit relations, and so forth. An intriguing feature of this theory is the degree to which it appears to be quite cogent and revelatory, on the one hand, and quite limited on the other (Young 1997). This combination makes sense in a condition of increasing post-Westphalianism; the theories and their impressions are intimations of this post-Westphalianism. Thus, on the one hand, one can suggest that the apparent cogency of these theories is rooted in the fact that in certain cases and in certain places, religions have begun to model themselves on capitalist enterprise. The reason that the theory works best in the United States is then because American religion has for some time been more entrepreneurial than religious in other parts of the world. Correspondingly, the reason that the theories are less cogent in other parts of the world, and especially for other periods, is because religion has not been modelling itself on an economy in those places and times. Therefore, in the contemporary world, where the theory seems to be most applicable or interesting, is not just the United States but various other countries like China, Brazil, or South Korea—places where certain forms of religion have manifestly attempted to take on some economic modelling. Such modelling allows them to behave more like private corporations than public and national institutions, permitting an easier transnationalism and a lesser tie to local national identities.

Similar observations suggest themselves for the modelling of religion on the mass media system. Since the early 20th century, religion around the world has gone beyond the mediation of writing and print, entering radio already from the 1920s and television from the 1970s (Hoover 1988). It has since manifested itself in all the subsequently developed electronic media. This is not just a neutral matter of putting 'old wine in new skins'. Just as writing and print radically changed what religion became once these media were introduced beginning some 2,500 years ago, so we should anticipate that these electronic media are affecting the reconstruction of contemporary religion along lines that, among other effects, redefine the range as well as the nature of religious communication (Dawson & Cowan 2004). Radio preachers, televangelists, and now evangelists of the blogosphere are the tip of another iceberg. Beneath the visible surface that they provide, participants can, much more radically than before, pick and choose what they want, where they want it, and in what combinations. Such religious communication not only escapes authoritative religious institutions; it takes place across whatever social boundaries one might imagine. For a long time, religious communication has been in part translocal and then transnational. Mass media religion dissolves or ignores such effective boundaries even more, although clearly not entirely. The result can only be a greater de-localisation of religion, especially as concerns Westphalian nation-state boundaries. It could also mean a greater fluidity of the boundaries of the religions themselves insofar as the Westphalian boundaries have been instrumental for this purpose over the past two to four centuries. This includes confessional and denominational boundaries which, as I have argued, are variations on the state religion rather than something completely different. In this regard, Stark and Bainbridge's 1970s analysis of the idea of 'cult' into audience cult, client cult, and cult movement (1985) may be instructive, but not in the way that they imagined. Rather than such cults being the precursors to the formation of the next churches, they may actually be a stable and continuing form of religion which mass media are ideally suited to carry. Again, however, none of this obliterates or transplants the Westphalian arrangements, but it does contribute to their further contingency, as one possibility among others.

LIVED POST-WESTPHALIAN RELIGION: AN ILLUSTRATION FROM MUSLIM YOUTH IN CANADA

In a research project carried out in Canada by myself and several colleagues between 2004 and 2006, we sought to discover, among other aims, how young Muslims who have grown up in Canada related to the religions of their heritage (see Beyer 2007, 2010; Ramji 2008a, 2008b). The results of this research are relevant to my arguments here in several ways. These young adults are an integral outcome of more recent transnational migration. Their inherited religion is thoroughly global and has a long history of such globality; Islam also has a significant history of incorporation into Westphalian models in numerous modern nation-states. In Canada, however, Islam is a minority religion. As young adults born in 'diaspora' but of 'heartland' origins, the participants in the research incorporated within themselves the question of multiple centres of authenticity and authority. They are also among those with strong transnational connections, especially through electronic mass media. With respect to them, therefore, it is relevant to ask to what extent they practise their religion in what I have been calling Westphalian and post-Westphalian modes.

One of the more remarkable consistencies among this group of young Muslims is that they shared a strong sense of what constitutes Islam and religion. Most of them understood religion as a way of life centred on clear rules: moral, ritual, and otherwise. Islam for them was centred on the five pillars and on a corresponding moral code that featured caring for one's fellow human and a disciplined personal life. Most of them were from moderately to highly practising. Those who were not still shared this view: in significant majority, then, they converged on a widespread global model of Islam.

This Islam, however, was not centred in one place more than another. They stressed the global *ummah* and the oneness of Islam, but they refused to locate this Islam as belonging more in one country or region than another. In fact, a great many of them expressly distanced themselves from an association of their inherited, usually national, culture with Islam; they also consistently criticised this melding in their parents. Correspondingly, relatively few of them felt that it would be easier being a Muslim in a Muslim-majority country, as compared with Canada. Several of them went so far as to declare Canada a more conducive place for practising their religion than Muslim-majority countries where, as it were, a Westphalian religio-nationalism would be enforced on them.

A number of prevalent features corresponded to this basic position. With respect to religious authority and authenticity, almost all of them declared that it was they, as individuals, which were responsible for understanding and finding true Islam. They did not receive this as tradition, passed on by religious authorities or their families and simply carried on by them. In almost all cases, they felt that they had to reconstruct Islam for themselves using a variety of sources and resources at their disposal, including their parents and relatives, a great deal of direct consultation of the Qur'an and Hadith, literature and Internet sources of all kinds. They looked for and found trusted sources, but they did this through their own critical faculties. They did not generally favour sources from one country over another. Like the medium as a whole, their Internet sources were selected and used in an almost entirely de-localised manner; it was the quality of the source as they understood it that mattered, not its location. In consequence, their Islam tended to be highly individually understood in a de-localised manner, even if it was not individualistically practised and practised almost entirely very locally.

On the whole, these Muslim young adults felt very comfortable living in Canada. They were well aware of being part of a demographic, religious, and cultural minority. Yet that minority status did not reflect itself in a sense of considering themselves Canadian citizens who didn't belong as much as the Christian and European-descended majority. They insisted that, even if Canada was still a majority Christian country, and even if Christianity still had a privileged status over other religions, they and their religion belonged just as much—but not more—than any other. Almost all of them valued not just a plurality of religions in Canada but gave a positive assessment of religious *pluralism* as an inherent good: as a condition that enabled Islam rather than inhibiting it. Correspondingly, for the most part they did not see themselves as fatally 'caught between two worlds', whether religiously or culturally. One might even say that they led hybridised lives if that did not imply the existence of self-evident and more natural purities that would be the subject of such hybridisation (Beyer 2005).

Perhaps one of the more notable features among this group of young Muslims is the virtually total absence of an expressed political Islam. In fact, very few indeed made any connection between religion and state, let alone between nation and state. This, of course, accords well with their valorisation of religious pluralism in Canada as elsewhere. Political Islam around the world, in spite of protestations to the contrary, is almost always centred in and on a particular state. These young Muslims did not make that connection and located genuine Islam away from and in abstraction from any particular state or even the state in general.

CONCLUSION

The question of Westphalian and post-Westphalian constructions of religion is a way of asking in what directions we are headed as concerns what religion will be. Are we witnessing the progressive deconstruction of religion in the form of systematic institutional entities? Are we heading much further down the road of a radical individualisation of religion? Or are we, as a result of these reconstructions, heading down the road of a more religious world? My argument in this presentation has been 'yes' and 'no' to all three of these questions. Deconstruction may be happening, but it is more a matter of loosening the hold of Westphalian assumptions about religion. This loosening may allow religions to appear less solid as regards the form a religion takes; but they show no signs of taking over. A 'spiritual revolution' (Heelas 2002) is consistent with the continuation of 'strong religion' (Almond, Appleby & Sivan 2000). Individualisation, while undoubtedly a real and strong trend, is probably best seen as the other face of reconstruction: as the old forms become less dominant and less sure, the individual perspective offers a way of looking at religion without having to adopt those old forms as the standard of what will count as religion. The change of optic reflects more the greater difficulty of observing self-evidently in the old ways than it does a shift of religion from the institutional and collective to the individual and private. And finally, whether we are inhabiting a more or less religious world may be a question that reveals more about the insecurity of the observer in his or her old assumptions than it does any measurable change in degree of religiousness, whatever this latter may mean.

If the thesis of an incipient post-Westphalianism does not allow a clear answer to such questions, that may not be the most important conclusion that it implies. The post-Westphalian thesis, in pointing to a greater manifest contingency of substantive religious forms, also indicates the contingency of assumed religious function. Undoing Westphalian self-evidence means that it is less and less possible to take for granted that, whatever form religion (and the state) takes, it is no more important in providing the foundation of social order and life than any other institutional system. Religion can be structured to be foundational and integrative, or not. It is not necessarily, except historically, the name for the basis of social cohesion, for the guarantor of meaning and the prophylactic against corrosive anomie. In the post-Westphalian condition, religion can appear as well as be nonfoundational, even instrumental; and if it is deemed to continue to represent the whole, then the whole will be just another part. And that includes 'the secular' and 'civil religion'.

NOTE

1. The long history of Islam in what is generally considered to be Europe (see, e.g., Al-Azmeh & Fokas 2007) notwithstanding, there is a strong historical sense in which the idea of Europe defines itself over against Islam. See, as a classic locus, Henri Pirenne (1957).

11 Voluntarism

Niche Markets Created by a Fissile Transnational Faith

David Martin

CONTESTED SITES: ORIGINS AND CULTURAL PROVENANCE

Pentecostalism belongs to the modern era of global communication, though it reaches back through Methodist traditions of holiness to Pietist forms of devotion that initially arose in territorial churches before also operating outside them in 'free churches' (Stephens 2008). It represents the most recent phase of those missionary traditions that first emerged over three centuries ago in an earlier phase of globalisation in Germany and England, and then in North America. Effectively, it is the alternative mode of missionary action to the one inaugurated by mainstream religious bodies at the major Edinburgh Missionary Conference of 1910.

Pentecostalism, or something like it, emerged in many parts of the world in the decades immediately before and immediately following the beginning of the 20th century, including places as far apart as India, Wales (in 1904) and Kansas (in 1901). It was in that sense multicentred in its origins, and some writers on Pentecostal history are keen to stress these varied sources. This is at least in part to counter other writers, some of them with political concerns, who are equally keen to argue that Pentecostalism represents the global diffusion of a peculiarly American style of enthusiastic Christianity. In the view of these latter writers, some of whom think well of such a global diffusion while others do not, Pentecostalism is an extension in religious form of American cultural power (Dempster, Klaus & Petersen 1999; Micklethwait & Wooldridge 2009).

These contradictory accounts of the origins of Pentecostalism indicate how contentious practically all aspects of Pentecostalism have been from its beginnings until now, though the ferment of debate was perhaps particularly violent at the beginning of the 1990s when my own overview of its progress in Latin America first appeared (D. Martin 1990). Indeed, to suggest anything positive about Pentecostalism at that time was to take one's academic life in one's hands (B. Martin 2011). This was because the expansion of Pentecostalism, which first took off in Latin America from about the middle of the 20th century, coincided with the rise of liberation theology and base communities. Pentecostalism was therefore cast as a form of counter-revolutionary religion covertly supported by the CIA, although it was also argued, for example by Anthony Gill, that the motives powering liberation theology included the need to preempt the evident appeal of Pentecostalism as well as the threat of Marxism (Gill 1998). It was not entirely clear in the heat and smoke of ideological controversy whether Pentecostalism was a response to liberation theology or the other way round, or indeed whether both were generated in the main by the condition and aspirations of the impoverished masses in Latin America.

Beyond this background of misery and aspiration there was the curious mix of traditions in Latin America for which Catholicism provided a potentially unstable sacred canopy. Reform, or at least change of some major kind, was waiting to happen, and when change occurred it took two different but in some ways complementary as well as contradictory forms. The Marxist analyst Roger Lancaster has made precisely this observation in his work on the varied appeals and social constituencies of liberation theology and Pentecostalism in Nicaragua (Lancaster 1988). Certainly the two movements fished in the same pools of discontent among the same classes, though perhaps the liberation theologians appealed to a constituency that was more sophisticated and better off (Burdick 1993).

Mainstream Protestants in Latin America were also critical of Pentecostalism, partly because it had succeeded in challenging Catholic hegemony in a way they had not, but also because of its inspired character, which could be regarded as regressive and could even plausibly be linked to a recrudescence of native American spiritism. Mainstream Protestants were provoked in particular by the spectacle of religious showmen trading on mass susceptibility to the miraculous in a world where modern medicine was only intermittently available and misdiagnosis all too common. For centuries the Virgin Mary and syncretic cults of the saints had dispensed what Protestants regarded as illusory consolations and healing powers. Now similar consolations were dispensed by supposedly 'Protestant' religious organisations like the flamboyant Universal Church of the Kingdom of God with its holy hustlers providing an uncomfortable mirror of the style associated with the Brazilian urban scene.

So Pentecostalism can be presented and understood, often polemically, both as an emanation of modern American cultural power and a manifestation of indigenous and very ancient sources of spiritism (Bastian 2003). It is simultaneously ancient and modern, alien and indigenous, and precisely these potent contradictions emerged when Pentecostalism took off in Africa a little later in the 1970s and 1980s. There was something to be said for both points of view, because Pentecostalism does indeed fuse the global and the local, and links the deep deposits of the religious past with the characteristic forms of a thoroughly modern faith, especially in its enthusiastic embrace of technology. A combination of very ancient and very modern is part of what lends it such widespread appeal. Depending on your criteria, and on how you evaluate the overlap with charismatic Christians generally,

Pentecostalism now embraces some quarter of a billion people, from persecuted house churches in Iran to megachurches in Buenos Aires, Singapore and Nigeria, and it does so precisely because it fuses varied elements to leap over hitherto impassable cultural barriers.

CONTESTED SITES: ORIGINS AND EXPANSION

Whatever the varied global origins claimed for Pentecostalism, it is clear that a special and mythic importance is attached to the religious explosion that took place under the aegis of a black preacher in Los Angeles in 1906 (Wacker 2001). Quite soon after that there was a starburst of missionary activity, often following trails laid down by preachers of holiness fanning out from Britain and the United States (Anderson 2007; Bergunder 2008). Similar charismatic manifestations also occurred in Chile and in Korea (Buswell & Lee 2006). The Chilean revival is particularly interesting because of the way it illustrated the mingling of the global with the local, of American missionary activity and Chilean appropriation. The American missionaries were Methodists and had not succeeded in making much impression in Chile. Then a revival occurred with manifestations like those attendant on early Methodist preaching in England and frontier America. The missionaries reacted as many in the established churches of England and America had reacted a century or more before when faced by Methodist revival. They sought to moderate what was happening and retain control, only to be faced with a lively local church controlled by Chileans which turned out to be remarkably successful. The Methodist Pentecostal Church is now ubiquitous in Chile and has hundreds of thousands of members.

It seems that even if the initial seed is dropped by Americans, which is by no means always the case, Pentecostalism is far more likely to take off under local auspices following local inspirations. It was, after all, black catechists rather than white missionaries who were mainly responsible for the original diffusion of Protestant Christianity in black Africa. It also seems that Pentecostalism, or some mixture of Pentecostal and autonomous Evangelical enterprises, has succeeded in achieving the goal of 'inculturation' long sought by the mainstream Christian bodies. That is because Pentecostalism fused black-and-white revivalism from its inception and so became preadapted to a wide range of global cultures.

The argument about whether Pentecostalism is an American export or a new expression of the local religious imagination naturally links up with the argument about authenticity, particularly as that is put forward by local cultural elites. It is an argument that illustrates the complicated relation between the global and the local, because the idea of authenticity is initially put forward by cosmopolitan elites and then picked up and elaborated by local national elites. Authenticity becomes a key concept in the hands of those seeking to define, on the basis of recently reconstructed or invented narratives, what forms of religiosity are consonant with a contemporary nationalist vision. The metropolis first develops the idea of authenticity, often through the work of anthropologists, in order to define what is appropriate for the local, and local elites then use anthropology and even deploy anthropologists for their own political and cultural projects (Marshall 2009). In the immediate postcolonial period, there was a marked tendency among anthropologists and Africanists to focus on what are now called African-Initiated Churches (AICs), which was based in part on ideological sympathy for them rather than for mainstream churches or for Pentecostals, though Pentecostals had not yet achieved their later prominence. The position was further complicated by the way some AICs harboured cultural genes from the Pentecostal pool.

David Lehmann offers a useful perspective on this site of contestation when he characterises Pentecostals in Brazil as indifferent to the sponsorship of local cultural elites (Lehmann 1996). Local spirit cults are patronised by 'the erudite' whereas Pentecostals are rejected by these elites on grounds of cultural nationalism, and, moreover, show no interest in attracting elite sponsorship. There appears, therefore, to be a widespread tension between Pentecostal churches and the ideological positions of educated local elites which plays into a historic tension between anthropology and Christian missions, and which is made more paradoxical by the major contributions of missionaries to the development of anthropology, not excluding Pentecostals (Harries 2007).

CHANGING ATTITUDES AMONG ANTHROPOLOGISTS AND THE CHRISTIAN MAINSTREAM

However, there have been major changes in the approach of anthropologists in the last couple of decades both to Christianity in general and Pentecostals in particular. This has been particularly marked among female anthropologists who might have a more sensitive understanding of the changes wrought by Pentecostalism in the texture of everyday life, including the status of women. When Pentecostalism was assimilated to the category of fundamentalism, it was easy to treat it as concerned with restoring patriarchal values in the domestic sphere, but blanket discussions of fundamentalism are less prevalent than they were, and there is a vastly enhanced understanding of the influence of Pentecostalism on mutuality in the home and of the way it allows men to escape the power of machismo. This reassessment began with the work of Elisabeth Brusco and has been continued in a series of distinguished monographs (Brusco 2010). Overall, anthropologists have focussed on the global changes associated with Pentecostalism rather than on what used to be seen as insensitive intrusion on the 'functioning' of local societies. Pentecostalism adds to the options in contemporary global society, and it makes little sense to commend pluralism at home and condemn it in postcolonial societies.

There have also been changes in the attitude of some mainstream churches. The initial impulse to blame the growth of Pentecostalism on the export of American religion, especially where it promoted a gospel of health and wealth, has given way to a realisation that there are reasons for its global appeal which lie in the local cultures themselves, particularly perhaps the partial failure of the modernisation promised by the development narrative. Mainstream churches have become aware of the extraordinary capacity of Pentecostalism to put down roots in Africa and Asia, to the point where many members of mainstream churches either join Pentecostal churches or attend them because they feel such churches are more authentically African than the mainstream. Anglicans in West Africa and Lutherans in East Africa, for example, have been obliged to take over some of the unique selling points of Pentecostalism, notably their style of worship. The global impact of Pentecostalism includes an infusion of charismatic fervour into the older, more established churches. Competition provokes emulation.

PENTECOSTALISM AND THE GLOBAL MARKET

The theme of competition brings us directly to the theme of pluralism and multiculturalism, and to the way Pentecostals are natural inhabitants of the global market in religion. That has led some commentators to link their rise to the rise of neoliberalism in the economic sphere, but it is not clear what this means, apart from the principle of competition in the religious market. Of course, Pentecostalism began in the voluntary sector where free competition for members was accepted as normal and state regulation of religion regarded as anathema, but that does not make Pentecostals automatic partisans of a market free-for-all. What Pentecostalism does is to create a strong community with clear boundaries between the state and the individual, offering services that the state does not provide or is too corrupt and venal to provide on an adequate scale. It is not in any strong sense individualistic, because all the benefits it offers, including a heightened sense of individuality and personal worth, are dependent on a combination of personal discipline and communal discipline. The unbounded enthusiasm and spontaneity of its worship is likewise dependent on a sense of order orchestrated by pastors acting as the religious version of a compère. Freedom of expression among Pentecostals is dependent on implicit rules and rituals generated by communal assent and overseen by the pastorate. These rules and rituals are not the established forms of mainstream bodies, which are accomplished through set forms and calendars and can therefore be performed without overt orchestration, but they are rituals all the same, however much Pentecostals might repudiate the term (Lindhardt 2011).

Nevertheless, the economic metaphor can go far in characterising the operation of Pentecostalism (B. Martin 2006). Pentecostals are free entrepreneurs on the religious market, using marketing devices and deploying market forms of organisation and dissemination. It is not simply a matter of the Protestant Ethic breeding disciplined economic endeavour, though that is certainly the case, but of modes of religious organisation that resemble the international corporation. Indeed the Pentecostal and para-Pentecostal megachurches are often international corporations providing a complete life-world with all associated facilities for their members (Ukah 2008). What some megachurches provide resembles the all-embracing environment provided by Japanese firms and Japanese New Religions. The analogy has not received much attention, but there is clearly a global form of religion transcending national and confessional borders which creates a complete protective environment that is very different from the differentiated sphere of religion in Europe though not unlike some of the major megachurches in the United States. This environment includes educational, medical and recreational provision; and even on occasion, financial institutions. Religion in this form really does mediate between the individual and the state and constitutes the main form of voluntary organisation, not just one voluntary organisation among others.

TRANSNATIONAL VOLUNTARISM AND ORGANIC TERRITORIALISM

The big contrast on the global scale is between transnational voluntarism, and those forms of religion based on a closed market, which regard certain territories as their peculiar and sacred preserve and further assume an isomorphic relation between kin, ethnicity and faith. The principle of the transnational voluntary organisation competes globally with the religions of place and ethnicity. To convert from these religions to another is to this or that extent to break with family, as well as with tribe or nation, and to opt out of the nexus and ethos of local culture. The sanctions against the exercise of choice through conversion run along a scale from mild disapproval to symbolic death or death itself. The global variations run along a scale from North America, where it is normal, to Western Europe and Australasia where it is accepted but not all that frequent, to the Arabian Peninsula, which is seen as Islamic territory by definition and where even foreigners cannot establish their own sacred buildings.

As usual, Western Europe is an exception because there the Westphalian principle still holds. It means that people grow up with a given religious identity but one which has only a weak and residual hold on their personal loyalty (Madeley 2003). The religious organisation of a more or less established church is available when needed, but people may believe though not belong, in Grace Davie's (1994) well-known formulation; or belong but not believe, as is the case in much of Scandinavia. These two forms of loose identification may well be parasitic on the active involvement of earlier generations and therefore be transitional.

Yet they still block the advance of a more active voluntary sector on the American model. Eastern Europe, and much of Central Europe, differ from Western Europe on account of a much closer fusion of religion and ethnicity, reinforced in most countries, except East Germany, the Czech Republic and Estonia, by the period of domination under the then-Soviet Union and its apparatus of state secularisation. This model inhibits the growth of the voluntary sector as effectively as the residual Westphalian model does in Western Europe. So, in effect, we have active voluntary sectors in the United States and, to a lesser extent, Canada; modest and not very lively voluntary sectors in Britain and Australasia, and some parts of continental Western Europe; while in Eastern Europe we have a strong relation between religion and ethnic identity, excepting successfully secularised countries like the former Deutsche Demokratische Republik (DDR).

The implications for Pentecostalism, as the most dramatic embodiment of a transnational voluntary organisation, are obvious. Pentecostalism becomes, first of all, a subordinate but lively and expansive sector within the mainstream Evangelical world of the United States, and it provides a further and lively addition to the free churches in Britain, in parts of Northern Europe and in Australasia. It makes very little headway in Eastern Europe where ethnicity and religion are fused together, though it can have an impact in transitional areas of mixed religion like Transylvania and the Western Ukraine. But neither North America nor Western/Eastern Europe are the areas of maximum expansion for Pentecostalism, because the voluntary sector is already fully developed in North America, and because in Europe the Westphalian model still operates to maintain a diffuse area of low temperature in the religious sphere which acts as a break on fresh developments in the voluntary sector. Pentecostals may create the liveliest churches in that sector, but they are not going to reverse its overall decline.

VOLUNTARISM AND TERRITORIALISM IN LATIN AMERICA AND SUB-SAHARAN AFRICA

As already indicated, Pentecostalism has taken off most dramatically in Latin America and Sub-Saharan Africa, but the relationship with the locally dominant religion based on territory is very different. In Latin America, Pentecostalism encountered a union of faith and territory in decay. Catholicism provided a sacred canopy over the whole continent, but within that canopy there flourished numerous spirit cults loosely intermingling with Catholicism, as well as native peoples whose ancient forms of religion had been partially assimilated to the pantheon of Catholic saints. Both the spirit cults and the native religions were at the point of forming more distinctive enclaves of independent religiosity, and it was at that juncture that Pentecostalism entered the religious field. It offered elements that appealed both to the spirit cults and the native religions and combined them with a Protestant discipline and the prospect of a conduit to international modernity. What most facilitated the emergence of a large voluntary sector and a major break in the sacred canopy of Catholicism was the vast growth of international communication and the break-up of tightly knit local communities, in particular as rural migrants made the great trek to large cities.

In one way, Africa presented just as variegated a scene as North America, leaving aside the Islamic North and the survival of Christianity in Egypt, Eritrea and Ethiopia. There were, of course, numerous forms of non-Christian religion often associated with local tribes and their territories. Then there were the territorial emplacements of Catholicism in Francophone Central Africa and the very partially Catholicised regions of Spanish and Portuguese Africa. Finally, there was the pluralistic religious scene of Anglophone Africa reproducing in a more extended form the voluntary sector and the varied territorial faiths of Britain, as well as the Lutheran emplacements in the former German colonies. Initially, Pentecostalism had a natural point of entry in South and West Africa, where it also influenced African-Initiated Churches (AICs) to some extent, but it extended to the whole of Anglophone Africa, before taking off in the increasingly deregulated religious markets of French- and Portuguese-speaking Africa.

VOLUNTARISM AND CULTURAL NATIONALISM IN ASIA AND THE PACIFIC RIM

Asia and the non-monotheistic East present rather different opportunities and challenges. Perhaps one can set aside places like Pakistan, where all Christians, let alone Pentecostals, are under threat of persecution by radical Islamists, and where conversion is only allowed in one direction, and simply consider the major non-monotheistic religious complexes. Many such cultures in Asia do not so much reject as absorb 'foreign' bodies, accepting Christian churches as just another manifestation of the numerous expressions of the divine; or another avenue to the ubiquitous spirit world; or even, in China, as another reasonable ethic like that of Confucius. Yet, as is the case everywhere else, including Latin America and Africa, the ideologies of Marxism and nationalism imported from the West are deployed to condemn Christianity (or in the case of Pentecostalism in Latin America, a new form of Christianity) as a Western and/or American import, above all where Marxism and nationalism combine in the notion of imperialism. Christianity, including a nonelite form like Pentecostalism, here takes the blame for Western/American imperial depredations. This provides cover for the wellnigh universal objection of cultural and political elites outside the North Atlantic world to pluralism and competition, and reinforces elite appeals to notions of some authentic and historic religious tradition. Given that Christianity, and to some extent Pentecostalism, are more likely to take off in deprived social sectors or in marginal and perhaps threatened ethnic groups, as in Burma, the scene is set for severe restrictions on religious liberty and competition, or for actual persecution fomented by nationalist parties, like that recently associated with the Bharatiya Janata Party (BJP) in Orissa, India. In China, during the Cultural Revolution, all religious activity was suppressed, and Christianity was defined as a form of imperialist cultural intrusion, though some paradoxical consequences followed as will be shown below. In Japan, pervasive cultural nationalism at all social levels ensured that Christianity had a quite restricted impact, even though its influence in the educated sector was very considerable.

If we take into account the variable role of Christianity in relation to local nationalisms, and its major role in education, we can compare the variable success of Christian expansion in the Pacific Rim, from Korea to Indonesia. One begins with Christianity in general because the challenges and opportunities found in the region affect all Christians, whether they belong to the first wave of the late 19th century or the later waves, including Pentecostalism. Obviously, the Philippines and the Pacific Islands are two special cases to be set aside because they were deeply affected by American and by European, especially British, influence respectively. In the Philippines and the Pacific Islands, Pentecostalism arrived simply as the second wave of Evangelical expansion, along with a more diffuse charismatic movement, Protestant and Catholic, among the better off. In some respects the Philippines is affiliated to the Latin American pattern, except that the erosion of Hispanic imperial influence by American political influence and cultural power after the Spanish-American War was much more far reaching than in Latin America. There are, as you might expect, many major megachurches, Pentecostal or charismatic, for example, in Manila and considerable Pentecostal expansion among the many ethnic subgroups, often carried out by Pentecostal missionaries from Korea.

When one considers the rest of the Pacific Rim, China included, Korea stands out as the one country where Christian expansion and the educational role of Christianity was most assisted by a positive association with Korean nationalism, over and against both of its more powerful neighbours, China and Japan. Whereas Chinese nationalism, and even more the insular nationalism of Japan, worked against the expansion of Christianity in general, in Korea the birth of nationalism and the growth of Christianity, Pentecostalism included, went forward hand in hand. Korea is now about 25% Christian, mostly Protestant, and Korean megachurches are among the largest and most successful in the world. One might have expected Taiwan, which has from time to time been part of China as well as intermittently independent, to be more receptive to Christianity than has in fact been the case. Taiwan experienced the same influence of Christian-inspired education, much of it Presbyterian, as Korea, but the Chinese nationalists who governed Taiwan after their expulsion from mainland China, were barely better disposed to Christianity than the Chinese Communists. In Taiwan, as in Japan, the functional equivalents of Christian voluntary movements were to be located in Buddhist New Religions. In Taiwan and China alike the proportion of Christians probably hovers in the region of 3–5%.

At the same time, the story of the expansion of Christianity during and after the ravages of the Cultural Revolution, and even more the expansion and continuing vitality of Pentecostalism, has been remarkable. Broadly speaking, it has taken two forms. One emerged among women and in the course of the Cultural Revolution took the form of Pentecostal-like house churches as recourse to temples became impossible for men. The other emerged among the educated and technologically sophisticated harbingers of modernity. The study by Nanlai Cao of 'Boss Christians' in the coastal city of Wenzhou, a linguistic and geographical enclave some 200 miles south of Shanghai, portrays a lively charismatic culture powerful in the commercial life of the city, and comprising some 15% of the population of six million (Cao 2011). This commercial culture with its mixture of Pentecostal and charismatic Christianity is also to be found in Singapore. Indeed Singapore is host to one of the most advanced, expensive and expansive megachurches in the world.

Another major manifestation of Christianity has occurred in the Chinese diaspora in the two predominantly Muslim countries of Malaysia and Indonesia. Here one encounters a theme to be developed below: the appeal of charismatic Christianity to marginal ethnic groups. The Chinese in Malaysia and Indonesia have been very successful and have encountered a degree of hostility that has reinforced what looks like an 'elective affinity' between the Chinese entrepreneurial ethos and the Protestant Ethic.

POINT OF INSERTION: MARGINAL ETHNICITIES

In discussing points of insertion, we begin with the appeal of Pentecostalism and/or charismatic Christianity to marginal ethnic groups before we look at its appeal to newly self-aware groups who challenge those who have already secured their position, as well as its appeal to new business and other middle class groups. Finally we can discuss its relation to the Great Trek to the megacity, and its participation in a global dispersion, including migration to Europe.

The appeal of Pentecostalism to marginal ethnicities might seem contradictory given it is a transnational and voluntary faith that is free of the ties to territory and ethnicity. However, it is perfectly understandable that some people belonging to marginal ethnic groups, including those on the territorial periphery of a major and more powerful nation, might opt for the kind of distinctive religious identity offered by Pentecostalism. Only some of the people belonging to a marginal ethnic group are likely to convert, which means that the group as a whole becomes religiously differentiated and fragmented, something that anthropologists used to regret.

Perhaps Wales offers a useful example of the creation of a distinct religious identity and of consequent cultural fragmentation. Wales is a territorial periphery with its own language. It maintained loyalty to Catholicism for longer than elsewhere in Britain, and it adopted Protestant nonconformity, in particular Methodism and Presbyterianism, more quickly and enthusiastically. Wales also revived its 'authentic' culture, partly in alliance with a historic local Christianity, partly in alliance with neopaganism, and adopted a proto-Pentecostalism which experienced a remarkable if final efflorescence in the revival of 1904–1905, just prior to the Los Angeles revival of 1906. Indeed some observers have posited a connection between the two revivals.

The re-creation of a national culture, and the religious revival in Wales, found combined expression in mass popular singing, choral societies and festivals. It has been said that 'Methodism was born in song', and that is also conspicuously true of the successor faith of Pentecostalism. In Wales, there was a conspicuous division between the saved who used their mouths to sing and the others who used their mouths to drink. In exactly the same way a division has emerged in some of the marginal ethnicities of the Andean region between those who *drink* competitively as part of the old faith and those who *sing* competitively as part of their newly respectable faith and identity. This is crucial, because the old identity was locally considered disreputable whereas the new identity reverses the stereotype. What was once subject to metropolitan contempt is now more 'respectable' than the surrounding dominant culture. During my own research in South and Central America, I had fleeting intimations of how Methodism (and Presbyterianism) in Wales, and Pentecostalism in the Hispanic world, might play very similar cultural roles. In one village on the territorial and ethnic periphery of Mexico, I came across on the one hand a derelict Catholic chapel; and on the other hand, a dispensary, a school and a replica of a Welsh Presbyterian chapel. In Merida, the regional capital, I also encountered a missionary hospital and a musical culture as singing groups of young women took their faith and their guitars from village to village. At a Two Choirs Festival in a new Pentecostal church in Campinas I encountered an undistinguished melange of popular musical items but was not remotely surprised when it all came to a climax with Handel's Hallelujah Chorus. There was a cultural initiation and educational aspiration in that Campinas church recognisable to anyone who has heard a Welsh choir. When I heard a choral concert in the new Baptist church, which had its own educational facilities attached, in Oradea, a peripheral region of Romania, I knew just as surely where I was in terms of spiritual inspiration and cultural aspiration.

Whether on the periphery of Britain, Mexico or Romania, parallel global developments acquire 'a local habitation and a name'. The Mapuche of Southern Chile, like the Maya of Western Mexico, long resisted conquest, and they were initially evangelised by Anglicans before a further Evangelical wave arrived with the Pentecostals. Now many of them are urban migrants and are to be found in the Pentecostal churches of Santiago. The aborigines of Australia were once categorised as among those 'first peoples' resistant to missions, though welfare services for them were in part provided by mainstream religious bodies (Brock 2005). It was when the services were withdrawn that Pentecostalism began making serious inroads, as though it finally offered a chosen autonomy. There have also been revivals of authentic aboriginal culture and recently some conversions to Islam, numbering perhaps a thousand. Yet aborigines also tend to adopt the secular urban culture of the dominant white population. Perhaps several processes are occurring simultaneously: Christian revivalism in successive waves, the reemergence of 'authentic historic cultures', for example, the revived Buddhism of Taiwan and Korea emulating some of the unique selling points of Christianity, and the growth of a religiously indifferent and secular culture, such as is to be found in Singapore, Korea and Australia. The appearance of this large secular sector encourages some observers to view Pentecostalism as part of the transition to secular society, parallel to the transition that has occurred in Wales in the course of the last decades of the 20th century.

One of the most interesting instances of the appeal of Pentecostalism to a marginal ethnicity is found in Europe, both in the east in Romania, and in the west in Spain and France. The course of Pentecostalism among the Roma of Spain offers an interesting site for analysis and one which also gives some idea of the broad character of the cultural transformations associated with Pentecostal conversion. Paloma Gay y Blasco has studied the expansion of the Philadelphia Church among Spanish *Gitanos* (Gay y Blasco 2004). She focussed both on the mobilisation of a marginal ethnic group, hitherto without a sense of the impetus of time, toward the embrace of modernity, and on the radical revision of relationships involved in that embrace. This autonomous revision offers a stark contrast to attempted reforms from without through social work programmes, such as obligatory reeducation and forced resettlement in remote colonies devised for 'marginal populations', though the trauma induced by these attempts may have provided further impetus to autonomous reformation and redefinition of what it meant to be a Roma people.

As is almost always bound to be the case, the initial seed was sown by outsiders, in this case non-Roma missionaries from France. Yet, as in the Chilean example already referred to, the burgeoning of the seed thereafter was entirely autonomous. Traditionally *Gitanos* are both preoccupied with their past identity and concerned with preventing the past from overflowing into the present. With the advent of Pentecostalism, however, the past was reimagined as though the *Gitanos* were a lost tribe of Israel who had as their founder not just Moses but later liberators like Martin Luther and Martin Luther King.

Modernity requires 'a Christian way' of doing things, whether in negotiating a fresh economic enterprise or dealing with a blood feud. Previously *Gitanos* had lived in potentially hostile and feuding patrigroups in which young men were the main actors through displays of sexual and violent prowess, as well as (more recently) addiction to drugs, while the older men were figures of respect negotiating a way out of the resulting conflicts. However, with the advent of the Philadelphia Church, feuding was replaced by an obligation to forgive and to exercise self-control negotiated by the young men themselves, many of them pastors. Women tended to approve of these changes, and mothers encouraged their daughters to find marriage partners among the 'new men'. None of this required the young men and women to cease being *Gitanos*. They were now 'better *Gitanos*, and a *truly* chosen people, through their reinterpretation of traditional values of respect and knowledge, and through their membership of a transnational politico-religious movement throughout Europe, both West and East.

This example typifies the changes associated with Pentecostalism, in particular its appeal to women who are tired of macho posturing and the effects of financial and sexual irresponsibility. Women suffering the consequences of male irresponsibility are not worried by the pejorative overtones attached to 'respectability' because they have much to gain from a reinterpretation of traditional male notions of 'respect'. Indeed, change is the more likely provided males can still enjoy respect in the reinterpreted form. If a notion of male headship is retained, it has to be morally earned through the mutual cooperation and consultation of man and wife and the replacement of the values of the street by those of the domestic table. The values of the street include easy resort to violence, much of it related to alcohol and drugs, and there is a great deal of evidence of the ability of Pentecostalism to create the new man and to negotiate imaginatively with people mired in the violence and chaos of the contemporary urban scene.

POINTS OF INSERTION: CHALLENGING ESTABLISHED GROUPS, MOBILISING NEW MIDDLE CLASSES

One way of looking at certain kinds of Pentecostalism is to understand them as challenges, on the part of newly self-conscious and mobilising groups, to those above or adjacent to them who have already achieved social recognition, perhaps through an earlier wave of conversion. Something of this appeared in the way charismatic Anglicanism has appealed to a number of newly well-off families in Santiago, Chile. These families found that the atmosphere of release and free expression in the Anglican charismatic milieu, combined with a more familiar Eucharistic ritual, 'got to them' in a way Catholicism did not. Presumably they had several alternatives open to them, including the house groups of a charismatic Catholicism as well as the older tradition of paternal social responsibility now reassembled after the Pinochet era through new religious orders and the schools they ran for the elite.

Likewise, in parts of Africa, the mainstream churches have become assimilated to the culture of nongovernmental organisations and of state-bearing elites, and Pentecostalism offers a milieu where those only recently self-conscious can reach out to a religious version of international modernity. In Nigerian universities, there are strong charismatic and Pentecostal groups for whom the corruption of the state is focussed in the echelons of the Islamic 'Other'. Perhaps one may see the distinctive culture of the so-called Boss Christians in China as a manifestation of a new technocratic and business elite on the rise. The same is true of the business-oriented Christians of the Chinese dispersion, though in their case charismatic Christianity provides both an environment in which 'executives may cry' and a haven against the envy of the majority population.

It is perhaps in the emerging powers of Nigeria and Brazil that one can observe the appeal of charismatic and Pentecostal Christianity to large new middle classes concerned about the corruption that invades their everyday existence and the tensions and uncertainties to which they are subject. The large church known as Rebirth in Christ provides an example from Brazil, and the Deeper Life movement an example from Nigeria. The Deeper Life Church has vast premises, and like its rival the Redeemed Christian Church of God, it provides a total environment for its members.

POINTS OF INSERTION: THE TREK TO THE MEGACITY

One of the most extraordinary developments in the major cities of the developing world, from Manila to Johannesburg, is the emergence in many areas,—but especially areas settled in by migrants—of sectors honey combed with religious enterprises. Each of them represents a buzzing hive of self-generated and autonomous social capital. In Johannesburg you find these enterprises in downtown areas, in Santiago in more distant housing estates. They may be quite small house churches run by a family with their friends, or they may be modest but nationwide denominations, or they may be vast religious emporia like the Rhema church in Soweto, the sprawling township suburb of Johannesburg. People set out from rural areas (or even from neighbouring countries) in search of a new life in the megacities of the developing world only to find themselves subject to chaotic conditions and tempted to turn to crime, drugs and prostitution. There are various ways in which they may hear the message of a better version of their 'new life'. Perhaps the most frequent is personal contact with someone who recommends the path of salvation as a way out of the chaos of existence. Alternatively, the message is delivered by the ubiquitous Evangelical radio or television stations. Part of what the new life has to offer is physical as well as psychic healing: few testimonies are complete without a witness to some experience of healing.

THE TRAILS OF GLOBAL MIGRATION

A transnational voluntary association not only lives by competition and the endless proliferation of new enterprises but by a constant circulation of religious migrants and entrepreneurs around the globe. Religious entrepreneurs are constantly on the move, perhaps in Oradea, Romania, one month and then in Buenos Aires the next. Given that people do not so much abandon their homelands as establish something approaching dual residency, with some family members more often in the original base and others working abroad, the Pentecostal churches act as way stations and homes from home. The New Testament Church of God in Birmingham may be a home from home for West Indians living in that city. The largest congregations in the cities of Northern Europe, from Amsterdam to Berlin, may well be made up of Africans who have brought their churches with them, though they are on occasion multicultural hubs for people from all over the world (Thompson 2005). Then there is the intriguing case of the Nigerian studying in Russia who ended up founding a large megachurch in Kiev in the Ukraine, many of whose members have now migrated to the United States (Wanner 2007). The African diaspora in Europe, and elsewhere, attracts less attention than the Islamic one, but it is substantial (van Dijk 2001).

In Africa itself, the extent of civil disturbance and outright war may mean that churches, both mainstream and Pentecostal, are made up of people who migrate for reasons of safety and are virtually refugees—for example, the large numbers of people from the Democratic Republic of Congo or from Zimbabwe who take refuge in the Republic of South Africa. The Zimbabwe Assemblies of God Africa spills over into several neighbouring countries, including Mozambique, (Maxwell 2006), and the Mossi people of Burkino Faso likewise take their business and their faith with them across borders.

Korea exports people and missionaries. Of course many Koreans migrate to Canada and the United States so that parts of the Pacific coastline of North America are populated by them. The Korean dispersion is perhaps disproportionately Christian, and it may also be that some of those Koreans who migrate to the United States become Christian on arrival. Some Koreans even disperse to Central Asia and there engage in risky missionary work, so that there is now a large Pentecostal church in Northern Kyrgystan (Pelkmans 2006).

Exactly the same is true of migration within Latin America, and of the migration of Latin Americans to North America. Parts of Boston are full of Brazilian Pentecostals. The para-Pentecostal church of *The Light of the World* provides way stations back and forth between its home base in Guadalajara and Dallas or Los Angeles. Its vast temple in Guadalajara, drawing on pre-Columbian architectural models, is a kind of Mecca for annual pilgrimage and it flies the flags of all the numerous countries where it has set up missionary embassies. Faith migrates within continents and between them. Missionaries from Brazil work in the Portuguese-speaking countries of Africa or in Portugal itself.

CONCLUSION

One or two strands are worth separating out from this discussion of the transnational voluntary association and its clash with the territorial emplacements of 'organic' religion, whether Catholic, Buddhist or Muslim. I have noted in particular the tension between the transnational flows of religious entrepreneurs and migrants based on choice and competition, and nationalist cultural elites and politicians claiming to foster and represent authentic historic culture. One major competitive advantage enjoyed by Pentecostalism is its capacity to create autonomous social capital as a buffer between the state and the individual in conditions where politics is widely perceived to have failed. Clearly the Marxist narrative of modernisation and change through state action and centralised control has failed, and the achievements of the liberal development narrative are patchy (Jones 2008). It is in these circumstances that the transnational voluntary association can build up what are often complete alternative societies and imagined communities across national frontiers and in so doing present an alternative master narrative of modernity. Though I have not discussed it here, Pentecostals are most exuberantly modern in their deployment of technology and all the means of global communication. It is simply on account of their equally exuberant supernaturalism that we in the West judge them inadequately modern and still enchanted by illusion, but it is precisely their appeal to the spirit in all its manifestations that makes them so strikingly successful in the modern world.

12 Women Perform ʾIjtihād

Hybridity as Creative Space for Interpretations of Islam

Els Vanderwaeren

In previous articles I have described how young, religious Muslim women recognise a female power inherent in Islam despite the image presented in public discourse of female Muslims (*Muslimahs*) as victims of authoritarian, androcentric and patriarchal structures (Vanderwaeren 2006, 2008). The present article is based on the conclusion of a qualitative doctoral research about the use of different methods regarding religious interpretations—which is called ʾijtihād[1]—and this by female Muslims of Moroccan origin in Flanders.[2] It presents the discourse that exists among *Muslimahs* in Flanders (Belgium). In the research, I revealed the religious actions and discursive patterns present among religious women when talking about themselves and their beliefs, and emphasised the significant potential for religious renewal that these discourses and actions contain.

This article provides information about the attempt of Muslim women to reconcile their religious way of being with the broader community in which they live. After an introductive contextualisation, the method of data collection is specified. Next, theoretical reflections regarding hybridity and hybridisation are given. The ways Muslim women formulate and disseminate their own perspectives on religious ideas and interpretations of Islam are finally described and subsequently discussed by means of the research question and the validation or falsification of the research hypotheses explained in the methodological paragraph.

THE DEVELOPMENT OF A FEMALE INFLUENCE

In most European societies, Muslims are actively contributing to contemporary religious discourse. However, with some notable exceptions (e.g., Fadil 2008; Pedziwiatr 2008), Belgian[3] scholars have paid scant attention to the existence of 'differentiating' discourses within Muslim communities, though it has become evident that such discourses exist.[4]

Questions about faith and normativity have become more relevant as Muslims in a diaspora context are confronted with 'the myriad shapes and colours of global Islam', as Mandaville (2001: 174) explained. Because of

Islam's nonhierarchical and decentralised structure, differences within Islam are more pronounced in this context. The internal differentiation creates conditions for religious renewal, as conventional hierarchies are interrupted and many traditional and cultural anchors disappear (Mandaville 2001: 136–137). Such a differentiation within the diaspora results in a certain disintegration of authenticity and authority. Consequently, Muslim diaspora communities all over the world must decide which aspects of Islam are contextual and negotiable (the concept of localisation), and which are essential and universal (the concept of universalisation) and therefore must remain undisturbed (Van Bruinessen & Allievi 2003). This leads to debates about authority since the central question is often who decides what is valid and legitimated. Authority becomes highly pluralised in terms of conceptual characteristics, of its ascription and acquisition, and in terms of who bears authority. Worldwide, traditional bearers of religious authority must accept new bearers of religious authority (Eickelman 1992: 648). Subordinated groups like younger generations and women see this as a chance to increase the influence of their point of views and interpretations of Islam, which they consider more relevant to their local situation.

Many studies about Islam in Europe have described profound changes initiated by women in both Muslim society and religion (e.g., Amiraux 2003; Babès 1997; Jonker 2003; Jouili 2009; Jouili & Amir-Moazami 2006).[5] For example, these researchers have noted that young Muslim women (and men) seem to have a more individualised interpretation of religious prescriptions and symbols than their parents do.[6] Their religiosity consists of a more personal construction of belief and belonging. It becomes clear that structural changes,[7] resulting from immigration provide new opportunities for women to assume nontraditional roles in religion and to access resources which were previously unavailable or substantially less available to them (Ebaugh & Chafetz 1999: 586). Women are seeking empowerment from within the traditional religious framework by choosing for themselves what they accept, what they believe, and what makes sense to them from within the prescribed framework.

In their search for an adequate religious discourse, Muslim women in Belgium, like Muslim women in other European countries (i.e., Jonker 2003; Jouili 2009; Jouili & Amir-Moazami 2008) have come to realise that they can no longer rely solely on the established religious authorities to understand and explain their religion. As the overall level of education among young Muslim women in European countries rises, these women are increasingly formulating their own insights into everyday issues, based on their understanding of Islam (Boubekeur 2004; Fadil 2005; Vanderwaeren 2005). In their own environment, they actively contribute to the renewal of religious discourse by challenging current versions of Islam as cultural artefacts and falsifications of something that was originally 'more just'.[8] Western societies, however, attribute mainly traditional identities and social roles to Muslim women. The acceptance of such images suggests that these women will be less inclined to adapt to a modern society. It also neglects the diverse and complex experiences of women in general and of Muslim women (with an immigrant background) in particular.

The new, female approach to Islam contains significant potential for social change that leading religious (male) authorities may perceive as threatening, especially since every instance of religious renewal in local forms of Islam by women (or men) represents a bid for emancipation that is aimed at the countries of origin and the cradle of Islam.[9] The transformation of Islam in Western Europe becomes visible with the democratisation of Islam and indicates that a process of pluralisation of religious authority structures is occurring. Such a democratisation of Islam is an unavoidable consequence of the higher, but not specifically religious, education of young European Muslims who claim for oneself the right to understand; the access to Islamic understanding that European Muslims gain when more and more Islamic sources are translated into European languages; and the penetration of Western educational ideas regarding independent thinking via education. Since changes in society and in the religious arena are closely connected with reformulations of religious authority (see Peter 2006a), the resulting democratisation of Islam and the subsequent call of European Muslims for more flexibility in interpretation and in arguing indicate a movement toward (theological) emancipation from institutionalised authority (Vertovec 2001: 110). The breakdown in attributing authority only to traditional religious authorities and the loss of influence by established religious authorities are clearly consequences of a more highly individualised religiosity (Amiraux 2000; Babès 1997; Césari 1994; Dassetto 1997; Dassetto, Maréchal & Nielsen 2001; Tietze 2002). Muslims are increasingly understanding that 'no one has a monopoly over the meaning of what God says' and more people are claiming the right to interpret the religious resources personally (see Barlas 2002, xii). How a more critical attitude has found its way among Muslims—and more specifically, Muslim women of Moroccan origin—in Flanders, and how the author has approached that critical attitude, is explained in the following sections.

THE COLLECTED DISCOURSES OF MUSLIM WOMEN

My analysis is based on data collected by means of 30 audiotaped semi-structured in-depth interviews and five focus groups. Both were conducted among Muslim women of Moroccan descent between April 2007 and February 2008 in Flanders (Belgium). The same group of women participated in both the interviews and the focus groups. The groups explored and further clarified the interview findings.

Participants were selected from young (with an age of 18 years or more) Muslim women living in Antwerp. All participants had to have an immigration experience in their personal or family history. This selection criterion is important since immigration, whether personal or family (parents or grandparents), affects the position, development, and experience of all family members (Vanderwaeren & Timmerman 2008: 9), especially gender relationships (Read 2002: 209). The study further reduced the available sample by adding the Moroccan ethnic element. The migratory and ethnic criteria were chosen to strengthen the validity of the results, given that assumptions could be made that all participants belong at least on a nominal level to the Moroccan Muslim community and more specifically to the Mālikī school of law.[10] Like others, Muslim children are born into and educated in a tradition that has a historical continuity and communal dimension (Waardenburg 2000: 58). This meant that this group could be seen as at least nominally belonging to Mālikism. Therefore, although participants might describe themselves as no longer belonging to a particular tradition, the assumption that they are Mālikī is reasonable because, as Renaerts (1999: 289) states, primary socialisation is 'likely to leave indelible traces'. The final consideration for selection was age. The minimum age of participants was 18 years old (the oldest participant was 38; no children, adolescents, or elderly women were included). All participants were studying or working and described their life in terms of marrying, educating children, and so on.

Within this profile, participants who considered themselves 'active believers' and 'emancipated women' were assembled randomly. They could define active, belief and emancipation in their own terms. I first contacted the participants by e-mail, and then set up appointments via telephone. Interviews were semistructured, and a list of major topics to be addressed was developed in advance. Topics were focused around whether and how young Muslim women in Flanders were searching for religious answers to modern, Western societal problems.

The research was influenced by the grounded theory approach (Glaser & Strauss 1967), in which theory derives from the data and participants are not given advanced knowledge of topics to be addressed. For this study, this meant that during interviews participants were asked what believing and acting religiously (~ 'doing religion' (Avishai 2008)),[11] ʾijtihād and authority meant to them, without being provided with a previously fixed definition of any of those terms. No definition was provided because any definition might have excluded potential meanings. The results of what those words meant to the participants, based on their responses to questions covering those topics, enriched the understanding whether and how Muslim women of Moroccan origin achieve religious authority in realising socioreligious changes by means of ʾijtihād in the current, Western (Flemish) society. This was the research question we tried to answer. That question was further developed into three hypotheses around which I concentrated my research results in a balanced answer to the research question. The first hypothesis reads as follows: *Muslimahs* hold a marginalised position regarding the institutional-religious level that, besides restrictions, contains opportunities for creativity and innovation. The second hypothesis holds that *Muslimahs* are realising sociotreligious change in theory and praxis. And the final hypothesis is that *Muslimahs* acquire religious authority on local and translocal levels by means of *'ijtihād* as a method in their search for answers to concrete life questions for their living in the West'.

The research question and hypotheses touch upon consciousness of the borders of multiculturalism, pluralism and the debate about social cohesion in society. Thinking about those issues is related to the level of recognising and acknowledging differences. Hybridity and hybridisation offer interesting insights regarding borders and boundaries, and therefore recognition and acknowledgement of differences.

FROM A GLOBAL MÉLANGE TO A HYBRID RELIGIOSITY

According to Verkuyten (1999: 5) processes of globalisation mark the way 'people see and place themselves and others'.[12] Since people take over and embrace global phenomena, globalisation affects the mindset of people and their behaviour in a community. Global phenomena conquer a place in the norms and values proper to a community and individuals. A unique, local content is given to the global phenomena, and values and norms receive their own local significance. This aspect of globalisation is called glocalisation and can best be described as an interaction between the global and local. According to the conceptualisation of this term by Robertson (1992: 172–174), glocalisation contradicts the superficial assumption that globalisation would lead to homogenisation (i.e., the idea of the world as one 'Global Village' (McLuhan 1964)). Glocalisation refers to the tandem effect of globalisation and localisation: on the one hand, there is a homogenising globalisation; on the other hand, we notice how a tendency towards local cultural identity is sought. These two trends work in interaction with each other and participate in various mixtures. The interaction between the global and the local shows how the local is spread and gains importance and how the world influences the local. In this sense, globalisation is viewed as a process that leads to *mélange*. The processes of melting, combining and mixing of elements, meanings and forms are indicated as hybridisation. Hybridity and hybridisation refer to terms indicating intercultural transitions and the identities belonging to such transitions.

Hybridity is as obviously as it is inconspicuously present in daily life. The reflexive relationship between the local and the global precisely establishes the hybrid (Iyall-Smith 2008: 3). People are living in a society to which they adapt, in which they negotiate and in which they are in a continuous process of change. To put it differently: a society in which they continuously melt, combine and mix. The analysis of this research demonstrates how the informants never possess just one identity. People simultaneously dispose of more identities which are not independent of each other, but which merge and influence each other. Hill Fletcher (2005: 86) explains this as follows:

In any given experience of the World or understanding of the World, it is not always possible to identify which feature or features of my identity (Christian, North-American, college educated, feminist, married, Midwestern, professorial, familial or otherwise) are informing my interpretation of that experience or understanding.

In Hill Fletcher's previous quote, she explains that considering the world as built on one identity is too simplistic. The hybrid constitution of everyone as a mix of different identities is central in my consideration of identities. The formation of such a hybrid constitution asks that identity be considered as a process and not so much as a description, as an ongoing 'becoming' and not a 'being' (Hall 1990).[13]

Given the mutual impact (and formation), an identity can only be understood in relation to the other identities studied. Unlike a single intersection of identities, I consciously choose hybridity and hybridisation since they indicate how a new identity is created which can no longer be traced back to the original elements. Bhabha (1994) expresses his vision on hybrid identities as follows: 'an identity that is "neither one nor the other", retaining the semblance of each yet ambiguously "in between"' (Bhabha 1994). According to Bhabha, hybridity is precisely the fact 'that when a new situation, a new alliance formulates itself, it may demand that you should translate your principles, rethink them, extend them' (Bhabha in Rutherford 1990: 216), that an alliance shall lead to something 'which is greater than the sum of its severed parts' (Anzaldúa 1987: 101–102).

Due to the individualistic dynamics in contemporary societies, and the abundance of cultural and religious information, hybridisation is increasingly an appropriate option for those who look for a way to make religion or spirituality meaningful for themselves. True multiple religious belonging and religious hybridity cannot simply be reduced to syncretism (or the merging of more than one tradition into a new construction) and goes beyond the idea of a Jew or a Christian adopting some Buddhist meditation practice (or *bricolage*). Zondervan (2008: 105) believes that understanding the hybrid religiosity (of youth) demands a reconsidering of what religion is in our time, and that we look at the places and forms in which it appears.[14] A similar message to review what is known is also present in Bhabha's *Signs Taken For Wonders: Questions of Ambivalence and Authority Under a Tree Outside Delhi, May 1817* (1985). Here he explains religious hybridity by means of how the missionary message is understood by local people based on their cultural filters. Thinking about religious hybridity is therefore about how belief systems interact with local and traditional cultural and religious frameworks. Hybridity manifests itself as a new option for individuals who experience discomfort within a tradition which for them has contradictory elements and who therefore do not fully comply or limit themselves to that. This resembles the model of Hervieu-Leger (1999) of the modern believer who chooses carefully and decides what is personally meaningful. These choices may be outside the traditional range of choices and can relate to aspects of other religious traditions. In this sense, a hybrid religious person does not abandon what is typical, nor is he limited to that feature. After all, hybridisation occurs in established and ongoing social processes (Stewart 1999) in which religious groups and individuals live and sense their own histories and religious personalities from dynamic interactions with the (religious) other. When religious traditions in new contexts—whether time or place or both—arrive, they reform their meanings and boundaries (Bender & Cadge 2006: 229). It is not different for the religion of immigrants.

Earlier, I reported how the research question was reformulated into three hypotheses. The validation or falsification of those hypotheses summarises the main results of the research and is discussed hereafter.

A CREATIVE PERIPHERAL POSITION OF HYBRID MUSLIM WOMEN IN AUTHENTICATING SOCIORELIGIOUS CHANGES

The first hypothesis mentioned—that the *Muslimahs* hold a marginalised position regarding the institutional-religious level that, besides restrictions, contains opportunities for creativity and innovation—is confirmed based on an analysis of the informants' positions.

It is of note that the informants do not take up a central role in their Orthodox Muslim community (e.g., a mosque), but are searching for a niche in their own faith by, for instance, attending living room meetings for and by women (Vanderwaeren 2010, 2012). Women are meeting with each other to reflect upon their religion, both publicly and privately, at home, in mosques, or in women's associations. Participants interviewed for this project are not only active in the women's spaces of mosques or Islamic associations, but approximately half also meet informally in domestic spaces, where they share religious information and discuss daily life and other topics related to Islam with other women. According to Ask & Tjomsland (1998: vii), the importance of religion is in its practice in daily life since it is 'something that takes place in everyday life and thereby is actively founded in the experience of the believing women.' There, *Muslimahs* are searching for their own niche or space in which to practice their religion based on their personal understanding of Islam. They gather, as Hafida (a participant) says, 'to, . . . erm, talk about Islam'. And, as Rahma notes, 'to remember God,' because 'out of the abundance of the heart the mouth speaks'.[15] Women meeting up with other women is not a new phenomenon. Ahmed mentions in *A Border Passage. From Cairo to America—A Woman's Journey* that women have always figured out religious issues and questions among themselves, and that this has resulted in a type of Islam that is essentially women's Islam (as opposed to an official, textual Islam, or a men's Islam) (Ahmed 1999: 123–124). Meetings in the home reveal the space that religion occupies in daily life.

The way they talk about their own 'niche', mosques and associations, express the interest of women to take up institutional-religious roles. In the analysis on social and religious activism, the women surveyed seem to find their way within the Muslim community and its structures, when they teach Islam in schools for example. However, the analysis around social change highlights how women emphasise the fact that more women need to follow a theological education. They consider this as a necessity in order to realise a conscious and often progressive socioreligious change that would not be the result of time and place. Currently, women increasingly appear in debates (according to e.g., Asma), follow a theological training course (Sabriya, Umaymah, Yettou), hold religious functions (Yettou, Umaymah) and collectively claim their rights (Yettou, Aisha, Nabila). Eventually, the informants themselves say they are prepared to take up functions in religious institutions such as the Board of Governors of (mosque) associations, or in the Executive Body of Muslims, also when this includes a leadership position, even the ʾimāma.[16]

The institutional-religious marginalised situation of the informants is not only shown in the literal niche—outside the mosques—that the informants seek and create for their faith and which would place them outside the direct scope of androcentric orthodoxy, but in a figuratively located niche. They consider their own position itself as more peripheral in respect of what they describe as the orthodoxy. However, the women simultaneously believe that their vision is supported by many people. The quote of Dounia below shows how the informants are not at the centre of the Orthodox spectrum although they do not consider themselves to be outside of what they consider as Orthodox either: 'While you now have the idea that you can fill in Islam yourself and that this is respected, it is understood.

The marginalised position of *Muslimahs* in Flanders in relation to institutional religion, however, offers potential for creativity and innovation in the managing of what they consider as Islam. It needs, as Ibtissame says, 'to be something personal. It is a direct link between yourself and God.' I find creativity and innovation in the way they combine their being Muslim(ah) all over again in their different identities, with all the ambivalences those cause and without considering them as problematic. Their position on the sidelines, or on the periphery, gives them space to handle their religion pragmatically and creatively, to bring it in line with their daily situation and in agreement with their hearts and also to understand it. How they do this brings me to the process of authentication that lies beneath the second hypothesis.

The idea that *Muslimahs* realise socioreligious change in theory and praxis is supported by the following findings. The informants belong, in accordance with their subidentities, to different groups. The interaction and the formation of these subidentities feed the hybrid religious identity with different (foreign) elements. The analysis shows how the processes of globalisation and hybridisation cause transformations in contemporary religious experience. Central to the hybrid state, I isolate the 'agency'[17] of Muslim women, which is shown in their pragmatic handling of religion. In their pragmatism they verify the limits of their (Orthodox) religious community, and they gradually shift those boundaries. They do this by considering Islam as something holistic—as explained below by Siham—and by authenticating not specifically religious or Islamic elements as religious or Islamic: 'For me, that is my way of life. That is . . . Islam is my religion. It is actually just the way of life. [. . .] For me, this is something obvious. For me, it is, yes, nature itself, because that is my nature.'

An example of authentication is the adoption of habits or celebrations such as celebrating birthdays as Zefira explains:

> There are many things that are so, yes, anything that is not written in texts is a bid'a, but phew! [. . .] Not everything is black and white or ḥalāl/ḥarām. I do not think so, hey, you also have an environment that it affects, and it also written in the Qur'an, that's so, that when you live in a country that uh . . . that is not Islamic, you have sometimes to admit to those traditions of that country, hey, then I do not think I depart from my faith! No, on the contrary, I. . . I try to live.'

Zefira justifies in the previous quote why she celebrates the anniversary of her children. She incorporates and legitimises—and therefore authenticates the celebration of birthdays—by referring to the celebration of the birth of the Prophet and by declaring that the intention has to prevail in acting. She adds that not everything is black and white or clearly ḥalāl/ḥarām. To authenticate and to make (religiously) acceptable one's own progressive ways of action also appears when they authenticate as Islamic a 'new' dress style, such as the combination of a scarf with a narrow top or tight jeans, which they actually discussed during a focus group. This authentication can be considered as another confirmation of the desire of women to continue to position themselves within the (Orthodox) religious community.

Their hybrid condition helps the informants to connect to continuity and change without cracks in time and space. They express a rolling interaction between centre and periphery, which they, through dealing with difference, creatively attempt to innovate by redrawing boundaries. This is also evident with respect to their parents. Azza says: 'the way of thinking [that] [is] different to theirs. I am Western, uh?' The informants speak of another way of believing (more conscious, more critical) than that of their parents. This other way of believing is no radical break, rather it has a certain continuity. In another quote, Siham illustrates this gentle continuity: 'Yes! This one is not, I mean, that is not contradictory, I mean, it is not one or it is not the other.' By choosing themselves in their search for their Islam, they use a discourse that is about their 'right' to understand and to orchestrate their lives.[18]

In my research, the informants seem to examine critically and creatively their ways of regarding various Islamic topics, and when there is more than one of them, without breaking with either. For this, they approach Islam not as something fixed, but as something discursively determined. Through their descriptions of what they consider as a 'correct' approach of a particular act, they connect theory and practice. Indeed, these descriptions have two functions: they serve to change their own implementation of that act till it is 'correct' or conforms to their description and to authenticate and religiously legitimate their own 'correct' implementation. In this sense, the hybrid constitution of identity and a pragmatic approach to Islam allow the informants to feel comfortable in the traditions of their faith community and those of the wider society.

HYBRIDISATION IN AUTHORITY DUE TO FEMALE INTERPRETATIONS

In this paragraph I come to the third hypothesis. I examine whether Muslim women acquire religious authority on local and translocal levels by the use of *ʾijtihād* as a method of finding answers to vital questions of practical life in the West. This needs a deconstruction since the hypothesis contains multiple elements that need separating.

A first element of the hypothesis is about the use of *ʾijtihād* by women. More and more Muslim women, such as my informants, are acquiring the necessary knowledge to shape their Islam. They claim their right to discuss it and reach the 'correct' arguments. The women get these arguments to interpret from the Koran itself, where there seems to be written that knowledge is superior to ignorance. The informants also know how to use the discourse of scholars to their own advantage and to distil arguments from it. They use for themselves the idea expressed by Jihane that 'one rule can be understood in very different ways'.

When analysing the respondent's provision to do *ʾijtihād*, it seems that they chose an outcome of a *ʾijtihād* done by an *ʿālim* (a scholar). In other words they chose from the different outcomes of *ʾijtihād* one that corresponded to their hearts. Their *ʾijtihād* then consists of a search for both sources and Islamic scholars, whose interpretation of a Qu'ranic verse or *ḥadīth* is consistent with their vision of Islam. Siham mentions: 'I actually follow what is most in tune with my own life'. And Rahma stresses that 'You need to follow what is close to your feelings, like here I feel comfortable with and I do not feel as if I do something wrong'.

Given the restrictions on who can practice *ʾijtihād*, several informants themselves decided to do a form of *ʾijtihād*. Interestingly, the doing of *ʾijtihād* by Muslim women in this study turns out to be first and foremost a discursive event. If Islam is a discursive tradition (Asad 1986)[19] and achieves a continuous (re-)interpretation due to the interaction between the participants in the discourse, we understand that a change in who participates in the discourse changes the interpretation (Bowen 1993). The possibilities for socioreligious changes, because of ʾijtihād by the informants, lie in this discursiveness itself and in the participation in its discourse.

The interpretation of ʾijtihād by informants is implicitly legitimated because it is an ʾijtihād on the outcome of an ʾijtihād. Their approach is mainly that of ʾijtihād as a variable instrument in the changed world (and less of that ʾijtihād as a fixed instrument in a changing world). In the approach of ʾijtihād as a variable instrument the Muslim women questioned consider their ʾijtihād as a tool to legitimise the positions or acts they have already taken. In this way they justify their personal vision of Islam, which also becomes authenticated. They realise in addition that those elected and 'in line with-their-heart' ʾijtihād of an ʿālim exists as a way of doing ʾijtihād that other Muslims regard as valid.[20]

A hybridisation of authority is also performed by the informants. In their search for their own 'niche' or religious space, the Muslimahs arouse the suspicion of those who do not want to lose or share their authority. The informants produce an understanding of Islam from which they distil what is just, what has legitimacy for them and therefore has authority. They also choose for themselves the necessary elements that attribute authority to someone or something. Umaymah remarks: 'the question is when do I follow an interpretation of someone, when do I find that good enough?' and emphasises, in saying this, the discursive construction of authority.[21] The idea of discursiveness should be brought into account since the legitimacy of Muslim scholars is shaped by the Islamic discursive context. In this way the informants fragment and diversify knowledge and authority. Given that obtaining knowledge is crucial to attributing authority to someone and that this knowledge is diversified by the women, this diversification causes a hybridisation in the profiles of those to whom authority is attributed. By this I mean that actors, other than the scholars or ulamā, acquire authority; for instance popular opinion leaders or lecturers such as Amr Khaled and Tariq Ramadan.

Having shown how the women interviewed during the research process perform ʾijtihād, and that the outcome is legitimate for third parties, we come now to the question whether women by means of their ʾijtihād acquire religious authority on a local level and beyond. The confirmation or refutation of the third hypothesis depends entirely on the interpretation we give to the local and translocal levels and to authority. I mean that depending on how we fill in the local and translocal level, the hypothesis will be confirmed or shown to be unanswerable.

When I consider the 'direct women' group (e.g., the women who participate in the (informal) living room meetings) as the local level and all who are not participating in those as belonging to the translocal level, I am able to confirm the hypothesis. But if I have another interpretation of the local and the translocal level (for example, by considering the religious community of Moroccan Muslims as local and the wider Muslim community as translocal), the hypothesis cannot be answered since the data is missing for either a strong confirmation or a clear weakening of the hypothesis.

However, the interpretation of authority is also important here. Informants fill this in from 'having influence' to 'the mandatory way that something should be understood'. Depending on which interpretation the informants emphasise, the hypothesis will either be confirmed or refuted. Here, I would finally like to add that there is an ambiguity in their discourse on authority. Although a 'female touch' is needed—as Umaymah told me—the informants hesitate and problematise the attribution of religious authority to women, such as indicating a woman as an ʿālim. I deduce that women are enclosed to this day—despite their discourse about their 'rights', their capability, and their options and opportunities—within the existing and Orthodox discursive tradition that is male oriented and has a centuries-old pattern. Whether Muslim women will be able to transcend their abstract and theoretical discourse, when they say that women have the possibilities, opportunities, rights and abilities to take up an equal role as men regarding Islam, is another question that remains and a challenge to further research.

FINAL REMARKS

Researchers often see Islam as a monolithic religion that controls all aspects of its adherents' lives, what Tohidi (1998: 278) considered as the reduction of women to their religious identity, and which is, in this case, considered a rigid identity. Therefore, any discussion concerning Muslim women risks essentialising them. This makes generalisations difficult, and they need to be avoided in this work or to be framed with the explicit remark that they are made with an awareness of the existing diversity among the research group of Muslim women and the contexts in which they live.[22]

Because of immigration, territorial disconnection and fragmentation often affect the transmission of Islam to Muslims in Europe, and this can lead to a particularly intensive search for and discussion of identity. In what is presented, Göle's (2005) remark that religion and culture no longer offer prearranged identities is endorsed. The use of the idea of hybridity and the process of hybridisation have made clear to me that Muslim women who are bound in their faith community (as in the wider society) to be the 'other', are on the periphery, even though it is a metaphorical 'third space' or 'border zone' in which they interact. The informants belong to different groups according to their various subidentities. The interaction and the formation of those identities influence the religious identity that becomes hybrid due to the different 'foreign' elements. The incorporation of 'foreign' elements appears in the analysis on transformations of religious systems (such as concepts and traditions) and the processes to authenticate and legitimate those changes. The processes to authenticate, legitimate and make their discourses authoritative shows how a holistic approach to their Islam, and a hybrid understanding of their Islam is necessary to understand the continuous changes in contemporary religious experiences.

Furthermore, I consider the 'agency' of Muslim women, which is shown in their pragmatism, as central to the hybrid state. It is a pragmatism that illustrates how they search creatively for a religious understanding of things in their daily lives. Doing this, they test the borders of their (Orthodox) religious community, and gradually shift them. They do this by considering Islam as something holistic and by authenticating (non-)Islamic elements as religious.

Besides all this, the *Muslimahs* negotiate with various other adherents of Islam about what constitutes Islam. Consequently, normative traditions—and by extension, religious authority—are continuously being revised. Muslims today consider authority, including religious authority, to be discursively constructed, that is, contextual. The question of who is considered an authority depends on time-, place- and culture-specific understandings.

The organic growth of this research—and the recurrence of the data in the theory and the theory in the data—has made its relevance to the current understanding of hybridity clear. The postmodern aspect of the concept clarifies the Hegelian teleology and vision of history or the more *Zuhause sein in der Welt* (Hegel 1793). Hegel believes that world history is changing the world and a process exists towards a being more 'at home' in the world. Hybridity as a transgressive concept also contains the ability to be 'at home' in different cultural settings, since it offers the space for the transformation and change of supposedly fixed identities and concepts based on essentials. All these elements have become clearer in this research.

NOTES

1. *'Ijtihād* is not easy to translate. The translation often used for this is interpretation. However, it should be noted that this only partially covers this loaded concept (Vikør 2005: 53ff). *'Ijtihād* refers to the collection of methods that derives (legal) implications of the Qur'an (text) and systematises the use of reason or human thought (see Vikør 2005: 53ff; EI2 ''idjtihād' (Schacht, MacDonald & Schacht 2010); and the discursive construction of *'ijtihād* among believing women (see Vanderwaeren 2010: 7, 39–50, 184–230).
2. As regards the analysis, the article is based on the illustrated text with citations for my doctoral defence. Detailed analysis can be found in Vanderwaeren (2010).
3. Belgium is a nation-state and Flanders is the northern, Dutch-speaking region of Belgium. The article results from research conducted among Muslim women of Moroccan descent living in Flanders.
4. Fadil (2005: 153) focuses on how 'Muslims individualize themselves through Islam rather than how they individualize themselves from Islam. Pedziwiatr (2008) focuses on the 'Islam of citizens', that is, the Islam of European-born citizens who are the new Muslim elites in European urban spaces. My research discussed here focuses on the discourses regarding the use of different Islamic instruments (especially *'ijtihād*) by Muslim women in their attempt to reconcile their religious way of being with the broader community.
5. Several studies have highlighted changes in Islam among Muslims in Western Europe (see Babès 1997; Klinkhammer 2000, 2003; Roy 2000; Schiffauer 2000; Tietze 2002).

6. Own research (Van der Heyden, Geets, Vanderwaeren & Timmerman 2005) and examinations of Césari (1994, 1998, 2007 & 2008), Nielsen (1995), Sunier (1996), Vertovec & Rogers (1998), Fadil (2001, 2005, 2008), Tietze (2002), Phalet, Van Lotringen & Entzinger (2002), Djaït (2003) and Phalet & Güngör (2004) show how young Muslims in Europe identify with Islam.
7. According to Giddens's understanding (2006: 45) of social change, three main factors have consistently influenced social change: physical environment, political organisation, and cultural factors. All three factors are omnipresent in an immigration context.
8. The idea of a 'just' Islam (in Arabic ʿadl, derived from ʿadala) is taken from a lecture by Azisah al-Hibri at the Worldwide Women's Day on 8 March 2005 at the Belgian Parliament in Brussels.
9. The core of the problem is the traditional Islamic religious authority structure in Muslim societies and diaspora communities, which follows an earlier, patriarchal tradition, despite other theoretical possibilities for legitimate authority. Religious renewal questions this accepted form of authority.
10. Socialisation in a Moroccan family and belonging, at least nominally, to one Islamic school of law is important because it means the research results are not a consequence of variation between different Islamic schools of law.
11. Avishai (2008: 412–413) decides to speak about 'doing religion' in relation to the identity category of religion. The 'doing religion' refers to an attitude and performance of identity. The aim is to become knowingly an authentic religious individual. '*Doing religion*' refers to the idea of 'doing gender' by West & Zimmerman (1987), but while 'doing gender' happens often unconsciously 'doing religion' is a half conscious and self-directed-project.
12. The processes are economic and cultural changes, continuing migration, the loss of dominant ideologies and of traditional symbols and stories about their own history, the rapid exchange of information, the high mobility of goods, services and people and the increasing number of national and international conflicts. For Verkuyten (1999: 5), these would then be responsible for the growing importance of identity issues.
13. Hall (1990) proposes that identity is always unfinished, always in the making, in other words, a product of an ongoing process. In his essay *Cultural Identity and Diaspora*, Hall discusses (1990) two approaches of (cultural) identity. One that defines identity in terms of a shared culture, a kind of overarching collective giving 'one true self' (Hall 1990: 223), and a quite different approach, in which similarities and differences are both recognised, and one can never speak for long and with accuracy about one experience or one identity.
14. To make his image of hybrid religious identity clearly, Zondervan (2008: 100–102) looks at the religious function of popular culture and the media-religion that develops among (young) people.
15. I try to represent the participants' voices by using quotes from the interviewed women since all collected data was audiotaped, transcribed, and coded for analysis.
16. The discrepancy between the intention of women to take on a role in the organisation of mosques, Muslim mosque associations and the Executive, and their current absence, seems an appropriate subject for further research. For a detailed analysis about the informants; reflections regarding a female ʾimāma, see Vanderwaeren (2010: 218–221).
17. The ability to act from religion, like the informants do, is explained by Korteweg (2008, 434) as being an agency embedded in social structures such as the intersecting social forces of domination and subordination. A consideration of agency, as something created by local and national, social,

cultural and political forces that traverse religion and that go beyond religion itself, can be found in McNay (2000), Ahaern (2001), Mahmood (2001) and Korteweg (2008). The agency of the Muslim women involved in this study is thus formed in direct relationship to structures of subordination.
18. It is precisely this discourse about rights that refers to a postmodern religiosity and binds the informants to a perception of feminism which is closely linked with postmodern feminism (see Tong: 1989).
19. In *The Idea of an Anthropology of Islam*, Asad (1986) described the way that Islam, for its believers and others, is a moral tradition that continues to develop through processes of normalisation of the correct praxis. This explains why instruction and discussion among Muslims about the correct praxis is important.
20. ʾal-Qaradawi considers the effort of a selective ʾ*ijtihād* as the putting next to each other and the evaluating of various legal opinions by 'revoir leurs preuves respectives fondées sur les sources ou l'ʾ*ijtihād* afin, au bout du compte, de pouvoir choisir celle qui nous paraît reposer sur la preuve la plus solide et l'argumentation préférable selon les nombreux paramètres de référence' (ʾal-Qaradawi (1993) in Ramadan 1999: 169). Moreover, such a choice should be adapted to the times, taking into account the current people and their interests, and protect them against evil.
21. Peter (2006b) notes in his article "Leading the Community of the Middle Way: A Study of the Muslim Field in France" how literature often focuses on actors of religious authority, which implies the alignment of religious authority with leadership and ignores the dependence on and entanglement with the existing Islamic discursive tradition (Peter 2006b: 111).
22. Generalising based on qualitative in-depth analysis raises questions. A common strategy for refuting most remarks is to interview people until 'theoretical saturation' (Glaser & Strauss 1967) occurs, meaning that no new information will be acquired by additional interviewing.

13 Processes of Localised and Globalised Islam among Young Muslims in Berlin

Synnøve Bendixsen

Muslim communities of Western Europe deal with a range of new and diverse challenges in their everyday life compared to Muslims in countries where the majority population follows Islam. Each European country presents distinct structural, political, and institutional approaches in how they deal with Muslim minority claims (see Triandafyllidou 2010), offering both opportunities and limitations in establishing Muslim institutions and in promoting religious practices. This continuous interaction between a minority Muslim population and non-Muslim majorities and institutions in different European countries impact how Islam is institutionalised and practised. Some scholars suggest that one consequence of this process is the formation of 'Euro-Islam', or 'German Islam', French Islam', etc. The Euro-Islam perspective (i.e., Bassam Tibi 2010), an imagined new branch of Islam which supposedly combines Islamic principles with contemporary European cultures and values, highlights the pluralistic and democratic character of the European public sphere. However, it is rightly critiqued for de-legitimising the mobilisation of Muslims that deviate from this '"enlightened" European system of values' (Amir-Moazami & Salvatore 2003: 52). Furthermore, such perceptions of Islam also fuel the practices by certain media, politicians, and researchers in Europe of depicting Islam as an unchanging unit with a particular set of characteristics (essentialisation of Islam), or as haphazardly chosen rules of behaviour which differ between the various sociocultural groups (fragmentation of Islam). For example, Khosrokhaver (1997) advances the idea of a fragmented Islam in his research. He says: 'There exists not one Islam in France, but several, each one of which obeys its proper dynamic which allows itself be influenced by the others only in a limited way' (1997: 23).[1] This artificial construction of a fragmented Islam ignores that '[t]he fact that local traditions developed; did not produce many Islams but rather many versions of a theme that was continuously developed in those local traditions, but within a greater tradition' (Manger 1992: 53).

In consequence, this research follows Asad's (1986) approach to Islam as a discursive tradition. According to Asad, 'Islam is neither a distinctive social structure nor a heterogeneous collection of beliefs, artifacts, customs, and morals. It is a tradition' (Asad 1986: 14). If we consider Islam as a discursive tradition, we can recognise that practitioners are induced to follow certain practices that are viewed as religiously 'correct' because of how these practices are situated within a Muslim discourse that is directed to a perception of the Islamic past and future, with orientation to a present Islamic practice (Asad 1986: 15). It is a mode of discursive engagement based on the sacred texts. While there is a tendency for each particular Islamic community to claim to represent the 'true Islam' (Yükleyen 2007), the fact that Islam can encompass a broad range of groupings remains unquestioned. In Europe, there are competing voices—all of whom claim to represent Islam, including educational institutions, intellectuals, media, Islamic organisations, communities and Internet portals. The place of Islam in people's daily lives, as Bringa (1995: 197) puts it, 'creates a community of Muslims and also communicates differences between Muslims in life-style, forms of religiosity, practices, and interpretations of the role of Islam in everyday life'. Indeed, there are always some Muslims who assert that what others take to be Islam is not Islam (Asad 1986).

This chapter seeks to examine how the local expression of religiosity in everyday life among Muslim youth in Germany is formed in relation to processes on various scales, some of which are global, others national and yet others, urban. It examines how Muslim youth take a particularly active part in the process of developing Islamic practices situated in Germany, and how they, in this process, also create a religious female youth culture. It also provides one example of how a transnational religion and feelings of religious belonging are formed by local life and come to represent the foundation of moral solidarity. In my research, I have conducted fieldwork with a group of young Muslim women who participate in the religious organisation *Muslimische Jugend in Deutschland* (MJD, Muslim Youth Germany) in Berlin.[2] I participated in weekly meetings, leisure activities, religious events and celebrations, weddings, engagement parties, home parties, high school events and shopping. Although the organisation consists of both men and women, the meetings are gender divided (they meet on different days), and my research gives an account of the female participants. After a short introduction of Muslims in Germany, the chapter will discuss four aspects of female youth's religiosity which this religious organization and the young participants illustrates particularly well: (1) (re)localisation of the universal message of Islam in Berlin, (2) modifications in power structures, (3) transnational forces, and (4) the formation of a religious youth culture.

A NEW GENERATION OF MUSLIMS

Germany is home to around 3.8 to 4.3 million Muslims, representing the largest Muslim population in Western Europe after France. Muslims in Germany are predominantly Sunni (74 per cent), and the majority's ethnic background is from Turkey.[3] Berlin has the largest population of Turks outside

Turkey, with approximately 2.6 million in Germany overall. Although not every Turkish migrant defines him or herself as a Muslim, a large percentage of them do even if their active participation in religious activities tends to vary. Germany's Muslims also consists of persons from Bosnia, Bulgaria and Albania (496,000 to 600,000), the Middle East (292,000 to 370,000), North Africa (including Morocco, 259,000 to 302,000) and a small number of people from central Asia, Iran, South-East Asia and Africa (Faas 2010). In the same way as the predominantly economic migration from Turkey, people from Morocco and Tunisia have parents who came as labour migrants to Germany through bilateral governmental agreements, while most people from Palestine, Iraq, and Lebanon arrived as political refugees, and a large part of people from Syria, as well as Palestinian Arabs, who came as students and then stayed on (al-Hamarneh 2008: 26). Estimates suggest that the Muslim population in Berlin is around 213,000: an estimate which includes both numbers of immigrants from countries where Islam is the main religion and converted Germans. The accuracy of the figure is problematic as it includes people that do not necessarily personally adhere to Islam; how to count 'Muslims' is both a political question and a research dilemma (Spielhaus & Färber 2006).

Muslim migrants in Germany, as in other European countries, have been setting up mosques since the early 1970s, both to provide themselves with a supportive community structure and also with an idea of raising their children so 'they would not be lost' to the 'other' culture. The role of Islamic communities and organisations has changed over time, in relation not only to the alteration of the status of 'migrants' but also, particularly, in relation to the social and religious needs of the younger generation born in Europe (see also Yükleyen 2007). Both Turkey and Germany have continued to try to bring Muslims under a greater degree of state control. In 1994, the Islamrat für die Bundesrepublik Deutschland (Islamic Council for the Federal Republic of Germany) was established on the model of the Central Council of Jews in Germany that aspires to represent the needs of the Muslim community by operating within a German legalistic framework.[4] Established in April 2007, the Koordinierungsrat der Muslime (KRM, Co-ordination Council of Muslims) attempts to coordinate the interests of its member organisations and represent them vis-à-vis the state and the public. It includes the four largest Muslim umbrella organisations, namely, the Zentralrat der Muslime in Deutschland e.V. (ZMD, Central Council of Muslims in Germany); the Turkish-Islamische Union der Anstalt für Religion e.V. (DITIB, The Turkish-Islamic Union for Religious Affairs, representing 52.3 per cent of organised Muslims with Turkish background); the Islamrat für die Bundesrepublik e.V. (IRD, The Council of Islam); and the Verband der islamischen Kulturzentren e.V. (VIKZ, Association of Islamic Cultural Centers, representing 13.66 per cent of organised Muslims with Turkish background). According to their own estimations, KRM represents around 410,000 believers from approximately 1,530 mosque organisations (Şen & Sauer 2006). However, as Barbara John argues, 'The direction which Islam will take in Germany, is decided neither by the gathering at the Islam-conference [DIK, Deutsche Islam Konferenz, the German Islam Conference] nor the co-ordination council of Muslims [KRM] of the affiliated umbrella organizations' (2007: 63).

The increasingly plural field of Muslim organisations in Germany also includes initiatives from youth in particular, often born in Germany. The religious youth organisation in focus here, *Muslimische Jugend in Deutschland e.V.*, was established in 1994 under Haus des Islam e.V (HDI, based in Lützelbach) by eight young Muslims of varying ethnic backgrounds and ages between 17 and 20. Starting modestly with the idea of providing religious teaching and activities to youth born in Germany, the initiative later split off from Haus des Islam e.V and registered itself independently in a small village in Baden-Württemberg.[5] Comprising approximately 50 branches across Germany, the organisation is today apparently the second largest Muslim youth organisation in Germany, after the Islamische Gemeinschaft Milli Görüş (IGMG).[6] Fatima (age 31) told me that during one Muslim tent camp in 1994, organised for youth all over Germany by Haus des Islam e.V, a Muslim 'brother' from the United Kingdom had talked about a youth organisation for Muslims in England.[7,8] Fatima recalls sitting around a campfire discussing 'would it not be great if, living in Hamburg but going to Aachen, you would know where to find other young Muslims who are actively practising their religion?'[9]

Weekly MJD meetings in Berlin attract relatively few people—often between 10 and 20 female youth—but annual national meetings are more popular, with an upper limit of approximately 1,200 participants from all over Germany. Similar Muslim youth organisations exist in Austria, France, Italy, Norway, Sweden and the United Kingdom, and MJD is represented at the European level by FEMYSO (Forum of European Muslim Youth and Student Organisations) established in Leicester (United Kingdom) in 1996. According to a *shura* (council) member and MJD's homepage, the German MJD is funded by an annual membership fee, events, donations (from earlier members, parents and friends), and income from the religious bookstore Green Palace, which had been owned by MJD since 2000–2001 but was closed down in 2010.

The general structure of this particular religious youth organisation consists of a *shura* with 10 members elected every 2 years by a membership meeting (which in 2008 consisted of 50 per cent males and females), and a male *Vorsitzende* (*Amir*, chairperson/president). The *shura*, whose members meet in different German cities or towns every four to six weeks, is responsible for all MJD activities and represents MJD at the national level. The *shura* is responsible for dealing with general questions from other organisations or local MJD groups, and for planning MJD events and their religious content. Individual assignments are delegated to different *AG* (working groups), such as the Editorial AG, Organisation AG, Handbook AG (which develop the branch handbooks used by the different local branches), Fun-Day AG, Regional AG, and Meeting AG.

The 'faith community' MJD represents a new kind of Muslim organisation: created by second-generation Muslims living in Europe, its structure challenges the more traditional Islamic organisations established by their parents. MJD in Berlin was not situated within a mosque for several years, although since 2010 it has moved, first to a Bosnian mosque situated in Kreuzberg and then to the premises of a German-speaking mosque in Wedding.[10] Still, it only seldom makes use of *Imams* (prayer leaders) or educated religious teachers. It is multicultural in the sense that it does not adhere to one specific national or ethnic belonging and specifically makes use of the German language during seminars. This organisation seeks to both carve out a public space for Islam in Germany and to offer youth with a migration background ways to live out Islam in a non-Muslim, secular society.

(RE)LOCALISING RELIGIOUS PRACTICE

Young women participating in MJD are primarily well-educated and socially upwardly mobile Muslims from immigrant families who are likely to be active in the future in representing Islam within the German public. The majority are educated in a Western intellectual tradition, are socially and politically well informed, and are active users of media and the Internet. It attracts young Muslims (15–30 years old) with various migration backgrounds, including Egyptian, Palestinian, Kurdish and Turkish, who are seeking a pure or true Islam across ethnic and national ties. The youth arrive at the weekly meetings of MJD largely motivated by a desire to cultivate themselves according to the ideals of how to be a correct Muslim, considered as universal and situated outside of time and space, an idea partly made possible due to new information technology and enhanced education.

The focus on knowledge and self-discipline as the correct way to Islam echoes similar processes taking place in several European societies (see, for example, Jacobson 1998: 158 for UK; Sahlin 2003 for Italy and Roy 2004 for France) and also in Islamic movements in Turkey (Sanktanber 2002) and Egypt (Mahmood 2005). Weight is given to how individual actors can choose between various interpretations and take 'individual assertions' with respect to Islam (Eickelman & Piscatori 1996; Mandaville 2004). This particular religious consciousness is usually understood as being realised through a process of modernisation, where the expansion of literacy and education play a role in diminishing the dependence on more traditionally defined religious authorities to make sense of one's religion (Eickelman & Piscatori 1996; Ismail 2004). Media and mass higher education have made it possible for an increasing number of actors to engage with and modify the religious tradition. This has led to a 'democratised' access to religious texts (Eickelman & Piscatori 1996: 111) and a 'democratisation' of religious authority (Hirschkind 2001)—a process in which MJD takes part.

The search for the religious truth by MJD can also be considered as one example of the dual process of universalisation and localisation which Islam has undergone in various societies and cultures.[11] Islam happened in a particular social, cultural and historical context of the Middle East. As van Bruinessen and Allievi (2003) have pointed out, in the process through which Islam reached other societies and cultures, it simultaneously went through a twofold process of *universalisation* and *localisation*.

The process of universalisation allows for the fact that the producers of Islamic knowledge can clarify which aspects of Islam are essential and non-negotiable, and which aspects can be abandoned on the grounds that they are specifically Arabic (van Bruinessen & Allievi 2003). The process of universalisation is an effort to separate what one consider as universal in Islam, from what is contingent on the sociohistorical, cultural context. In MJD Berlin, efforts to perform a pure, true or real Islam are pursued by going back to the sources (Qur'an, hadith and Sunna), obtaining knowledge, understanding the religious practices, and being reflective on where knowledge comes from in order to judge whether or not it is valid. The participants of MJD, as well as other religiously oriented Muslims with whom I had discussions, learn through peers, lectures and discussions to be conscious of the roots of a religious practice—whether it derives from the traditional customs of their parents or can be situated in relation to universal sources. Frequently, participants are challenged to explain where they take their knowledge from and to clarify their ideas. In the mosque or during events youths often ask each other 'where have you heard that from?', 'where does it say that?', and 'is it an innovation?' followed by discussions and even heated arguments on what is 'the correct answer'. Young people are seldom reserved or meek when it comes to disputing someone else's religious knowledge. Here is an example:

> One of the new participants is saying that she has heard that if you laugh in prayer then the prayer becomes invalid. Somaya (17) responds: 'Yes, but try to remember where you have heard that from, 'cause remember that hearing something is not the same as it being correct.'

In case of uncertainty or in discussions of different opinions the youth organiser stops the discussion, saying, 'I will check that for next time' or asks the attendees to 'check it' with an imam or in a book. The continuous religious authority of imams, even when none are officially linked to the organisation, is revealing here. The youths are encouraged to ask questions, to seek answers in books, on the Internet, and to participate in organised events. MJD also infrequently invites a young imam for a dedicated Question & Answer meeting in which the youth are invited to ask concrete questions.

The second step is the process of *localisation*, namely, the adaptation of what is considered to be a universalised message to more localised customs and needs (van Bruinessen & Allievi 2003), a process through which it becomes part of the local context. Discussing Hinduism and Islam in India, de Kruijf (2006: 129–130) refers to religious localisation as the following:

> The process in which a system of thoughts and practices is modified to meet the requirements of a particular (new) locale and thus to ensure its relevance and survival. More than anything, it involves a divergence from the developmental trajectory of the 'original' system which is prompted by alterations in people's (re)creative possibilities, by shifted boundaries of the productive field.

Although the aim of the youth in MJD is that of practising a 'universal' or 'pure' Islam, all religious practices must be socially performed and in that process they are accommodated, in various degrees and at various times, to the specific sociohistorical context. In the weekly MJD meetings, religious ideals (*adab*) or a religiously defined ethos, are promoted through debates, presentations, lectures, comments and everyday expectations of the young participants. At the MJD gatherings, events and seminars, the attendees listen to presentations on practices that (Sunni) Muslims consider as duties, such as prayer and fasting. The participants, to a various degree, seek to learn 'universal' ideals in their endeavour to be or become a 'good' or 'pious' Muslim. However, in practice, there is creativity in the form, style or performance of the youth's religiosity, and far from being universal, it is firmly localised in time and space. Religious ideals that are considered universal are, for example, localised by the specific examples used by the participants during discussions and by the contextualisation of specific difficulties, challenges, and opportunities that living in Berlin as a 'good' Muslim bring forth. For example, one of the organisers, Leila (21) gives a presentation, saying, 'When we are sitting in the underground and there are no other Muslims there, one feels like an outsider and does not dare to take the Qu'ran out to read. Why are we ashamed of ourselves to do that? People are looking anyways.' Leila then refers to a verse in the Qu'ran and a history from the life of Muhammad where the moral is that one should be proud to be who one is, also in front of other people. She says, 'What did Umar Ibn al-Khattab [the second Caliph] do when he took up [converted to] Islam or what did a young man do at a university—praying in the middle of the university? When everyone is doing this, there is a (positive) chain reaction. Trust yourself. Just do it'.

Leila makes a direct link here between historical time and today: born in the year 580, Umar converted the same day as he planned to assassinate Muhammad and later became the second Caliph (634–644). Accordingly, his conversion improved the confidence of Muslims to practice Islam openly, including in the subway, as nobody dared to obstruct Umar's prayer at the *Ka'ba* (Islam's central house of worship, located in Mecca). Appealing to the women to be self-conscious, to not be ashamed of openly practicing Islam is done also through emphasising (directly or indirectly) that they are part of the larger Muslim society (the *ummah*). Daring to perform their religious practices openly in the Berliner streets can also inspire other Muslims to perform their religion openly. Professing one's religion openly can be a form of *da'wa*, which means 'call' or 'invitation' in Arabic and is an invitation to Islam (not unlike the Christian notion of evangelising). Thus, the religious dimension cannot be omitted here. The emphasis within the youth group is that it is normal to be a practising Muslim, and that this should be the starting point of an effort to take Islam into the public sphere and out of an abnormal position in Germany. Visibility of their practice of Islam here becomes a feature of the struggle of recognition in which visibility can become a source of power, and the invisibility or suppression of the visible act becomes a sign of subjugation (cf. Fraser 2000: 119).

Additionally, many of the MJD meetings are concerned with how the youth can live in a non-Muslim society without embracing too much of the secular environment. In discussions, presentations, and debates, the leaders invite them to reflect upon the overlapping value concerns held by both Germans and Muslims. Values which are viewed as shared by both Muslims and Germans, such as freedom, equal opportunities, concern with the environment, the poor and ill are contrasted with values that both Muslims and Germans disapprove of, such as discrimination, oppression and that money is ruling the world. Islam, the young people argue, promotes equality and helps the poor, which are ideals that Germans also support at an ideological level. Certain values, such as punctuality', honesty and hard work are advanced in MJD as valued both in Islam and in the German culture. After a weekly meeting which had been dedicated to discussions on how punctuality was not only valued by Germans (indeed a very typical trait associated with Germans), but also in Islam, I asked one of the more knowledgeable participants whether it says anything in the Qu'ran about punctuality? She looked at me with unease and explained that in fact she had been wondering about the exact same thing and acknowledged that she could not come up with any sources. It is my impression that emphasising that certain values and characteristics which they consider as appreciated in Germany are also Islamic values, facilitates the effort to amalgamate a 'Muslim' and 'German' identity.[12]

Processes of localisation should be understood in relation to changes in productive conditions. Indeed, '[a]lterations in practical circumstances that facilitate or even instigate the production or reproduction of a system make adaption inevitable' (de Kruijf 2006: 130). Immigration brings along a constellation of new conditions which alters how religion is produced and transmitted. Modification of (re-)creative opportunities due to migration consist of new financial situations, changed access to authentic knowledge, and a new legislative system in the country of settlement. Additionally, social alienation and frustration related to migration have an impact on ethnic and religious identification. In the process of moving, 'religion and tradition cease to be prearranged identities' (Göle 2003: 813). Migration also brings forth a new social makeup of the body of believers which, as Eickelman & Piscatori (1996) have pointed out, makes the immigrant familiar with different ways of performing a ritual or religiously defined act and she or he becomes aware of outsiders' (often critical) viewpoints on her or his ways of performance. When they moved to Germany, Muslim migrants from various backgrounds brought with them Islam in different localised forms, such as more popular practices and authorities that are localised orientations of the scriptures.

MODIFICATIONS IN POWER STRUCTURES

Localisation processes are also linked with modifications in power structures, a frequent consequence of the relocation of people or a cultural system (de Kruijf 2006). For example, improved access to higher education in Germany increases the generational gap and, to some extent, contributes to the deconstruction of the authority of elders and, some have argued, to an individualisation of religion (Cesari 2003; Roy 2004). Simultaneously, globalisation has an effect in this process given that religious concepts, practices, and organisations are shaped by transnational forces everywhere, not only in migratory contexts. The transnational aspects will be further elaborated in the next section. I will here briefly discuss two aspects of the modifications of the context in which the youth practise Islam: first, performing religion in a minority situation in which Islam is perceived negatively; and second, changes in religious authority.

First, the negative representation of Islam, escalating post 9/11, promoted by the media and also right-wing politicians includes a view of Islam as a 'backward', 'traditional' and 'misogynist' religion and Muslims as 'terrorists'. Yet simultaneously, rather than leading to a decrease in identifying with Islam and Muslims among the young generation with a migration background, it has intensified it. The media has contributed to an increased consciousness of being Muslim and belonging to a Muslim community (Spielhaus 2010). The 'turn to Islam' as a main form of identification may well have specific local characteristics in that it can be one strategy of youth born in Germany to deal with the feeling of not being accepted as German by media, politicians and in everyday social interactions, as well as a reaction towards the German public's simplification of Islam as embracing and representing everything negative.[13] In my fieldwork, it became clear to me through everyday conversations that the female youth were regularly stopped by strangers on the street who asked them whether they were forced to wear the veil; or who hurled insulting remarks, such as 'you look stupid with the headscarf', 'Taliban!' or 'another one of those Mummies'. Verbal abuse was a frequent topic of conversation among the young friends and provoked amusement, frustration and incredulity. Verbal abuse suggests that people in general consider the young women in this study as representatives of Islam who have an obligation to respond to questions considered as somehow related to Islam (be they cultural, social or political). Although negative situations seemed to happen frequently with veiled youth, that is, youth who already *visually* identified with Islam, discriminatory episodes were also revealed to me by unveiled youth who dressed as 'typically' German with tight jeans and short sweaters.

Being a religious minority in a secular society shapes both the process of forming and practicing the youth's religiosity and their relations to their parents and religious authorities. Within MJD, in particular, the perception of the female youth's roles as representing Islam is situated within a religious discourse, namely, as *da'wa* (invitation to Islam) and thus a religious duty. Accordingly, several youth consider it as their religious obligation to alter the stereotypical view of Islam and Muslims in Europe. Such counteraction includes things like the youth reminding each other to smile to strangers on the *U-Bahn*, and to be friendly and helpful to German non-Muslims. More importantly, during the seminars it is emphasised how important it is to behave as a good Muslim woman in public in order to show, both to Muslims and non-Muslims, how 'real' Muslims are. I consider this effort also as participating in a public struggle of who can define or at least help shape the normative content within the stained category Muslim.

Second, for some young females, the search for conduct befitting 'true' Islam can emancipate them to some extent from their parents and ethnic social field, which may entail a pluralisation of religious authority. This aspect is part of a more general process of pluralisation and fragmentation of religious authority in the Islamic tradition (Eickelman & Piscatori 1992) which, rather than advancing secularisation, opens up to an expansion of religious education. Educated Muslims are given or constructing spaces to participate in discussions on the Islamic tradition and how Islam is applicable within democracy, civil society and human rights (Casanova 2001). Such spaces tended to be filled only by Muslim intellectuals or the traditional *ulama*. According to Casanova (2001), Islam here follows the confrontation of all world religions in reacting to modernity, partly by repositioning the traditions in an attempt to fashion their own version of modernity. In Germany, many female youths find that their parents trust them more and are willing to provide them with more freedom to participate in the public sphere when they don the veil. When these youths are religiously knowledgeable, their parents are not only more likely to grant them more freedom of movement, but they are also more prone to argue against their parents' rules often traditionally motivated. That said, the discourse of 'true' Islam also emphasises the value and place of parents in Islam, illustrating a potential *re-accentuation of parental authority* (Bendixsen 2010). As parents are highly valued in Islam, the youth learn to respect them and their wishes, and to avoid breaking with the family. This double-edged emancipation also exists when looking at education as a means for the so-called empowerment of young women: insofar as females acquire knowledge and master

Islamic discourse, language and laws, they can set their own agenda within the otherwise patriarchal structure typically found in any of the world religions (Cooke 2001). Simultaneously, however, the fact that these females want to use their educational attainments not to reform their community but to defend it from the negative stereotypes prevalent in German society, means that they decide (consciously or unconsciously) to subordinate the construction of an emancipating agenda. As noted, the manner in which the women have chosen to fight the idea of Islam as 'traditional', 'patriarchal' and 'backward looking', is through presenting themselves as 'good Muslim women', an ideal informed by their understanding of their scripture. In this struggle, personal and social pressure is placed on young women both by themselves and their peers to conform to the standard of a good Muslim woman—a pressure which can itself be transformed into a means of social control by the self and others in regard to the female's public behaviour.

While these modifications largely take place in a minority situation, the turn towards a 'pure' or 'real' Islam should not be understood as a mere trend of migration given that it also takes place outside the European and North American context. The 'turn towards a religious lifestyle', which is broader than what is commonly called 'Islamic revival', since similar trends for religious renewal can be found in Christianity and New Religious Movements, is a phenomenon taking place on a global scale, encompassing several countries around the world. This kind of religiosity needs to be situated as part of a larger ongoing process within the Muslim tradition as a "living tradition" embracing continued negotiations and struggles of interpretation and authority (Amir-Moazami & Salvatore 2003: 53–54). One should not consider the youth's living of Islam merely as a return to tradition, a re-Islamification, coming out as Muslims, or only as a consequence of the specific European migration situation—to do so would ignore the dynamics within Islam. The youth's beliefs and practice (the religious culture) of Islam must be situated within a discursive Muslim tradition which is constantly subjected to internal transformations (cf. Amir-Moazami & Salvatore 2003; Asad 1986). One needs to emphasise the continuity of an internal logic of interventions within all the Islamic traditions. Nevertheless, the specific European social, political and historical context in which young female Muslims decide to assume a religious identification undoubtedly informs the expressions of this religiosity and the localisation processes of Islam in Germany.

TRANSNATIONAL ISLAMIC KNOWLEDGE AND CONSUMPTION

Similar to contemporary youth cultures, the religiosity of these female youth also needs to be conceptualised as 'constellations of temporary coherence' within a multifaceted interaction between local and global cultural flows (Massey 1998: 123). Clearly the localities within which youth cultures coalesce do play an important role in these interactions, but in an increasingly interconnected world, geographical conceptualisations of cultures fail to account for the complex social interactions that extend beyond localities (Massey 1998). Transnational and global flows are part of shaping the youth's religiosity in terms of religious authorities, dress style and general Islamic consumption. The transnational aspects of migrants, Muslims in Europe and the emergence of global Muslim identities have been increasingly analysed (see, for example, Basch, Glick Schiller & Szanton Blanc 1994; Eickelman & Salvatore 2002; Mandaville 2004). The term 'transnational' is meant to capture the processes through which immigrants (re-)produce social fields across geographical, cultural and political borders (Basch & Glick Schiller 1994: 7). It emphasises the multiplicity of relationships developed by migrants—including familial, economic, social, organisational, political, and religious, which traverse the country of residence (ibid.), something particularly made possible through new technological developments.

Throughout the last couple of years, Muslims in Europe have increasingly generated a large body of knowledge on Islam, including books, magazines, newspapers or newsletters, Internet sites and television presentations. In particular, Muslim youth have also produced Islamic culture, including Islamic fashion, music such as hip hop, and comedy shows in the larger European cities (see Moors 2009). These multiple voices represent different home countries and streams within more transnational forces and various political, social and cultural frameworks in the European country of residence.

How is the religiosity of these female youths also shaped by transnational forces? Religious consumption, such as shopping extensively during the holidays in their parents' home countries plays extensive part in the process of forming an 'authentic' Muslim self and in providing an understanding of one's identity and life world, just as does the consumption of Arab and Turkish media. Young girls utilise websites for Muslim-branded clothes such as www.MuslimGear.com; or German-based, religiously ethical products, such as T-shirts with 'I love my prophet'.[14] For example, Janna (19) tells me:

> On Arabic television they have a show telling you different ways to put it [the headscarf] on. There are women who show different ways of how you can have your headscarf. One day I had this with three different layers, it looked really professional! I had seen on television.

TV shows, religious authorities and influential figures among youth in Europe and in the Middle East, including transnational charismatic figures, such as Tariq Ramadan, Amr Khalid, and Yusuf al-Qaradawi, help shape the religious knowledge of the youth. As Janna's statement suggests, populist talk shows even form the basis for headscarf fashion in Berlin.

During MJD weekly, monthly and annual meetings, the participants are made familiar with transnational authorities, such as Tariq Ramadan, Yusuf al-Qaradawi, and the Egyptian television preacher Amr Khalid, who through their activities online and on cable TV channels are reaching Muslim youth all over the world.[15] The messages of these authorities are not followed entirely; whereas some aspects of Qaradawi's teachings, such as 'women who are allowed to travel alone' are pursued, a recent call to jihad against Israel is rejected. Furthermore, whereas some members might be attracted to Khalid's profile, other members will find him objectionable and too populist. Like most organisations, MJD has developed a particular organisational culture or content, which successive *shura* (council) uphold with some modifications. According to the (male) leader of the *shura*, changes in what is religiously acceptable or not (for instance, whether or not hip hop is suitable at religious meetings) could be understood as a consequence of the increased experience of the organisers, of becoming adults and thus less afraid of doing something which is not Islamically correct.

The religious knowledge communicated by these relatively new forms of authority particularly appeals to youth with their form of dress, rhetorical style, and choice of themes. The style of Khalid is youthful, with his clean-shaven face, dressed in jeans and polo shirts, or in suit and necktie. Bayat explains Khalid's success through the observation that Khalid 'simultaneously embodies the hip-ness (rewish) of Amr Diab (Egypt's most revered pop-star), the persuasive power of evangelist Billy Graham, and the unsubtle therapy of Dr Phil, an American popular talk-show host' (Bayat 2002: 23). The family values clips of Ali Gawhar and video music clips of the popular singer Sami Yusuf, which use pop'conventions to articulate messages of Islamic piety and devotion, are further popular references. Amr Khalid encourages young Muslims to be active, both socially and religiously, in the society in which they live. Apparently he promotes a 'civil jihad' in the name of Islam, where the goal is to improve Islam's image. Amr Khalid is a popular figure among youth in Middle Eastern countries as well, which is confirmed in the journalist-style book *Muhajababes* (Stratton 2006).

During one MJD presentation to explain her point, Somaya refers to the film clip 'the Haram police' on 'Ummah Films', suggesting that the others 'check out' this funny—and even attractive—guy called 'Baba Ali'. This recent religious personality, Baba Ali who is on YouTube, although not a religious authority or a religious preacher, is a source of inspiration for youth in the United States and in Europe. Since 2006, the 33-year old Web designer Ali Ardekani, known as Baba Ali has been presenting a one-man show with video blogs on YouTube called 'Ummah films'. This young, American-Iranian Muslim, creatively contributes to a transnational Muslim youth culture with his funny, satirical clips in a stand-up comedian style. Baba Ali's clips, which last between four and eight minutes each, provide ironic critiques of the Muslim community worldwide, such as 'Seasonal Muslims' and 'Ramadan-Muslims'. In 'The Haram Police', he makes fun of Muslims who only practice Islam during Ramadan, and in the clip 'That's not hijab', he makes fun of young veiled females who do not wear their headscarves correctly.

He also satirises how non-Muslim society relates to Islam with the popular postings 'Who Hijacked Islam?' or 'Muslim while flying'. Since 2008 he has started the show 'Ask Baba Ali' where he answers questions e-mailed to him from youth all over the world (i.e., 'Racism and pride!').

Baba Ali's (or Ali Ardekani's) authority arrives from his eloquent ability to clearly communicate many of the contemporary problems and urgent issues that the youth experience in their everyday life, playing on the generational gap and social relations with non-Muslims. Dressed in cool T-shirts and interacting playfully with the camera, he represents a new form of authority. He emphasises that he is not 'knowledgeable' about Islam, and that he 'is saying this to himself before anyone else', positioning himself as 'just like them'. Some of the clips, for example 'Muslim Characters at Work' have German subtitles—others are translated into Bosnian, Arabic, Italian, Russian and French.[16] In his discourse, he distinguishes between 'tradition' and 'true Islam' and particularly targets youths living in non-Muslim societies. His YouTube clips are enjoyed by MJD youth, situating them as part of a wider religious youth movement than just that of Berlin, a transnational religious youth culture.

In short, transnational Islamic consumption enforces the vision of a global *ummah* by strengthening the imaginary bonds between Islamic actors worldwide. The experience of belonging to a globally imagined *ummah* is the starting point for looking at the self as part of an extensive and powerful force, and identification with such a community can be one way to construct a positive self-image.

RELIGIOUS YOUTH CULTURE

The young women I have studied hold a vision of modernity dissimilar to the Western models—an alternative modernity which combines more typical Western ideas of modernity, such as Western-style urban clothing, an emphasis on education and working life, taking pleasure in (Islamic) hip hop, and marking a distance from their parent's generation with deep religiosity, namely, a strong place for religion and practical religious observance, as well as pious fun and religious consumption.[17]

Young people make a complex amalgamation by leading a life that is both religiously observant while staying young, modern, urban individuals. European discourses suggest that this amalgamation is contradictory, since they perceive it to be impossible to be both modern and religious, and in particular to be both modern and Muslim. Islam and Muslim in the European media stand for all that is traditional, conservative and conventional. Salwa Ismail (2006) argues that '[t]he view of Islamism as antimodern rests on the assumption that modernization is associated with secularization and the retreat of religion from the public sphere. Islamism thus appears as an expression of an antimodern strand that, for some, is inherent in the religion' (Ismail 2006: 3). Instead of considering Islamism as an antimodern movement, Ismail refocuses our attention on its rejection of the perceived Western hegemonic ownership or meganarrative of the modern.

Indeed, my research suggests that young Berliner Muslims do not believe that there are contradictions between their consuming what they consider a modern lifestyle and being religiously diligent. The youth, for example, perform a Muslim fashion show to teach each other how they can dress fashionably and yet still appropriately with a veil (Bendixsen 2010). One of the characteristic features of (late) modernity is the tight coupling between identity and consumer goods (Bauman 2001; Friedman 1994). In their free time and during the events, youths draw on the slowly developing 'Islamic popular culture' (Sanktanber 2002). The last couple of years have seen a development of a religious youth culture, partly visible in commodities like music, clothes and consumption, such as 'Mecca cola'. For special events, MJD invites Muslim hip hop singers who perform Islamic songs, like the converted German (with Ethiopian background) Ammar 114 from Frankfurt who performs in the German language and pop singers like Yusuf Islam (formerly known as Cat Stevens) and Sami Yusuf who perform in the English language. They also stage interviews with famous Muslims, such as the former German-Turkish pop star Hülya Kandemir who withdrew from her famous pop life and turned to living as a practising Muslim. Music groups like 'skit skatch' are also popular among the Muslim youth as they perform social critiques through songs like 'es warn' (it was) which pinpoints the discrimination against the Arabic population in German society.

This religious youth culture is an *aesthetic practice* guided by specific values and religiously defined orders, which in turn carve out spaces, belonging and mark social borders. The female youth styles are part of the process of growing up as young, female and Muslim in a Western society, creating a type of consumption which becomes a significant, vigorous aspect of crafting a young religious self (Bendixsen 2009). In the process of interacting with religious texts and normative ideas and participating in specific religious spaces, the youths also localise their religious youthfulness as a specifically 21st-century Berliner religious youth culture. The young female individuals negotiate between enjoying modern consumerist society while dedicating themselves to their religion and its practices—and they see no contradiction in the two. In this process, the youth are creating a *female youth culture* which is becoming increasingly publicly visible and in which the youth position themselves vis-à-vis their (parent's) ethnic social circle, peers, family, and other youth.

Indirectly, this normalises Islam as part of a modern way of life—at least for the practising youth. Religious spaces like MJD promote and put forward ways for youth to live an active, religiously oriented youth life in a Western society. They carve out alternative local spaces where being young and having fun can take place, oriented by religious norms and forms, including endorsing a proper religiously oriented gender order as well as being oriented by the existing (nonreligious) youth culture. Furthermore, the young participants in MJD consider that their chosen path to craft the self is more modern than a path which remains affiliated to ethnically oriented group discourses, which they view as traditional, uneducated and misinformed. The youth's focus on moral values and universality can be seen in light of two positions; on the one hand, they react towards what they consider to be a secular, materialistic, and Eurocentric majority society in which religion is forgotten, morality is lost, and where the contribution of their parents' forefathers to the (secular) knowledge production of the world is ignored. On the other hand, their religious and social practices are a reaction against what they consider to be the traditional, cultural, local and nostalgic orientation of their parents and the overall migrant community, in that ethnic belonging is still significant in organisation of mosques and religious organisations, and many of their parents perform religious rites and practices habitually or with reference to their past, but without scriptural knowledge. In this youth space, specialised knowledge, which becomes a kind of symbolic capital (Bourdieu 1990), is valued more than the question of class, national or ethnic background.

CONCLUSION

The forces of localisation and globalisation are part of parallel catalysts of change, and rather than being mutually exclusive these processes coexist and are even interconnected (de Kruijf 2006: 128). Jonathan Friedman has pointed out how fragmentation and homogenisation 'are not two arguments, two opposing views of what is happening in the world today, but two constitutive trends of global reality' (2002: 233). The Muslim youth's religiosity is formed by complex spheres of social practices that cross geographical, cultural and political borders, through media, consumption, and family relations outside of Germany. Religious ideas and concepts accessed and discussed online or through cable TV are further debated and (re-) interpreted locally, within the friendship group based in Berlin.

At this moment in history, when Islam is being socially, political and culturally positioned in European society, young people play an extensive, visual and creative role in the establishment of new institutions and structures like MJD, which specifically targets young people. Among the aims of this Muslim youth organisation is to raise awareness among young Muslims as to how they should behave in daily interaction with non-Muslims and how they should represent Islam to the German public as good Muslims. The youth increasingly identify with a nonethnically defined, universally oriented religious sphere, while at the same time their religious practices become localised in the Berlin context, encouraging them to find ways to practice Islam in the way that is best for their specific sociocultural sphere. The organisational approach of MJD is part of a struggle to provide a social space where the youth can learn or affirm that it is not contradictory to be modern and to be Muslim. The upward social mobility among the youth, mostly acquired through higher education and entering public working life through pursuing a professional career, also brings with it a move from home to outside, from private to public life.

Noticeably, the youth who are most attracted to this religious youth organisation are not uneducated youth but those who in many ways are the best equipped among the second-generation migrant youth, in the sense that they master the German language, focus on higher education and have ambitions for a future working career. At the same time as localising themselves through the urgency of improving the image of Islam in Germany, they also transcend the physically bounded site by drawing on globalised networks and sources of inspiration, (re-)capitalising on the Islamic notion of community, the *ummah*.

NOTES

1. Il n'existe pas un Islam en France, mais plusieurs, chaque forme obéissant à sa propre dynamique et ne se laissant influencer par les autres que de manière limitée'; personal English translation from the original French. This may well be a continuation of the endeavour by Hamid (1977) who argued that there are several Islams.
2. The data for this paper is derived from lengthy fieldwork (March 2005–June 2007) with 40 young female Muslims in Berlin, many of whom participate in MJD. During this period of time, I participated in the weekly meetings and the regular events organised by MJD. This was part of my PhD thesis '"It's like doing SMS to Allah". Young Female Muslims Crafting a Religious Self in Berlin' defended April 2010. In addition to empirical data gathered through fieldwork, I make use of the organisation's publications, websites, brochures, newspapers, magazines and both semistructured interviews and informal conversations. I have chosen to rely less on interviews with the young women I have worked with and have instead sought an understanding and reflection based on social situations and encounters with the women which could not be captured by collections of narratives or interviews.
3. This is only a rough estimate since precise statistical data does not exist, primarily because the German government does not keep statistics on, or make distinctions concerning, religious affiliation. In order to make estimates, statistical details about foreign nationals from predominantly Muslim countries and numbers of naturalisations of former Turkish citizens are taken into consideration (Spielhaus & Färber 2006). See Spielhaus and Färber (2006) for a discussion on the problems of numbers with regard to Muslims, religious organisations and mosques. Muslims in Germany also comprise Alevis (13 per cent), Shi'ites (7%) and a small proportion of Ahmadis, Sufis/Muslim mystics and Ibadis.
4. This exemplifies the perception that immigrant groups and minorities are orienting their behaviour towards each other, and that more recent immigrants take their predecessor's narrative as a model.
5. According to their webpage, the HDI is member of the ZMD (Zentralrat der Muslime in Deutschland), an umbrella organisation of Islamic organisations

and communities. Their webpage also states that the HDI, in the framework of youth work in Germany, works together with the MJD. Accordingly, the MJD makes use of, in infrequent intervals, the spaces of HDI, and members of the MJD help with the youth work at HDI. See www.hausdesislam.de, accessed 8 December 2007.
6. The Islamische Gemeinschaft Milli Görüş (IGMG) is closely linked with political Islam in Turkey, including the Refah Partisi (Welfare party) and its predecessors (Henkel 2004). The nature and quality of this relationship is highly disputed.
7. The national British Muslim Youth Organization (YM UK, Young Muslims UK) established as a national youth moment in 1984 springs from the Islamic Youth Movement (IYM), established in the 1970s. The focus is second-generation Muslims. It was inspired by the influential Jammati-Islam ideologue Khurram Murad who found the time ready to 'provide opportunities for the development of an educated elite that would provide ways of connecting with and provide leadership to a new generation of Muslim young people' (Hamid 2009: 4). For an analysis of the organisation's establishment, structure and ideology, see Hamid (2009).
8. All names in this study have been altered in order to ensure the anonymity of the interviewees. Additionally, the ages of the interviewees at the entrance of my fieldwork are provided in brackets and have been slightly altered in order to further ensure anonymity.
9. All names of youths have been altered to comply with academic ethics.
10. For several years MJD Berlin used the premises of the bookshop and publishing firm Green Palace. When this publishing firm was reorganised, they left the premises. Consequently, MJD had to find a new meeting place.
11. It also parallels similar processes which new movements go through as discussed by Alberoni (1984). Frequently, in the 'birth phase' of movements, the group is apt to generate a unanimous view or model about the essential issues. The movement searches for the 'truth'—the 'unique truth'—against old institutions (Alberoni 1984).
12. By this, I do not mean to suggest that such values are not also found in the Islamic context. My point is that there is a large selection from which one can choose which aspect to emphasise. This choice is neither 'universal' nor 'haphazard', but must be understood as informed by a socio-historical and cultural context.
13. In the beginning of the 1990s, researchers considered that youth turned to Islam as the only option available, owing to the conflicting demands of the majority society and their ethnic group (Sahgal 1992). The new Islamic revival observed among second-generation migrants in the European cities is largely explained as a response to external forces like discrimination (Cesari 2002, 2003), daily racism, and a way out for youth who are more or less excluded or rejected from the society and search for a sense in life (Khosrokhavar 1997).
14. Other popular online links are www.islam-online.net, www.styleislam.com, TheHijabShop.com, TheNasheedShop.com, TheMuslimBabyShop.com, and TheHalalHealthShop.com at www.dukkaan.net, accessed 15 November 2008. The webpage www.myumma.de is a German speaking Internet site which links active Muslims across the German-speaking world, accessed 20 December 2008.
15. The controversial Swiss thinker Tariq Ramadan was presented as one of the 100 most powerful and influential people in the world by *Time* magazine April 2006, and referred to as the leading Islamic thinker among Europe's second- and third-generation Muslim immigrants, see www.time.com/time/

magazine/article/0,9171,993913,00.html, accessed 21 November 2008). Yusuf al-Qaradawi is considered as one of the main intellectual characters in the contemporary Islamic Revival (Mahmood 2005: 61).
16. See youtube.com/ummahfilms, accessed 9 December 2007.
17. Modernity is here discussed as an 'emic' term—thus, it is concerned with the youth's understanding of 'modern'. The researcher is not seeking to promote the all too often overemphasised dichotomy between 'tradition' and 'modernity' at an analytical level.

14 Towards Cultural Translation

Rethinking the Dynamics of Religious Pluralism and Globalisation through the Sathya Sai Movement

Tulasi Srinivas

RELIGION AND GLOBALISATION: INHERITED LEGACIES AND IMMEDIATE FUTURES

As the march of globalisation converts, or appears to convert, most, if not all, participating societies into plural entities, the reputation of religion in the minds of democratic citizens all over the world is rapidly becoming, or has already become, tarnished. Popular cynicism regarding the role of religion as a force for locating and engaging a common good has flourished, mediated through global news networks, popular cinema and everyday texts and experiences. Religion is now perceived as the viscous locus around which the discussions of parochial forces that appear to impede globalisation coalesce. Given this popular perception, it is important to critically interrogate the role of religion in contemporary society, and to examine the intersection between religion and globalisation more thoroughly (Tilly 2005).

The virtually unbroken consensus in social sciences, drawn historically from Western modernist secularist paradigms (Berger and Luckman 1966), was the accepted empirical assumption that with democratisation and modernisation religion would be confined to the private sphere (Shah, Stepan & Duffy-Toft 2012: 2–3). The normative assumption that happily fused 'description with prescription' was that it *should* be so, and it was thought that what was true, or thought to be true, in the historical trajectory for Western nations would be true of non-Western ones as well (Shah & Stepan 2012: 2). In reality, of course, religion has never been absent from the public realm. Some might even argue that in the face of modernisation, religion has actually become stronger. The phenomenon of a resurgent modern religion in the public sphere (Beyer 1994; Beyer & Beaman 2007; Casanova 1994), within the compressing and expanding forces of globalisation (Appadurai 1991; Harvey 1989, 2005; Stiglitz 2006;) has been the cause of some theoretical handwringing in the West. Scholars have suggested various polemical frameworks, both for understanding the phenomenon and dealing with it in the arena of world affairs (Barber 1995; Huntington 1996).

The cultural turn in international affairs (Bauman 1998; Beyer & Beaman 2007; Giddens 1991, 2003; Tomlinson 1999) has shifted the discourse to acknowledge the stubborn longevity of religion and the rooted nature of 'other' moral and ethical communities in the face of 'progressive' modern forces (Nandy 2005). The subsuming of religion under the broader rubric of culture in theoretical models indicated by the use of the term 'cultural globalisation' focuses on the interaction and play of intimacy between cultures that the political economy of globalisation encourages (Bhagwati 2004). I approach religion as being a foundation of culture, while also supported by it, weaving through it, and surrounding it, and while I recognise that religion and culture are not coequal, using the broader rubric of culture in this chapter allows us to more fully rethink broader patterns and the apparatus of process in cultural interaction.

Paradoxically however, while religion has been stubborn in its refusal to retreat to the private sphere, equally surprisingly, the old consensus of the role of religion as withering away has also been stubborn in the face of evidence to the contrary. Our inherited legacy of a fixed array of conceptual ideas and language distinctions remains firmly lodged and deeply divisive, despite it being obviously frayed. I see three principal conceptual problems of inheritance that prevent the articulation of a new way of thinking about religion and globalisation: the definitional ambiguity of globalisation, dialectical thinking of local/global paradigms leading to conceptual sterility, and a reified understanding of culture within which religion is often subsumed (Srinivas 2010).

Definitions of globalisation have emerged from studies that address transformations in religion directly and indirectly due to a variety of attributed causal factors, such as international migration and diasporic cultures (Berger and Huntington 2001; Stiglitz 2002, 2006); global political policy and civil society (Huntington 1996); threats to secular religion and the public sphere in the West (Barber 1995; Friedman 2000); democracy (Fukuyama 1992) nationalist identities (Van Der Veer 1994); and cosmopolitanism, cultural dialogue and valorisations of morality (Appiah 2006; Hannerz 2002; Nussbaum 2007). The sheer variety of definitions hints at intricate and intimate ties to disciplines and subdisciplines within which the discussions of globalisation theory have been bounded, and at the politics maintaining that boundary (Fischer 2004). The problem is that the *options to think and rethink then get delimited* by these definitions. Further, I suggest that the *how* of the process of globalisation has become lost, and the reality is far more nuanced than the definitional array allows for. Attempting to make sense of the links between religion and these varied spheres involves a challenge and opportunity that is created by the tensions between the 'theory only' route of globalisation studies and the 'empirical realities' of globalisation (Beck 2005: 20; Hannerz 1990, 2002). Facing this definitional array allows us to call productively for a focus on both the empirical realities of globalisation as defined by the larger populist discourse (Friedman 2000, 2007) and to call for a more complex understanding of the politics of experience of the global, through a focus on the dynamics of culture, particularly religion (Jameson 1991).

Within social science's early grappling with the problem of globalisation and culture (Abu Lughod 1991; Bourdieu 1977; Fox & King 2002; Ortner 1984), the multidimensionality of globalisation is celebrated, as local and indigenous cultures are set against the bland uniformity of the global. But this dialectic vocabulary is fraught with problematic paradoxes (Cvetkovich & Kellner 1997) in its description of active dynamic processes and has simplified their inherent complexity (Srinivas 2010). It imposes a dualist template on what is, in effect, a cultural ecosystem in which a hierarchy of cultures is fluid, negotiable, dependent upon the context and the perspective of the viewer, and in which religion moves in and out of focus as a structuring paradigm for behaviours. In this dualistic framework, religion is seen simply as an obstacle to progress, rooted in the local, embedded culture that prevents a global mindset. But to those outside the secular West, the removal of religion from the debate is seen as an imperialist exercise by Western neocolonial forces deeply inimical to local traditions, bent on global homogeneity to further capitalist domination (Nandy 2005). Thus, religion is seen by both sides of the debate as a bulwark for issues of identity politics, such as class warfare or anomic disenfranchisement, uncomfortably fusing with nationalist or ethnic paradigms to create the perfect storm of ideology often ending in violence (Tambaih 1996). In these cases, religious pluralism is seen cynically as a stand in for ghettoisation or new racism, and this view is stoked by the rhetoric of cultural misunderstanding.

So religion has been othered and seen as located problematically in the other. This has led to a theory that problematises the other through an emphasis on religious difference. For example, Samuel Huntington's problematic, yet influential, vision of the 'clash of civilizations' is a natural outcome of this view as is scholarship focused on the 'challenge of pluralism' (Eck 2006, in Ammerman 2006; Levitt 1999, 2007) and the appearance, or lack thereof, of tolerance and acceptance.[1] Both these theories share the assumption that Western-style globalisation is inevitable, leading to an elimination of difference and resulting in a bland homogeneity. All societies and cultures are classified in relationship to the West, which implies, mutatis mutandis, that the West, that is, Euro-America, has the 'primacy model of globalisation'[2] and, to put it bluntly, the 'right' way to do globalisation (Nederveen-Pieterse 2003). This complex and often misconstrued relationship between modern, Western thinking and cultural difference (Kurasawa 2004: 2), is one in which the theoretical tension between the universalism of globalisation, 'the transhistorical and transcultural applicability' of modern, Western culture (Kurasawa 2004: 2–3) and the spatial and temporal embeddedness of contextual theorising, 'a radical particularism'—has made the theorising of religion in the global frame a pursuit dogged by charges of ethnocentrism and lack of subject agency. To account for non-Western forms and routes of cultural globalisation, some contemporary social scientists argue that globalisation indeed comprises a series of 'alternate' (Eisenstadt 2002) or 'multiple' modernities (Hefner 1998)[3]—alternatives to the Western secular concept of modernity (Vertovec 1997)—which enable a hybrid combination of a deeply religious attitude with a modern consciousness (Weller 2001).

But in all these conceptual understandings, religion is seen as external and other to the capital, secular processes of globalisation. As I see it, there are two primary understandings of religion *within* the global frame. The first is the rise of non-Western religion (Goody 1996) and the focus on fundamentalist religion and its growth and spread, specifically the way the West has seen Islam (Barber 1995) which deals primarily with world affairs and politico-economical approaches. The second is the decline of religion, primarily in the West, and the rise of an individualist spirituality, met by either a celebratory understanding of the modern individualist's turn towards spirituality (Heelas & Woodhead 2000, 2005); or an elegiacal one that frames the rise of spirituality as the loss of traditional religion (Carrette & King 2004) and which primarily deals with individualism and the loss of moral community to capitalist enterprise. It speaks to the anxiety of loss of traditional understandings of religion, primarily within academia but also in the broader society. For our purposes of building new theory located in process, it signals the urgent need to envision a new horizon for the immediate future of religion.

In this chapter, I will therefore try to get beyond these two articulations of religion in globalisation. I use religion as a tool to disinter *the economies of faith* through a meditation on the neo-Hindu, syncretic, Indic, civil religious movement called the Sathya Sai movement. As I do so, I call for an idealistic third place from which to view the promises and perils of religious pluralism, which productively challenges the established binary theoretical spaces of secularism and fundamentalism, and that productively upsets the established disciplinary and scholarly categories of religion and globalisation. The reclaiming of the vocabulary of civil religion to encourage discourses of civility and pluralism is a powerful intra and intersubjectivity exercise to begin an interrogation, not only of modernity and globalisation, but of the vital relationship between our imaginings of the world and the place of the other within it. So I focus upon the problem of encouraging cosmopolitanism and plurality.

As I trace the movement of this little-known, and sometimes misunderstood, charismatic religious movement from its inception in a small village in Southern India to its current large and successful global presence, I offer a broader reflection on cultural mobility and cultural interaction within the frame of the political economy of globalisation. Taking into account both the politics of knowledge (the cultural context before analysis and the fuzzy praxis of cultural engagement), which provides the epistemological framework, and the politics of interpretation (loaded as it is with affectivity), provides a productive tension. I suggest that as religious forms become dis-embedded from their geographical and cultural locations and become dynamic and mobile, they morph and shift. Focusing on this shape-shifting aspect of cultural interaction allows us to explore the *usually invisible processes of cultural translation that happen at these intersections*.

Let me note that in using the term 'cultural translation' as a strategic manoeuvre within globalisation, embedded in everyday performance, I am signalling a wider strategy than text. Talal Asad, in his magisterial essay on cultural translation, uses the term as a lens to reflect upon the enmeshed power within textual strategy that reflexively focuses upon the writing of ethnography by the anthropologist (Asad 1986), where the anthropologist as cultural translator needs to be made sensitive to the inherent invisible power structures of his pedagogic practice. While I agree with Asad about the reconsideration of the implicit power in text creation, I expand the term 'cultural translation' beyond the ethnographic text to the agentive subject. In this story, it is the Sai devotees who are cultural translators; and as such, I suggest that cultural translation is a agentive performative term that signals a multiplicity of subjective sources, rather than a reflexive textual term located in questions of authoritative voice (Asad 1986: 161). So I unpack the *processes of cultural translation* and indicate possible avenues of rethinking it as a strategy that reaches beyond text in the contemporary context. In so doing, I explore the 'implicit' and ambiguous meanings within it that might possibly allow for a varying inclusivity and plurality and new ethical ways of being, a productive and plastic 'strategic ambiguity' that, I tentatively suggest, may offer new ways of seeing and being cosmopolitan in a plural world.

New ways of seeing and being cosmopolitan are necessary as the primary model of cosmopolitanism, the Euro-American model, rests on what F.G. Bailey has termed 'the civility of indifference' (1996). The chapter leads to a tentative critical conclusion regarding the nature and importance of an 'engaged cosmopolitanism' that, I argue, has different roots from the Euro-American model and therefore engages plurality through a *civility of difference*. Therefore, although my work is about one Indian religious movement, it also suggests a way of facing the more complex reality of threatening tensions within plural societies and interlayering the complexities without thereby provoking the discussion of what it takes to share a public space that is linked willy-nilly to the wider world (Nussbaum 2007).

I attempt to build an apparatus (even if it is a recognisably flawed and limited exercise) of cultural translation, located in four dyadic pairs of processes.[4] The focus on process speaks to the inherent problems in our current understandings of globalisation (both techno-economical and cultural) and our apprehensions and applications of religious pluralism which are limited to the increasingly fuzzy and yet hard boundaries of the nation state. Yet I simultaneously attempt to destabilise this apparatus as I am alert to its problematic postulation of culture as "bounded". So the larger aim of this chapter is to problematise how religion and religious sensibilities move and change in contexts of contemporary globalisation and its accompanying discourses, stores of knowledge and technologies in order to privilege the concept of pluralism and the accompanying discourses of multiculturalism and cosmopolitanism.

In the following pages, therefore, I turn to ethnography and begin with an outline of the transnational Sathya Sai movement—a charismatic, religiocultural, Indic, civil, movement of approximately 20 million devotees in 137 countries—in several locations including, but not limited to, the United Kingdom, Australia, Germany, Italy, the United States, India and Japan. Using examples from my nine-year international ethnographic study of the Sai movement's successful globalisation, I build, and simultaneously critique, my tenuous model of cultural translation through the articulation and exploration of four dyadic pairs of translation processes. Last, I meditate upon plastic ontologies and ambiguous vocabularies as ways of allowing for difference that are productive of new engagements with plurality.

My ethnographic, participant observation among Sai devotees took place over nine years and is the product of a postdoctoral study in six countries across the world including India, the United States, Japan, and the United Kingdom. In so doing I combined a multisited approach with a networked optic to consider what I call 'mobile description', a thick description à la Geertz (1996) made suitable for mobile subjects such as those of the Sai movement. Most fieldwork was based on traditional ethnographic participant observation, though it often took place in emergent spaces of mobility such as airports and bus stops, with intense interviews over several years through a rolling sample of Sai devotees and anti-Sai activists. This study, unusually, engaged the politics of belief through the accounts of devotees but also a hermeneutics of suspicion through the accounts of anti-Sai activists (Srinivas 2010), thereby creating an understanding of religious belief in the round. I travelled with devotees as they made their way to see Sai Baba in India and saw how they lived their lives while visiting the ashram in India. Overall, I interviewed 115 devotees. Some fieldwork, especially that of anti-Sai activism, was done over the Internet and through phone calls and Skype sessions, proof of the deployment of global technologies in media and knowledge that create these new global worlds of being and knowing.

THE SATHYA SAI BABA MOVEMENT, NEW KNOWLEDGE AND TRANSNATIONAL GLOBAL RELIGIOUS INFLUENCE

The Sathya Sai Baba movement (SSB) is a transnational religiocultural charismatic movement approximately 65 years old. The movement had a single identifiable leader called Shri (honorific) Sathya Sai Baba who was the titular head of a large global charismatic organisation (Taylor 1987) and who died on 27 April 2011, leaving the organisation in the hands of the powerful Satya Sai Trust. The Satya Sai movement currently attracts a self-reported 50 million followers worldwide (though the Indian news magazine *India Today* estimated the SSB following to be 20 million in 2007 and their net worth to be six billion US dollars that was corrected to nine billion US dollars after Sai Baba's death) through a message promoting the universal values of truth, righteousness, peace, love, nonviolence and charitable service. The growth of the movement from a small rural group in South India in the late 1940s to an international movement with a presence in 137 countries today has been rapid and consistent, and their cultural influence has broadened simultaneously. The number of Sai centres originally in India and their locations underlines this explosive growth, first in India and later globally. In 1988 there were 3,864 Sai centres in India which expanded to 8,447 by 2002, a growth of, on average, 118% (Srinivas 2008: 133). In the overseas organisation of the Sai movement, the growth was equally rapid. In 1969, a Sai centre was started in Tustin, California, followed by centres in London (1969), Durban (1973), Rome (1974), Berlin (1977), and Mauritius (1978). By the 1980s, Sai centres had been established in Australia, the West Indies and Brazil; and the number of centres and their locations suggested a division into "zones" based on geographic regions. In 2000, zone 3, which included Asia and Australia, had 598 Sai centres (Srinivas 2008:137), and there were over 2,000 centres worldwide with over 10,000 registered members in the United States alone.[5]

Further, the Sai transnational following is not confined to the Indian, primarily Hindu diaspora (Babb 1986; Klass 1991), though they form a significant part of the devotional base, but has expanded to include the middle classes of many different countries and cultures (Srinivas 2002). I met devotees from Chile, Japan, Mexico, Singapore, the United Kingdom, the United States, the Netherlands, Italy and Australia in one trip of a few days to the Sai ashram in South India. The devotees—professional, technocratic, 'Westernized' (Kent 2004), or what sociologist S. Srinivas calls an 'urban following' (2008)—are characterised by their mobility, their affluence, and their focus on creating a healthy union between body, spirit, and mind (Heelas & Woodhead 2005: 75–79), and Sai Baba is what Weiss calls 'a prophet of the jet-set more than he is a guru of peasants' (2005: 7). Socially, they strive for a better society, defined as less poverty, cruelty, inequality, and other forms of repression.

The story of Sai Baba's incredible life from peasant boy in a remote town in rural India to global godman/guru, has been recorded in over 600 texts, some devotee based and others by scholars (Babb 1983; Kent 2004; Klass 1991; Nagel 1994; Shepherd 1986; S. Srinivas 2008; T. Srinivas 2002, 2010; Urban 2002). The accounts of devotees suggest that Sathya Sai Baba's charisma, his healing abilities, his god-like being and his capacity to perform miracles (Murphet 1971, 1977) are all significant for their construction of belief (Sandweiss 1975). From his own discourses and many prophesies, devotees suggest that he is and remains even post his passing, a charismatic guru (teacher), a reincarnated Muslim seer (faqir), a saint, or an avatar (incarnation) of God (S. Srinivas 2008). The movement seamlessly draws on philosophical and theological strands from several great religious traditions of the subcontinent—Sufi mysticism, popular Vaishnavite Hinduism, Shaivite Hindu iconography, Vedanta and Advaita philosophy, contemporary Christian teachings, and indigenous healing rituals—to weave a constantly evolving Indic urban syncretism in which the problems of dogma, creed, and literature appear to magically fade into the background as also do problems arising from divisions of caste, class, nationality, and religion (Srinivas 2010). Devotees from various cultures and nation states abide by what Sai Baba says in his sermons and talks, and it is his articulation of any intention, problem, or solution that is important in the devotee's mind (Lee 1982).

Lawrence Babb describes the Sai doctrine as having 'relatively little to dwell upon, or at least nothing very distinctive: philosophical views are simplistic, eclectic and entirely unoriginal' (1983: 117). In reality the lack of doctrinal originality allows for the contention that Sai faith 'rekindles awareness of eternal truths not to invent new ones' (Kent 2004: 57). Their simplicity makes them accessible to a broad audience, and their eclecticism makes them appealing to people of many cultures though they are often read variously in different cultures.

The Sai case suggests, in the larger frame, that some religions are capable of going global (Srinivas 2010). Religion, itself a complex epistemological and ontological structuring mechanism, further complicates the globalisation process by creating an ambiguous, plastic yet multidimensional matrix with new ways of being, new alliances and new formulations to create registers of meaning and regimes of value for devotees. In sum, mobile culture, as exemplified in the Sai case (made easily mobile through the processes of techno-economic globalisation), makes new links to space and territory in new contexts. For every de-territorialization move (where cultural forms and ideas are removed from one context), there is a re-territorialization move (cultural forms re-inscribe culture with new context-based time-space meanings) (Inda & Rosaldo 2002: 12), a double movement of meaning making. The problem that this itinerant culture raises is that of cultural congress and interaction: what happens when two or more cultures meet?; of the asymmetry and efficacy of the process; and its outcome in terms of new knowledge, as cultures influence each other and reinvent themselves in the process. I locate this work in the examination of the dynamics of cultural interaction and the description of the processes of cultural reinvention as a way out of the pitfalls of social theory towards a critical understanding of cross-cultural interaction.

The argument here is that the presence of the Sathya Sai movement and its growth across the globe indicates that globalisation is about understanding interactions and networks within a new space and new modalities of knowledge. I suggest that apprehending this new world of knowledge—theatres of action and emotion, of value and meaning—both shapes it and imbues it with meaning, which is itself an act of cultural reading and production. So, as cultural forms are made mobile and make their way across the global network they structure new moments of reinvention and, consequently, new cultural translation dynamics.

THE DYNAMICS OF CULTURAL TRANSLATION

The complex process of cultural translation is composed of the four dyadic pairs of subprocesses or stages that I have identified, which occur in a progression as a cultural form or ideology is made mobile: (1) cultural awareness and dis-embedding, (where the cultural form is taken out of its originating culture or ideology and is separated from its location); (2) codification and universalisation (where the cultural assumptions of the originating culture are codified for transfer); (3) latching and matching (where the cultural form is taken overseas to a new receiving culture and given new meaning, re-linking it in new and innovative ways to the originating culture to give it authenticity and value); and last, (4) contextualisation (where the cultural form or ideology is linked to the larger cultural matrix of the receiving culture and made relevant) and re-embedding (where the cultural form is embedded into the host culture). These processes of cultural translation are, I argue, a key part of the practical problem of creating and maintaining any dynamic, successful, transnational, cultural movement. I will use brief examples from my rich ethnography to extract the subprocess dyads of cultural translation and discuss them in some detail.

Cultural Awareness and Dis-Embedding

The first stage of mobility is the dis-embedding of the cultural form from its parent context, the originating culture. Dis-embedding requires cultural reflexivity to determine which parts are integral to the phenomenon itself and also those than can be translated. What must occur in the originating culture for cultural forms to be able to contemplate mobility? First, the culture must develop a sense of itself within the larger world; that it feels it has something to offer culturally is very important. In essence, it is a reflexive understanding of being part of the global game with something to offer. Accompanying this position is a sense of power and agency over the process of cultural translation. Let me give an example from my field notes:

> October 22, 2006, Bethesda, Maryland; the home of Mrs. Susan Ratner (57). The entire basement of this four-bedroom home had been converted into a Sai Baba shrine. Walking into the mirrored basement tricked one into believing that Sai Baba was standing there. Other walls of the room held garlanded and framed pictures of Sai Baba at various stages of his life, giant close-ups of his smiling head, and photos of his feet, hands, and eyes. In front were a series of small tables on which stood images of Krishna, Rama, the Buddha, Hanuman, Jesus Christ, and Sathya Sai Baba. One of the large garlanded pictures was a holograph where if you looked at it one way it showed Sai Baba's face and at another angle, it seemed to be a recognisable image of the Hindu god Shiva, with snakes in his hair and a tigerskin robe. Yet another image fused Sai Baba with

Jesus Christ, and in another one Sathya Sai Baba was superimposed on his Sufi Islamic mendicant predecessor Shirdi Sai Baba.

As my vignette shows, for devotees, Sai Baba encompasses many forms of divinity in one. Sai Baba himself suggests through his life story that the plurality of divinity is engaged through three primary forms: as guru or teacher, as fakir or Sufi mystic, and as Hindu avatar or a reincarnated form of God on earth. He extended his divinity through bold imaginative connections to divinities and semi-divine beings from world religions other than Hinduism: Sufi Islam, Shaivite and Vaishnavite Hinduism and Christianity (Kasturi 1968). This creates a universally appealing charismatic figure who transcends the human-divine chasm to create a future divinity. These representational categories help construct a new language and tradition within the movement. Thus, it becomes possible for devotees to be both devotees of Sai Baba and devout Christians. Finally, this 'extension by affiliation strategy' is subtly applied to the devotional base arguing for a racial, ethnic, national and linguistic pluralism.

Sai Baba had in his life time created a divine persona that is nomadic in spite of, or perhaps because of, the fact that traditional Hinduism (not reform elements) has no proselytising mechanism. The productive ambiguity around the sacred person of Sai Baba allows for an extension by affiliation strategy to other great divine and semi-divine figures. The sacred personhood of Sai Baba is dis-embedded from the original religiocultural milieu in which it is embedded, and is free to travel across the global network across space while he was alive and across time after his passing. This extension of divinity enables a bringing together of temporal (*avataras* spanning many *yugas* or eras), spatial (transgeographical and national boundaries) and interactive frames (the life story is told through multimedia) into a coherent whole, simultaneously engaging the possibility of travel as well as the possibility of becoming grounded in one place.

Here pluralism is not about choice as it is usually understood in contemporary culture but about the possibility of multiple commitments. The competition here is about adding meaning, not about excluding it. The fourfold divinity of Sai Baba articulated in his life story extends his divinity to the possibility of including gods, demigods, saints, and gurus, all of whom are considered equally valid by the devotee base (Padmanaban 2000; Palmer 2005). So, while devotees might feel a sense of agency in "picking" the form of godhood they feel a kinship to, the underlying principle of plural forms is never diminished by this choice. Teleological pluralism,—that is, what has evolved as a response to the fragmentation of Western Judeo-Christian culture and finds its way into contemporary discourses on cosmopolitanism and pluralism, is about the replacement of a single, lost sacredness (Juergensmeyer 1991). In a sense, then, theorists are struggling to understand the contemporary gestalt, in which people find it possible to hold multiple meanings as they break away from the assumption of a singular commitment. Hence, the concept of pluralism itself is political and subject to various meanings based on its derivation.

Codification and Universalisation

In the second stage, the integral parts are codified to make them accessible to various peoples. The codified parts are then made accessible to a larger number of people through various tactics of diffusion such as affiliation or extension. For cultural translation of a particular cultural form, the originating culture[6] must codify the cultural matrix within which the cultural form resides. The world that was taken for granted is made explicit so that the particular cultural form can be easily contextualised. The codification of the cultural matrix of the originating culture into a series of regulatory principles or patterns of knowledge that is transferable enables the cultural form to become mobile, and the code maybe abstract or literal.

For example, in the Sai case, indigenous, Indian, embodied ascetic practices called *sattvica*, drawn from medical moral practices of the subcontinent, from *Ayurvedic* (Hindu) and *Unani* (Islamic) texts and regimes which determine embodied controls for food and drink, modest clothing, sexual relations, and even thought, argue in favour of a soteriological quest as I have written about previously (Srinivas 2010). In Hindu philosophy, the dominant philosophical paradigm in the Sai tradition, the understandings of the separateness and opposition between the 'this-worldly' paradigm, comprising the body and its desires, and the 'otherworldly' world of the soul and its soteriological quest to find self-knowledge and liberation, is the centrepiece of the human quest. The body and its spirit are connected but have different goals and motivations; the purpose of the monadic soul that lives within the gross corporeal body is to realise self-knowledge, liberation and truth, through the disciplined service and controlled asceticism of the body. In this way the Sai body is seen by devotees as a workable site for self-creation.

By virtue of its global presence, the Sai movement is engaged in the interplay between the codified conception of embodied, Indic, embedded, sattvic disciplinary practice for transnational audiences on the one hand and its individual expression, often based in global consumption practices (Harvey 2005), on the other. The Sai devotee moves between the two ideational poles, living everyday life in the capitalistic discourse of satisfaction of desires (which is an accepted lifestyle choice), all the while striving toward a therapeutic 'self-betterment' program (which is increasingly gaining legitimacy as an alternative 'spiritual' lifestyle choice) of simple living. To enable the Sai devotees to achieve sattvica, the Sai movement has codified a 'Ceiling on Desires Program' ('Do not waste Food . . . do not overindulge in food. Do not waste energy, electricity, water, your own energy—too much talking, anger, jealousy and other negative expressions are equally a waste of Divine energy—do not waste Time, . . . do not waste Money'), that included a 'Nine point Code of Conduct' that structures embodied ways of being and worship. It is published in a range of multimedia.

The literal codification both of the Ceiling on Desires Program and the Nine point Code of Conduct enables the idea of sattvica to be disembedded from the cultural matrix. The cultural form of sattvica is disassembled, that is, the cultural form itself is taken apart and examined. What is deemed extrinsic to the form is discarded, and what is seen as intrinsic for the form to have meaning and power is retained. The intrinsic meaning gives the form its legitimacy and authenticity in the new culture. The cultural form is ready to be made mobile upon the back of the engines of globalisation: migrations of people, new technology and economic institutions. In the Sai worldview, ascetic practices are made explicit and codified to enable people of different cultural milieus to follow them. The Sai identity of a 'public, moral and virtuous devotee' is constructed through a reflexive and strategic codified process tied into a disciplining of the body and its feelings and desires, according to a moral code set down by the Sai organisation, which contests the contemporary embedded assumption of therapeutic well-being through a celebration of the body (Scuzzarello, Kinnval & Monroe 2008).

Latching and Matching

The third dyadic process I have termed 'latching and matching' by which I mean that as cultural ideas are made mobile, they encounter different cultures as they travel and "latch" on to them. Because these ideas often mean something quite different elsewhere with different sets of rules, it creates several possibilities of meaning, thereby making the idea more elastic, ambiguous and inclusive. Cultures that have efficient systems of latching are more mobile in spreading cultural forms and ideologies and in absorbing them as well. The imported cultural forms match certain desires or needs in the host society. When the latching mechanism is efficient, and the match is effective, then the new cultural form is engaged to the point where it becomes part of the everyday consciousness of people. They forget that it was imported and embedded in the host culture. Roach has argued that we use 'processes of surrogation' whereby we 'substitute' something we are familiar with, for something that is strange and unknown (1996).

To return to the example of the ascetic practice of sattvica, for Sai devotees in other parts of the world, particularly in the United States, Sai understandings of sattvica are seen, not as an embodiment towards purity and salvation, but as a therapeutic self-improvement program, creating a different moral value for the concept of sattvica. Sattvica in the United States focuses on the purity of mind through physical exercise akin, I was told, 'to the calmness and detachment one can achieve in going to the gym and doing meditation', a 'mindfulness' of self that has penetrated psychotherapeutic programs as well. An American Sai devotee seemed relatively unperturbed when he broke Sai rules about the body such as the eating of meat and when I asked him what he thought, he said, with a smile, 'it's like eating cake on a diet' (Srinivas 2010) indicating that it was possible to recover from this misdemeanour. However, in the Indian understanding of sattvica, any such lapse jeopardizes the soul in its quest for liberation, a misdemeanour of quite different dimensions. So the concept of sattvica undergoes some elastic stretching to fit it to the lives of the Sai devotees in different parts of the world. The language and conceptual shifting is functionally derived and designed to fit the needs of a postmodern society. The latching mechanism matches the goals of the larger culture of therapeutic self-improvement and self-awareness using language and ideas that are familiar to frame concepts that are otherwise culturally 'alien'[7] and might be rejected.

Contextualisation and Re-Embedding

Finally after its travels, the cultural code is re-embedded in a new culture. Re-embedding is accompanied by appropriate contextualisation manoeuvres. For example, in the Sai case, the encoded prescription of asceticism is reconfigured in the Western context as 'abstention', and the Nine point Code of Conduct makes these abstentions workable in everyday life by using terms such as 'awareness', 'mindfulness', 'vigilance' and 'control' that devotees are familiar with in other parts of their lives. The language and imaginative elasticity aid in (re-)constructing it as a lifestyle choice, submerging the deep aspect of belief that encodes the bodily prescriptions. It also enables prospective and existing devotees to imbue it with differing meanings and values according to their level of comfort, what S. Srinivas calls 'multiplicity rather than singularity' (2008: 215), where symbols and meanings occur across geographical spaces as well as time spans and reorient space and reconstruct time to fit another reality. So a cultural, embedded understanding of embodiment is given new forms and meanings appropriate to the local culture making it appear to fit seamlessly into the culture. However, since every culture is dynamic and changing, other processes influence this process of contextualisation as well; it is a dynamic process that is constantly changing. But the authenticity and ability to trace the lineage and origins of cultural forms become critical for the cultural form to be adopted.

Let us not, however, delude ourselves that translation is a one-to-one concordance. There is, occasionally, incommensurability between the culturally embedded ideas of the Sai movement and the culturally embedded ideas of devotees from other cultures. When different, culturally embedded, spatio-temporal understandings come into congress, intercultural communication grinds to a halt and contestations arise. The contestations are symptomatic of "cultural gaps" in translation. Any one of these four dyadic processes can have gaps and wrong turns, leading to conflict and failure to adapt to a global stage.

STRATEGIC AMBIGUITY, MATRICES OF MULTIPLE MEANINGS AND PLASTIC ONTOLOGIES

The ambiguity surrounding meaning allows for polysemic symbols and multiple interpretations of any image or event. The readily universalising moral/religious tool kit, with individually and culturally based mediation, is the essence of a successful global religion. This enables displaced transmission and the adaptation of historic practices to changing conditions and differing locales. New traditions may also be invented and others overturned. The paradox of the restoration of behaviour resides in the phenomenon of repetition itself: no action or sequence of actions is performed the same way twice; they must be reinvented or re-created at each appearance (Hervieu-Léger 2001). This repetition with revision program, which the Sai movement effectively engages in, 'illuminates the theoretical and practical possibilities of restored behaviour not merely as the recapitulation but as the transformation of experience through the displacement of its cultural forms and improvisation creeps into these forms and gets ritualised. Thus, the dominant notion that cultural transmission results in a repetition that is static, rigid, conventional, predictable and uniform is a fallacy. As Rosaldo writes in his analysis of culture (1993: 20), culture and cultural transmission nodes are 'busy porous intersections' where 'distinct processes criss-cross from within and beyond its borders'.

Multiple possible interpretations of the porous intersections enable an escape from the stifling dialectics of a unitary understanding of a culture of origination and cultures of reception toward both 'ontological complexity'—one where the ontology becomes mouldable and plastic (the inherent complexity of social systems and hybrid cultures)—and 'semiotic complexity' (our understandings of these complexities and the signs we use to denote them), where semiotics becomes fluid and nonoppositional. In the Sai movement, symbols, metaphors and tropes (oral, sensual, textual, and visual) act as accessible, complex, and ambiguous vehicles for meanings, emotions, and experiences that can be infinitely interconnected, leading to the possibility of an array of different meanings.

All these fluid meanings and the plasticity of being are deemed acceptable, creating what I term a 'matrix of meanings' where the agency of the devotee is located in the interpretation of knowledge. Individual choice thus becomes a complex and critical component of the mediation of the matrix. Devotees feel that their contributions become essential for the creation of this overarching matrix, as they transform both their selves and their *habitus* (Bourdieu) through the ideal of devotion performed daily (Csordas 1994:

68–69) into a quotidian poetics. Their thoughts, bodies, lives and stories all enrich the matrix, and for them the value resides not in the dualisms of the modern or the traditional, but in the multistranded ambiguity of the plural and global—what I have argued is a plastic ontological stance—a 'strategic ambiguity' that enables ever-greater expansion of meaning.

Strategic ambiguity enables the same praxis to be understood differently in different times and contexts without posing the expected problems of text and translation. Asad, in his critique of anthropologists performing cultural translation (1993), suggests that viewing culture as a text enables . . . categorization and reification and it is these precise problems that strategic ambiguity allows the Sai movement to overcome. Strategic ambiguity enables the culture to remain open ended and plastic whereby it can allow many significations within the same apparent praxis, and so paradoxes and seeming oppositions cease to be significant. The Sai movement, including devotees and institutions, exploits the matrix of possible meanings and deploys strategic ambiguity through a theological and symbolic ecumenism that makes the movement more inviting to people of different cultures, faiths, ethnicities and nationalities.

The matrix of possible meanings articulates different systems of ordering that are not based 'a priori on dualisms of subjects and objects' and enables a dissemination of 'accumulated intelligence' (Van Loon 2006: 309) through the 'interconnectedness of a multiplicity of agency that sits quite comfortably alongside non-Western belief systems' (Van Loon 2006: 309). To return to the essential question of pluralism, I suggest that the Sai movement, through adequate cultural translation, enables a matrix of possible meanings. Devotees feel agency in doing so and in crafting their own devotional identity, making this a postmodern devotion par excellence. Thus, the achievement of imagination in the Sai movement is the creation of a metastructure of meaning production that is rooted in the plural, the ambiguous, the plastic and the layered.

Today the question that remains is this: can religiously based varieties of cosmopolitanism (Beck 2007; Van der Veer 2003) be effective if their very appeal requires prior acceptance of their religious premises? Secularisation theorists may argue that the seemingly chaotic structures and forms of the Sai movement are only meaningful to an insider, and therefore such techtonics of strategic ambiguity and multiplicity of meanings is limited in its application and reach. Religious movements such as the Sathya Sai movement, in their sheer ambitious conceptual and strategic inventiveness, *suggest a repository of ingenious concepts and vocabularies for assuaging or attenuating some of the problems of global modernity.* Is it possible for such a cosmopolitanism, rooted in an embedded plurality, to spread beyond the limited confines of the movement to other more seemingly secular milieus? Speculatively, one could argue that the matrix of multiple meanings and their strategic ambiguity would allow for those on the margins of the movement, or perhaps outside it, to be drawn in, but there is neither space nor time here to consider this in any detail. I suggest hopefully that it is in this productive critical intersection that a new ecology of flourishing pluralism could emerge.

NOTES

My thanks to Christiane Timmerman, UCSIA, for the invitation to the conference on *Religion and Culture in a Globalised World* held in Antwerp in August 2010; and to all the conference participants for their generous sharing of ideas, including Maja Veselič, Inna Naletova, Jeffrey Haynes, David Martin and Peter Beyer. Thanks to John Hitchins, whose comments made this work more thoughtful, and more particularly to Robert W. Hefner and Jeremy Carrette for their encouragement in the writing of this chapter. Finally, I owe thanks to Andrew McDowell and Namita Dharia for their close reading of this work despite their intense travel and work schedules.

1. This formulation of the problem has been accepted by both critics and believers alike and has been received with some hesitancy, some fear, and some warmth by the various quarters.
2. The problem of Europe is the tendency of social science scholarship to conceive of Europe as the primary habitus of the modern. Thus India's—or indeed any other culture's—varied transitions merely become a footnote to the European move towards a fuller modernity.
3. The use of 'multiple' modernities still suggests that the primary model is the Euro-American model which, while true in a historical context, is often conflated, wrongly, with a structural primacy which should be unpacked and problematised.
4. I am grateful to Andy McDowell of Harvard University for bringing this significant critique of cultural translation models to my attention, and also for sharing his thoughts regarding cultural translation derived from his rich data on a Rajasthani village.
5. This strikes me as a conservative estimate. However, accurate figures are difficult to obtain since many Sai devotees who attend worship at the Sai centres are not dues paying, registered members of the organisation.
6. Scholars will disagree with me since this implies that a culture in some senses inviolate, and people can be a closed group. That is not, however, what I intend. I merely argue that some parts of a culture are more local than others and can be easily identified. For example, nobody can dispute even in an era of rapid dissemination of knowledge that Yoga is definitely South Asian in origin.
7. Of course some anthropologists would argue that to suggest that some ideas are 'alien' is itself an admission that I am treating culture as bounded, but I would venture to suggest that I am merely distinguishing one culture form another (and cultures are bounded in that understanding) and that I am not discussing culture qua culture as a whole.

15 Ghanaian Films and Chiefs as Indicators of Religious Change among the Akan in Kumasi and Its Migrants in Southeast Amsterdam

Louise Müller

The argument of this chapter is that the migration of the Akan people from Ghana (Kumasi) to the Netherlands (the Bijlmer district, a neighbourhood of Amsterdam that is geographically distinct from the rest of the Dutch capital) has caused a transformation in their religious identity.[1] Ghanaian films and the mediatory role of Akan chiefs are used as indicators of their religious change. This is a phenomenon, which can be explained by focusing on the differences in the notion of home of the Akan people in both localities. I will first concentrate on the nature of the religious change in the identity of the Akan migrants in Southeast Amsterdam. Then I will provide evidence to support this change by sharing the results of my research on the mediatory role of Akan chiefs and my study of the reception of Ghanaian films in both Ghana and the Netherlands. In the final part, I would like to provide an explanation for the Akan people's religious change by delving into existing theories on the different notions of home for people in their country of origin and migrants in their country of residence.

But first I would like to introduce the Akan people and the Akan as an analytical term. The Akan are cultural groups that originate from the Ivory Coast, Togo and Ghana (Braffi 2002: 8; Ogot 1992: 204).[2] In Ghana, 49.1 % of an estimated 17 million people belong to the Akan. Most of the roughly 1.5 million Ghanaians abroad are also of Akan descent. Historically, Akan has been a problematic concept. The term was first used in 1602 by Portuguese map makers who drew the first map of Guinea. This was based on details of the Gold Coast that they collected during a Portuguese mission to the interior in 1573 (Cortesão & Teixeira da Mota 1962: 67–69, plate 362).[3] The Portuguese map makers commented on two interior states known as 'Acanes grande' and 'Acanes pequenos', which in actual fact never existed but were drawn by cartographers on the maps of Guinea of 1606, 1616 and 1729. As a result, travelers from different countries referred to these imaginary states as 'Akkany' until 1819 when the states were removed from all maps of Guinea. By then, however, the term 'Akan' was widespread. In 1875 the Danish missionary J.G. Christaller further contributed to the popularity of the term 'Akan' by including an entry in his dictionary regarding this cultural group (singl. *Akànni*, pl. *Akanfo*) (Müller 2010).

Figure 15.1 "I am the shining light of the world"; photo taken by the author.

Historically therefore, the *Akanfo* were never real, but Portuguese mapmakers and a Danish missionary spread the myth of their existence. Most historians who work on Ghana, such as Ivor Wilks, Thomas C. McCaskie, Jean Allman, John Parker, Larry W. Yarak, Joseph K. Adjaye and Thomas J. Lewin are aware of this history. Most often they prefer to refer to the Asante and the Fante, which are the names of cultural groups that were created by the people themselves, instead of using the historically inaccurate term 'Akan'. Christaller, however, has influenced most scholars of religion, such as Jan G. Platvoet, George Parrinder, Joseph B. Danquah and philosophers from Ghana, such as Kwame Gyekye and Kwasi Wiredu. As a result, they refer to 'the Akan' as a cultural-linguistic term and their unit of analysis.

Because this article is mainly about the religious identity of people and belongs more in the field of religious studies than history, I use the term 'Akan' as a cultural-linguistic unit of analysis without making a further differentiation into subgroups. The Akan share many cultural characteristics, such as naming ceremonies, puberty rituals and burial rites. They all speak Kwa languages, such as Twi, and dialects, such as Akuapem Twi, Asante Twi and Fante Twi. Twi is a Niger-Congo tonal language that has been connected linguistically to the Ewe, the Fon, and other cultural groups that live eastward.

THE RELIGIOUS IDENTITY OF THE AKAN IN KUMASI AND IN THE BIJLMER DISTRICT: A COMPARISON

In this section, I will provide insight into the religious identity of the Akan people in Kumasi (Ghana) and of the Akan migrants in Southeast Amsterdam (the Netherlands). I will conclude by comparing the two.

Kumasi

Since the 15th century, Kumasi has been at a junction of important trade routes in West Africa. In 1701 it became the Asante kingdom's capital, and today it is the second largest city in Ghana after Accra, as well as the most important commercial and administrative center in the Asante region. Because of trade and its huge open-air market, Kumasi has always been a place that attracted people from very distant places and different cultural and religious backgrounds. Among the inhabitants of Kumasi are, for instance, many cultural groups who are Muslims, such as the Frafra; the Dagomba; the Kusasi; the Bisa; the Asante *Nkramo*; the Mossi and the Hausa people. These Muslims, who all have their own headmen, live in distinct areas of Kumasi, which are known as *zongos* or settlements. Other cultural groups, of whom the majority are both African indigenous religious believers and Christians, are the Fante, the Akuapem and the Asante. The latter form the majority of all Akan groups in Kumasi. Ghanaians of non-Akan stock who are mostly Christians such as the Ewe and the Ga also reside in this town (Dienst Onderzoek en Statistiek 2006; Ghana, Statistical Service 2002a). Furthermore, since the 1950s, the city is also host to Lebanese and Syrian families, Iranians and Indians, which gives the town a cosmopolitan outlook (Appiah 2007).

The belief of the Akan people in Ghana comprises a number of Akan indigenous religions, Christianity (mainstream Methodist, Catholic, Anglican and the Presbyterian Churches, new traditional religious African movements, new religious movements including the Pentecostal-Charismatic Church) and Islam (Orthodox Hausa Islam, the Suwarian Islamic tradition, the Ahmadiyya, Tijaniyya, Ahlus-Sunnah wal-Jama'ah and Wahhabi movements) (Müller 2009).

Most of the Akan in Ghana claim membership of one of the Christian churches (68.8%), and most Christians (24.1% of the population) belong to one of the Pentecostal-Charismatic churches. Around 15.9 % of the population consists of Muslims, and 8.5 % are adherents of an African indigenous religion (Ghana, Statistical Service 2002b). There is also a very small minority (0.7 %) of Hindus, Buddhists, Jews, and adherents of the Bahá'í faith (Ghana, Information Services Department 1991). A significant characteristic of the Akan believers in Ghana is that they are religiously pluralistic. They are most often both Akan indigenous religious believers and either Christians or Muslims.

The Bijlmer District

Since the 1970s, the Akan have migrated (especially from Accra and Kumasi) to a number of European countries including the United Kingdom, France, Germany, Italy, Spain and the Netherlands. Two-thirds of the Akan in the Netherlands live in Southeast Amsterdam (the Bijlmer), which is a very multicultural neighbourhood with over 130 nationalities. The majority of them are of African descent (including the Afro-Surinamese and the Moroccan population) (Centraal Bureau voor de Statistiek 2011). The neighbourhood is also known as 'Little Africa' because it includes an African-Surinamese market, various shops that sell African and Surinamese foods and culturally related products, such as African music and films, African hairdressers, Surinamese travel agencies, African boutiques with Adinkra cloth and/or souvenirs from Africa and the Caribbean. The Bijlmer therefore has a clearly visible African community with its own religious-cultural characteristics including a film culture. During the author's fieldwork in the Bijlmer, some West African film stars visited the neighbourhood to promote their latest films and provide their numerous fans with leaflets, free films and signatures. Akan chiefs from Ghana also frequently visit the Bijlmer, for instance, during the festival 'Dancing with Kings' which is celebrated annually in the heart of the neighbourhood.

In January 2011 the Bijlmer counted 82,008 residents. Immigrants from non-Western countries made up 64.3% of the population. The Akan are estimated at over 10,000 officially registered members and a large undocumented population, and they make up 10% of the Bijlmer population (Centraal Bureau voor de Statistiek 2011; Dienst Onderzoek en Statistiek 2007, 2011; Mazzucato & Kabki 2007). The majority of the Akan in Southeast Amsterdam are Pentecostal-Charismatic Christians and all others are Muslims. Unlike in Ghana, Pentecostal-Charismatic Akan believers in the Netherlands do not adhere to any of the Akan indigenous religious beliefs. The Akan in Ghana do believe that indigenous religious spirits can travel outside their country (de Witte 2010; Dienst Onderzoek en Statistiek 2006). However, the Akan in the Bijlmer do not regard the belief in these spirits as a religion, but as an aspect of Akan culture (Dienst Onderzoek en Statistiek 2006; Müller 2011). In Ghana, the Akan chiefs and 'queen mothers'[4] are the representatives of the Akan indigenous religions and use that religion to legitimise their traditional political institution, the so-called institution of chieftaincy. In Ghana, these religious leaders, who thus also have a political function, deal with indigenous religious matters and solve relational and interreligious conflicts, but they are also there to help their subjects with more mundane matters such as finding a job and housing (Bartels & de Jong 2007; Müller 2009; Ray & Redy 2003; ter Haar 1998). In the Netherlands, as well as in other European countries like Germany and North America, the Akan chiefs are highly involved in development projects in the corresponding villages of their communities in Ghana and have a significant secular function (Bob-Milliar 2009; Kleist 2011; Mazzucato & Kabki 2007; Nieswald 2008; ter Haar 1998). They also help newcomers in the Bijlmer who come from the same village as they do; nevertheless, their main focus is on collecting remittances from among Akan migrants to connect to and help their communities in Ghana (interview with a Bijlmer chief in Southeast Amsterdam, 17 February 2010). The church leaders and imams are also very much involved in helping migrants in the initial period in their new country of residence to go through a religious rite of passage to provide them with a sense of identity and self-worth in their country of residence. The church and the mosque have both a religious and a social function (Bartels & de Jong 2007; ter Haar 1998; Tonah 2007).

The Africans in Southeast Amsterdam, of whom a significant number are Akan, have founded at least 65 churches—the majority of which are Pentecostal-Charismatic (van der Meulen 2009). These churches are either branches of churches that originate in Africa, such as 'The Bijlmer Redeemed Christian Church of God' or they are founded in Europe, such as the 'True Teachings of Christ Temple'. The church leaders of African migrants offer them moral and religious support and also help in finding, for example, jobs, shelter and acquiring a residence permit (Hunt & Lightly 2001; ter Haar 1998). The churches enable African Christians to build a religious community together with other non-African Christians on a global and local level, at least in theory. The aim of the 'Candle', a multifunctional church building in the Bijlmer that brings together a large number of the African churches is to serve all Christians, no matter what their cultural background (e.g., Surinamese, Antillean, Ghanaian or Dutch) (van der Meulen 2009).

The churches in the Candle are locally embedded and aim to offer Africans a connection to both the local and transnational Christian community. For them, their world religion is more important than each other's cultural background. The churches are involved in the integration of Africans in a global Christian community that includes Caucasian Europeans. In its ideology the African churches open the door for African migrants to become part of Europe and the native, Christian, culturally rooted and dominant North Atlantic world of which they are often excluded on the basis of ethnicity. My interview data make clear that for many Akan migrants in Southeast Amsterdam, the African churches in Europe, including the Netherlands, are therefore more interesting to join than the local branches of community organisations of the institutions of Akan chieftaincy.

With respect to the Muslims in the Netherlands, recent research demonstrates that Islamic religious leaders are generally more divided than the Christian leaders and that Islamic organisations are more often divided along ethnic-cultural lines (Waardenburg 2001). In the Bijlmer, Muslims are more ethnically divided than the Christians, whose churches are mainly filled with members of the same ethnic-cultural origin. Muslims of 17 nationalities including Surinamese, Pakistani and Ghanaians worship together in the Taibah mosque. This Islamic religious institution is affiliated with the Orthodox Islamic organisations *Ahle Sunnat Wal Djam'at* and the World Islamic Mission, which aims to be an umbrella organisation for all ethnically divided Hindustani Muslim organisations in the Netherlands (Landman 1991; Nielsen 2004). The World Islamic Mission (WIM) was founded in Mecca in 1972 and aims to build a global Islamic community of Muslims, but so far the WIM has not succeeded in uniting all Hindustani Muslims in the Netherlands (Landman 1991). A group of Dutch citizens inspired by various Sufi movements in Iran, Pakistan and India have founded their own Sufi order in the Netherlands, but despite their good contacts with Muslim immigrant communities in the country, they form a different group (Landman 1992). The same pattern can be found among Akan Christians, who are not much integrated with the Dutch churches, even though they maintain links with them. The Islamic organisation behind the Taibah mosque is also well connected internationally to Surinam and Pakistan. The majority of their members, including their leader, Gaffaer, are Surinamese (den Uyl & Brouwer 2009; Vernooij 2004).

With the help of the Internet and chat rooms, the (Akan) Muslim youth in the Bijlmer also create a more individualistic Dutch Muslim identity that is not necessarily connected to the group's country of origin. They seek a universal form of Islam free from the particularities of local customs of their parents' country of origin, but do combine global Islam with elements of their local Islamic religious practices in the Bijlmer. A 25-year-old Akan Sufi Muslim said: 'I do not go to the Taibah mosque. I use my own prayer carpet at home and at work, which includes a compass to find the location of Mecca wherever I am. I also spend a lot of time on the Internet to look at American websites to find new religious items and new Islamic ideas. I do not buy these things online, but I look for it in shops in the Bijlmer and also in religious specialist shops in Amsterdam' (Interview with a 25-year-old Akan Sufi Muslim, 17 February 2010). My findings correspond with the results of scholars who conducted research on the media consumption of Muslim migrants in Europe. Shavit's empirical research results demonstrates, for instance, that in Frankfurt and Mainz in Germany, especially for the younger Muslims among his respondents, 'Islamic Internet sites and satellite programs are a major source of Muslim legal instruction, spiritual guidance and general information' (Shavit 2009: 187).

To conclude this section, the main difference in the religious identity of the Akan in Kumasi and in that of the migrants in Southeast Amsterdam is that in the former locality, the majority of the Akan are dual believers, who combine their Akan indigenous religion with the membership of one of the above-mentioned Islamic or Christian denominations. In the Bijlmer, instead, the majority of the Akan are Pentecostal-Charismatic Christians. One characteristic of that religion is a tendency to condemn the Asante indigenous religion and to transfer several of its expressions to the field of culture rather than religion.

AKAN CHIEFTAINCY IN GHANA AND THE AKAN DIASPORA IN SOUTHEAST AMSTERDAM AS INDICATORS OF RELIGIOUS CHANGE[5]

In this section, I would like to explain why the Akan chiefs are indicators of religious change. To do this, it is necessary to enhance our understanding of the style of leadership and the practice of the mediatory role of the Akan chiefs in both Kumasi and Southeast Amsterdam, taking into account the different societal context in which the Akan chiefs operate. Mediation is a form of conflict management by bringing together the disputants and trying to make them bridge their differences. Mediators can operate in very different ways. In modern Western societies, mediators often take a neutral position and operate as outsiders who leave after the conflict is resolved. Their style of mediation is also known as 'outsider mediation'. In many traditional societies, however, mediators solve conflicts on the basis of long enduring relationships based on trust and connectedness with the disputants. This means that the mediators are not neutral but insiders who mediate from within the conflict. This style of guidance is currently referred to as 'insider-partial' mediation (Wehr & Lederach 1991).

Kumasi

The Akan chiefs in Kumasi, the majority of whom are Asante, are 'insider-partial' mediators. They are chosen and enthroned ('enstooled') by their subjects on the basis of personal characteristics, such as trustworthiness and their oratory skills, which these subjects hope will enable their chief to help them to resolve conflicts together (interview with the Akan Chief Oboguhene Owusu Asiama II, 21 April 2006). The Akan chiefs generally know their subjects very well and earn their respect and legitimacy on the basis of the creation and preservations of customary laws that are embedded in the Akan indigenous religion. On the basis of that religion, the Asante subjects perceive their chiefs also as the custodians of ancestral land, which gives them an economic basis of power (90% of all land in Ghana belongs to the traditional authorities). The Muslim headmen are hosts on this land of the Asante chiefs, who all fall under the authority of the Asante king (the Asantehene). Thus, in terms of mediation, the Akan chiefs in Kumasi fulfil distinguished mediatory roles in the juridical-political and indigenous religious fields.

In a juridical-political sense, the Akan chiefs in Kumasi mediate between their subjects and the secular authorities of the local government of the Ghanaian nation-state. The chiefs have a unique position in that state, because when Ghana gained independence in 1957, their traditional political institution, known as 'chieftaincy', was incorporated in the Ghanaian democratic political order. The Akan chiefs thus represent a form of traditional leadership, which is legitimised on the basis of their indigenous religion and is embedded in the legal system of the Ghanaian state. Within that system they are entitled to create and preserve the exercise of the customary laws that derive from indigenous religious customs, such as traditional marriage rituals and funeral rites. Apart from this, the chiefs do not have much jurisdiction, and all other laws are created and controlled by the Ghanaian state and its local representatives. The chiefs and the state represent separate, decentralised political institutions, which are organised hierarchically; and their representatives meet one another on the same horizontal level in their hierarchies. At the top of the institution of chieftaincy stands the Asanteman Council that is represented by the Asante king, followed by, in descending order, the National House of Chiefs, the Regional Houses of Chiefs, the Traditional Councils and, at the bottom, the Unit Committees. The national government that falls under the political authority of the president of Ghana is subdivided in a hierarchical descending order in the District Assemblies, the Town or Area Councils and the Unit Committees. The representatives of the institutions of chieftaincy and the government both have seats in the District Assemblies (DAs). The chiefs form part of the interest groups in a society that also comprises religious organisations and youth associations. These groups are not elected but nevertheless occupy one third of the seats in the DAs. The local politicians, who represent their voters rather than the ancestral spirits, occupy the other two thirds of the seats. The interest groups and the politicians are partners in development. The chiefs negotiate on behalf of their community to receive the type of help and resources from the government that are necessary for their community, for example, for the building of toilet blocks or schools (interview with Akan Chief Brefo Gyededu Kotowko II, chief of Gyamasi,[6] 13 March 2006). The local politicians in turn use the chiefs to collect taxes and to reach the population during elections, even though the chiefs are not allowed to participate in partisan politics (Boafo-Arthur 2001). In Kumasi, the local politicians and the chiefs thus cooperate to serve the people of Ghana both as citizens and subjects. However, the difference in legitimacy also causes tensions and conflicts between the chiefs and the politicians, who are respectively sacred and secular leaders. Many of these conflicts are about the question of authority over the Akan people and over the chiefs' land ('stool' land). The chiefs perceive themselves as the custodians of the ancestral land, but in practice they have to give away over half of the revenue of their land to the DAs. No doubt, this causes problems between the chiefs and the politicians. One politician said: 'The chiefs have to give the revenues of their 'stool' land to the District Assemblies, but they often keep part of the money for themselves or sign contracts with developers without informing the Assembly. They then tell us that we should trust them, because they are chiefs. They deny any accountant who the District Assembly send over to enter the palace in which they live and check their accounts, and tell them that they are not allowed and should not interfere with their chieftaincy affairs, as it negatively affects their image' (Interview with a local politician in Kumasi, 10 February 2006).

The chiefs are, however, equally often negative about the politicians, whom they accuse of being corrupt and not spending the revenues of the land that belongs to their 'stool' or throne in such a way that it is beneficial to the community (interview with Oboguhene Owusu Asiama II, 21 April 2006). In Kumasi, (Nana) Brefo Gyededu Kotowko II, acknowledged that there are conflicts in the District Assembly around issues of 'stool' land, and that there is a power struggle between the chiefs and politicians, and said: 'Ideally, the chiefs and the politicians cooperate and make important decisions together. In practice there are a lot of fights between these sacred and secular leaders, but decisions cannot be made without the consent of both' (interview in Kumasi with the Akan chief Brefo Gyededu Kotowko II, 13 March 2006).

Besides mediating between their subjects and politicians, the Akan chiefs also play two religious mediatory roles. The chiefs are (a) the occupants of the throne (or better 'stool') in which the communal spirit (*sunsum-kra*) is housed and through which they can connect to the ancestral spirits and which also enables them to connect and represent the *abusua*, the extended family unit or lineage of both the living and the living-dead. The ritual of 'enstoolment' enables the chief to mediate between those spirits and the social world. This creates a ritual bond between the chief and his subjects, whom they represent and with whom they are united by the performance of indigenous religious rituals. During these rituals, libation is poured and animals are slaughtered (e.g., chickens or goats) for the ancestral spirits. The continuation of these rituals is significant for the community because by feeding the spirits, the chief protects the interests of the community in the spiritual world. Besides, the chiefs are (b) also significant in maintaining peace in the (religious) public space. In Ghana, the Akan chiefs are not religiously neutral, as they are the representatives of the Akan indigenous religion, but they may mediate between Christian and Islamic religious groups with the help of their indigenous religion. Ghana is a secular state with Christians, Muslims and indigenous believers, who are free to practice their religion. However, in cooperation with the interest groups in the District Assemblies and the Regional House of Chiefs the chiefs create bylaws and regulations that are meant to streamline the religious practices of various religious denominations. In this way, the chiefs play a crucial role in maintaining peace between all religious groups in the city. Theoretically, they seek similarities in Christianity and Islam and emphasise the commonality of both religions. The Akan indigenous religion is the glue that brings Christianity and Islam closer to one another as aspects of both of these world religions are incorporated into the indigenous religion. The traditional authorities that represent the Akan indigenous religion make sure that all religious leaders and believers observe the regulations and actively bring together the headmen of the Islamic communities and the priests and pastors of the various Christian denominations. None of the Christian and/or Islamic communities fulfils this same mediatory function as the Akan chiefs. Islamic and Christian religious leaders solve intrareligious conflicts by helping the people of their own congregations, but they do not solve interreligious disputes. The chiefs and queen mothers are the only religious heads who help any member of their community irrespective of their religious affiliation.

The legal position of the chief as the creator and preserver of customary laws and bylaws stimulates and sometimes forces ordinary people to be dual believers to demonstrate both their loyalty to their local chiefs as adherents of the Akan indigenous religion and to a form of either Christianity or Islam. The jurisdiction of the chiefs is limited, but their presence and authority give the Akan people a sense of belonging and a religious identity that appeals to them as subjects. Besides, they are also modern citizens. The legitimacy of the Ghanaian state is economically and symbolically weak and is based on legality. Unlike the chieftaincy institution, which is religiously rooted, the state does not directly appeal to people in search of a religious and cultural identity. In their capacity as citizens, they therefore often feel attracted to either Christianity or Islam, which are religions with a more worldly character than the Akan indigenous religions (Müller 2008, 2009, 2010).

The Bijlmer District

In the Bijlmer district, the way in which the Akan chiefs can fulfil their mediatory role between beings from the spiritual and the visible world is different and more limited than in Kumasi. In Southeast Amsterdam, the chiefs do not have the juridical authority to create and preserve the exercise of customary laws, which puts severe limitations on the exercise of their juridical-political role. Some Akan chiefs who live in the Bijlmer, like Barima Asamoah Kofi IV, have strengthened their role in this respect by becoming politically active. In the period 2002–2006, the Akan Chief (Nana) Barima (known in private as S.K. Oduro) was, for instance, a district council member of Southeast Amsterdam for the Dutch Labour Party (PvdA).[7] Politically, he fulfilled his mediatory role by combining his membership of the council (which is part of the Dutch local government structure) with that of Ghanaian organisations in the Netherlands that promote their interests, such as the Manstiman Association and the Okyeman Foundation (van der Wijst 2009). The latter two organisations do not have any political power, however, and are in that sense incomparable with the function of the Akan chieftaincy institutions in Ghana. Economically the Akan chiefs, who are both 'enstooled' in Ghana and in the Bijlmer (like Barima Asamoah Kofi IV), can be the custodians of 'stool' land in Ghana. In the Bijlmer they also have a different profession, like Nana Barima who is a health information counsellor for the Municipal Public Health Authority (GG&GD). Due to their custodianship over land, the Akan chiefs in Southeast Amsterdam are thus juridico-politically but not necessarily economically disempowered, and some Akan chiefs play a significant role in the collection and sending of the remittances from the Akan migrants to Ghana (Kabki, Mazzucato & Appiah 2004: 95). Furthermore, the Akan chiefs also help new members of the migrant community search for work, get housing, and getting a passport (interview with Akan chief in Southeast Amsterdam, 16 February 2010).

Because of the lack of juridical-political power, however, the religious mediatory roles of the Akan chiefs in the Bijlmer are also limited. In Kumasi, the chiefs can claim the loyalty of their subjects by the exercise of laws that are inspired by the Akan indigenous religion and on the basis of that same religion they give their subjects a community identity and a sense of belonging to the past, includeing the spirits of their forefathers. The ancestral spirits are there to help the living in times of need. In the Bijlmer, the Akan chiefs are also ritually 'enstooled' and have organised themselves in the 'Council of Ghanaian chiefs in The Netherlands'. They cannot, however, claim any political or religious power on the basis of their role as representatives of the Akan indigenous religions because the Bijlmer-Akan chiefs lack legal authority. The absence of the juridical power of the chiefs also undermines their religious mediatory role as peacekeepers between Christians and Muslims, because none of these world religious believers is juridically obliged to adhere to the Akan indigenous religion of their chiefs, who only legitimise their institution of chieftaincy on the basis of that religion. Unlike in Kumasi, none of the Akan respondents of the research I carried out in the Bijlmer said that they were dual believers.

GHANAIAN VIDEO FILMS AS INDICATORS OF RELIGIOUS CHANGE

In this section, I will first describe the research methodology that I used to investigate the way Ghanaian video films can be understood as indicators of religious change. Second, I will discuss the history, characteristics and the different types of these films. Finally, I will describe the differences in the choice of types of films between the Akan in Kumasi and those in the Bijlmer district.

Research Methodology

This research is mainly the result of five months of fieldwork on Ghanaian films that I conducted in the Bijlmer district and in Kumasi in the period between 2009–2011.[8] In that period, I realised three sets of interviews and a structural and content analysis of Ghanaian films. First, I carried out a general study of two months on the media consumption of the Akan migrants in the Bijlmer district, which made clear that its members frequently consumed Ghanaian video films (data set 1). These results are confirmed by earlier research in Ghana (see Meyer 1995, 1996, 2001, 2006, 2010; and Mitchell 2007).

Second, to analyze the content of the films, I further made use of existing analyzes of Ghanaian films conducted in film studies departments (Diawara

1988; Garritano 2000; Haynes 2010a, 2010b; Meyer 1996, 2001, 2007, 2008; Oha 2000; Reid 1991; Wendl 2001; Wright 2006). One of the research findings was that Ghanaian films all cover religious themes and—implicitly or explicitly—contain religious messages. In most parts of Africa, including Ghana, religion is not a separate sphere of life. Because of the chieftaincy, customary laws in these countries, which are based on the traditions of African indigenous religions, religion is embedded in all spheres of life and forms the foundation of all activities of social, economic, or political nature (Mbiti 1992; Müller 2009; Platvoet 1992). This means that even though the Ghanaian filmmakers do not always consciously put religious themes and messages in their films they are nonetheless always included. As the Kenyan philosopher Mbiti put it, 'Africans are notoriously religious' (Mbiti 1992:1).

Finally, in another three months of fieldwork, I conducted interviews in Kumasi (data set 2) and Southeast Amsterdam (data set 3) about the Akan people's choice of movies—in the latter case alongside my research on the Akan chiefs. I viewed 47 Ghanaian films, most of which were viewed together with Akan families in the Bijlmer, and another 45 Ghanaian films, together with Akan families in Kumasi and received permission to interview the Akan people individually and to record the interviews, alongside the making of field notes. The interviews were all face to face, in depth and semistructured, which has the advantage that they generate open-ended answers, puts emphasis on the elaborating points of interests of the interviewees and provides detailed data on their emotions, experiences and feelings (Denscombe 2004). The age of the interviewees ranged from 15 to 65. The interviews were transcribed manually and analyzed by using the database software FileMaker pro. The results of the research on the differences in the Akan people's choice of Ghanaian films were found by comparing the answers of the interviewees in the FileMaker pro boxes 'religious beliefs of the Akan people' and 'favorite types of Ghanaian films categorized by their religion' (see next section on types of Ghanaian video films) and by analysing field notes and observations.

In the following section, I will demonstrate how and why I have used Ghanaian films as indicators of the transformation of the religious identity of the Akan migrants in Kumasi when migrating to the Bijlmer district. The points of focus will thereby be on the finance of the Ghanaian film industry. First, however, I will give a short introduction about the nature of Ghanaian video films.

Ghanaian Video Films

The Ghanaian video films that one can buy in both Kumasi and the Bijlmer district were first created in Ghana in the 1980s. The makers of these video films often did not receive formal education at one of the state academies for filmmaking in West Africa and were not connected to the West African State Film Industry Corporations. The birth story of these films is that ordinary

West Africans started to use digital video cameras that flooded the West African markets to retell stories and tell new stories that derived from their oral tradition and were close to the reality of life in their communities. This new technology allowed individuals situated outside the state-controlled realm of cultural production to produce films that gave space to their own concerns and views of life. Most of these films were based in West Africa and were created without the help of financial resources from the Western world. As a result, the budgets of these films were, and still are, most often very low. To reduce costs, many of these films are produced quickly and often in no more than two weeks. The production crews are small and shots are made in real localities, which give the films a highly realistic outlook, despite their occult themes (Garritano 2008). A favourite theme of these films is, for instance, the deceit of witchcraft mothers and false prophets or the devil who buys a person's soul in exchange for money that he or she receives by the performance of money rituals (*sakawa*). Initially the actors and actresses in these films were non-professionals, but today many of the films are made with a (semi) professional crew who are educated at the local film schools that have mushroomed in the urban areas of West Africa. In the Bijlmer, Ghanaian films are the most popular because most of the West Africans in the district are of Ghanaian descent. In the shopping centers 'the Amsterdamse poort' and 'Kraaiennest plaza' Ghanaian video films are sold in several shops alongside grocery products and in some video shops that specialise in African highlife, hip life, soul and gospel music and in these films.

In terms of narratives, these types of music, and especially the Ghanaian video films, appeal to the religious life and experience of the Bijlmer's Akan migrants. One of their recurrent themes is the practice of witchcraft, which is believed to bring misfortune. A very high percentage of Akan worldwide believe in witches and the effects of witchcraft. In West African culture, evil witches are believed to be the cause of most misfortunes in life such as infertility, difficulties in finding a spouse, conjugal problems, poverty and illness. For many Akan the way out of becoming victim to any of these problems is to convert to Christianity or Islam. They believe that these world religions can empower them spiritually and protect them against witchcraft. The members of the Akan migrants in the Bijlmer, the majority who are Pentecostal-Charismatic Christians, view the Ghanaian films because they feel that the messages in these media help them to strengthen their faith in God. They see Pentecostal-Charismatic Christianity as a form of protection against evil witches and as a source of white witchcraft that can bring them wealth and prosperity, like native Westerners.

The songs and films are full of examples of Akan people who live in nice mansions and drive big cars. The moral message of many of these songs and films is that anyone who is not in connection with the evil spirits of, for instance, witches can gain prosperity, wealth and 'personhood', which in the Akan religious context refer to a high social status that is related to social achievements, and are beneficial to the community. According to the

Ghanaian philosopher Wiredu (Ceton 2002), in the Akan culture, everybody is born a human being (*onipa*) but to achieve 'personhood' or to become a person (*onipaa paa*) one needs to make one's talents beneficial to the cultural group. However, when one such as a witch or someone in contact with these devils, gains these avidities in life by some sort of deception and at the cost of others, one's glamour will be short lived. Only by conversion to either Islam or to Pentecostal-Charismatic Christianity, one can count on eternal 'personhood', which means that one will be remembered in the afterlife. A recurrent theme in these popular art forms is 'what you sow is what you reap', which implies that only those who live a good life will receive good, and vice versa. This belief is embedded in the Akan indigenous religions, but it also makes conversion to a world religion beneficial. In the Bijlmer, messages in the Pentecostal-Charismatic songs and films are most popular because they resonate most with the religious life and religious experiences of the Akan migrants, who form the majority of the members that show an interest in these popular African art forms. The songs and the films bring a message of hope because, in the light of the Holy Spirit, wealth, prosperity and 'personhood', that mainly used to be the privileges of the Akan traditional authorities and wealthy traders, come within reach of every believer regardless of one's personal situation (Adinkrah 2008; Müller 2011; van der Geest 2009).

The Ghanaian films are, however, not only significant because they link up with the religious beliefs and experiences of their Ghanaian audiences. Because the films are low cost, they are also highly commercial and only offer a very popular form of entertainment. It is for this reason that the religious and moral messages of the films that are hidden in their theme songs and in the preaching of the Pentecostal-Charismatic pastors often contradict the aesthetic representations of urban life in the films. The actors and actresses often drive expensive cars and live in big mansions, whereas the main message of the film is that one should convert oneself to Pentecostal-Charismatic Christianity and save money for the church community to help the poor rather than spending it all. The films are mass produced and mass marketed, but they are mainly distributed outside the channels of the official national and international West African film industry. The films are low budget and self-financed and as a result, the video makers are also businessmen and businesswomen, who must produce films that sell by making them comprehensible to a large audience. As Birgit Meyer puts it, 'the boundaries between production and consumption become blurred' (Meyer 2007: 98). The religious messages in the films that do not sell are adjusted to the wishes of the audience until the filmmaker and distributor have found the right formula of religious ideas and visual images that turn their films into economic successes. The video filmmakers seem only to link up with the religious views and experiences of Ghanaians on a commercial basis, which means that the Ghanaian video film industry can only survive if it has found a formula that appeals to its audience. Consequently, Ghanaian filmmakers create video films that provide a form of 'edutainment'; a term that refers to the combination of entertaining visual images and religious moral messages inside these films.

One of the results of my more general media reception study was that these edutaining Ghanaian video films are significant for the Akan people's religious identity. The films are part and parcel of their daily religious life alongside other products that are in line with their beliefs; such as *halal* food for the Muslims among them, and the Akan mainly buy films that fit with their existing religious beliefs and affiliations. The fact that the same video films are viewed in both localities, Ghana and Amsterdam, makes the films useful as indicators of any transformations in the religious identity of the Akan migrants due to their (generational) stay outside Ghana, and they can be inferred from the type of films that the community consumes.

Types of Ghanaian Video Films

I distinguish between Christian, Islamic and African indigenous religious Ghanaian films, all of which come with their own subcategories (see Table 15.1).

The Christians create their films in such a way that they are attractive to members of all Christian congregations, which are the mainstream churches

Table 15.1 Types of Ghanaian Video Films

Type of films	Subthemes
1. Christian films	(a) films with proselytising messages
	(b) films with Christian themes
2. Islamic films	(a) films with proselytising messages
	(b) films with Islamic themes
3. African indigenous religious films (Conversion is not an aspect of the African Indigenous Religions nor these type of films)	(a) films with indigenous religious themes that are the result of an 'invention of tradition' and use a symbolic language and colourful image to portray an imaginary past (in a village setting),
	(b) films with indigenous religious themes that are the result of an 'invention of tradition' and a symbolic language and colourful imagery to portray an imaginary present (in an urban setting),
	(c) films with indigenous religious themes in the present that give a realistic account of the Indigenous Religion and the outlook of their representatives (the traditional priest(ess) and the traditional authorities) and believers.

(Anglican, Methodist, Catholic, Protestant) and the Pentecostal-Charismatic churches, who dominate the Ghanaian film industry. The Muslims, on the contrary, spread a large variety of religious messages belonging to the various Islamic Sunni or Sufi denominations in Ghana. The overwhelming majority of Ghanaian Muslims are Sunni who subscribe to the Maliki legal tradition, while a significant minority follows the Shafi'i school of thought. Sufi orders in the country are the Qadiriyya, the Tijaniyya, and the Qadiani faction of the Ahmadiyya movement that is currently dominant among the Akan Sufi Muslims (Azuma 2000). Second in importance among this cultural group is the modest Sunni Islamic tradition of the Soninke scholar (*ulama*) Al-Hajji Salim Suwari (1523/24–1594). Since the 1800s, its scholars (*ulama*) drew elements from the Qadiriyya Sufi order, such as *batin*, which is an occult aspect of Islam (Austen 2010).

The Choice of Ghanaian Video Films of the Akan in Kumasi and in the Bijlmer District

The aim of this section is to demonstrate that Ghanaian films are indicators of transformations in the religious identity of the Akan migrants, since the choice of these films resembles their religious beliefs.

Kumasi

In Kumasi and Southeast Amsterdam, the strongest link between the Akan people's choice of Ghanaian films and the practice of their religion was found among Pentecostal-Charismatic believers. In Kumasi, a female Pentecostal said, 'In the evening I often watch Ghanaian films with Pentecostal-Charismatic evangelic messages, because it encourages me to be a good Christian and to pray. These films, such as the miracle production *Nyame ye Nyame*, contain prayer and deliverance sessions by popular pastors of churches here in Kumasi, such as Apostle John Prah. During these sessions, the pastor invokes the Holy Spirit (*sunsum kronkon*) in order to fight the evil spirits inside the bodies of some of the church members. The films make me aware of where I would be without the protection of God. The deliverance sessions make clear that one should have strong faith in the Lord in order not to fall into the hands of the powers of darkness' (interview with a female Pentecostal in Kumasi, 13 March 2010; see Figure 15.2). Religious adherents of mainstream Christianity and of Islam in Kumasi had a less distinct preference for Ghanaian films that corresponded with their religion.

In Kumasi, both of these groups of believers said that they also watched films that represent religious beliefs other than their own. A male Anglican Christian said, 'I prefer to watch Ghanaian films with Christian themes, such as for instance Kumasi *yonko*, a movie that makes people aware of the dangers of being too unsuspecting and shows that those who behave wrongly

Figure 15.2 An aesthetic representation of a traditional priest in the indigenous religious Akan Ghallywood film (3a) Wedlock of the Gods.

will sooner or later meet the wrongdoing of others. However, I also view Islamic films. I have many friends who adhere to a modest form of Islam that contains elements of the Akan indigenous religion, like that of the Asante *Nkramo*. When I am with them, we view Ghanaian films of Islamic producers in Twi, such as, for instance, *Dipantiche*, an Akan Islamic movie with proselytising messages. This film is about a woman who as a consequence of evil spirits that dwell inside her wakes up with a lot of money in her bed each time a person in her direct environment is being killed. The only way she can be healed is by visiting the Asante *Nkramo* Imam (*nsumankwahene*), who begins a spiritual fight with the evil spirits inside the woman's body and heals her by driving out these spirits' (interview with a male Anglican Christian in Kumasi, 12 March 2010; see Figure 15.3).

A female Methodist Christian in Kumasi, who also occasionally visited a traditional Akan priest, said: 'I like to watch the films that are about my traditional beliefs, such as "Homeda", a movie that emphasises the importance of traditional marriage and being obedient to the traditional authorities. I dislike watching Christian Ghanaian films because they portray our traditional belief very negatively. In Homeda the traditional priest is a person who uses his spiritual powers to protect his daughter against misfortune, which is good. In Christian films such as "Mogya apam" (blood covenant), however, the traditional priestess is portrayed as a woman whose aim is to make money rather than to heal her clients, which is something I do not like at all' (interview with a female Methodist Christian in Kumasi, 11 March 2010). This respondent also detested Islamic Ghanaian films that, according to her, portray all the indigenous religious deities as evil spirits just like in Christian films. In terms of story lines, these Akan Islamic films of the

Ghanaian Films and Chiefs as Indicators of Religious Change 263

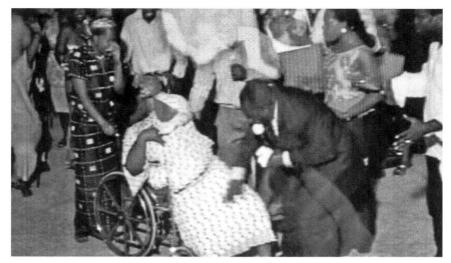

Figure 15.3 An aesthetic representation of a pastor in the Christian Akan Ghallywood film (1a) Nyame ne Nyame.

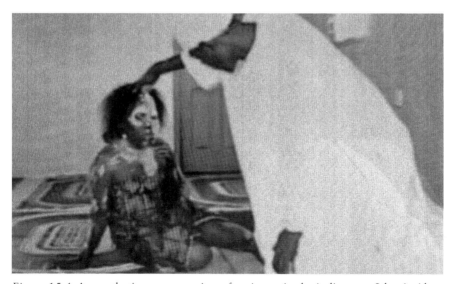

Figure 15.4 An aesthetic representation of an imam in the indigenous Islamic Akan Ghallywood film (2a) Dipantiche.

Suwarian tradition are very similar to the Christian films with proselytising messages. The main difference between the two is that in the Christian films, the pastor leads the deliverance sessions that take place in his church, whereas in the Islamic films these sessions are exercised in the mosque under the guidance of a chief imam.

The Bijlmer District

In Southeast Amsterdam, however, the respondents did not view films of all the above-mentioned religions in the Ghanaian film industry. An Akan male Christian respondent said, 'I like to view Christian films with strong religious messages. My favourite is "Agyenkwa", about a boy who wins a spiritual fight against witches that killed a pregnant woman. He succeeds with the help of his Bible that he holds firmly and the power of the Holy Spirit that protects him against all evil'. The respondent did not view Islamic films and/or films about indigenous beliefs. He said, 'The only Ghanaian films I view are Christian films especially those with prayer sessions. I do not have Islamic friends in the Bijlmer. They have their own network. I do not view films about traditional belief' (interview with an Akan male Christian respondent in Southeast Amsterdam, 17 February 2010). Other Christian and Islamic Akan respondents in the Bijlmer gave similar answers. An Akan male Muslim said, 'I like to view films that are about a spiritual fight between the traditional priest and Muslims who are strong in faith. My favourite movie is "Zoka de Allah" [LM: Hausa for the intelligence of God/a man of God], about a Muslim who shows that Allah is more powerful than the deities and who tries to convert the people of Manpa (a village in Ghana) to Islam. I do not view Christian films or films that are only about traditional belief because they are not "halal" and therefore my Imam and my religion do not permit me to view them' (interview with an Akan male Muslim in Southeast Amsterdam, 16 February 2010).

In conclusion, the Akan people in Kumasi are used to viewing films of all religious beliefs including their indigenous religion. Members of the Akan diasporic community in Southeast Amsterdam prefer to view films that represent their Christian or Islamic religious beliefs, practices and religious organisational affiliation.

NOTIONS OF HOME: AN EXPLANATION FOR TRANSFORMATIONS IN THE RELIGIOUS IDENTITY OF THE AKAN MIGRANTS

The emphasis in this chapter is on the observation that the religious identity of the Akan in Kumasi differs from that of the Akan migrants in the Bijlmer. Ghanaian films and chiefs were used as indicators of transformations in the Akan religious identity as a consequence of migration. In this section, I will use the theory of Ralph and Staeheli (2011) on the 'notion of home' to explain why the religious identity of the Akan in Ghana and the migrants in Southeast Amsterdam is not the same. Ralph and Staeheli write that 'migrants, more than those who stay at home, are more subject to processes of categorisation, incorporation and exclusion, as they negotiate belonging inter subjectively in multiple homes. Because individual migrants often fail to meet normative expectations of behaviour, language, appearance, eating habits, and countless other materiality's and context-dependent etiquettes, they are in consequence perceived and discursively constructed as a group as being different to dominant others' (Ralph & Staeheli 2011: 524). They also remark that by excluding migrants, the host society confirms its own-shared commonalities and strengthens the identity of the group. However, by blending with the members of the host society's normative expectations, among others, migrants can gradually 'begin to belong' to their countries of settlement, which is a coming together of migrants' own feelings of fitting in that society and being accepted by the members of that society. The observations of ter Haar (1998), for instance, that Ghanaian Christians in the Bijlmer refer to themselves as 'International Christians' reveals that these Akan are doing their best to become part of and belong to the world Christian community and no longer want to be associated with the Akan indigenous religions. The experience of adjusting and belonging to a different (religious) group than before, transforms people's (religious) identity, which is also the case with those Akan migrants whose Islamic members are focussed on and have succeeded in becoming members of the Islamic world religious community (*ulama*). However, despite the disassociation of Akan Christians and Muslims in the Bijlmer with the Akan indigenous religions, they also long to maintain a connection with the people in Ghana. As Ralph and Staeheli put it: 'Home is like an accordion in that it both stretches to expand outwards to distant home and remote places, while also squeezing to embed people in their proximate and immediate local and social relations. In this way, home seems to extend outward and to be mobile, but also to be grounded and sedentary' (Ralph & Staeheli 2011: 518). For the Akan in the Bijlmer, this theory is applicable to the formation of their religious identity because the majority of the respondents said not only that they felt a sense of belonging to the society in their new country of residence but also to that of their country of origin. Understandably, they secularised the indigenous religious part of their religious identity and transformed it into a world religious identity.

CONCLUSION

The aim of this chapter was to diagnose and provide evidence for my observation that the religious identity of the Akan in the Bijlmer district has been transformed. The majority of the Akan in Ghana (whereby Kumasi is taken as an urban area in this country that is dominated by the Akan people) are dual believers and demonstrate their loyalty to their traditional authorities by adhering to one of the Akan indigenous religions alongside their Christian or Islamic faith. The Akan in the Bijlmer are by contrast monotheistic and are either Islamic or Christian world religious believers. The empirical evidence for the religious change of the Akan in the Bijlmer district was found by delving into the different ways in which Akan chiefs in both localities fulfill their mediatory roles and in the Akan people's choice for Ghanaian films in Kumasi (Ghana) and Southeast Amsterdam (the Netherlands). Chiefs and Ghanaian films were thus used in this research as indicators of religious change. What the two indicators share is that they both play a significant role in the identity of the Akan people either as a popular cultural expression of that identity or as the human face of a network of reciprocal social relationships with human and nonhuman entities. This research reveals that when one wants to find evidence for such complicated phenomena as the religious change of migrants, one should look for indicators that might not be the most self-evident but that touch on the core of what religious identity is and that, by having themselves an element of constancy, can map the aspects of change.

NOTES

1. A significant number of the Akan in Southeast Amsterdam belong to the same social network as the Akan in Kumasi (Kabki, Mazzucato & Appiah 2004).
2. The term 'cultural group' is also used in relation to the Asante and the Akan (Stoeltje 2003).
3. See map collection Universiteit van Amsterdam: http://dpc.uba.uva.nl.
4. A queen mother is legally 'the mother' of a chief or king, but in actuality, she is not his real mother but in most cases his sister.
5. These results are based on the doctoral research I conducted between 2004–2009 at the University of Edinburgh, Scotland (Centre of African Studies) concerning the religious mediatory roles of Akan chiefs and 'queen mothers' in the Kumasi Metropolis. My research was both historical and anthropological and included a year of fieldwork in the Kumasi Metropolis, where I conducted 56 semistructured face-to-face interviews with Akan (mainly Asante) traditional authorities and their subjects: Akan traditional priests, Muslim headmen and their subjects, chief imams, religious leaders of various mainstream Christian denominations, New African Traditional Religious movements, and New Religious Movements and politicians. For my postdoctoral research at Utrecht University, I conducted interviews with Akan chiefs and leaders of local Ghanaian organisations in the Bijlmer district and held conversations with Akan people about their chiefs alongside my research on Ghanaian films.
6. Gyamasi is located 25 miles north of Kumasi, near Mampong.
7. Barima Asamoah Kofi IV is the Abakomahenene of the Abrem traditional area in the Komenda-Edina- Eguafo-Abrem district in the central region of Ghana.
8. Initially, I conducted this research as a postdoctoral member of the Cultures and Identities Research Focus Group of Utrecht University, the Netherlands. Currently, I am affiliated with the African Studies Centre in Leiden.

Contributors

Synnøve Bendixsen, Postdoctoral Researcher, IMER Bergen Uni Rokkansenteret

Peter Beyer, Full Professor, Department of Classics and Religious Studies, University of Ottawa

Jeremy Carrette, Head of Religious Studies and Professor of Religion and Culture, Department of Religious Studies, School of European Culture and Languages, University of Kent

Suna Gülfer Ihlamur-Öner, Lecturer in the Department of Political Science and International Relations, Marmara University, Istanbul

Jeffrey Haynes, Associate Dean, Research and Postgraduate Studies; Faculty of Law, Governance and International Relations; and Director of the Centre for the Study of Religion, Conflict and Cooperation, London Metropolitan University

Robert W. Hefner, Professor of Anthropology and Director of the Institute on Culture, Religion, and World Affairs (CURA), Boston University

John Hutchinson, Reader in Nationalism, Department of Government, London School of Economics

Norah Karrouche, Doctoral Researcher at the Erasmus School of History, Culture and Communication (ESHCC), Erasmus University Rotterdam

Francesco Marone, Postdoctoral Fellow in Political Science, Department of Political and Social Sciences; University of Pavia, Italy

David Martin, Emeritus Professor of Sociology, London School of Economics; Fellow of the British Academy and Adjunct Professor, Liverpool Hope University

Sara Mels, Project Coordinator, University Centre Saint Ignatius Antwerp (UCSIA)

Louise Müller, Research Fellow at the African Studies Centre, Leiden

Inna Naletova, Lecturer at the Institut für Praktische Theologie, Katholisch-Theologische Fakultät, Universität Wien; and Senior Researcher at J. M. Dawson Institute of Church-State Studies, Baylor University

Tulasi Srinivas, Assistant Professor of Sociology and Anthropology, Department of Communication Studies, Emerson College

Christiane Timmerman, Director of the Centre for Migration and Intercultural Studies (CeMIS), University of Antwerp; and former Academic Director of UCSIA

Els Vanderwaeren, Postdoctoral Researcher, Centre for Migration and Intercultural Studies (CeMIS), University of Antwerp

Maja Veselič, PhD, Lecturer in the Department of Asian and African Studies, Faculty of Arts, University of Ljubljana

Bibliography

'A Christian Perspective on the Future European Constitution' (January–March 2003). *News Bulletin of the Romanian Patriarchate*, 1–3, p. 5.
'Activitatea Sectorului Biserica și Societatea' (2002). *Biserica Ortodoxa Romana* [Official Bulletin of the Romanian Orthodox Church], 120(1–6), pp. 672–673.
'Activitatea Sectorului IV al Administratiței Patriarhale—Biserica și Societatea' (1998). *Biserica Ortodoxa Romana* [Official Bulletin of the Romanian Orthodox Church], 116(1–6), p. 374.
'Activitatea Sectorului Relații Externe Bisericești' (2001). *Biserica Ortodoxa Romana* [Official Bulletin of the Romanian Orthodox Church], 119(1–6), p. 487.
'Clergy and Laity Ask Patriarch Kirill to Announce fast and National Repentance to Fight Heat' (2010). *Interfax, Moscow*, August 6. Retrieved 7 March 2012 from http://www.interfax-religion.com/?act=news&div=7564
'Globalizare și Ortodoxie: Sesiunea celei de-a IX-a Adunări Generale Interparlamentare Europene a Ortodoxiei, București, Palatul Parlamentului, 27–30 iunie, 2002' (2002). *Biserica Ortodoxa Romana*, [Official Bulletin of the Romanian Orthodox Church], 120(1–6), p. 162.
'More Than 500,000 Euro on Behalf of the Romanian Orthodox Church for the Victims of the Natural Calamities in the South-East of Asia' (March 2005). *News Bulletin of the Romanian Patriarchate*, 1–2, p. 6.
'News in Brief: A "Health and Faith"—Social Programme of the Romanian Patriarchate in Partnership with a Pharmaceutical Company' (April–June 2003). *News Bulletin of the Romanian Patriarchate*, 4–6.
'News in Brief: A Collaboration between the Romanian Patriarchate and the Ministry of the Interior in View of Preventing and Combating the Trafficking in Persons' (Jan–Mar 2003). *News Bulletin of the Romanian Patriarchate*, 1–3, p. 9.
'Patriarch Kirill Reminded the President About a Symphony of Two Powers'. (2009). *Russkaya Liniya*, 2 February. Retrieved 7 March 2012 from http://rusk.ru/news-data.php?idar=730102 (in Russian).
'Patriarch Teoctist Urges All Romanians to Love and Tolerance for Those Suffering of AIDS/HIV' (January–February 2004). *News Bulletin of the Romanian Patriarchate*, 1, p. 4.
'Președintelui României' [President of Romania] (n.d.). Retrieved 20 August 2011 from http://www.presidency.ro/?lang=ro.
'Temei nr. 3806/2006 Referatul Sectorului Biserica și Societatea cu privire la concluziile întâlnirii anuale a coordonatirilor eparhiali ai activităților de asistență socială (Tismana, 1–3 noiembrie 2006)'. (2006). *Biserica Ortodoxa Romana* [Official Bulletin of the Romanian Orthodox Church], 124(7–12), p. 33.
'UK Calls for G8 Financial Aid for "Arab Spring"' (2011). BBC News. Retrieved 11 June 2011 from http://www.bbc.co.uk/news/uk-politics-13565532.

'Yisilanjiao fazhan yinhang daibiao fang Hua [Representative of Islamic Development Bank Visits China]' (1990). *Zhongguo musilin* 2, p. 8.
Aarab, M. (2009). *De vergeten geschiedenis van het Marokkaanse Rif*. Utrecht: Stichting Observatoire.
Abttoy (2008). *Cartoons van een Berber*. Amsterdam: XTRA.
Abu-Lughod, L. (1991). 'Writing against Culture', in R. G. Fox (ed.), *Recapturing Anthropology: Working in the Present*. Santa Fe, NM: School of American Research Press, pp. 137–162.
Adinkrah, M. (2008).'Witchcraft Themes in Popular Ghanaian Music'. *Popular Music and Society*, 31(3), pp. 299–311.
Adogame, A. (2000). 'Mission from Africa: The Case of the Celestial Church of Christ in Europe'. *Zeitschrift für Missionswissenschaft und Religionswissenschaft*, 84, pp. 29–44.
Agadjanian, A. & Roudometof, V. (2005). 'Introduction: Eastern Orthodoxy in a Global Age—Preliminary Considerations', in V. Roudometof, A. Agadjanian & J. Pankhurst (eds.), *Eastern Orthodoxy in a Global Age: Tradition Faces the Twenty-First Century*. Oxford: AltaMira Press, pp. 1–26.
Agourides, S. (1964). 'The Social Character of Orthodoxy', in A.J. Philippou (ed.), *The Orthodox Ethos: Essays in Honour of the Centenary of the Greek Orthodox Archdiocese of North and South America Studies in Orthodoxy*. Oxford: Holywell Press, Vol. 1, pp. 209–221.
Ahearn, L. (2001). 'Language and Agency'. *Annual Review of Anthropology*, 30, pp. 109–137.
——— (1999). *A Border Passage. From Cairo to America. A Woman's Journey*. New York: Penguin Books.
Akbar, M. J. (2002). *The Shade of Swords: Jihad and the Conflict between Islam & Christianity*. London: Routledge.
Al-Azmeh, A. & Fokas, E. (Eds.) (2007). *Islam in Europe: Diversity, Identity and Difference*. Cambridge: Cambridge University Press.
Al-Hamarneh, A. (2008). 'Arab-German Remigration'. *ISIM Review*, 21, pp. 26–27.
Al-Qaraḍāwī, Y. (1993). *Al-ijtihād al-mu'āṣir, bayna al-inḍibāt wal-infirāṭ*. Quoted in T. Ramadan (1999). *Être musulman européen, Étude des sources islamiques à la lumière du contexte européen*. Lyon: Éditions Tawhid.
Alberoni, F. (1984). *Movement and Institution*. New York: Colombia University Press.
Albrow, M. (1996). *The Global Age*. Cambridge: Cambridge University Press.
Alfeyev, H. (Archbishop Hilarion) (2004). 'Orthodoxy in a New Europe: Problems and Perspectives'. *Religion in Eastern Europe*, 24(3), pp. 18–34.
Allès, E. (2000). *Musulmans de Chine. Une anthropologie des Hui du Henan*. Paris: Éditions de l'École des Hautes Études en Sciences Sociales.
Almond, G. A., Appleby, R. S. & Sivan, E. (Eds.) (2000). *Strong Religion: The Rise of Fundamentalisms Around the World*. Chicago: University of Chicago Press.
American Friends Service Committee (1955). *Speak Truth to Power: A Quaker Search for an Alternative to Violence*. New York: AFSC.
Amir-Moazami, S. & Salvatore, A. (2003). 'Gender, Generation, and the Reform of Tradition: From Muslim Majority Societies to Western Europe', in S. Allievi & J. Nielsen (eds.), *Muslim Networks and Transnational Communities in and across Europe*. Leiden: Brill, pp. 52–77.
Amiraux, V. (2000). 'Jeunes musulmanes turques d'Allemagne. Voix et voies d'individuation', in F. Dassetto (ed.), *Paroles d'Islam. Individus, sociétés et discours dans l'Islam européen contemporain/Islamic Words. Individuals, Societies and Discourse in Contemporary European Islam*. Paris: Maisonneuve et Larose, pp. 101–123.
——— (2003). 'Discours voilés sur les musulmanes en Europe: Comment les musulmans sont-ils devenus des musulmanes?' *Social Compass*, 50(1), pp. 85–96.

Ammerman, N. T. (Ed.) (2006). *Everyday Religion: Observing Modern Religious Lives*. New York: Oxford University Press.
Ananta, A., Arifin, E. N. & Suryadinata, L. (2005). *Emerging Democracy in Indonesia*. Singapore: Institute of Southeast Asian Studies.
Anderson, A. (2007). *Spreading Fires: The Missionary Nature of Early Pentecostalism*. Maryknoll, NY: Orbis.
Anderson, B. (1991). *Imagined Communities: Reflections on the Origin and Spread of Nationalism*. London: Verso.
Andreescu, L. (2007). 'The Construction of Orthodox Churches in Post-Communist Romania'. *Europe-Asia Studies*, 59(3), pp. 451–480.
Annan, K. (1998). 'The Quiet Revolution'. *Global Governance*, 4, pp. 123–138.
Ansell, C. (2006). 'Network Institutionalism', in R. A. W. Rhodes, S. A. Binder & B. A. Rockman (eds.), *The Oxford Handbook of Political Institutions*. Oxford: Oxford University Press, pp. 75–89.
Anzaldúa, G. (1987). *Borderlands/La Frontera: The New Mestisa*. San Francisco: Aunt Lute Books.
Appadurai, A. (1991). 'Global Ethnoscapes: Notes and Queries for a Transnational Anthropology', in R. G. Fox (ed.), *Recapturing Anthropology: Working in the Present*. Santa Fe, NM: School of American Research Press, pp. 191–238.
Appiah, K. A. (2007). *Cosmopolitanism: Ethics in a World of Strangers*. London: Penguin Books.
——— (2006). *Cosmopolitanism: Ethics in a World of Strangers*. New York: Norton.
Asad, T. (1973). *Anthropology and the Colonial Encounter*. New York: Humanities Press.
——— (1986). 'The Concept of Cultural Translation in British Social Anthropology', in J. Clifford & G. Marcus (eds.), *Writing Culture: The Poetics and Politics of Ethnography*. Berkeley: University of California Press, pp. 141–164.
——— (1986). *The Idea of an Anthropology of Islam*. Occasional Papers Series. Washington DC: Center for Contemporary Arabe Studies, Georgetown University.
——— (1993). *Genealogies of Religion: Discipline and Reasons of Power in Christianity and Islam*. Baltimore: Johns Hopkins University Press.
——— (2003). *Formations of the Secular: Christianity, Islam, Modernity*. Stanford, CA: Stanford University Press.
Ashiwa, Y. & Wank, D. L. (Eds.) (2009). *Making Religion, Making the State. The Politics of Religion in Modern China*. Stanford, CA: Stanford University Press.
Ask, K. & Tjomsland, M. (1998), 'Preface', in K. Ask & M. Tjomsland (eds.). *Women and Islamization. Contemporary Dimensions of Discourse on Gender Relations*. Oxford: Berg, pp. vii–viii.
Assmann, A. (2008). 'Transformations between History and Memory'. *Social Research*, 75(1), pp. 49–72.
Aust, S. (2008). *Der Baader Meinhof Complex*. Hamburg: Hoffman und Campe Verlag; English translation, *Baader-Meinhof: The Inside Story of the R. A. F.* Oxford: Oxford University Press, 2009.
Austen, R. A. (2010). *Trans-Saharan Africa in World History*. New York: Oxford University Press.
Avishai, O. (2008). '"Doing Religion" in a Secular World. Women in Conservative Religions and the Question of Agency'. *Gender & Society*, 22(4), pp. 409–433.
Aynan, A. (2007). *Veldslag en andere herinneringen*. Amsterdam: Atlas.
Azuma, J. (2000).'Controversy and Restraint in Ghana'. *Transformation: An International Journal of Holistic Mission Studies,* 17(1), pp. 23–26.
Babb, L. A. (1983). 'Sathya Sai Baba's Magic'. *Anthropological Quarterly*, 56(3), pp. 116–124.
——— (1986). *Redemptive Encounters. Three Modern Styles in the Hindu Tradition*. Berkeley: University of California Press.

Babès, L. (1997). *L'Islam positif. La religion des jeunes musulmans de France*. Paris: Éditions de l'Atelier/Éditions ouvrières.
Bagader, A. A. (2009[1981]). 'Muslims in China: Some Popular Middle Eastern Perspectives', in M. Dillon (ed.), *Islam in China. Key Papers. Volume 1*. Folkestone: Global Oriental, pp. 86–91.
Bai, S. (2003). *Zhongguo Huihui minzu shi* [*The History of Hui Nationality*]. Beijing: Zhonghua shuju.
Bailey, F. G. (1996). *The Civility of Indifference: On Domesticating Ethnicity*. Ithaca, NY: Cornell University Press.
Bailey, S. D. (1985). 'Non-Official Mediation in Disputes: Reflections on Quaker Experience'. *International Affairs*, 62(2), pp. 205–222.
Barber, B. R. (1995). *Jihad versus McWorld: How Globalism and Tribalism Are Reshaping the World*. New York: Ballantine.
Barkin, J. S. (2006). *International Organization: Theories and Institutions*. London: Palgrave Macmillan.
Barkun, M. (2007). 'Appropriated Martyrs: The Branch Davidians and the Radical Right'. *Terrorism and Political Violence*, 19(1), pp. 117–124.
Barlas, A. (2002). *'Believing Women' in Islam: Unreading Patriarchal Interpretations of the Qur'ān*. Austin: University of Texas Press.
Bartels, E. & de Jong, I. (2007).'Civil Society on the Move in Amsterdam: Mosque Organizations in the Slotervaart District'. *Journal of Muslim Minority Affairs*, 27(3), pp. 455–470.
Bartholomew I, His All Holiness Ecumenical Patriarch (2008). *Encountering the Mystery: Understanding Orthodox Christianity Today*. New York: Doubleday.
Basch, L. G., Glick Schiller, N. & Szanton Blanc, C. (1994). *Nations Unbound: Transnational Projects, Post-Colonial Predicaments and Deterritorialized Nation-States*. Amsterdam: Gordon & Breach Science Publishers.
Bastian, J.-P. (2003). *La mutación religiosa de America Latina*. Mexico City: Fonda de Cultura Económica.
Bauman, Z. (1998). *Globalisation: The Human Consequences*. New York: Columbia University Press.
——— (2001). *Community. Seeking Safety in an Insecure World*. Malden, MA: Blackwell.
Baumann, M. M. (2009). 'Transforming Conflict Toward and Away from Violence: Bloody Sunday and the Hunger Strikes in Northern Ireland'. *Dynamics of Asymmetric Conflict*, 2(3), pp. 172–180.
Bayat, A. (2002). 'Piety, Privilege and Egyptian Youths'. *ISIM Newsletter*, 10, pp. 23–24.
Baylis, J. & Smith, S. (2001). *The Globalization of World Politics: An Introduction to International Relations*. New York: Oxford University Press.
Bayly, C. A. (2002). '"Archaic" and "Modern" Globalization in the Eurasian and African arena, c. 1750–1850', in A. G. Hopkins (ed.), *Globalization in World History*. London: Pimlico, pp. 46–73.
Bayly, C. A. (2004). *The Birth of the Modern World*. Oxford: Blackwell.
Bays, D. (2003). 'Chinese Protestant Christianity Today', in D. L. Overmyer (ed.), *Religion in China Today*. The China Quarterly Special Issues No. 3. Cambridge: Cambridge University Press, pp. 182–98.
BBC (1980). 'China in the Role of Protector of Islam.' BBC Summary of World Broadcasts, 11 July 1980.
——— (2004). *Secret Swami*. Television documentary.
Beck, U. (2005). *Power in the Global Age*. Cambridge, MA: Polity Press.
——— (2007). *Cosmopolitan Vision*. Cambridge, MA: Polity Press.
Beckford, J. A. (2004). 'New Religious Movements and Globalization', in P. C. Lucas & T. Robbins (eds.), *New Religious Movements in the Twenty-First Century*:

Legal Political and Social Challenges in Global Perspective. New York: Routledge, pp. 205–214.
Beeson, M. & Bell, S. (2009). 'The G-20 and International Economic Governance: Hegemony, Collectivism, or Both?' *Global Governance*, 15, pp. 67–86.
Belguendouz, A. (2009). *Le conseil de la communauté marocaine à l'étranger. Une nouvelle institution en débat*. Research Report CARIM-RR 2009–01, Florence: European University Institute.
Bell, D. S. (2005). 'Mythscapes: Memory, Mythology and National Identity'. *British Journal of Sociology*, 54(1), pp. 53–81.
Ben-Rafael, E. & Sternberg, Y. (2005). 'Introduction', in E. Ben-Rafael & Y. Sternberg (eds.), *Comparing Modernities: Pluralism versus Homogeneity. Essays in Homage to Shmuel N. Eisenstadt*. Brill: Brill Academic Publishers, pp. 1–27.
Bender, C. & Cadge, W. (2006). 'Constructing Buddhism(s): Interreligious Dialogue and Religious Hybridity'. *Sociology of Religion*, 67(3), pp. 229–247.
Bendixsen, S. (2009). 'Being Muslim or Being 'German'? Islam as a New Urban Identity', in G. Tibe Bonifacio & V. S. M. Angeles (eds.), *Gender, Religion and Migration: Pathways of Integration*. Lanham, MD: Lexington Books, pp. 95–115.
——— (2010). *'It's Like Doing SMS to Allah.' Young Female Muslims Crafting a Religious Self in Berlin*, unpublished PhD thesis, Humboldt Universität (Berlin)/Ecole des Hautes Etudes en Sciences Sociales (Paris).
Berger, J. (2003). 'Religious Nongovernmental Organizations: An Exploratory Analysis'. *Voluntas: International Journal of Voluntary and Nonprofit Organizations*, 14(1), pp. 15–39.
Berger, P. L. (1969). *Sacred Canopy: Elements of a Sociological Theory of Religion*. New York: Anchor Books.
——— (1990). *The Sacred Canopy: Elements of a Sociological Theory of Religion*. New York: Anchor Books.
——— (1999). 'The Desecularization of the World', in P. L. Berger (ed.), *The Desecularization of the World: Resurgent Religion and World Politics*. Grand Rapids, MI: W. B. Eerdmans Publishing Company, pp. 1–18.
——— (2001). 'Reflections on the Sociology of Religion Today'. *Sociology of Religion*, 62, pp. 443–454.
——— (2002). 'The Cultural Dynamics of Globalization', in P. L. Berger & S. Huntington (eds.), *Many Globalizations: Cultural Diversity in the Contemporary World*. New York: Oxford University Press, pp. 1–17.
——— (2005). 'Orthodoxy and Global Pluralism', *Demokratizatsiya*, keynote address at the Conference 'The Spirit of the Orthodoxy and the Ethic of Capitalism', on 7–9 March at the Institute for Human Sciences, Vienna, Austria.
——— (2005). 'Orthodoxy and Global Pluralism'. *Demokratizatsiya, the Journal of Post-Soviet Democratization*, 13(3), pp. 437–448.
——— (Ed.) (1999). *The Desecularization of the World: Resurgent Religion and World Politics*. Grand Rapids, MI: Wm. B. Eerdmans.
——— & Huntington, S. P. (2001). *Many Globalizations*. Oxford: Oxford University Press.
Berger, P. L. & Luckman, T. (1966). *The Social Construction of Reality: A Treatise in the Sociology of Knowledge*. Garden City, NY: Anchor Books.
Berger, P. L., Davie, G. & Focas, E. (2008). *Religious America Secular Europe? A Theme and Variations*. Aldershot: Ashgate Publishing Limited.
Bergunder, M. (2008). *The South Indian Pentecostal Movement in the Twentieth Century*. Grand Rapids, MI: Eerdmans.
Berkey, J. (1992). *The Transmission of Knowledge in Medieval Cairo: A Social History of Islamic Education*. Princeton, NJ: Princeton University Press.
Berman, H. J. (1983). *Law and Revolution: The Formation of the Western Legal Traditions*. Cambridge, MA: Harvard University Press.

Bertelsmann Stiftung (2009). *Religion Monitor-2008*. Gütersloh: Verlag Bertelsmann Stiftung.
Berzano, L. & Cassinasco, A. (1999). *Cristiani d'Oriente in Piemonte*. Turin: L'Harmattan.
Beyer, P. (1994). *Religion and Globalisation*. Thousand Oaks, CA: Sage.
────── (1998). 'The City and Beyond as Dialogue: Negotiating Religious Authenticity in Global Society'. *Social Compass*, 45, pp. 61–73.
────── (2003). 'De-Centring Religious Singularity: The Globalisation of Christianity as a Case in Point'. *Numen*, 50, pp. 357–386.
────── (2005). 'Au croisement de l'identité et de la différence: les syncrétismes culturo-religieux dans le contexte de la mondialisation'. *Social Compass*, 54, pp. 417–429.
────── (2006). *Religions in Global Society*. London: Routledge.
────── (2007). 'Can the Tail Wag the Dog? Diaspora Reconstructions of Religion in a Globalized Society'. *Nordic Journal of Religion and Society*, 20(1), pp. 41–63.
────── (2007). 'Globalization and the Institutional Modeling of Religions', in P. Beyer & L. Beaman (eds.), *Religion, Globalization and Culture*. Leiden: Brill, pp. 167–186.
────── (2010). 'Differential Reconstruction of Religions among Second Generation Immigrant Youth in Canada'. *Annual Review of the Sociology of Religion*, 1, pp. 1–28.
────── [1994] (2000). *Religion and Globalization*. London: Sage.
Beyer, P. & Beaman, L. (2007). 'Introduction', in P. Beyer & L. Beaman (eds.), *Religion, Globalization and Culture*. Leiden: Brill, pp. 1–8.
Beyer, P. & Beaman, L. (Eds.) (2007). *Globalisation, Religion and Culture*. Leiden: Brill.
Bhabha, H. (1985). 'Signs Taken for Wonders: Questions of Ambivalence and Authority Under a Tree Outside Delhi, May 1817'. *Critical Inquiry*, 12(1), pp. 144–165.
────── (1994). *The Location of Culture*. London: Routledge Classics.
Bhabha, H. K. (1990). 'Introduction: Narrating the Nation', in H. K. Bhabha (ed.), *Nation and Narration*. London: Routledge, pp. 1–7.
────── (1994). *The Location of Culture*. London: Routledge.
Bhagwati, J. (2004). *In Defense of Globalisation*. New York: Oxford University Press.
Bickerton, C., Cunliffe, P. & Gourevitch, A. (Eds.) (2007). *Politics without Sovereignty: A Critique of Contemporary International Relations*. London: University College London Press.
Biggs, M. (2006). 'Dying Without Killing: Self-Immolations, 1963–2002', in D. Gambetta (ed.), *Making Sense of Suicide Missions*. Oxford: Oxford University Press, pp. 173–208.
Binns, J. (2002). *An Introduction to the Christian Orthodox Churches*. Cambridge: Cambridge University Press.
Biserica Ortodoxa Romana [Romanian Orthodox Church] (n.d.). 'Sectorul comunităţi externe' [Externa Community Sector]. Retrieved 20 August 2011 from http://www.patriarhia.ro/ro/administratia_patriarhala/sectorul_comunitati_externe.html
Bloom, M. M. (2004). 'Palestinian Suicide Bombing: Public Support, Market Share, and Outbidding'. *Political Science Quarterly*, 119(1), pp. 61–88.
────── (2005). *Dying to Kill: The Allure of Suicide Terror*. New York: Columbia University Press.
Bloom, M. M. & Horgan, J. (2008). 'Missing Their Mark: The IRA's Proxy Bomb Campaign'. *Social Research*, 75(2), pp. 579–614.
Boafo-Arthur, K. (2001).'Chieftaincy and Politics in Ghana Since 1982'. *West Africa Review*, 3(1), pp. 10–21.
Bob-Milliar, G. M. (2009).'Chieftaincy, Diaspora and Development: The Institution of Nkɔsuohene in Ghana'. *African Affairs*, 108(433), pp. 541–558.

Bobrinskoy, B. (2003). 'La Diaspora Ortodossa in Europa Occidentale: Un Ponte tra le Due Tradizioni Europee?', in A. Pacini (ed.), *L'Ortodossia nella Nuova Europa: Dinamiche Storiche e Prospettive*. Turin: Giovanni Agnelli, pp. 303–319.
Bogomilova, N. (2004). 'Reflections on the Contemporary Religious "Revival" Religion, Secularization, Globalization'. *Religion in Eastern Europe*, 24(4), pp. 2–10.
Borowik, I. (2006). 'Orthodoxy Confronting the Collapse of Communism in Post-Soviet Countries'. *Social Compass*, 53(2), pp. 267–278.
—— (2010). 'Why Has Religiosity in Poland Not Changed Since 1989? Five Hypotheses'. *Politics and Religion*, 3(2), pp. 262–275.
Boubekeur, A. (2004). 'Female Religious Professionals in France'. *ISIM Newsletter*, 14, pp. 28–29.
Bourdieu, P. (1977). *Outline of a Theory of Practice*. New York: Cambridge University Press.
Bowen, J. R. (1993). *Muslims through Discourse: Religion and Ritual in Gayo Society*. Princeton, NJ: Princeton University Press.
—— (2003). *Islam, Law and Equality in Indonesia: An Anthropology of Public Reasoning*. Cambridge: Cambridge University Press.
—— (2009). *Can Islam be French?: Pluralism and Pragmatism in a Secularist State*. Princeton, NJ: Princeton University Press.
Braffi, E. K. (2002). *Akwasidae and the Odwira Festival*. Krofrom-Kumasi: Bayoba Limited.
Brand, L. A. (2008). *Citizens Abroad: Emigration and the State in the Middle East and North Africa*. Cambridge: Cambridge University Press.
Brett, R. (2008). 'Why Quakers Work at the United Nations'. *Quaker News*, 66, p. 11.
Brettell, C. B. (2006). 'Introduction: Global Spaces/Local Places: Transnationalism, Diaspora, and the Meaning of Home'. *Identities: Global Studies in Culture and Power*, 13, pp. 327–334.
Bria, I. (1995). *Romania: Orthodox Identity at a Crossroads of Europe*. Gospel and Cultures Pamphlet 3, Geneva: WCC Publications.
Bringa, T. (1995). *Being Muslim the Bosnian Way: Identity and Community in a Central Bosnian Village*. Princeton, NJ: Princeton University Press.
Brock, P. (Ed.) (2005). *Indigenous Peoples and Religious Change*. Leiden: Brill.
Brown, G. C. (2001). *The Death of Christian Britain: Understanding Secularization 1800–2000*. London: Routledge.
Brubaker, R. (1996). *Nationalism Reframed: Nationhood and the National Question in the New Europe*. Cambridge: Cambridge University Press.
—— (2005). 'The "Diaspora" Diaspora'. *Ethnic and Racial Studies*, 28(1), pp. 1–19.
Brubaker, R. & Cooper, F. (2000). 'Beyond "Identity"'. *Theory and Society*, 29, pp. 1–47.
Bruce, S. (2001). 'The Social Process of Secularization', in R. K. Fenn (ed.), *The Blackwell Companion to Sociology of Religion*. Oxford: Blackwell, pp. 249–263.
—— (2003). *God Is Dead: Secularization in the West. Religion and Spirituality in the Modern World*. Oxford: Blackwell.
—— (2006). 'Secularization and the Impotence of Individualized Religion'. *The Hedgehog Review*, Vol. spring and summer, pp. 35–45.
Brusco, E. (1995). *The Reformation of Machismo: Evangelical Conversion and Gender in Colombia*. Austin: University of Texas Press.
—— (2010). 'Gender and Power', in A. Anderson, M. Bergunder, A. Droogers & C. van der Laan (eds.), *Studying Global Pentecostalism: Theories + Methods*. Berkeley: University of California Press, pp. 74–92.
Brym, R. (2008). 'Religion, Politics, and Suicide Bombing: An Interpretive Essay'. *Canadian Journal of Sociology / Cahiers canadiens de sociologie*, 33(1), pp. 89–108.
Bull, H. [1977] (2002). *The Anarchical Society: A Study of Order in World Politics*. Basingstoke, Hampshire: Palgrave Macmillan.

Burawoy, M. & Verdery, K. (1999). 'Introduction', in M. Burawoy & K. Verdery (eds.), *Uncertain Transition: Ethnographies of Change in the Postsocialist World*. Boston: Rowman and Littlefield Publishers, pp. 1–19.

Burdick, J. (1993). *Looking for God in Brazil: The Progressive Church in Urban Brazil*. Berkeley: University of California Press.

Burke, E. III (1973). 'The Image of the Moroccan State in French Ethnological Literature: A New Look at the Origin of Lyautey's Berber Policy', in E. Gellner & C. Micaud (eds.), *Arabs and Berbers: From Tribe to Nation in North Africa*. London: Duckworth, pp. 175–199.

—— (2007). 'The Creation of the Moroccan Colonial Archive: 1880–1930'. *History and Anthropology*, 18, pp. 1–9.

Bush, E. L. (2007). 'Measuring Religion in Global Civil Society'. *Social Forces*, 85(4), pp. 1645–1665.

Buss, A. E. (2003). *The Russian-Orthodox Tradition and Modernity*. Leiden: Brill.

Buswell, R. & Lee, T. S. (Eds.). (2006). *Christianity in Korea*. Honolulu: University of Hawai'i Press.

Byrd, R. O. (1960). *Quaker Ways in Foreign Policy*. Toronto: University of Toronto.

Calhoun, C., Juergensmeyer, M. & van Antwerpen, J. (Eds.) (2011). *Rethinking Secularism*. New York: Oxford University Press.

Campbell, C. (1987). *The Romantic Ethic and the Spirit of Modern Consumerism*. Oxford: Blackwell.

Camus, A. (1950). *Les Justes*. Paris: Gallimard; English translation, *The Just Assassins*. London: Penguin, 1970.

—— (1951). *L'homme révolté*. Paris: Gallimard; English translation, *The Rebel*. London: Penguin, 2000.

Cao, N. (2011). *Constructing China's Jerusalem: Christians, Power and Place in Contemporary Wenzhou*. Stanford, CA: Stanford University Press.

Carp, R. (2007). 'Biserica Ortodoxa Romana si pozitia laicilor fata de integrarea europeana: elemente de discurs in spatiul public', in R. Coman & A.M. Dobre (eds.), *Politici Publice Romanesti in Context European*. Institutul Europan: Iasi.

Carrette, J. R. (2007). *Religion and Critical Psychology: Religious Experience in the Knowledge Economy*. London: Routledge.

—— (2012). 'Religion and Globalization', in King, R. (ed.), *Theory/Religion/Culture: Classic and Contemporary Approaches*. New York: Columbia University Press, forthcoming.

Carrette, J. R. & King, R. (2004). *Selling Spirituality: The Silent Takeover of Religion*. London: Routledge Press.

Casanova, J. (1994). *Public Religions in the Modern World*. Chicago: The University of Chicago Press.

—— (2001). 'Civil Society and Religion: Retrospective Reflections on Catholicism and Prospective Reflections on Islam'. *Social Research*, 68(4), pp. 1041–1080.

—— (2001). 'Globalizing Catholicism and the Return to a "Universal Church"', in P. Beyer (ed.), *Religion in the Process of Globalisation*. Würzburg: Ergon Verlag, pp. 201–225.

—— (2006). 'Rethinking Secularization; A Global Comparative Perspective'. *The Hedgehog Review*, vol spring and summer, pp. 7–22.

—— (2012). 'Rethinking Public Religions', in T. S. Shah, A. Stepan, & M. D. Toft (eds.), *Rethinking Religion and World Affairs*. New York: Oxford University Press, pp. 25–35.

Castells, M. (1996). *The Rise of the Network Society*. Oxford: Blackwell.

Cavatorta, F. (2010). 'The Jamiat al-Adl wal-Ihsan: Religion, Political Opposition and Stalled Democratisation in Morocco', in J. Haynes (ed.), *Religion and Politics in Europe, the Middle East and North Africa*. London: Routledge, pp. 162–176.

Centraal Bureau voor de Statistiek. (2011). 'Kerncijfers wijken en buurten 2004-2010' [Core Figures Districts and Neighbourhoods 2004-2010], Retrieved 18 July 2011 from http://statline.cbs.nl/StatWeb/publication/?DM = SLNL&PA=70904NED.
Cesari, J. (1994). *Être musulman en France: associations, militants et mosquées.* Paris: Karthala.
——— (1998). *Musulmans et républicains: les jeunes, l'Islam et la France.* Bruxelles: Éditions Complexes.
——— (2002). 'Islam in France: The Shaping of a Religious Minority', in Y. Yazbeck- Haddad (ed.), *Muslims in the West: From Sojourners to Citizens.* London: Oxford University Press, pp. 36–51.
——— (2003). 'Muslim Minorities in Europe: The Silent Revolution', in J. Esposito & F. Burgat (ed.), *Modernizing Islam: Religion in the Public Sphere in the Middle East and in Europe,* London: Hurst & Company, 2003, pp. 251–269.
——— (2006). *When Islam and Democracy Meet: Muslims in Europe and in the United States.* New York: Palgrave Macmillan.
——— (2007). 'The Hybrid and Globalized Islam of Western Europe', in Y. Samad & S. Kasturi (eds.), *Islam in the European Union, Transnationalism, Youth and the War on Terror.* Karachi: Oxford University Press, pp. 108–122.
——— (2008). 'Muslims in Western Europe After 9/11: Local and Global Components of the Integration Process', in G. Motzkin & Y. Fischer (eds.), *Religion and Democracy in Contemporary Europe.* London: Alliance Publishing Trust, pp. 153-167.
Ceton, C. (2002).'Onipa—Mens—Onipapa—Heel erg mens: Een interview met Kwasi Wiredu'. *Filosofie Magazine,* 11(5), pp. 12–15.
Chandler, D. (2007). 'Deconstructing Sovereignty: Constructing Global Civil Society', in C. Bickerton, P. Cunliffe & A. Gourevitch (eds.), *Politics without Sovereignty: A Critique of Contemporary International Relations.* London: University College London Press, pp. 150–167.
Chang, H.-J. (2003). *Globalisation, Economic Development and the Role of the State.* London: Zed Books.
Chang, Q. (1999). 'Yisilanjiao fazhan yinhang daibiao fang Hua [Delegation of Islamic Development Bank Visits China]'. *Zhongguo musilin* 6, p. 29.
Chatterjee, P. (1995). 'History and the Nationalisation of Hinduism', in V. Dalmia & H. von Stietencron (eds.), *Representing Hinduism.* New Delhi: Sage, pp. 103–128.
Chen, N. N. (2003). 'Healing Sects and Anti-Cult Campaigns', in D. L. Overmyer (ed.), *Religion in China Today.* The China Quarterly Special Issues No. 3. Cambridge: Cambridge University Press, pp.199–214.
Chérif-Chebbi, L. (2004). 'Brothers and Comrades. Muslim Fundamentalists and Communists Allied for Transmission of Islamic Knowledge in China', in S. Dudoignon (ed.), *Devout Societies vs. Impious States. Transmitting Islamic Learning in Russia, Central Asia and China, Through the Twentieth Century.* Berlin: Klaus Schwarz Verlag, pp. 61–90.
Chesnut, R. A. (2003.) *Competitive Spirits: Latin America's New Religious Economy.* Oxford: Oxford University Press.
Ciobotea, D., Metropolitan of Moldavia and Bucovina (2003). 'La Chiesa e la Fede Ortodossa nella Società Romena Contemporanea', in A. Pacini (ed.), *L'Ortodossia nella Nuova Europa: Dinamiche Storiche e Prospettive.* Turin: Giovanni Agnelli, pp. 323–330.
Clark, A. M., Friedman, E. & Hochstetler, K. (2005). 'The Sovereign Limits of Global Civil Society: A Comparison of NGO Participation in UN World Conferences on the Environment, Human Rights and Women', in R. Wilkinson (ed.), *The Global Governance Reader.* London: Routledge, pp. 292–321.
Clark, I. (1997). *Globalisation and Fragmentation.* Oxford: Oxford University Press.

Clark, S. D. (1948). *Church and Sect in Canada*. Toronto: University of Toronto Press.
Clément, O. (2005). *La Chiesa Ortodossa*. P. Crespi (Trans.). Brescia: Editrice Queriniana.
Cohen, P. A. (1985). *Discovering History in China*. Columbia, NY: Columbia University Press.
Coleman, S. (1995). 'America Loves Sweden: Prosperity Theology and the Cultures of Capitalism', in R. H. Roberts (ed.), *Religion and the Transformations of Capitalism: Comparative Approaches*. London: Routledge, pp. 161–179.
Confino, M. (2005). 'Religion and Power in the History of the Eastern Orthodox Church', in E. Ben-Rafael & Y. Sternberg (eds.), *Comparing Modernities: Pluralism versus Homogeneity. Essays in Homage to Shmuel N. Eisenstadt*. Brill: Brill Academic Publishers, pp. 339–363.
Conovici, I. (2006). 'The ROC after 1989: Social Identity, National Memory, and the Theory of Secularization'. Paper presented at the ISORECEA Conference, 14–16 December.
Cook, D. (2007). *Martyrdom in Islam*. Cambridge: Cambridge University Press.
Cook, M. (2000). *Commanding Right and Forbidding Wrong in Islamic Thought*. Cambridge: Cambridge University Press.
Cooke, M. & Lawrence, B. (2005). 'Introduction', in M. Cooke & B. Lawrence (eds.), *Muslim Networks from Hajj to Hip Hop*. Chapel Hill: University of North Carolina Press, pp. 1–28.
Cortesão, A. & Teixeira da Mota, A. (1962). *Portugaliae Monumenta Cartographica* Lisbon: Comissão Executiva Das Comemorações do V Centenario da Morte do Infante D. Henrique.
Cottaar, A. & Bouras, N. (2009). *Marokkanen in Nederland. De pioniers vertellen*. Amsterdam: J. M. Meulenhoff.
CPOST (Chicago Project on Security and Terrorism) (2011). *Suicide Attack Database*. Retrieved 16 February 2012 from http://cpost.uchicago.edu/search.php.
Crawford, D. & Hoffman, K. E. (2000). 'Essentially Amazigh: Urban Berbers and the Global Village', in K. Lacey (ed.), *The Arab-African and Islamic World: Interdisciplinary Studies*. New York: Peter Lang, pp. 117–131.
Csordas, T. (1994). *The Sacred Self: A Cultural Phenomenology of Charismatic Healing*. Berkeley: University of California Press.
Cvetkovich, A. & Kellner, D. (Eds.) (1997). *Articulating the Global and the Local: Globalisation and Cultural Studies*. Boulder, CO: Westview.
Dale, S. (1988). 'Religious Suicide in Islamic Asia: Anticolonial Terrorism in India, Indonesia and the Philippines'. *Journal of Conflict Resolution*, 23(1), pp. 37–59.
Dassetto, F. (1997). *Facettes de l'Islam Belge*. Louvain-la-Neuve: Bruylant Academia.
Dassetto, F., Maréchal, B. & Nielsen, J. (eds.) (2001). *Convergence musulmanes. Aspects contemporains de l'Islam, dans l'Europe élargie*. Louvain-la-Neuve: Academia Bruylant.
Davie, G. (1994). *Religion in Britain Since 1945: Believing without Belonging*. Oxford: Blackwell.
——— (1999). 'Europe: The Exception That Proves the Rule?' in P. L. Berger (ed.), *The Desecularization of the World: Resurgent Religion and World Politics*. Washington, DC: Ethics and Public Policy Center, pp. 65–85.
——— (2000). *Religion in Modern Europe: A Memory Mutates*. Oxford: Oxford University Press.
——— (2001). 'Patterns of Religion in Western Europe: An Exceptional Case', in R. K. Fenn (ed.), *The Blackwell Companion to Sociology of Religion*. Oxford: Blackwell, pp. 264–278.
——— (2003). *Europe: The Exceptional Case: Parameters of Faith in the Modern World*. London: Darton, Longman & Todd.

——— (2007). 'Vicarious Religion: A Methodological Challenge', in N. Ammerman (ed.), *Everyday Religion: Observing Modern Religious Lives*. New York: Oxford University Press.
——— (2010). 'Resacralization', in B. S. Turner (ed.), *The New Blackwell Companion to the Sociology of Religion*. Chichester: Wiley-Blackwell, pp. 160–177.
Dawson, L. L. & Cowan, D. E. (Eds.) (2004). *Religion Online: Finding Faith on the Internet*. New York: Routledge.
De Haas, H. (2007). 'Morocco's Migration Experience: A Transitional Perspective'. *International Migration*, 45, pp. 39–70.
——— (2009). 'International Migration and Regional Development in Morocco. A Review'. *Journal of Ethnic and Migration Studies*, 35, pp. 1571–1593.
de Kruijf, J. G. (2006). *Guyana Junction: Globalization, Localization and the Production of East Indianness*. Doctoral thesis Utrecht University, Igitur, Utrecht Publishing & Archiving Services. Retrieved 10 January 2011 from http://igitur-archive.library.uu.nl/dissertations/2006-0829-201225/index.htm.
De La Calle, L. & Sánchez-Cuenca, I. (2011). 'What We Talk About When We Talk About Terrorism'. *Politics and Society*, 39(3), pp. 451–472.
de Witte, M. (2010). 'Religious Media, Mobile Spirits: Publicity and Secrecy in African Pentecostalism and Traditional Religion', in G. Huwelmeier & K. Krause (eds.) *Travelling Spirits: Migrants, Markets and Mobilities*. New York: Routledge, pp. 83–101.
della Cava, R. (2001). 'Transnational Religions: The Roman Catholic Church in Brazil & the Orthodox Church in Russia'. *Sociology of Religion: Special Issue: Religion and Globalization at the Turn of the Millennium*, 62(4), pp. 535–550.
Délumeau, J. (1983). *Le péché et la peur: La culpabilisation en Occident, XIIIe–XVIIIe siècles*. Paris: Fayard.
Dempster, M. W., Klaus, B. D. & Petersen, D. (Eds.) (1999). *The Globalisation of Pentecostalism*. Oxford: Regnum.
den Uyl, M. & Brouwer, L. (2009). '"Mix, Just Mix and See What Happens": Girls in a Super-Diverse Amsterdam Neighbourhood', in S. Alghasi, T. H. Eriksen & H. Ghorashi (eds.), *Paradoxes of Cultural Recognition: Perspectives from Northern Europe*. Burlington, CO: Ashgate, pp. 201–219.
Denscombe, M. (2004). *The Good Research Guide: For Small-scale Social Research Projects*. Berkshire, UK: MacGraw-Hill Education.
Department for External Church Relations of the Moscow Patriarchate (n.d.). 'Bases of the Social Concept of the Russian Orthodox Church', Chapter VI. 5. Retrieved 7 March 2012 from http://orthodoxeurope.org/print/3/14.aspx.
DeSoucey, M., Pozner, J.-E., Fields, C., Dobransky, K. & Fine, G. A. (2008). 'Memory and Sacrifice: An Embodied Theory of Martyrdom'. *Cultural Sociology*, 2(1), pp. 99–121.
Despland, M. (1979). *La religion en occident: Evolution des idées et du vécu*. Montreal: Fides.
Diamond, L. (1999). *Developing Democracy. Toward Consolidation*. Baltimore, MD: The Johns Hopkins University Press.
Diamond, L., Plattner, M. & Brumberg, D. (Eds.) (2003). *Islam and Democracy in the Middle East*. Baltimore, MD: The Johns Hopkins University Press.
Diawara, M. (1988). 'Popular Culture and Oral Traditions in African film'. *Film Quarterly*, 41(3), pp. 6–14.
Dienst Onderzoek en Statistiek, Gemeente Amsterdam. (2006). 'Overige niet-westerse allochtonen in Amsterdam [Other Non-western Immigrants in Amsterdam]'. *Fact sheet*, 2, Amsterdam. Retrieved 27 March 2012 from http://www.os.amsterdam.nl/pdf/2006_factsheets_2.pdf.
——— (2007). *Feiten en cijfers [Facts and Numbers]*. Amsterdam: Gemeente Amsterdam.

—— (2011). *Kerncijfers Amsterdam 2011 [Core Figures Amsterdam 2011]*. Amsterdam: Gemeente Amsterdam. Retrieved 27 March 2012 from http://www.os.amsterdam.nl/pdf/2011_kerncijfers_amsterdam.pdf.
Dingley, J. & Kirk-Smith, M. (2002). 'Symbolism and Sacrifice in Terrorism'. *Small Wars and Insurgencies*, 13 (1), pp. 102–128.
Dingley, J. & Mollica, M. (2007). 'The Human Body as a Terrorist Weapon: Hunger Strikes and Suicide Bombers'. *Studies in Conflict and Terrorism*, 30(6), pp. 459–492.
Djaït, B. (2003). 'Sociale en etnische identiteit in de multiculturele samenleving. Een exploratief onderzoek naar identiteitsbeleving(en) bij allochtone jongeren in Gent', in M.-C. Foblets & E. Cornelis (eds.), *Migratie, zijn wij uw kinderen? Identiteitsbeleving bij allochtone jongeren*. Leuven: Acco, pp. 81–98.
Dobbelaere, K. (2007). 'Secularization', in G. Ritzer (ed.), *The Blackwell Encyclopedia of Sociology. Volume VIII*. Oxford: Blackwell Publishing, pp. 4140–4148.
Dragon, G. (2003). *Emperor and Priest. The Imperial Office in Byzantium*. Cambridge: Cambridge University Press.
Duara, P. (1995). *Rescuing History from the Nation: Questioning Narratives of Modern China*. Chicago: University of Chicago Press.
Duffield. M. (2001). *Global Governance and the New Wars*. London: Zed Books.
Dungaciu, D. (2006). 'Davie's "Europe" and the Secularization Thesis', in M. Franzmann, C. Gärtner & N. Köck (eds.), *Religiosität in der säkularisierten Welt: Theoretische und empirische Beiträge zur Säkularisierungsdebatte in der Religionssoziologie*. Wiesbaden: VS Verlag für Sozialwissenschaften.
Durkheim, É. (1915). *The Elementary Forms of the Religious Life. A Study in Religious Sociology*, translated from French by Joseph Ward. Swain, London: George Allen and Unwin.
—— (1965). *The Elementary Forms of the Religious Life* (J. W. Swain, Trans.). New York: Free Press.
Ebaugh, H. & Chafetz, J. (1999). 'Agents for Cultural Reproduction and Structural Change: The Ironic Role of Women in Immigrant Religious Institutions'. *Social Forces*, 78(2), pp. 585–613.
Eck, D. (2006). *A New Religious America: How a 'Christian Country' Has Become the World's Most Religiously Diverse Nation*. San Francisco: Harper.
Eickelman, D. (1992). 'Mass Higher Education and the Religious Imagination in Contemporary Arab Societies'. *American Ethnologist*, 19(4), pp. 643–655.
Eickelman, D. F. & Piscatori, J. P. (1992). 'Preface', in D. F. Eickelman & J. P. Piscatori (eds.), *Muslim Travellers: Pilgrimage: Migration and the Religious Imagination*. Berkeley: University of California Press.
Eisenstadt, S. N. (2002). *Multiple Modernities*. Edison NJ: Transaction.
—— (Ed.) (2002). *Multiple Modernities*. New Brunswick, NJ: Transaction.
El Aissati, A. (2010). 'The Amazigh Language in the Media of the Diaspora: Proficiency, Use and Attitudes'. *Colloques et séminaires*, 166, pp. 285–295.
El Ayoubi, M. (2000). *Les merveilles du Rif: contes berbères*. Driebergen: Houtsma Stichting.
Elias, N. (1982). *Über die Einsamkeit der Sterbenden in unseren Tagen*. Frankfurt: Suhrkamp; English translation, *The Loneliness of the Dying*. Oxford: Basil Blackwell, 1985.
Elster, J. (2006). 'Motivations and Beliefs in Suicide Missions', in D. Gambetta (ed.), *Making Sense of Suicide Missions*. Oxford: Oxford University Press pp. 233–258.
Enev, T. N. (2001). 'Catholicism and Eastern Orthodoxy: Cultural Influences on the Transition in Central and Eastern Europe'. Dissertation submitted to the University of Delaware in partial fulfilment of the requirements for the degree of Doctor of Philosophy in Sociology.
Ergil, D. (2000). 'Suicide Terrorism in Turkey'. *Civil Wars*, 3(1), pp. 37–54.

Erickson, J. H. (1999). *Orthodox Christians in America*. New York: Oxford University Press.
Essadki, A. (1997). *Strijdkreet van de aarde. Riffijnse gedichten*. Utrecht.
Faas, D. (2010). 'Muslims in Germany: From Guest Workers to Citizens?', in A. Triandafyllidou (ed.), *Muslims in 21st Century Europe. Structural and Cultural Perspectives*. New York: Routledge, pp. 59–77.
Fadil, N. (2001). *Eenheid in de diversiteit. Een cultuursociologische studie naar de etnische identiteit van Marokkaanse adolescente meisjes*. Master thesis. Leuven: Katholieke Universiteit Leuven.
—— (2005). 'Individualising Faith, Individualising Identity: Islam and Young Muslim Women in Belgium', in J. Césari & S. McLoughlin (eds.), *European Muslims and the Secular State*. Farnham: Ashgate, pp. 143–154.
—— (2008). *Submitting to God, Submitting to the Self: Secular and Religious Trajectories of Second Generation Maghrebi in Belgium*. PhD dissertation. Leuven: Katholieke Universiteit Leuven.
Falk, R. (1993). 'The Making of Global Citizenship', in J. Brecher, J. B. Childs & J. Cutler (eds.), *Global Visions: Beyond the New World Order*. Boston: South End Press, pp. 39–50.
Fällman, F. (2010). 'Useful Opium? "Adapted Religion" and "Harmony" in Contemporary China'. *Journal of Contemporary China* 19(67), pp. 949–969.
Fantini, P. (2008). 'Metropolitan Kirill on Economic Globalization and the Social Consensus'. *Religion & Liberty*, 18(2). Retrieved 6 March 2012 from http://www.acton.org/pub/religion-liberty/volume-18-number-2/metropolitan-kirill-economic-globalization-and-soc.
Fattah, M. A. (2006). *Democratic Values in the Muslim World*. Boulder, CO: Lynne Rienner.
Ferguson, N. (2003). 'What Is Power?' *Hoover Digest*, 2, pp. 1–4. Retrieved 29 February 2012 from http://www.hoover.org/publications/hoover-digest/article/7682.
Fischer, M. M. J. (2004). *Emergent Forms of Life and the Anthropological Voice*. Durham, NC: Duke University Press.
Fitzgerald, T. (2000). *The Ideology of Religious Studies*. New York: Oxford University Press.
—— (2011). *Religion and Politics in International Relations: The Modern Myth*. London: Continuum.
Flanagan, K. & Jupp, P. C. (Eds.) (2007). *A Sociology of Spirituality*. Aldershot: Ashgate.
Flora, G. & Szilagyi, G. (2005). 'Church, Identity, Politics: Ecclesiastical Functions and Expectations Toward Churches in Post-1989 Romania', in V. Roudometof, A. Agadjanian & J. Pankhurst (eds.), *Eastern Orthodoxy in a Global Age: Tradition Faces the Twenty-First Century*. Oxford: AltaMira Press, pp. 109–143.
Foblets, M.-C. (2007). 'Moroccan Women in Europe: Bargaining for Autonomy'. *The Washington and Lee Legal Review*, 64, pp. 1385–1415.
Fokkema, T. & Harmsen, C. (2009). 'Herkomst en vestiging van de eerste generatie Marokkanen'. *Demos*, 25(5), pp. 1–4.
Foley, M. W. & Edwards, B. (1996). 'The Paradox of Civil Society'. *Journal of Democracy*, 7(3), pp. 38–52.
Först, J. (2006). 'Die unbekannte Mehrheit: Sinn- und Handlungsorientierungen 'kasualienfrommer' Christ/inn/en', in J. Kügler (ed.), *Die unbekannte Mehrheit: Mit Taufe, Trauung und Bestattung durchs Leben? Eine empirische Untersuchung zur 'Kasualienfrömmigkeit' von Katholiken–Bericht und interdisziplinäre Auswertung*. Münster: Lit Verlag, pp. 13–54.
Fosztó, L. (2007). 'Born Again in Postsocialist Romania: Ritual, Personhood, and Conversion among the Roma in a Transylvanian Village'. Unpublished PhD Thesis. Halle-Wittenberg: University of Martin-Luther, Faculty of Philosophy.

Foucault, M. (1975). *Surveiller et punir: naissance de la prison*. Paris: Gallimard; English translation, *Discipline and Punish: The Birth of the Prison*. New York: Random House, 1977.

——— [1976] (1990). *The History of Sexuality: An Introduction*. London: Penguin.

Fox, J. (2001). 'Religion as an Overlooked Element of International Relations'. *International Studies Review*, 3(3), pp. 53–73.

Fox, J. & Sandler, S. (2006). *Bringing Religion into International Relations*. New York: Palgrave Macmillan.

Fox, R. G. & King, B. (2002). *Anthropology Beyond Culture*. Oxford: Berg.

Fraser, A. & Crossland, B. (2011). 'Egypt: You Can't Eat Democracy'. *Hurriyet Daily News*, 19 May. Retrieved 11 June 2011 from http://www.hurriyetdailynews.com/n.php?n = egypt-you-cant-eat-democracy-2011-05-19.

Fraser, N. (2000). 'Rethinking Recognition'. *New Left Review*, 3, pp. 107–120.

Freedom of Religious Belief in China (1997). Retrieved 10 May 2011 from http://www.china.org.cn/e-white/Freedom/index.htm.

Freston, P. (2001). *Evangelicals and Politics in Asia, Africa and Latin America*. Cambridge: Cambridge University Press.

——— (2008). 'The Many Faces of Evangelical Politics in Latin America', in P. Freston (ed.), *Evangelical Christianity and Democracy in Latin America*. Oxford: Oxford University Press, pp. 3–36.

Friedman, J. (1994). *Cultural Identity and Global Process*. London: Sage.

——— (2002). 'Globalization and Localization', in J. X. Inda & R. Rosaldo (eds.), *The Anthropology of Globalization: A Reader*. Oxford: Blackwell Publishing, pp. 233–246.

Friedman, T. (2000). *The Lexus and the Olive Tree: Understanding Globalisation*. New York: Farrar, Straus and Giroux.

——— (2007). *The World Is Flat: A Brief History of the Twenty-First Century*. New York: Picador.

Frijhoff, W. (2007). *Dynamisch erfgoed*. Nijmegen: SUN.

Frisch, H. (2005). 'Has the Israeli-Palestinian Conflict Become Islamic? Fatah, Islam, and the Al-Aqsa Martyrs' Brigades'. *Terrorism and Political Violence*, 17(3), pp. 391–406.

Fukuyama, F. (1992). *End of History and the Last Man*. New York: Free Press.

Fuller, G. (2003). *The Future of Political Islam*. New York: Palgrave.

Gabriel, E. (2007). 'Performing Persecution: Witnessing and Martyrdom in the Anarchist Tradition'. *Radical History Review*, 98(2), pp. 34–62.

Gallagher, N. (2007). *Quakers in the Israeli-Palestinian Conflict: The Dilemmas of NGO Humanitarian Activism*. Cairo: The American University of Cairo Press.

Gambetta, D. (2006b), 'Epilogue to the Paperback Edition', in D. Gambetta (ed.), *Making Sense of Suicide Missions*. Oxford: Oxford University Press, pp. 301–333.

——— (ed.) (2006a). *Making Sense of Suicide Missions*. Oxford: Oxford University Press.

Garritano, C. (2000). 'Women, Melodrama, and Political Critique: A Feminist Reading of "Hostages", "Dust to Dust", and "True Confessions"', in J. Haynes (ed.), *Nigerian Video Films*. Athens: Ohio University Centre for International Studies, pp. 165–192.

——— (2008). 'Contesting Authenticities: The Emergence of Local Video Production in Ghana'. *Critical Arts: South-North Cultural and Media Studies,* 22(1), pp. 21–48.

Gay y Blasco, P. (2004). 'Evangelical Transformations of Forgetting and Remembering: The Politics of *Gitano* Life', in F. Pine, D. Kaneff & I. Haukanes (eds.), *Memory, Politics and Religion: The Past Meets the Present in Europe*. Münster: Lit Verlag, pp. 255–272.

Geertz, C. (1966). 'Religion as a Cultural System', in M. Banton (eds.), *Anthropological Approaches to the Study of Religion.* New York: Praeger Press.
Gellner, E. (1983). *Nations and Nationalism.* New York: Cornell University Press.
Ghana, Information Services Department. (1991). *An Official Handbook of Ghana.* Information Services Department. Accra: New Times Corporation.
Ghana, Statistical Service. (2002a). '2000 Population and Housing Census. Summary/Report of Final Results: 22: Table 4-Ethnic Groups of Ghanaians by Birth and by Region'. Ghana, Ministry of Finance and Economic Planning Head Office, Retrieved 12 July 2011 from http://www.statsghana.gov.gh/.
────── (2002b). '2000 Population and Housing Census. Summary/Report of Final Results: Table 7 'Religious Affiliation of Population by Region'. Ghana, Ministry of Finance and Economic Planning Head Office, Retrieved 12 July 2011 from http://www.statsghana.gov.gh/.
Ghannoushi, S. (2011). 'Cairo Haunts Riyadh Again'. *The Guardian*, 8 June.
Ghazal, M. (2010). 'Islamic Banking Can Boost Trade between China, Muslim States'. *Xinhuanet*, Xinhua News Agency, 10 March 2010. Retrieved 15 February 2011 from http://news.xinhuanet.com/english2010/indepth/2010–03/10/c_13205448.htm.
Giddens, A. (1990). *The Consequences of Modernity.* Cambridge: Polity.
────── (1991). *Modernity and Self-Identity: Self and Society in the Late Modern Age.* Stanford, CA: Stanford University Press.
────── (2003). *Runaway World.* New York: Routledge.
────── (2006). *Sociology.* Cambridge, MA: Polity Press.
────── (2009). *Sociology.* Cambridge: Polity Press.
────── [1999] (2002). *Runaway World: How Globalization Is Reshaping Our Lives.* London: Profile Books.
Gill, A. (1998). *Render unto Caesar: The Catholic Church and the State in Latin America.* Chicago: University of Chicago Press.
Gill, P. (2007). 'A Multi-Dimensional Approach to Suicide Bombing'. *International Journal of Conflict and Violence*, 1(2), pp. 142–159.
Gillet, O. (1995), 'Orthodoxie, nation et ethnicité en Roumanie au XXe siècle: Un problème ecclésiologique et politique', in M. Crăciun & O. Ghitta (eds.), *Ethnicity and Religion in Central and Eastern Europe.* Cluj, Romania: Cluj University Press, pp. 345–362.
Gladney, D. C. (1991). *Muslim Chinese: Ethnic Nationalism in the People's Republic.* Cambridge, : Council on East Asian Studies, Harvard University Press.
────── (2008). 'Islam and Modernity in China. Secularization or Separatism?', in M. M. Yang (ed.), *Chinese Religiosities. Afflictions of Modernity and State Formation.* Berkeley: University of California Press, pp. 179–205.
Glaser, B. & Strauss, A. (1967). *The Discovery of Grounded Theory: Strategies for Qualitative Research.* Chicago: Aldine Publishing Company.
Göle, N. (2000). 'Snapshots of Islamic Modernities'. *Dædalus* 129(1), pp. 91–117.
────── (2003). 'The Voluntary Adoption of Islamic Stigma Symbols'. *Social Research*, 70(3), pp. 809–828.
────── (2005). 'De islam in Europa'. *Eutopia*, 11, pp. 9–14.
Goodman, J. E. (2005). *Berber Culture on the World Stage. From Village to Video.* Bloomington: Indiana University Press.
Goody, J. (1996). *The East in the West.* Cambridge: Cambridge University Press.
Goossaert, V. (2008). 'Republican Church Engineering: The National Religious Associations in 1912 China', in M. M. Yang (ed.), *Chinese Religiosities. Afflictions of Modernity and State Formation.* Berkeley: University of California Press, pp. 209–232.
Goossaert, V. & Palmer, D. A. (2011). *The Religious Question in Modern China.* Chicago: The University of Chicago Press.

Gorski, P. S. & Altinordu, A. (2008). 'After Secularization'. *Annual Review of Sociology*, 34, pp. 55–85.
Gorski, P. S. (2003). 'Historicizing the Secularization Debate: An Agenda for Research', in M. Dillon (ed.), *Handbook of the Sociology of Religion*. Cambridge: Cambridge University Press, pp. 110–123.
Goverde, H., Cerny, P. G., Haugaard, M. & Lenter, H. (2000). *Power in Contemporary Politics: Theories, Practices, Globalizations*. London: Sage.
Grever, M. (2009). 'Geen identiteit zonder oriëntatie in de tijd. Over de noodzaak van chronologie'. *Bijdragen en mededelingen betreffende de geschiedenis der Nederlanden*, 124, pp. 397–410.
Gross, J. E. & McMurray, D. A. (1993). 'Berber Origins and the Politics of Ethnicity in Colonial North African Discourse'. *Political and Legal Anthropology Review*, 16, pp. 39–58.
Guibernau, M. (2001). 'Globalization and the Nation-State', in M. Guibernau & J. Hutchinson (eds.), *Understanding Nationalism*. Oxford: Polity, pp. 242–268.
Guitton, R. (2011). 'The Fate of Minorities in the Arab Spring'. *Hurriyet Daily News*, 19 May. Retrieved 11 June 2011 from: http://www.hurriyetdailynews.com/n.php?n = the-fate-of-minorities-in-the-arab-spring-2011–05–19.
Gunning, J. & Jackson, R. (2011). 'What's So "Religious" About "Religious Terrorism"?' *Critical Studies on Terrorism*, 4(3), pp. 369–388.
Habermas, J. (2010). *An Awareness of What Is Missing: Faith and Reason in a Post-Secular Age*. Cambridge, UK: Polity Press.
Haddad, Y. Y. & Esposito, J. L. (Eds.) (1998). *Muslims on the Americanisation Path?* Atlanta: Scholars Press.
Hafez, M. M. (2006a). *Manufacturing Human Bombs: The Making of Palestinian Suicide Bombers*. Washington, DC: United States Institute of Peace Press.
——— (2006b). 'Rationality, Culture, and Structure in the Making of Suicide Bombers: A Preliminary Theoretical Synthesis and Illustrative Case Study'. *Studies in Conflict and Terrorism*, 29(2), pp. 165–185.
——— (2007). *Suicide Bombers in Iraq: The Strategy and Ideology of Martyrdom*. Washington, DC: United States Institute of Peace Press.
Halikipoulou, D. & Vasilopoulou, S. (Eds.) (2011). *Nationalism and Globalisation*. London: Routledge.
Hall, D. D. (Ed.) (1997). *Lived Religion in America: Toward a History of Practice*. Princeton, NJ: Princeton University Press.
Hall, S. (1990). 'Cultural Diversity and Diaspora', in J. Rutherford (ed.), *Identity: Community, Culture, Difference*. London: Lawrence & Wishart, pp. 222–237.
Hamid el-Zein, A. (1977). 'Beyond Ideology and Theology: The Search for the Anthropology of Islam'. *Annual Review of Anthropology*, 6, pp. 227–254.
Hammond, P. E. (Ed.) (1985). *The Sacred in a Secular Age: Toward Revision in the Scientific Study of Religion*. Berkeley: University of California Press.
Hammoudi, A. (1997). *Master and Disciple: The Cultural Foundations of Moroccan Authoritarianism*. Chicago: The University of Chicago Press.
Hannerz, U. (1990). *Cultural Complexity: Studies in the Social Organization of Meaning*. New York: Columbia University Press.
——— (2002). *Transnational Connections*. New York: Taylor and Francis.
Hansen, T. B. (1999). *The Saffron Wave: Democracy and Hindu Nationalism in Modern India*. Princeton, NJ: Princeton University Press.
Haraldsson, E. & Osis, K. (1977). 'The Appearance and Disappearance of Objects in the Presence of Sri Sathya Sai Baba'. *Journal of the American Society for Psychical Research*, 71, pp. 33–43.
Harries, P. (2007). *Butterflies and Barbarians: Swiss Missionaries and Systems of Knowledge in South Africa*. Oxford: James Currey.

Harrison, P. (1990). *"Religion" and the Religions in the English Enlightenment.* Cambridge: Cambridge University Press.
Hart, D. (s.d.). *De Aith Waryaghar van het Marokkaanse Rifgebied.* The Hague: SMDN.
Harvey, D. (1989). *The Condition of Postmodernity: An Enquiry into the Origins of Cultural Change.* Oxford: New York.
——— (2005). *A Brief History of Neoliberalism.* New York: Oxford University Press.
Hassan, R. (2011). *Life as a Weapon: The Global Rise of Suicide Bombings.* London: Routledge.
Hastings, A. (1997). *The Construction of Nationhood: Ethnicity, Religion, and Nationalism.* Cambridge: Cambridge University Press.
Hayek, F. (1973, 1976, 1979) *Law, Legislation, and Liberty.* Vols. 1–3. Chicago: University of Chicago Press.
——— [1948] (1980). *Individualism and Economic Order.* Midway Reprint, Chicago: University of Chicago.
Haynes, J. (1996). *Religion, Fundamentalism and Ethnicity: A Global Perspective.* Discussion Paper no. 65, Geneva: UNRISD.
——— (2005). *Comparative Politics in a Globalizing World.* Cambridge: Polity.
——— (2007). *An Introduction to International Relations and Religion.* London: Pearson.
——— (2010). 'Religion and Politics in Europe, the Middle East and North Africa', in J. Haynes (ed.), *Religion and Politics in Europe, the Middle East and North Africa.* London: Routledge, pp. 1–19.
——— (2010a). 'A Literature Review: Nigerian and Ghanaian Videos'. *African Cultural Studies,* 22(1), pp. 105–120.
——— (2010b). 'Nollywood: What Is in a Name?'. *Film International,* 28(1), pp. 106–108.
——— (2011). 'Turkey and Europe: Religion, Nationalism and International Relations', in L. Leustean (ed.), *Representing Religion in the European Union: Does God Matter?* London: Routledge.
Haynes, J. & Ben-Porat, G. (2010). 'Introduction: Globalisation, Religion and Secularisation—Different States, Same Trajectories?'. *Totalitarian Movements and Political Religion,* 11(2), pp. 125–132.
Heelas, P. (2002). 'The Spiritual Revolution: From "Religion" to "Spirituality"', in L. Woodhead, P. Fletcher, H. Kawanami & D. Smith (Eds.), *Religion in the Modern World.* London: Routledge, pp. 357–377.
Heelas, P. & Woodhead, L. (2000). *Religion in Modern Times: An Interpretive Anthology.* Malden, MA: Wiley Blackwell.
Heelas, P. & Woodhead, L. (2005). *The Spiritual Revolution: Why Religion Is Giving Way to Spirituality.* Oxford: Blackwell Publishing.
Hefner, R. W. (1998). 'Multiple Modernities: Christianity, Islam, and Hinduism in a Globalizing Age'. *Annual Review of Anthropology,* 27, pp. 83–104.
——— (2000). 'Democratization in an Age of Religious Revitalization', in R. W. Hefner (ed.), *Civil Islam: Muslims and Democratization in Indonesia.* Princeton, NJ: Princeton University Press, pp. 3–20. Retrieved 10 January 2011 from http://press.princeton.edu/chapters/s6966.pdf.
——— (2009). 'The Politics and Cultures of Islamic Education in Southeast Asia', in R. W. Hefner (ed.), *Making Modern Muslims: The Politics of Islamic Education in Southeast Asia.* Honolulu: University of Hawaii Press, pp. 1–54.
——— (2010). 'Muslims and Modernity: Culture and Society in an Age of Contest and Plurality', in R. W. Hefner (ed.), *Muslims and Modernity: Culture and Society Since 1800.* The New Cambridge History of Islam, vol. 6. Cambridge: Cambridge University Press, pp. 1–35.

——— (2011). 'Where Have all the *Abangan* Gone? Religionization and the Decline of Non-standard Islam in Contemporary Indonesia', in M. Picard & R. Madinier (eds.), *The Politics of Religion in Indonesia: Syncretism, Orthodoxy, and Religious Contention in Java and Bali*. London: Routledge, pp. 71–91.
Hefner, R. W. & Zaman, M. Q. (2007). *Schooling Islam: The Culture and Politics of Modern Muslim Education*. Princeton, NJ: Princeton University Press.
Hegel, G. W. F. (1984 [1793]). *Three Essays 1793–1795: The Tübingen Essay, Berne Fragments, The Life of Jesus*. Edited and translated with introduction and notes by Peter Fuss & John Dobbins. Notre Dame, IN: University of Notre Dame Press.
Held, D. & McGrew, A. (eds.) (2002). *Governing Globalization: Power, Authority and Global Governance*. Cambridge: Polity.
Held, D., McGres, A., Goldblatt, D. & Perraton, J. (1999). *Global Transformations: Politics, Economics, and Culture*. Stanford, CA: Stanford University Press.
Hellemans, S. (2001). 'From 'Catholicism against Modernity' to the Problematic Modernity of Catholicism'. *Ethical Perspectives*, 8(2), pp. 117–127.
——— (2005). 'Die Transformation der Religion und der Grosskirchen in der zweiten Moderne aus der Sicht des religiösen Modernisierungsparadigmas'. *Schwedische Zeitschrift Schweizerische Zeitschrift für Religions- und Kulturgeschichte* (SZRKG), 99, pp. 11–35.
Henkel, H. (2004). 'Rethinking the dâr al-harb: Social Change and Changing Perceptions of the West in Turkish Islam'. *Journal of Ethnic and Migration Studies*, 30(5), pp. 961–977.
Herberg, W. (1960). *Protestant, Catholic, Jew: An Essay in American Religious Sociology*. Garden City, NY: Anchor Books.
Heristchi, C. & Teti, A. (2006). 'Rethinking the Myths of Islamic Politics', in J. Haynes (ed.), *The Politics of Religion: A Survey*. London: Routledge, pp. 25–36.
Hervieu-Léger, D. (1993). *La religion pour mémoire*. Paris: Cerf.
——— (1999). *Le pèlerin et le converti. La religion en mouvement*. Paris: Flammarion.
——— (2001). 'The Twofold Limit of the Notion of Secularization', in L. Woodhead, P. Heelas & D. Martin (eds.), *Peter Berger and the Study of Religion*. London: Routledge, pp. 112–125.
——— (2001). *Religion as a Chain of Memory*. New Brunswick, NJ: Rutgers University Press.
Hill Fletcher, J. (2005), *Monopoly on Salvation? A Feminist Approach to Religious Pluralism*. New York: Continuum.
Hill, P. (2006). 'Kamikaze, 1943–5', in D. Gambetta (ed.), *Making Sense of Suicide Missions*. Oxford: Oxford University Press, pp. 1–42.
Hirschkind, C. (2001). 'Civic Virtue and Religious Reason: An Islamic Counter Public'. *Cultural Anthropology*, 16 (1), pp. 3–34.
Hoffman, B. (2006). *Inside Terrorism*. New York: Columbia University Press.
Hoffman, K. E. (2010). 'Internal Fractures in the Berber-Arab Distinction: From Colonial Practice to Post-National Preoccupations', in K. E. Hoffman & S. Gilson Miller (eds.), *Berbers and Others: Beyond Tribe and Nation in the Maghrib*. Bloomington: Indiana University Press, pp. 39–61.
Hoffman, K. E. & Gilson Miller, S. (2010). 'Introduction', in K. E. Hoffman & S. Gilson Miller (eds.), *Berbers and Others: Beyond Tribe and Nation in the Maghrib*. Bloomington: Indiana University Press, pp. 1–12.
Hoisington, W. A. (1978). 'Cities in Revolt: The Berber Dahir (1930) and France's Urban Strategy in Morocco'. *Journal of Contemporary History*, 13(3), pp. 433–448.
Holmes, S. (2006). 'Al-Qaeda, September 11, 2001', in D. Gambetta (ed.), *Making Sense of Suicide Missions*. Oxford: Oxford University Press, pp. 131–172.
Hoover, S. M. (1988). *Mass Media Religion: The Social Sources of the Electronic Church*. Newbury Park, CA: Sage.

Hopgood, S. (2006). 'Tamil Tigers, 1987–2002', in D. Gambetta (ed.), *Making Sense of Suicide Missions*. Oxford: Oxford University Press, pp. 43–76.
Hornemann, M. (2007). '"Religious Communists" and Religious Freedom'. *Forum 18 News Service*, 13 February 2007. Retrieved 25 July 2007 from http://www.forum18.org/Archive.php?article_id=910.
Horowitz, M. C. (2010). 'Nonstate Actors and the Diffusion of Innovations: The Case of Suicide Terrorism'. *International Organization*, 64(1), pp. 33–64.
Howe, M. (2005). *The Islamist Awakening and Other Challenges*. New York: Oxford University Press.
Hsiao, K. (1975). *A Modern China in a New World: K'ang Yu-wei, Reformer and Utopian, 1958–1927*. Seattle: University of Washington Press.
Hu, J. (2007). 'Jianding bu yi fazhan shehui zhuyi minzhu zhenngzhi' [Unswervingly Develop Socialist Democracy]. *Renmin wang*, 15 October. Retrieved 4 May 2011 from http://politics.people.com.cn/GB/1024/6378600.html (in Chinese).
Hunt, S. & Lightly, N. (2001). 'The British Black Pentecostal "Revival": Identity and Belief in "New" Nigerian Churches'. *Ethnic and Racial Studies*, 24(1), pp. 104–124.
Huntington, S. P. (1991). *The Third Wave. Democratization in the Late Twentieth Century*. Norman: University of Oklahoma Press.
——— (1997). *The Clash of Civilizations and the Remaking of World Order*. London: Touchstone Books.
——— (1996). *The Clash of Civilisations and the Remaking of World Order*. New Delhi: Viking Penguin.
Hutchinson, J. (2008). 'In Defence of Transhistorical Ethnosymbolism: A Reply to My Critics'. *Nations and Nationalism*, 14, pp. 18–27.
——— (2011). 'Globalisation and Nationalism in the Longue Duree', in D. Halikiopoulou & S. Vasilopoulou (eds.), *Nationalism and Globalisation: Conflicting or Complementary*. London: Routledge, pp. 84–99.
Inda, J. X. & Rosaldo, R. (Eds.) (2002). *The Anthropology of Globalisation: A Reader*. Malden, MA: Blackwell.
Inglehart, R. (1997). *Modernisation and Postmodernisation: Cultural, Economic, and Political Change in 43 Societies*. Princeton, NJ: Princeton University Press.
Institutul National de Statistica (18–27 March 2002). 'Populatia Dupa Etnie Si' [Population by Etnicity]. *Recensamantul Populatiei şi Al Locuintelor* [Population and Housing Census]. Retrieved 28 January 2012 from http://www.insse.ro/cms/files/RPL2002INS/vol1/tabele/t51.pdf.
——— (18–27 March 2002). 'Structura Populatiei Dupa' [Population Structure]. *Recensamantul Populatiei şi Al Locuintelor* [Population and Housing Census]. Retrieved 28 January 2012 from http://www.insse.ro/cms/files/RPL2002INS/vol1/tabele/t50a.pdf.
Introvigne, M., Zoccatelli, P., Macrina, N. I. & Roldàn, V. (eds.) (2001). *Enciclopedia delle Religioni in Italia*. Turin: Elledici.
Ismail, S. (2006). *Rethinking Islamist Politics. Culture, the State and Islamism*. London: I. B. Tauris.
Israeli, R. (1978). *Muslims in China. A Study in Cultural Confrontation*. London: Curzon Press.
Issawi, C. (1989). 'Empire Builders, Culture Makers and Culture Imprinters'. *Journal of Interdisciplinary History*, 20, pp. 177–196.
Iyall-Smith, K. (2008). 'Hybrid Identities: Theoretical Examinations', in K. Iyall-Smith & P. Leavy (eds.), *Hybrid Identities. Theoretical and Empirical Examinations*. Leiden: Brill, pp. 3–11.
Jacobse, F. & Johannes, L. (2009). 'Conflicted Hearts: Orthodox Christian "Social Justice" in an Age of Globalization', 11 September. Retrieved 11 January 2011 from http://www.aoiusa.org/2009/09/conflicted-hearts-orthodox-christian-%E2%80%98social-justice%E2%80%99-in-an-age-of-globalization.

Jacobson, J. (1998). *Islam in Transition. Religion and Identity among British Pakistani Youth*. London: Routledge.
Jaffrelot, C. (1996). *The Hindu Nationalist Movement in India*. New York: Columbia University Press.
James, P. (2006). *Globalism, Nationalism, Tribalism: Bringing Theory Back In*. London: Sage.
Jameson, F. (1991). *Postmodernism or the Cultural Logic of Late Capitalism*. Durham, NC: Duke University Press.
Jenkins, P. (2007). *The Next Christendom: The Coming of Global Christianity*. New York/Oxford: Oxford University Press.
Jensen, L. M. (1997). *Manufacturing Confucianism: Chinese Traditions and Universal Civilisation*. Durham, NC: Duke University Press.
Jensen, R. B. (2004). 'Daggers, Rifles, and Dynamite: Anarchist Terrorism in Nineteenth Century Europe'. *Terrorism and Political Violence*, 16(1), pp. 116–153.
John, B. (2007). 'Kulturelle anpassungsleistungen muslimischer Jugendlicher', in D. Dettling & J. Gerometta (eds.). *Vorteile Vielfalt*. Wiesbaden: VS Verlag für Sozialwissenschaften, pp. 57–66.
—— (2008). *Beyond the State in Rural Uganda*. Edinburgh: Edinburgh University Press.
Jonker, G. (2003). 'Islamic Knowledge through a Woman's Lens: Education, Power and Belief'. *Social Compass*, 50(1), pp. 35–46.
Joshi, S. (2002). 'Republicizing Religiosity: Modernity, Religion, and the Middle Class', in D. Peterson & D. Walhof (eds.), *The Invention of Religion: Rethinking Belief in Politics and History*. New Brunswick, NJ: Rutgers University Press, pp. 79–99.
Jouili, J. (2009). 'Negotiating Secular Boundaries: Pious Micro-Practices of Muslim Women in French and German Public Spheres'. *Social Anthropology/Anthropologie Sociale*, 17(4), pp. 455–470.
Jouili, J. & Amir-Moazami, S. (2006). 'Knowledge, Empowerment and Religious Authority among Pious Muslim Women in France and Germany'. *The Muslim World*, 96(4), pp. 617–642.
Jubilee Campaign NL. (2003). 'Religious Freedom in New and Future EU Member-States Law and Practice'. Retrieved 13 September 2008 from http://www.forum18.org/PDF/EUaccession.pdf.
Juergensmeyer, M. (1991). *Radhasoami Reality: The Logic of a Modern Faith*. Princeton, NJ: Princeton University Press.
—— (1993). *The New Cold War? Religious Nationalism Confronts the Secular State*. Berkeley: University of California Press.
—— (2001). *Terror in the Mind of God: The Global Rise of Religious Violence*. Berkeley: University of California Press.
—— (2005) 'The Role of Religion in the New Global Order'. Retrieved 18 April 2006 from http://www.maxwell.syr.edu/moynihan/programs/sac/paper%20pdfs/marks%20paper.pdf.
—— (2005). 'The Role of Religion in the New Global Order', in R. Rieman (ed.), *Europe: A Beautiful Idea?* Tilburg: Nexus Institute, pp. 17–25.
—— (2008). *Global Rebellion: Religious Challenges to the Secular State*. Berkeley: University of California Press.
Kabki, M., Mazzucato, V. & Appiah, E. (2004). '"Wo benanε a εyε bebree": The Economic Impact of Remittances of Netherlands-based Ghanaian Migrants on Rural Ashanti'. *Population, Space and Place*, 10(2), pp. 85–97.
Kalyvas, S. N. & Sánchez-Cuenca, I. (2006). 'Killing Without Dying: The Absence of Suicide Missions', in D. Gambetta (ed.), *Making Sense of Suicide Missions*. Oxford: Oxford University Press, pp. 209–232.

Karl, T. L. (1995). 'The Hybrid Regimes of Central America'. *Journal of Democracy*, 6(3), pp. 72–86.
Karpov, V. (2010). 'Desecularization: A Conceptual Framework'. *Journal of Church and State*, 52(2), pp. 232–270.
Kasturi, N. (1968). *Sathyam Sivam Sundaram. The Life of Bhagavan Sri Sathya Sai Baba*. 4 vols. 1961–1980. Prasanthi Nilayam: Sri Sathya Sai Books and Publications.
Katzenstein, P. J. (2006). 'Multiple Modernities as Limits to Secular Europeanization', in T. A. Byrnes & P. J. Katzenstein (eds.), *Religion in an Expanding Europe*. Cambridge: Cambridge University Press, pp. 1–34.
Kee, H. C. (1993). 'From Jesus Movement Toward Institutional Church', in R. W. Hefner (ed.), *Conversion to Christianity: Historical and Anthropological Perspectives on a Great Transformation*. Berkeley: University of California Press, pp. 47–63.
Kennett, P. (Ed.) (2008). *Governance, Globalization and Public Policy*. Cheltenham: Edward Elgar.
Kent, A. (2004). 'Divinity, Miracles and Charity in the Sathya Sai Baba Movement of Malaysia'. *Ethnos*, 69 (1), pp. 43–62.
Keohane, J. S. (1984). *After Hegemony: Cooperation and Discord in the World Political Economy*. Princeton, NJ: Princeton University Press.
Keohane, R. (2002). 'The Globalization of Informal Violence, Theories of World Politics, and the "Liberalism of Fear"'. *Dialog-IO*, Spring 2002, pp. 29–43.
Keohane, R. O. & Nye, J. S. (2000). 'Introduction', in J. S. Nye & J. D. Donahue (eds.), *Governance in a Globalizing World*. Washington, DC: Brookings Institution Press, pp.1–41.
Kepel, G. (1994). *The Revenge of God*. Oxford: Blackwell.
——— (2004), *Fitna. Guerre au cœur de l'islam*. Paris: Gallimard; English translation, *The War for Muslim Minds: Islam and the West*. Cambridge, MA: Harvard University Press, 2004.
Kesich, V. (1961). 'The Orthodox Church in America'. *Russian Review*, 20(3), pp. 185–193.
Khan, M. (Ed.) (2006). *Islamic Democratic Discourse. Theories, Debates and Philosophical Perspectives*. Lanham, MD: Rowman and Littlefield.
Khosrokhavar, F. (1997). *L'islam des jeunes*. Paris: Flammarion.
——— (2002). *Le nouveaux martyrs d'Allah*. Paris: Flammarion; English translation, *Suicide Bombers: Allah's New Martyrs*. London: Pluto Press, 2005.
Kidnopp, J. & Harmin, C. L. (eds.) (2004). *God and Caesar in China. Policy Implications of Church-State Tensions*. Washington, DC: Brookings Institution Press.
Kille, K. J. (Ed.) (2007). *The UN Secretary-General and Moral Authority: Ethics and Religion in International Leadership*. Washington, DC: Georgetown University Press.
Kirill (Metropolitan of Smolensk and Kaliningrad) (1999). 'The Circumstances of Modern Life: Liberalism, Traditionalism, and Moral Values of a Uniting Europe'. *Nezavisimaya Gazeta: Religii*, 26 May.
——— (2000). 'Standards of Faith as Norms of Life'. *Nezavisimaya Gazeta: Religii*, 17 February.
——— (2001). 'The Orthodox Church in the Face of World Integration, the Relations between Traditional and Liberal Values'. *Ecumenical Review*, 53(4), pp. 477–485.
——— (October 2001). 'The Orthodox Church in the Face of World Integration: The Relation between Traditional and Liberal Values'. *The Ecumenical Review*. Retrieved 1 January 2011 from http://findarticles.com/p/articles/mi_m2065/is_4_53/ai_81223342/?tag = content;col1.

Klass, M. (1991). *Singing with Sai Baba. The Politics of Revitalization in Trinidad*. Boulder, CO: Westview Press.

Kleist, N. (2011). 'Modern Chiefs: Tradition, Development and Return among Traditional Authorities in Ghana'. *African Affairs*, 110(441), pp. 629–647.

Klinkhammer, G. (2000). *Modern Forms of Islamic Life: A Qualitative-Empirical Investigation of the Religiousness of Turkish Women in Germany Shaped by Sunnite Tradition*. Marburg: Diagonal-Verlag.

—— (2003). 'Modern Constructions of Islamic Identity. The Case of Second Generation Muslim Women in Germany'. *Marburg Journal of Religion*, 8(1), pp. 1–16.

Korteweg, A. (2008). 'The Sharia Debate in Ontario. Gender, Islam, and Representations of Muslim Women's Agency'. *Gender & Society*, 22(4), pp. 434–454.

Kramer, M. (1991). 'Sacrifice and Fratricide in Shiite Lebanon'. *Terrorism and Political Violence*, 3(3), pp. 30–47.

Kratochwil, G. (1999). 'Some Observations on the First Amazigh World Congress (27–30 August 1997, Tarifa, Canary Islands)'. *Die Welt des Islams*, 39, pp. 149–158.

—— (2002). *Die Berberbewegung in Marokko. Zur Geschichte der Konstruktion einer ethnischen Identität (1912–1997)*. Berlin: Klaus Schwarz Verlag.

Kurasawa, F. (2004). *The Ethnological Imagination: A Cross-Cultural Critique of Modernity*. Minneapolis: University of Minnesota Press.

Kurien, P. A. (2007). *A Place at the Multicultural Table: The Development of an American Hinduism*. New Brunswick, NJ: Rutgers University Press.

Kurtz, L. (1995). *Gods in the Global Village: The World's Religions in Sociological Perspective*. Newberry Park, CA: Pine Forge Press.

Lakatos, P. (1998a). 'Denominational and Cultural Models and a Possible Ecumenical Strategy from a Romanian Context'. *Religion in Eastern Europe*, 18(5). Retrieved 12 January 2009 from http://www.georgefox.edu/academics/undergrad/departments/soc-swk/ree/Lakatos_Denominational-Part%20I.html.

—— (1998b). 'Denominational and Cultural Models and a Possible Ecumenical Strategy from a Romanian Context—Part II: The Christian Churches and Social Responsibility'. *Religion in Eastern Europe*, 18(6). Retrieved 12 January 2009 from http://www.georgefox.edu/academics/undergrad/departments/soc-swk/ree/Lakatos_Denominational-Part%20II_Dec%201998.pdf .

Lamb, G. (2003). 'American Friends? Hardly'. *FrontPageMagazine.Com*, Thursday 5 June. Retrieved 20 March 2012 from http://archive.frontpagemag.com/readArticle.aspx?ARTID=17849.

Lancaster, R. N. (1998). *Thanks to God and the Revolution: Popular Religion and Class Consciousness in the New Nicaragua*. New York: Columbia University Press.

Landman, N. (1991). 'Muslims and Islamic Institutions in the Netherlands'. *Institute of Muslim Minority Affairs*, 12(2), pp. 410–432.

—— (1992). 'Sufi Orders in the Netherlands. Their Role in the Institutionalization of Islam', in W. A. R. Shadid & P. S. Van Koningsveld (eds.), *Islam in Dutch Society: Current Developments and Future Prospects*. Kampen: Kok Pharos Publishing House, pp. 26–39.

Lee, R. L. M. (1982). 'Sai Baba, Salvation and Syncretism: Religious Change in a Hindu Movement in Urban Malaysia'. *Contributions to Indian Sociology* (NS), 16(1), pp. 125–140.

Leerssen, J. (2006). 'Nationalism and the Cultivation of Culture'. *Nations and Nationalism*, 12, pp. 559–578.

Legea Nr. 489/2006 Privind Libertatea Religioasă și Regimul General al Cultelor [Law Nr. 489/2006 on Religious Freedom and the General Regime of Cults]. Retrieved 20 December 2011 from http://www.crestinism-ortodox.ro/TEXTE/LegeaCultelor-Nr489-2006.pdf.

Lehmann, D. (1996). *Struggle for the Spirit: Religious Transformation and Popular Culture in Brazil and Latin America.* Cambridge: Polity.
Lemopoulos, G. (2000). 'Orthodox Diaspora in Europe: An Attempt to Describe a Range of Old and New Issues'. Retrieved 29 March 2011 from http://www.deltapublicaciones.com/derechoyreligion/gestor/archivos/07_10_00_895.pdf.
Lerner, D. (1958). *The Passing of Traditional Society: Modernizing the Middle East.* Glencoe, IL: Free Press.
Leustean, L. N. (2009). *Orthodoxy and the Cold War: Religion and Political Power in Romania, 1947–65.* Houndmills: Palgrave Macmillan.
Levitt, P. (1999). *Transnational Villagers.* Berkeley: University of California Press.
—— (2006). 'Immigration', in H. R. Ebaugh (ed.), *Handbook of Religion and Social Institutions.* New York: Springer, pp. 391–410.
—— (2007). *God Needs No Passport: Immigrants and the Changing American Religious Landscape.* New York: New Press.
Levy, D. (1999). 'Katallactic Partiality: Exploring the Link between Co-operation and Language'. *American Journal of Economics and Sociology*, 58(4), pp. 729–747.
Lewis, J. W. (2007). 'Precision Terror: Suicide Bombing as Control Technology'. *Terrorism and Political Violence*, 19(2), pp. 223–245.
—— (2008). 'Self-Sacrifice as Innovation: The Strategic and Tactical Utility of Martyrdom'. *Dynamics of Asymmetric Conflict*, 1(1), pp. 66–87.
Li, Y. (2011). 'Back after the Hajj, Muslims Reminisce'. *China Daily*, 5 November 2011. Retrieved 6 March 2012 from http://www.chinadaily.com.cn/china/2011–12/05/content_14210981.htm.
Liebman, C. S. & Don-Yehiya, E. (1983). *Civil Religion in Israel: Traditional Judaism and Political Culture in the Jewish State.* Berkeley: University of California Press.
Lindhardt, M. (ed.) (2011). *Practicing the Faith: The Ritual Life of Pentecostal-charismatic Christians.* Oxford: Berghahn.
Lipman, J. N. (1997). *Familiar Strangers. A History of Muslims in Northwest China.* Seattle: University of Washington Press.
Lobonț, F. (2009). 'Romanian Orthodoxy, between Ideology of Exclusion and Sécularisation Amiable'. *Journal for the Study of Religions and Ideologies*, 8(24), pp. 46–69.
Lokosov, V. & Synelina, J. (2008). 'Vsaimosvias' religiosnych i politicheskich orientazii pravoslavnych rossian' [Relations Between Political and Religious Orientations of Russians], in P. P. Mchedlov (ed.), *Religia v samosoznanii naroda* [Religion in the Consciousness of People]. Moscow: Institute of Sociology of the Russian Academy of Science Press, pp 135–158. Retrieved 7 March 2012 from http://www.isras.ru/files/File/Publication/Monografii/Glava_6_2.pdf (in Russian).
Lorenz, C. (2010). 'Unstuck in Time: The Sudden Presence of the Past', in K. Tilmans, F. van Vree & J. Winter (eds.), *Performing the Past. Memory, History and Identity in Modern Europe.* Amsterdam: Amsterdam University Press, pp. 67–104.
Luckmann, T. (1967). *The Invisible Religion: The Problem of Religion in Modern Societies.* New York: Macmillan.
—— (1990). 'Shrinking Transcendence, Expanding Religion?' *Sociological Analysis*, 50(2), pp. 314–355.
—— (1991). *Die unsichtbare Religion (suhrkamp taschenbuch wissenschaft).* Frankfurt am Main: Suhrkamp.
Luhmann, N. (1997). *Die Gesellschaft der Gesellschaft.* Frankfurt/M: Suhrkamp.
Lyotard, J.-F. (1984). *The Condition of Postmodernity.* Manchester: Manchester University Press.
Ma, Q. (2006). *Liudong de jingshen shequ–renleixue shiye xia de guangzhou musilin zhemati yanjiu* [A Fluid Spiritual Community: Guangzhou Jamaat in an Anthropological Perspective]. Beijing: Zhongguo shehui kexue chubanshe.

Ma, T. (2000[1983]). *Zhongguo Yisilan jiaopai yu menhuan zhidu shilue* [*Historical Sketch of Sects and Fraternities in Chinese Islam*]. Yinchuan: Ningxia renmin chubanshe.

Macar, E. (2003). *Cumhuriyet Dönemi'nde İstanbul Rum Patrikhanesi* [*Istanbul Greek Orthodox Patriarchate During the Republican Era*]. Istanbul: İletişim Yayınları.

MacInnis, D. E. (1989). *Religion in China Today. Policy and Practice*. Maryknoll, NY: Orbis.

Maddy-Weitzman, B. (2006). 'Ethno-Politics and Globalisation in North Africa: The Berber Culture Movement'. *The Journal of North African Studies*, 11, pp. 71–83.

—— (2007). 'Berber/Amazigh "Memory Work"'. B. Maddy-Weitzman & D. Zisenwine (eds.), *The Maghreb in the New Century. Identity, Religion and Politics*. Gainseville: University Press of Florida, pp. 95–126.

Madeley, J. T. S. & Enyedi, Z. (eds.) (2003). *Church and State in Contemporary Europe: The Chimera of Neutrality*. London: Cass.

Mahmood, S. (2001). 'Feminist Theory, Embodiment, and the Docile Agent: Some Reflections on the Egyptian Islamic Revival'. *Cultural Anthropology*, 16 (2), pp. 202–236.

—— (2005). *Politics of Piety. The Islamic Revival and the Feminist Subject*. Princeton, NJ: Princeton University Press.

Makrides, V. N. (2005). 'Orthodox Christianity, Rationalization, Modernization: A Reassessment', in V. Roudometof, A. Agadjanian & J. Pankhurst (eds.), *Eastern Orthodoxy in a Global Age: Tradition Faces the Twenty-First Century*. Oxford: AltaMira Press, pp. 179–209.

—— (2007). 'Religions in Contemporary Europe in the Context of Globalization', in P. Beyer & L. Beaman (eds.) *Religion, Globalization and Culture*. Leiden: Brill, pp. 549–570.

Maliepaard, M., Lubbers, M. & Gijsberts, M. (2009). 'Generational Differences in Ethnic and Religious Attachment and Their Interrelation: A Study among Muslim Minorities in the Netherlands'. *Ethnic and Racial Studies*, 33(3), pp. 451–772.

Mandaville, P. (2001). 'De informatietechnologie en de verschuivende grenzen van de Europese islam', in D. Douwes (ed.), *Naar een Europese Islam? Essays*. Amsterdam: Mets & Schilt, pp. 135–162.

—— (2001). *Transnational Muslim Politics: Reimagining the Umma*. London: Routledge.

—— (2004). *Transnational Muslim Politics: Reimagining the Umma*. London: Routledge.

—— (2007). *Global Political Islam*. London: Routledge.

Manger, L. (1992). 'On the Study of Islam in Local Contexts'. *Forum for Development Studies*, 1, pp. 51–65.

Marcussen, M. & Kaspersen, L. B. (2007). 'Globalization and Institutional Competitiveness'. *Regulation and Governance*, 1, pp. 183–196.

Marone, F. (2008). 'Il terrorismo suicida nel caso palestinese: una ricerca empirica (1993–2005)'. *Quaderni di scienza politica*, 15(2), pp. 207–249.

—— (2010). 'Attacchi suicidi e competizione interna: Palestina, 1993–2005', in S. Costalli & F. N. Moro (eds.), *La guerra nello Stato. Forme della violenza nei conflitti intrastatali contemporanei*. Milan: Vita e Pensiero, pp. 181–208.

Marshall, R. (2009). *Political Spiritualities: The Pentecostal Revolution in Nigeria*. Chicago: Chicago University Press.

Martens, K. (2005). *NGOs and the United Nations: Institutionalization, Professionalization and Adaptation*. New York: Palgrave Macmillan.

Martin, B. (2001). 'The Pentecostal Gender Paradox: A Cautionary Tale for the Sociology of Religion', in R. Fenn (ed.), *The Blackwell Companion to the Sociology of Religion*. Oxford: Blackwell, pp. 52–66.

—— (2006). 'Limits of the Market Metaphor', in *Exchange*, 35(1), pp. 161–191.
—— (2011). 'Interpretations of Latin American Pentecostalism: 1960s to the Present', in C. L. Smith (ed.), *Pentecostal Power: Expressions, Impact and Faith of Latin American Pentecostalism*. Leiden: Brill, pp. 111–136.
Martin, D. (1978). *A General Theory of Secularization*. New York: Harper & Row.
—— (1990). *Tongues of Fire: The Explosion of Protestantism in Latin America*. Oxford: Blackwell Publishing.
—— (1999). 'The Evangelical Upsurge and Its Political Implications', in P. Berger (ed.), *The Desecularization of the World: Resurgent Religion and World Politics*. Washington, DC: Ethics and Public Policy Center, pp. 37–49.
—— (2002). *Pentecostalism: The World Their Parish*. Oxford: Blackwell Publishing.
—— (2008). 'Is There an Eastern European Pattern of Secularization?', in S. Marincak (ed.), *Religion: Problem or Promise? The Role of Religion in the Integration of Europe*. Kosice, Slovakia: Orientalia at Occidentalia, pp. 129–144.
Marty, M. E. & Appleby, R. S. (Eds.) (1991–1995). *The Fundamentalism Project*. 5 vols. Chicago: University of Chicago Press.
Massey, D. (1998). 'The Spatial Construction of Youth Cultures', in T. Skelton & G. Valentine (eds.), *Cool Places: Geographies of Youth Cultures*. London: Routledge, pp. 121–129.
Masuzawa, T. (2005). *The Invention of World Religions*. Chicago: University of Chicago Press.
Matsumoto, M. (2006). 'Rationalizing Patriotism among Muslim Chinese. The Impact of the Middle East on the *Yuehua* Journal', in S. Dudoignon, H. Komatsu & Z. Kosugi (eds.), *Intellectuals in the Modern Islamic World: Transmission, Transformation, Communication*. London: Routledge, pp. 117–142.
Matsuzato, K. & Sawae, F. (2010). 'Rebuilding a Confessional State: Islamic Ecclesiology in Turkey, Russia and China'. *Religion, State and Society* 38(4), pp. 331–360.
Maxwell, D. (1998). '"Delivered from the Spirit of Poverty?": Pentecostalism, Prosperity, and Modernity in Zimbabwe'. *Journal of Religion in Africa*, 28(3), pp. 350–373.
—— (2006). *African Gifts of the Spirit: Pentecostalism and the Rise of a Transnational Religious Movement*. Oxford: James Currey.
Mazzucato, V. & Kabki, M. (2007). 'Small Is Beautiful: The Micro-Politics of Transnational Relationships between Ghanaian Hometown Associations and Communities Back Home'. *Global Networks*, 9(2), pp. 227–251.
Mbiti, J. S. (1992, first published in 1969). *African Religions & Philosophy*. Nairobi: Heinemann.
McCarthy, S. (2005). 'If Allah Wills It: Integration, Isolation and Muslim Authenticity in Yunnan Province in China'. *Religion, State and Society* 33(2), pp. 121–136.
McCutcheon, R. T. (1997). *Manufacturing Religion: The Discourse on Sui Generis Religion and the Politics of Nostalgia*. Oxford: Oxford University Press.
McDougall, J. (2003). 'Myth and Counter-Myth: The "Berber" as National Signifier in Algerian Historiographies'. *Radical History Review*, 86, pp. 66–88.
McGuire, M. (2008). *Lived Religion: Faith and Practice in Everyday Life*. New York: Oxford University Press.
McKinley, B. (1987). '"A Religion of the New Time": Anarchist Memorials to the Haymarket Martyrs, 1888–1917'. *Labor History*, 28(3), pp. 386–400.
McLeod, H. (2003). 'Introduction', in H. McLeod & W. Usorf (eds.), *The Decline of Christendom in Western Europe, 1750–2000*. Cambridge: Cambridge University Press, pp. 1–26.
McLuhan, M. (1964). *Understanding Media*. New York: Mentor.
McNay, L. (2000). *Gender and Agency: Reconfiguring the Subject in Feminist and Social Theory*. Cambridge, MA: Polity Press.

Merari, A. (1990). 'The Readiness to Kill and Die: Suicidal Terrorism in the Middle East', in W. Reich (ed.), *Origins of Terrorism: Psychologies, Ideologies, Theologies, States of Mind*. Cambridge: Cambridge University Press, pp. 192–207.
—— (1993). 'Terrorism as a Strategy of Insurgency'. *Terrorism and Political Violence*, 5(4), pp. 213–251.
—— (2006). 'Psychological Aspects of Suicide Terrorism', in B. Bongar, L. M. Brown, L. E. Beutler, J. N. Breckenridge & P. G. Zimbardo (eds.), *Psychology of Terrorism*. Oxford: Oxford University Press, pp. 101–115.
Merdjanova, I. (2000). 'In Search of Identity: Nationalism and Religion in Eastern Europe'. *Religion, State & Society*, 28(3), pp. 233–263.
Metcalf, B. (2003). 'Travelers Tales in the Tablighi Jamaat'. *The ANNALS of the American Academy of Political and Social Science* 588, pp. 136–148.
Meyendorff, J. (1996). *The Orthodox Church: Its Past and Its Role in the World Today*. Revised and expanded edition by N. Lossky, Crestwood, NY: St. Vladimir's Seminary Press.
Meyer, B. (1995). 'Delivered from the Powers of Darkness: Confessions About Satanic Riches in Christian Ghana'. *Africa*, 65(2), pp. 255–263.
—— (1996). 'Modernity and Enchantment: The Image of the Devil in Popular African Christianity', in P. van der Veer (ed.), *Conversion to Modernities : The Globalization of Christian Modernities*. New York: Routledge, pp. 199–231.
—— (1999). *Translating the Devil: Religion and Modernity Among the Ewe in Ghana*. IAL-Series. Trenton, NJ: Africa World Press.
—— (2001). 'Money, Power and Morality: Popular Ghanaian Cinema in the Fourth Republic'. *Ghana Studies*, 4(1), pp. 65–84.
—— (2004). 'Christianity in Africa: From African Independent to Pentecostal-Charismatic Churches'. *Annual Review of Anthropology*, 33, pp. 447–474.
—— (2006). 'Impossible Representations: Pentecostalism, Vision and Video Technology in Ghana', in B. Meyer & A. Moors (eds.), *Religion, Media and the Public Sphere*. Bloomington: Indiana University Press, pp. 290–312.
—— (2007). 'Religious Remediations: Pentecostal Views in Ghanaian Video Movies', in J. Mitchell & S. B. Plate (eds.), *The Religion and Film Reader*. New York: Routledge, pp. 95–102.
—— (2008). 'Powerful Pictures: Popular Christian Aesthetics in Southern Ghana'. *Journal of the American Academy of Religion*, 76(1), pp. 82–110.
—— (2010). 'Ghanaian Popular Video Movies between State Film Policies and Nollywood: Discourses and Tensions', in M. Saul & R. A. Austen (eds.), *Viewing African Cinema in the Twenty-First Century*. Athens: Ohio University Press, pp. 42–62.
Mezran, K. (2001). 'Negotiating National Identity in North Africa'. *International Negotiation*, 6, pp. 141–173.
Micklethwait, J. & Wooldridge, A. (2009). *God Is Back: How the Global Revival of Faith Is Changing the World*. New York: Penguin.
Millward, J. A. (2010). 'Introduction: Does the 2009 Urumchi Violence Mark a Turning Point'? *Central Asian Survey* 28(4), pp. 347–360.
Milner, H. V. & Moravcsik, A. (Ed.) (2009). *Power, Interdependence, and Nonstate Actors in World Politics*. Princeton, NJ: Princeton University Press.
Ministry of Cults (1949). 'STATUT Nr. 4593 din 17 februarie 1949 pentru organizarea si functionarea Bisericii Ortodoxe Romane'. *Buletinul Oficial* Nr. 0, 23 February 1949. Retrieved 1 February 2012 from http://www.legex.ro/Statut-Nr.4593-din-17.02.1949–198.aspx.
Mitchell, J. (2007). 'Towards an Understanding of the Popularity of West African Video Film', in J. Mitchell & S. B. Plate (eds.), *Religion and Film Reader*. New York: Routledge, pp. 103–112.
Moberg, D. O. (1962). *The Church as a Social Institution: The Sociology of American Religion*. Englewood Cliffs, NJ: Prentice-Hall.

Moghadam, A. (2006a). 'Defining Suicide Terrorism', in A. Pedahzur (ed.), *Root Causes of Suicide Terrorism: The Globalization of Martyrdom*. London: Routledge, pp. 13–24.

——— (2006b). 'The Roots of Suicide Terrorism: A Multi-Causal Approach', in A. Pedahzur (ed.), *Root Causes of Suicide Terrorism: The Globalization of Martyrdom*. London: Routledge, pp. 81–107.

——— (2008). *The Globalization of Martyrdom: Al-Qaida, Salafi Jihad, and the Spread of Suicide Attacks*. Baltimore: Johns Hopkins University Press.

Moors, A. (2009). 'Islamic Fashion in Europe: Religious Conviction, Aesthetic Style, and Creative Consumption'. *Encounters*, 1(1), pp. 175–201.

Mu, E. (2008). 'Apply to Join the Qiang Nationality in Fengxian, Shaanxi'. *Danwei*, 23 December 2008. Retrieved 10 January 2009 from http://www.danwei.org/front_page_of_the_day/you_can_choose_either_to_be_a.php.

Müller, L. F. (2008). 'The Reality of Spirits: A Historiography of the Akan Concept of Mind'. *Quest: An African Journal of Philosophy*, XXII(1–2), pp. 163–185.

——— (2009). *Religion and Chieftaincy in Ghana*. Edinburgh: Unpublished PhD thesis, University of Edinburgh.

——— (2010). 'Dancing Golden Stools'. *Fieldwork in Religion*, 5(1), pp. 31–54.

——— (2011). 'Spirits of Migration Meet the Migration of Spirits Among the Akan Diaspora in Amsterdam in the Netherlands'. *African and Black Diaspora: An International Journal*, 4(1), pp. 75–97.

Müller, O. & Pollack, D. (2009). 'Churchliness, Religiosity and Spirituality: Western and Eastern European Societies in Times of Religious Diversity', in Bertelsmann Stiftung (ed.), *What The World Believes: Analyses and Commentary on the Religion Monitor 2008*. Gütersloh: Verlag Bertelsmann Stiftung, pp. 399–416.

Mungiu-Pippidi, A. (1998). 'The Ruler and the Patriarch: The Romanian Eastern Orthodox Church in Transition'. *East European Constitutional Review*, 7(2). Retrieved 6 March 2012 from http://heinonline.org/HOL/Page?handle = hein.journals/eeurcr7&div=25&g_sent=1&collection=journals.

Muntean, A. (2005). 'Church-State Relations in Romania: Problems and Perspectives of Inter-Denominational Cooperation at the Level of Church-Based NGOs'. *Journal for the Study of Religion and Ideologies*, 12, pp. 84–100.

Murphet, H. (1971). *Sai Baba: Man of Miracles*. London. [Reprinted by Samuel Weiser, York Beach, 1973 and subsequently.]

——— (1977). *Sai Baba Avatar. A New Journey into Power and Glory*. San Diego: Birth Day Press.

Nadrani, M. (2008a). *Ben Abdelkrim, Emir van de Rif. Marokko 1920–22. Oorlog tegen de Spanjaarden*. Amsterdam: XTRA.

——— (2008b). *'Jaren van Lood', het complex. Mijn eerste 480 dagen in de geheime gevangenis in Marokko*. Amsterdam: XTRA.

Nagel, A. (1994). *De Sai paradox: Tegenstrijdigheden van en rondom Sathya Sai Baba* [The Sai Paradox: Contradictions of and Surrounding Sathya Sai Baba]. Series Religieuze bewegingen in Nederland [Religious Movements in the Netherlands], 29, Free University of Amsterdam.

Naletova, I. (2009). 'Other-worldly Europe? Religion and the Church in the Orthodox Area Eastern Europe'. *Journal of Religion, State and Society*, 37(4), pp. 375–403.

——— (2010). 'Life as a Pilgrimage. Religious Messages of the Post-Soviet Russian Cinema', in J. Juhant & B. Žalek (eds.), *Art of Life: Origins, Foundations and Perspectives*. Berlin: LIT Verlag, pp. 213–221.

——— (2012). 'Human Right: Confronting the Basis of the Social Concept and Survey Data', in A. Brüning & E. van der Zweerde (eds.), *Orthodoxy and Human Rights*. Leuven: Peeters Publishers, pp. 98–123.

Nandy, A. (2005). 'Imperialism as a Theory of the Future', in B. Hamm & R. Smandynch (eds.), *Cultural Imperialism: The Political Economy of Domination*. Toronto: University of Toronto Press.

Nederveen-Pieterse, J. (2003). *Globalisation and Culture: Global Melange*. New York: Rowan and Littlefield.

Nelson, B. (1969). *The Idea of Usury: From Tribal Brotherhood to Universal Otherhood*. Chicago: University of Chicago Press.

Niebuhr, R. [1932] (1960). *Moral Man and Immoral Society*. London: Continuum.

Nielsen, J. (1995). *Muslims in Western Europe*. Edinburgh: Edinburgh University Press.

——— (2004). *Muslims in Western Europe*. Edinburgh: Edinburgh University Press.

Nieswald, B. (2008). 'Ghanaian Migrants in Germany and the Social Construction of Diaspora'. *African Diaspora* 1(1/2), pp. 28–52.

Nora, P. (1989). 'Between Memory and History. Les Lieux de Mémoire'. *Representations*, 26, pp. 7–24.

Norris, P. & Inglehart, R. (2004). *Sacred and Secular: Religion and Politics Worldwide*. Cambridge: Cambridge University Press.

Noyon, J. (2003). *Islam, Politics and Pluralism. Theory and Practice in Turkey, Jordan, Tunisia and Algeria*. London: Royal Institute of International Affairs.

Nussbaum, M. (2007). *The Clash Within: Democracy, Religious Violence, and India's Future*. Cambridge, MA: Belknap.

Nye, J. (2002). 'Globalism versus Globalization'. *The Globalist* ('The Daily Online Magazine on the Global Economy, Politics and Culture'), 15 April. Retrieved 29 February 2012 from http://www.theglobalist.com/StoryId.aspx?StoryId=2392.

Nyman, M. (2006). *Democratizing Indonesia: The Challenges of Civil Society in the Era of Reformasi*. Copenhagen: NIAS Press.

Oberoi, H. (1994). *The Construction of Religious Boundaries: Culture, Identity, and Diversity in the Sikh Tradition*. Chicago: University of Chicago Press.

Ogot, B. A. (1992). *General History of Africa: Vol. 5, Abridged Edition: Africa from the Sixteenth to the Eighteenth Century*. London: James Currey, California, Unesco.

Oha, O. (2000). 'The Rhetoric of Nigerian Christian Videos: The War Paradigm of "the Great Mistake"', in J. Haynes (ed.), *Nigerian Video Films*. Athens: Ohio University Centre for International Studies, pp. 192–200.

Olick, J. K. & Robbins, J. (1998). 'Social Memory Studies: From "Collective Memory" to the Historical Sociology of Mnemonic Practices'. *Annual Review of Sociology*, 24, pp. 105–140.

Olwig, K. F. (2004). 'Place, Movement and Identity: Processes of Inclusion and Exclusion in a "Caribbean" Family', in K. Waltraud, K. Tölölyan & C. Alfonso (eds.), *Diaspora, Identity and Religion: New Directions in Theory and Research*. London: Routledge, pp. 53–71.

Ortner, S. (1984). 'Theory in Anthropology Since the Sixties'. *Comparative Studies in Society and History*, 26, pp. 126–166.

Overmyer, D. L. (ed.) (2003). *Religion in China Today*. The China Quarterly Special Issues, New Series, No. 3. Cambridge: Cambridge University Press.

Pacini, A. (2000). *Le Chiese Ortodosse [Orthodox Churches]*. Turin: Elledici.

——— (2003). 'L'Ortodossia nell'Europa Contemporanea', in A. Pacini (ed.), *L'Ortodossia nella Nuova Europa: Dinamiche Storiche e Prospettive*. Turin: Giovanni Agnelli, pp. 165–184.

Pacurariu, M., Reverend (n.d.) 'Short History of the ROC'. Retrieved 19 November 2011 from http://www.patriarhia.ro/en/roc_structure/history7.html.

Padmanaban, R. (2000). *Love Is My Form: The Advent, 1926–1950*. Puttaparthi: Sri Sathya Sai Towers.

Palmer, N. (2005). 'Baba's World: A Global Guru and His Movement', in T. Forsthoefel & C. Humes (eds.), *Gurus in America*. Albany: SUNY Press, pp. 97–122.

Pandey, G. (1992). *The Construction of Communalism in Colonial North India*. Delhi: Oxford University Press.
Pang, K.-F. (1996). 'Being Hui, Huan-nang, and Utstat Simultaneously. Contextualizing History and Identities of the Austronesian-speaking Hainan Muslims', in M. J. Brown (ed.), *Negotiating Ethnicities in China and Taiwan*. Berkeley: University of California Press, pp. 183–207.
Pape, R. A. (2005). *Dying to Win: The Strategic Logic of Suicide Terrorism*. New York: Random House.
Pape, R. A. & Feldman, J. K. (2010). *Cutting the Fuse: The Explosion of Global Suicide Terrorism and How to Stop It*. Chicago: The University of Chicago Press.
Parker, C. (1996). *Popular Religion and Modernisation in Latin America: A Different Logic* (R. R. Barr, Trans.). Maryknoll, NY: Orbis Books.
Passmore, L. (2009). 'The Art of Hunger: Self-Starvation in the Red Army Faction'. *German History*, 27(1), pp. 32–59.
Paul, C. (2010). 'As a Fish Swims in the Sea: Relationships between Factors Contributing to Support for Terrorist or Insurgent Groups'. *Studies in Conflict and Terrorism*, 33(6), pp. 488–510.
Payne, D. P. (2007). 'Nationalism and the Local Church: The Source of Ecclesiastical Conflict in the Orthodox Commonwealth'. *Nationalities Papers*, 35(5), pp. 831–852.
Pedahzur, A. (2005). *Suicide Terrorism*. Cambridge: Polity Press.
Pedziwiatr, K. (2008). *The New Muslim Elites in European Cities: Religion and Active Social Citizenship amongst Young Organized Muslims in Brussels and London*. PhD dissertation. Leuven: Katholieke Universiteit Leuven.
Pehoiu, G. & Costache, A. (2010). 'The Dynamics of Population Emigration from Romania—Contemporary and Future Trends'. *World Academy of Science, Engineering and Technology*, 66, pp. 607–612.
Pelkmans, M. (2006). 'Asymmetries in the "Religious Market" in Kyrgystan', in C. Hann & the 'Civil Religion' Group (eds.), *The Postsocialist Religious Question: Faith and Power in Central Asia and East-Central Europe*. Berlin: Lit Verlag, pp. 29–46.
Peter, F. (2006). 'Individualization and Religious Authority in Western European Islam'. *Islam and Christian-Muslim Relations*, 17(1), pp. 105–118.
——— (2006a). 'Leading the Community of the Middle Way: A Study of the Muslim Field in France'. *The Muslim World*, 96(4), pp. 707–736.
——— (2006b), 'Islamic Sermons, Religious Authority and the Individualisation of Islam in France', in M. Franzmann, C. Gärtner & N. Köck (eds.), *Religiosität in der Säkularisierten Welt. Theoretische und empirische Beiträge zur Säkularisierungsdebatte in der Religionssoziologie*. Wiesbaden: VS Verlag, pp. 303–320.
Petito, F. & Hatzopoulos, P. (Eds.) (2003). *Religion in International Relations: The Return from Exile*. Basingstoke: Palgrave Macmillan.
Phalet, K. & Güngör, D. (2004). *Moslim in Nederland: Religieuze dimensies, etnische relaties en burgerschap: Turken en Marokkanen in Rotterdam*. Den Haag: Sociaal Cultureel Planbureau.
Phalet, K., Van Lotringen, C. & Entzinger, H. (2002). *Islam in de multiculturele samenleving. Opvattingen van jongeren in Rotterdam*. Utrecht: Universiteit Utrecht, European Research Centre on Migration and Ethnic Relations.
Pickel, G. & Müller, O. (eds.) (2009). *Church and Religion in Contemporary Europe: Results from Empirical and Comparative Research*. Wiesbaden: VS Verlag für Sozialwissenschaften.
Pirenne, H. (1957). *Mohammed and Charlemagne*. Cleveland, OH: Meridien.
Platvoet, J. G. (1992). 'African Traditional Religions in the Religious History of Humankind', in Ter Haar, G., Moyo, A. & Nondo, S. J. (eds.). *African Traditional Religions in Religious Education: A Resource Book with Special Reference to Zimbabwe*. Utrecht: Theologische Faculteit Universiteit Utrecht, pp. 11–28.

Polak, R. (Ed.) (2006). *Religion kehrt wieder. Handlungsoptionen in Kirche und Gesellschaft*. Ostfidern: Schwabenverlag.

Poloma, M. M. & Green, J. C. (2010). *The Assemblies of God: Godly Love and the Revitalization of American Pentecostalism*. New York: New York University Press.

Potter, P. B. (2003). 'Belief in Control: Regulation of Religion in China', in D. L. Overmyer (ed.), *Religion in China Today*. Cambridge: Cambridge University Press, pp. 11–31.

Pouessel, S. (2010). *Les identités amazighes au Maroc*. Paris: Non Lieu.

Quaker United Nations Office (QUNO) (2010). *Annual Review 2010*. Geneva: QUNO.

Ralph, D. & Staeheli, L. A. (2011). 'Home and Migration: Mobilities, Belongings and Identities'. *Geographical Compass*, 5(7), pp. 517–530.

Ramet, P. (Ed.) (1984). *Religion and Nationalism in Soviet and East European Politics*. Durham, NC: Duke Press Policy Studies.

Ramet, S. P. (2006). 'The Way We Were—and Should Be Again? European Orthodox Churches and the "Idyllic Past"', in T. A. Byrnes & P. J. Katzenstein (eds.), *Religion in an Expanding Europe*. Cambridge: Cambridge University Press, pp. 148–176.

―――― (1998). *Nihil Obstat: Religion, Politics and Social Change in East-Central Europe and Russia*. Durham, NC: Duke University Press.

Ramji, R. (2008a). 'Being Muslim and Being Canadian: How Second Generation Muslim Women Create Religious Identities in Two Worlds', in K. Aune, S. Sharma & G. Vincett (eds.), *Women and Religion in the West: Challenging Secularisation*. Aldershot: Ashgate, pp. 195–205.

―――― (2008b). 'Creating a Genuine Islam: Second Generation Muslims Growing Up in Canada'. *Canadian Diversity / Diversité canadienne*, 6(2), pp. 104–109.

Ranstorp, M. (2009). 'Mapping Terrorism Studies After 9/11: An Academic Field of Old Problems and New Prospects', in R. Jackson, M. Breen Smyth & J. Gunning (eds.), *Critical Terrorism Studies: A New Research Agenda*. London: Routledge, pp. 13–31.

Rapoport, D. C. (1984). 'Fear and Trembling: Terrorism in Three Religious Traditions'. *American Political Science Review*, 78(3), pp. 658–677.

―――― (2004), 'The Four Waves of Modern Terrorism', in A. K. Cronin & J. M. Ludes (eds.), *Attacking Terrorism: Elements of a Grand Strategy*. Washington, DC: Georgetown University Press, pp. 46–73.

Ray, D. I. & Reddy, P. S. (2003). 'Ghana: Traditional Leadership and Rural Local Governance', in D. I. Ray, P. S. Reddy & IASIA (eds.), *Grassroots Governance ? Chiefs in Africa and the Afro-Caribbean*. Calgary: University of Calgary Press, pp. 83–122.

Read, J. (2002). 'Challenging Myths of Muslim Women: The Influence of Islam on Arab-American Women's Labor Force Participation'. *Muslim World*, 96(1), pp. 19–38.

Reid, M.A. (1991). 'Dialogic Modes of Representing Africa (s): Womanist Film'. *Black American Literature Forum*, 25(2), pp. 375–388.

Religion and Public Policy at the UN. (2002). Washington, DC: Religion Counts.

Renaerts, M. (1999). 'Process of Homogenisation in the Muslim Educational World in Brussels'. *International Journal of Educational Research*, 31(4), pp. 283–294.

Reuter, C. (2002). *Mein Leben ist eine Waffe*. Munich: Bertelsmann; English translation, *My Life Is a Weapon: A Modern History of Suicide Bombing*. Princeton: Princeton University Press, 2004.

Reychler, L. (1997). 'Religion and Conflict'. *The International Journal of Peace Studies*, 2(1), pp. 1–16. Retrieved 29 February 2012 from http://www.gmu.edu/academic/ijps/vol2_1/Reyschler.htm.

Ricolfi, L. (2006). 'Palestinians, 1981–2003', in D. Gambetta (ed.), *Making Sense of Suicide Missions*. Oxford: Oxford University Press, pp. 77–129.
Roach, J. R. (1996). *Cities of the Dead: Circum-Atlantic Performance*. New York: Columbia University Press.
Robbins, J. (2004). 'The Globalization of Pentecostal and Charismatic Christianity'. *Annual Review of Anthropology*, 33, pp. 117–143.
Robertson, R. (1992). *Globalisation: Social Theory and Global Culture*. London: Sage.
——— (2001). 'Foreword', in V. Roudometof, *Nationalism, Globalization, and Orthodoxy: The Social Origins of Ethnic Conflict in the Balkans*. Westport, CT: Greenwood Press, pp. xi–xiv.
Robinson, F. (1979). 'Islam and Muslim Separatism', in D. Taylor & M. Yapp (eds.), *Political Identity in South Asia*. London: Curzon Press, pp. 78–112.
Rosaldo, R. (1989, new edition 1993). *Culture and Truth: The Remaking of Social Analysis*. Boston: Beacon Press.
Rosenau, J. N. (2002). 'Governance in a New Global Order', in D. Held & A. McGrew (eds.), *Governing Globalization: Power, Authority and Global Governance*. Cambridge: Polity, pp. 70–86.
Rosenberg, J. (1994). *The Empire of Civil Society: A Critique of the Realist Theory of International Relations*. London: Verso.
Rosenblum, N. L. (Ed.) (2000). *Obligations of Citizenship and Demands of Faith: Religious Accommodation in Pluralist Democracies*. Princeton, NJ: Princeton University Press.
Roudometof, V. (2001). *Nationalism, Globalization, and Orthodoxy: The Social Origins of Ethnic Conflict in the Balkans*, Westport, CT: Greenwood Press.
——— (2008). 'Greek Orthodoxy, Territoriality, and Globality: Religious Responses and Institutional Disputes'. *Sociology of Religion*, 69(1), pp. 67–91.
Rousseau, J. J. (1977). *Du contrat social*. Paris: Editions du Seuil.
Roy, O. (2000). 'L'individualisation dans l'Islam européen contemporain', in F. Dassetto (ed.), *Paroles d'Islam. Individus, sociétés et discours dans l'Islam européen contemporain/Islamic Words. Individuals, Societies and Discourse in Contemporary European Islam*. Paris: Maisonneuve et Larose, pp. 69–85.
——— (2002). *L'Islam mondialisé*. Paris: Seuil; English translation, *Globalized Islam: The Search for a New Ummah*. New York: Columbia University Press, 2004.
——— (2004). *Globalized Islam: The Search for a New Ummah*. New York: Colombia University Press.
——— (2008). *La sainte ignorance. Le temps de la religion sans culture*. Paris: Seuil; English translation, *Holy Ignorance: When Religion and Culture Part Ways*. New York: Columbia University Press, 2010.
——— (2010). 'Religious Revivals as a Product and Tool of Globalization'. *Quaderni di Relazioni Internazionali*, 12, pp. 22–34.
Rudolph, S. H. & Piscatori, J. (Eds.) (1997). *Transnational Religion and Fading States*. Boulder, CO: Westview.
Rutherford, J. (1990). 'The Third Space: Interview with Homi K. Bhabha', in J. Rutherford (ed.), *Identity: Community, Culture, Difference*. London: Lawrence & Wishart, pp. 207–221.
Sahgal, S. (1992). 'Secular Spaces: The Experiences of Asian Women Organizing', in S Sahgal & N. Yuval-Davies (eds.), *Refusing Holy Orders: Women and Fundamentalism in Britain*. London: Virago, pp. 169–204.
Said, E. W. (1978). *Orientalism: Western Conceptions of the Orient*. Harmondworth: Penguin.
——— (1993). *Culture and Imperialism*. London: Vintage.
Sampson, C. (1994). '"To Make Real the Bond Between Us All": Quaker Conciliation during the Nigerian Civil War', in D. Johnston & C. Sampson (eds.),

Religion, The Missing Dimension of Statecraft. New York: Oxford University Press, pp. 88–118.
Sandweiss, S. (1975). Sai Baba: The Holy Man and the Psychiatrist. San Diego: Birth Day Press.
Sanktanber, A. (2002). '"We Pray Like You Have Fun": New Islamic Youth in Turkey Between Intellectualism and Popular Culture', in D. Kandiyoti & A. Sanktanber (eds.), Fragments of Culture. London: I.B. Tauris, pp. 254–277.
Sater, J.N. (2010). Morocco: Challenges to Tradition and Modernity. London: Routledge.
Schacht, J., MacDonald, D. B. & Schacht, J. (2010). 'Idjtihād', in P. Bearman, Th. Bianquis, C. E. Bosworth, E. van Donzel & W. P. Heinrichs (eds.), Encyclopaedia of Islam, 2nd Edition [Electronic Version]. Retrieved 22 January 2010 from http://referenceworks.brillonline.com/browse/encyclopaedia-of-islam-2.
Schiffauer, W. (2000). Die Gottesmänner. Türkische Islamisten in Deutschland. Eine Studie zur Herstellung religiöser Evidenz. Frankfurt am Main: Suhrkamp Verlag.
Scholte, J. A. (2000). Globalization: A Critical Introduction. London: Macmillan.
―――― (2005). 'Civil Society and Democracy in Global Governance', in R. Wilkinson (ed.), The Global Governance Reader. London: Routledge, pp. 322–340.
Schrover, M. & Penninx, R. (2001). Bastion of bindmiddel. De organisatie van migranten in historisch perspectief. Amsterdam: Instituut voor Migratie- en Etnische Studies.
Schwalgin, S. (2004). 'Why Locality Matters: Diaspora Consciousness and Sedentariness in the Armenian Diaspora in Greece', in K. Waltraud, K. Tölölyan & C. Alfonso (eds.), Diaspora, Identity and Religion: New Directions in Theory and Research. London: Routledge, pp. 72–92.
Scuzzarello, S., Kinnval, C. & Monroe, K. (2008). On Behalf of Others: The Psychology of Care in a Global World. Oxford: Oxford University Press.
Sedgwick, M. (2004). 'Al-Qaeda and the Nature of Religious Terrorism'. Terrorism and Political Violence, 16(4), pp. 795–814.
Şen, F. & Sauer, M. (2006). 'Religiöse Praxis und organisatorische Vertretung türkischstämmiger Muslime in Deutschland'. Zeitschrift für Ausländerrecht und Ausländerpolitik (ZAR), 1, pp. 14–22.
Shah, T., Stepan, A. & Duffy-Toft, M. (2012). Rethinking Religion and World Affairs. New York: Oxford University Press.
Shavit, U. (2009). The New Imagined Community: Global Media and the Construction of National and Muslim Identities of Migrants. Eastbourne: Sussex Academic Press.
Sheffer, G. (2003). Diaspora Politics: At Home Abroad. New York: Cambridge University Press.
Shepherd, K. R. D. (1986). Gurus Rediscovered: Biographies of Sai Baba of Shirdi and Upasni Maharaj of Sakori. Cambridge, UK: Anthropographia.
Shimazono, S. (2008). 'Individualization of Society and Religionization of Individuals: Resacralization in Postmodernity (Second Modernity)'. Pensiamento, 64 (242), pp. 603–619.
Silke, A. (2006). 'The Role of Suicide in Politics, Conflict, and Terrorism'. Terrorism and Political Violence, 18(1), pp. 35–46.
Silverstein, P. (2004). Algeria in France: Transpolitics, Race and Nation. Bloomington: Indiana University Press.
Silverstein, P. (2010). 'The Local Dimensions of Transnational Berberism: Racial Politics, Land Rights, and Cultural Activism in Southeastern Morocco', in K. E. Hoffman & S. Gilson Miller (eds.), Berbers and Others. Beyond Tribe and Nation in the Maghrib. Bloomington: Indiana University Press, pp. 83–102.
Silverstein, P. (2011). 'Masquerade Politics: Race, Islam and the Scale of Amazigh Activism in Southeastern Morocco'. Nations and Nationalisms, 17(1), pp. 65–84.

Simmel, G. (1908). 'Group Expansion and the Development of Individuality', in D. E. Levine (ed.), *On Individuality and Social Forms*. Chicago, IL: University of Chicago Press, pp. 251–293.

Simmel, G. (1971). 'How Is Social Order Possible', in D. N. Levine (ed.), *On Individuality and Social Forms: Selected Writings*. Chicago: University of Chicago Press, pp. 6–22.

Slyomovics, S. (2001). 'A Truth Commission for Morocco'. *Middle East Report*, 218, pp. 18–21.

Smith, A. D. (2009). *Ethno-Symbolism and Nationalism. A Cultural Approach*. Oxon: Routledge.

Smith, L. B. (2008). 'Can Martyrdom Survive Secularization?' *Social Research*, 75(2), pp. 435–460.

Smith, W. C. (1991). *The Meaning and End of Religion*. Minneapolis, MN: Fortress Press.

Speckhard, A. & Ahkmedova, K. (2006). 'The Making of a Martyr: Chechen Suicide Terrorism'. *Studies in Conflict and Terrorism*, 29(5), pp. 429–492.

Spickard, J. (2001). 'Tribes and Cities: Towards an Islamic Sociology of Religion'. *Social Compass*, 48, pp. 103–116.

——— (2003). 'What Is Happening to Religion? Six Sociological Narratives'. Working Paper. Retrieved 29 February 2012 from http://www.ku.dk/Satsning/Religion/indhold/publikationer/working_papers/what_is_happened.PDF.

Spielhaus, R. (2010). 'Media Making Muslims: The Construction of a Muslim Community in Germany through Media Debate'. *Contemporary Islam*, 4, pp. 11–27.

Spielhaus, R. & Färber, A. (2006). *Islamisches Gemeindeleben in Berlin*. Berlin: Der Beauftragte des Senats für Integration und Migration.

Srinivas, S. (2008). *In the Presence of Sai Baba: Body, City and Memory in a Global Religious Movement*. Leiden: Brill Press.

Srinivas, T. (2002). 'A Tryst with Destiny: The Indian Case of Cultural Globalisation', in P. L. Berger & S. P. Huntington (eds.), *Many Globalisations*. New York: Oxford University Press, pp. 89–116.

——— (2010). *Winged Faith: Rethinking Religion and Globalisation through the Sathya Sai Movement*. New York: Columbia University Press.

Stan, L. & Turcescu, L. (2007). *Religion and Politics in Post-Communist Romania*. Oxford: Oxford University Press.

Stark, R. & Bainbridge, W. S. (1985). *The Future of Religion: Secularisation, Revival, and Cult Formation*. Berkeley: University of California Press.

——— (1996). *A Theory of Religion*. New Brunswick, NJ: Rutgers University Press.

Stark, R. & Finke, R. (2000). *Acts of Faith: Explaining the Human Side of Religion*. Berkeley: University of California Press.

Statutul Pentru Organizarea şi Funcţionarea Bisericii Ortodoxe Române 1989. (1990). *Biserica Ortodoxa Romana* [Official Bulletin of the Romanian Orthodox Church], 108(7–10), p. 222.

Steger, M. (2009). *Globalisms: The Great Ideological Struggle of the 21st Century*. Lanham, MA: Rowman & Littlefield.

Stephens, R. J. (2008). *The Fire Spreads: Holiness and Pentecostalism in the American South*. Cambridge, MA: Harvard University Press.

Stewart, C. (1999). 'Syncretism and Its Synonyms: Reflections on Cultural Mixture'. *Diacritics*, 29(3), pp. 40–62.

Stiglitz, J. E. (2002). *Globalisation and Its Discontents*. New York: Norton.

——— (2006). *Making Globalisation Work*. New York: Norton.

Stoeltje, B. J. (2003). 'Asante Queen Mothers: Precolonial Authority in a Postcolonial Society'. *Research Review*, 19(2), pp. 1–19.

Stoica, I. (2007). 'Romanian Orthodox Theology between Tradition and Modernity—Missionary Aspects: New Confrontations, Illusions and Hopes', in A. Stan,

(ed.), *Convergent World Religions: Comparative Law, Order and Discipline*. Bucharest: Editura Ialpress Slobozia, pp. 183–219.
Stratton, A. (2006). *Muhajababes*. London: Constable.
Sunier, T. (1996). *Islam in beweging*. Amsterdam: Het Spinhuis.
Swallow, D. A. (1982). 'Ashes and Powers: Myth, Rite, and Miracle in an Indian Godman's Cult'. *Modern Asian Studies*, 16, pp. 123–158.
Sweeney, G. (1993). 'Irish Hunger Strikes and the Cult of Self-Sacrifice'. *Journal of Contemporary History*, 28(3), pp. 421–437.
Szonyi, M. (2009). 'Secularization Theories and the Study of Chinese Religions'. *Social Compass* 56(3), pp. 312–327.
Sztompka, P. (2005). 'From East Europeans to Europeans', in E. Ben-Rafael & Y. Sternberg (eds.), *Comparing Modernities: Pluralism versus Homogeneity. Essays in Homage to Shmuel N. Eisenstadt*. Brill: Brill Academic Publishers, pp. 527–543.
Tahtah, M. (1999). *Entre pragmatisme, reformisme et modernisme: Le rôle politico-religieux des Khattabi dans le Rif jusqu'a 1926*. Leuven: Peeters Publishers.
Tambaih, S. J. (1996). *Leveling Crowds: Ethnonationalist Conflicts and Collective Violence in South Asia*. Comparative Studies in Religion and Society. Berkeley: University of California Press.
Tan, Z. (2010). 'Tuijin Zhongguo yu shijie musilin diqu jiaoliu yu hezuo [Promoting Exchange and Cooperation Between China and World Muslim Areas]'. *Duiwai chuanbo* 9, pp. 26–27.
Tanasescu, A. I. (2005). 'Nationalism, Religion and Tourism in Postcommunist Romania: An Examination of Church-State Relations, Reinvigorated Orthodox Miracle and Pilgrimage Amidst Global Flows'. MA Thesis, Faculty of Graduate Studies and Research, Department of Anthropology, University of Alberta.
Tappe, E. (1977). 'The Rumanian Orthodox Church and the West', in D. Baker (ed.), *The Orthodox Churches and the West: Papers Read at the Fourteenth Summer Meeting and the Fifteenth Winter Meeting of the Ecclesiastical History Society*. Oxford: Blackwell.
Taylor, D. (1987). 'Charismatic Authority in the Sathya Sai Baba Movement', in R. Burghart (ed.), *Hinduism in Great Britain*. London: Tavistock Publications, pp. 119–133.
ter Haar, G. (1998). *Half Way to Paradise: African Christians in Europe*. Cardiff: Cardiff University Press.
Ternon, Y. (2006). 'Le terrorisme russe (1878–1908)', in G. Chaliand & A. Blin (eds), *Histoire du terrorisme. De l'Antiquité à Al Qaida*. Paris: Bayard, pp. 145–188; English translation, 'Russian Terrorism, 1878–1908', in G. Chaliand & A. Blin (eds.), *The History of Terrorism: From Antiquity to Al Qaeda*. Berkeley/Los Angeles: University of California Press, 2007, pp. 132–174.
Thal, S. (2002). 'A Religion That Was Not a Religion: The Creation of a Modern Shinto in Nineteenth-Century Japan', in D. Peterson & D. Walhof (eds.), *The Invention of Religion: Rethinking Belief in Politics and History*. New Brunswick, NJ: Rutgers University Press, pp. 100–114.
The Basis of the Social Concept. Russian Orthodox Church, official website of the Department for External Church Relations. Retrieved 5 August 2011 from http://www.mospat.ru/en/documents/social-concepts/xvi.
The Statutes for the Organisation and Functioning of the ROC General Stipulations, pp. 65–66. Retrieved 5 May 2008 from http://www.patriarhia.ro/_upload/documente/121438488425759490.pdf.
Thomas, S. M. (2005). *The Global Resurgence of Religion and the Transformation of International Relations: The Struggle for the Soul of the Twenty-First Century*. New York: Palgrave Macmillan.
Thompson, D. (2005). *Waiting for Antichrist: Charisma and Apocalypse in a Pentecostal Church*. Oxford: Oxford University Press.

Thual, F. (1993). *Géopolitique de l'orthodoxie*. Paris: Dunod.
Tibi, B. (2010). 'Euro-Islam: An Alternative to Islamization and Ethnicity of Fear', in Z. Baran (ed.), *The Other Muslims: Moderate and Secular*. New York: Palgrave Macmillan.
Tietze, N. (2002). *Jeunes musulmans de France et d'Allemagne. Les constructions subjectives de l'identité*. Paris: L'Harmattan.
Tilly, C. (1992). *Coercion, Capital and European States, AD 990–1992*. Cambridge, MA: Blackwell.
—— (2005). *Identities, Boundaries, and Social Ties*. New York: Paradigm.
Tohidi, N. (1998). 'The Issues at Hand', in H. Bodman & N. Tohidi, *Women in Muslim Societies. Diversity within Unity*. London: Lynne Rienner Publishers Inc., pp. 277–294.
Tomlinson, J. (1999). *Globalisation and Culture*. Chicago: University of Chicago Press.
Tonah, S. (2007). 'Ghanaians Abroad and Their Ties Home: Cultural and Religious Dimensions of Transnational Migration'. *COMCAD Arbeitspapiere—Working Papers*, 25, pp. 1–23.
Tong, R. (1989). *Feminist Thought: A More Comprehensive Introduction*. Boulder, CO: Westview Press.
Tosini, D. (2009). 'A Sociological Understanding of Suicide Attacks'. *Theory, Culture and Society*, 26(4), pp. 67–96.
Trentmann, F. (2000). *Paradoxes of Civil Society: New Perspectives on Modern German and British History*. New York: Berghahn.
Triandafyllidou, A. (ed.) (2010). *Muslims in 21st Century Europe. Structural and Cultural Perspectives*. Routledge: New York.
Troeltsch, E. (1931). *The Social Teachings of the Christian Churches*. New York: Macmillan.
Turcescu, L. & Stan, L. (2000). 'The ROC and Post-communist Democratisation'. *Europe-Asia Studies*, 52(8), pp. 1467–1488.
Turner, B. S. (1978). *Marx and the End of Orientalism*. London: Allen and Unwin.
—— (1994). *Orientalism, Postmodernism and Globalism*. London: Routledge.
—— (2006). 'Religion'. *Theory, Culture, Society*, 23, pp. 437–444.
Ukah, A. (2008). *A New Paradigm of Pentecostal Power: A Study of the Redeemed Christian Church of God in Nigeria*. Trenton: Africa World Press.
UN Commission on Global Governance (1995). *Our Global Neighbourhood: The Report of the Commission on Global Governance*. Oxford: Oxford University Press.
UN General Assembly (2004). *We the People: Civil Society, the United Nations and Global Governance*. Report of the Panel of Eminent Persons on UN-Civil Society Relations, Report A/58/8127.
Urban, H. B. (2002). 'Avatar for Our Age: Sathya Sai Baba and the Cultural Contradictions of Late Capitalism'. *Religion*, 33, pp. 73–93.
Urry, J. (2003). *Global Complexity*. Cambridge: Polity.
Valdman, T. (2007). Personal Interview at the ROC in Milan, 18 July.
Van Amersfoort, H. & van Heelsum, A. (2007). 'Moroccan Berber Immigrants in the Netherlands, Their Associations and Transnational Ties: A Quest for Identity and Recognition'. *Immigrants & Minorities*, 25, pp. 234–262.
van Bruinessen, M. (2011). 'Producing Islamic Knowledge in Western Europe: Discipline, Authority, and Personal Quest', in M. van Bruinessen & S. Allievi (eds.), *Producing Islamic Knowledge: Transmission and Dissemination in Western Europe*. London: Routledge, pp. 1–27.
Van Bruinessen, M. & Allievi, S. (2002). *The Production of Islamic Knowledge in Western Europe*, Discussion paper for workshop 3 at the Fourth Mediterranean Social and Political Science Meeting, Robert Schuman Centre, European University Institute, Florence, 19–23 March 2003.

van Bruinessen, M. & Allievi, S. (2003). *The Production of Islamic Knowledge in Western-Europe*. Workshop abstract of Fourth Mediterranean Social and Political Research Meeting 19–23 March. Firenze: European University Institute.

van Bruinessen, M. & Howel, J. D. (2007). *Sufism and the 'Modern' in Islam*. London: I. B. Tauris.

van der Geest, S. (2009). '"Anyway!": Lorry Inscriptions in Ghana', in J. B. Gewald, S. Luning & K. Van Walraven (eds.), *The Speed of Change: Motor Vehicles and People in Africa*. Leiden: Brill, pp. 253–293.

Van der Heyden, K., Geets, J., Vanderwaeren, E. & Timmerman, C. (2005), *Identiteit en islambeleving bij hoogopgeleide moslimjongeren in Vlaanderen. Gelijke kansen vanuit een moslimperspectief*. Antwerpen: Universiteit Antwerpen, Steunpunt Gelijke Kansenbeleid & Onderzoeksgroep Armoede, Sociale Uitsluiting en de Stad.

van der Meulen, M. (2009). 'The Continuing Importance of the Local: African Churches and the Search for Worship Space in Amsterdam'. *African Diaspora*, 2, pp. 159–181.

Van der Valk, I. (1996). *Van migratie naar burgerschap. Twintig jaar Komitee Marokkaanse Arbeiders in Nederland*. Amsterdam: Instituut voor Publiek en Politiek.

van der Veer, P. (1994). *Religious Nationalism: Hindus and Muslims in India*. Berkeley: University of California Press.

——— (2003). 'Colonial Cosmopolitanism', in S. Vertovec & R. Cohen (eds.), *Conceiving Cosmopolitanism: Theory, Context, and Practice*. Oxford: Oxford University Press, pp. 165–180.

van der Wijst, H (2009). *De wereld op zijn kop: Hella en de Ghanese koning [The World Upside Down: Hella and the Ghanaian King]*.KRO TV programme, 15 February. Retrieved 27 March 2012 from http://www.uitzendinggemist.nl/afleveringen/1135823.

van Dijk, R. (2001). 'Time and Transnational Technologies of the Self in the Ghanaian Pentecostal Diaspora', in A. Corten & R. Marshall-Fratani (eds.), *Between Babel and Pentecost: Transnational Pentecostalism in Africa and Latin America*. London: Hurst, pp. 216–235.

Van Heelsum, A. (2001). *Marokkaanse organisaties in Nederland. Een netwerkanalyse*. Amsterdam: Het Spinhuis.

Van Loon, J. (2006). 'Network'. *Theory, Culture & Society*, 23 (2/3), pp. 307–314.

Vanderwaeren, E. (2005). 'Moslima's aan de horizon. Islamitische interpretaties als hefbomen bij de emancipatie van moslima's', in G. Coene & C. Longman (eds.), *Eigen emancipatie eerst: Over de rechten en representatie van vrouwen in een multiculturele samenleving*. Gent: Academia Press, pp. 113–132.

——— (2006), *The Existing Conditions for Women to Conduct 'Ijtih d in the European Islamic Diaspora*. Paper presented at the Seventh Mediterranean Social and Political Research Meeting, organised by the Mediterranean Programme of the Robert Schuman Centre for Advanced Studies at the European University Institute, Florence & Montecatini Terme, Italy, 22–26 March 2006.

——— (2008). 'Religieuze beschouwingen onder hoger opgeleide moslims in Vlaanderen', in E. Vanderwaeren & C. Timmerman (eds.), *Diversiteit in islam. Over verschillende belevingen van het moslim zijn*. Leuven: Acco, pp. 45–72.

——— (2010). *Vrouwen doen aan 'ijtihād. Hybriditeit als creatieve ruimte bij interpretaties van islam*. PhD dissertation. Antwerpen: University of Antwerp.

——— (2012). 'Muslimahs' Impact on and Acquisition of Islamic Religious Authority in Flanders', in B. Masooda & H. Kalmbach (eds.), *Women, Leadership and Mosques: Changes in Contemporary Islamic Authority*. Leiden: Brill, pp. 301–322.

Vanderwaeren, E. & Timmerman, C. (2008). 'Inleidende beschouwingen op diversiteit in islam. Over verschillende belevingen van het moslim zijn', in E. Vanderwaeren

& C. Timmerman (eds.), *Diversiteit in islam. Over verschillende belevingen van het moslim zijn*. Leuven: Acco, pp. 9–14.
Verkuyten, M. (1999). *Etnische identiteit. Theoretische en empirische benaderingen*. Amsterdam: Het Spinhuis.
Vernooij, J. (2004). *Pentecostalism and Migration: The Dutch Case*. Paper for the IAMS Assembly in Malaysia, pp. 1–21. Retrieved 27 March 2012 from http://missionstudies.org/archive/conference/1papers/fp/Joop_Vernooij_pentecostalism_Full_Paper.pdf.
Vertovec, S. (1997). 'Three Meanings of "Diaspora", Exemplified Among South Asian. Religions'. *Diaspora*, 6(3), pp. 277–299.
——— (2001). 'Moslimjongeren in Europa: vermenging van invloeden en betekenissen', in D. Douwes (ed.), *Naar een Europese islam? Essays*. Amsterdam: Mets & Schilt, pp. 95–116.
Vertovec, S. & Rogers, A. (1998). 'Introduction', in S. Vertovec & A. Rogers (eds.), *Muslim European Youth: Reproducing Ethnicity, Religion, Culture*. Aldershot: Ashgate, pp. 1–24.
Veselič, M. (2011). 'Managing Religion in Contemporary China. The Case of Islam'. *Treatises and Documents: Journal of Ethnic Studies* 65, pp. 114–137.
Vikør, K. (2005). *Between God and the Sultan. A History of Islamic Law*. London: Hurst Company.
Voicu, M. (2007). 'Religiosity and Religious Revival in Romania', in E. Révay & M. Tomka (eds.), *Church and Religious Life in Post-Communist Societies*. Papers of ISORECEA Conferences, Budapest: Pázmány Társadalomtudomány, 7, pp. 13–33.
Volkov, D. (2005). 'Living Eastern Orthodox Religion in the United States', in V. Roudometof, A. Agadjanian & J. Pankhurst (eds.), *Eastern Orthodoxy in a Global Age: Tradition Faces the Twenty-First Century*. Oxford: AltaMira Press, pp. 224–244.
Waardenburg, J. (2000). 'Normative Islam in Europe', in F. Dassetto (ed.), *Paroles d'Islam. Individus, sociétés et discours dans l'Islam européen contemporain/ Islamic Words. Individuals, Societies and Discourse in Contemporary European Islam*. Paris: Maisonneuve et Larose, pp. 49–68.
Waardenburg, J. D. J. (2001). *Institutionele Vormgeving Van De Islam in Nederland Gezien in Europees Perspectief*. Den Haag: Wetenschappelijke raad voor het regeringsbeleid.
Wacker, G. (2001). *Heaven Below: Early Pentecostals and American Culture*. Cambridge, MA: Harvard University Press.
Wallis, R. & Bruce, S. (1992). 'Secularization: The Orthodox Model', in S. Bruce (ed.), *Religion and Modernization: Sociologists and Historians Debate the Secularization Thesis*. Oxford: Clarendon Press, pp. 8–30.
Wanner, C. (2007). *Communities of the Converted: Ukrainians and Global Evangelism*. Ithaca, NY: Cornell University Press.
Warburg, M. (2001). 'Religious Organisations in a Global World: A Comparative Perspective'. Paper presented at the 2001 international conference *The Spiritual Supermarket: Religious Pluralism in the 21st Century*, April 19–22, London School of Economics. Retrieved 11 April 2012 from http://www.cesnur.org/2001/london2001/warburg.htm.
Ware, T. (1997). *The Orthodox Church*. London: Penguin Books.
Warner, M., Van Antwerpen, J., & Calhoun, C. (2010). *Varieties of Secularism in a Secular Age*. Cambridge, MA: Harvard University Press.
Warner, S. (1993). 'Work in Progress Toward a New Paradigm for the Sociological Study of Religion in the United States'. *American Journal of Sociology*, 98, pp. 1044–1093.
Waugh, M. (2001). 'Quakers, Peace and the League of Nations: The Role of Bertram Pickard'. *Quaker Studies*, 6(1), pp. 59–79.

Wehr, P. & Lederach, J. P. (1991). 'Mediating Conflict in Central America'. *Journal of Peace Research*, 28(1), pp. 85–98.
Weiss, R. (2005). 'The Global Guru: Sai Baba and the Miracle of the Modern'. *New Zealand Journal of Asian Studies*, 7(2), pp. 5–19.
Weiss, T. G. & Gordenker, L. (1996). *NGOs, the UN and Global Governance*. Boulder, CO: Lynne Rienner.
Weller, R. P. (2001). *Alternate Civilities: Chinese Culture and the Prospects for Democracy*. Boulder, CO: Westview Press.
Wendl, T. (2001).'Visions of Modernity in Ghana: Mami Wata Shrines, Photo Studio and Horror Films'. *Visual Anthropology*, 14(3), pp. 269–292.
Werner, M. & Zimmermann, B. (2006). 'Beyond Comparison. Histoire Croisée and the Challenge of Reflexivity'. *History and Theory*, 45, pp. 30–50.
West, C. & Zimmerman, D. (1987). 'Doing Gender'. *Gender and Society*, 1(2), pp. 125–151.
Westerlund, D. (Ed.) (1996). *Questioning the Secular State: The Worldwide Resurgence of Religion in Politics*. New York: St. Martin's Press.
Wilkinson, R. (Ed.) (2005). *The Global Governance Reader*. London: Routledge.
Willetts, P. (Ed.) (1996). *'The Conscience of the World': The Influence of Non-Governmental Organisations in the UN System*. London: Hurst and Company.
Woodhead, L. (2010). 'New Forms of Public Religion: Spirituality in Global Civil Society', in W. Hofstee & A. van der Kooij, *Religion, Public or Private?* Leiden: Brill.
Woods, N. (2002). 'Global Governance and the Role of Institutions', in D. Held & A. McGrew (eds.), *Governing Globalization: Power, Authority and Global Governance*. Cambridge: Polity, pp. 25–45.
Woodward, K. (1997). 'Concepts of Identity and Difference', in K. Woodward (ed.), *Identity and Difference*. London: Sage, pp. 8–50.
Wright, M. (2006). *Religion and Film*. London: I. B.Tauris.
Wu, J. (2007). 'Religious Believers Thrice the Estimate.' *China Daily*, 7 February 2007. Retrieved 10 March 2010 from http://www.chinadaily.com.cn/china/2007-02/07/content_802994.htm.
Wuthnow, R. (2004). *Saving America? Faith-Based Services and the Future of Civil Society*. Princeton, NJ: Princeton University Press.
Yang, F. & Ebaugh, H. R. (2001). 'Religion and Ethnicity among New Immigrants: The Impact of Majority/Minority Status in Home and Host Countries'. *Journal for the Scientific Study of Religion*, 40(3), pp. 367–378.
Yang, M. M. (ed.) (2008). *Chinese Religiosities: Afflictions of Modernity and State Formation*. Berkeley: University of California Press.
Yang, Z. (1991). 'Yisilan fazhan yinhang daibiao tuan lai woguo fangwen [Delegation of Islamic Development Bank Visits Our Country]'. *Zhongguo musilin* 2, 45–46.
Yang, Z. & Zhang, F. (1991). 'Yong Alabo zijin fazhan wo go xibei jingji [Using Arab Capital to Develop the Economy of Our Northwest]'. *Kaifa yanjiu* 7, pp. 21–23.
Yarrow, C. H. M. (1978). *Quaker Experience in International Conciliation*. New Haven: Yale University Press.
Yazigi, P. Metropolitan of Aleppo. (n.d.). 'Globalization'. Retrieved 5 August 2011 from http://www.orthodoxresearchinstitute.org/articles/misc/paul_yazigi_globalization.htm.
Young, L. A. (Ed.) (1997). *Rational Choice Theory and Religion: Summary and Assessment*. London: Routledge.
Young, M. (2000). *Inclusion and Democracy*. Oxford: University of Oxford.
Young, R. J. C. (2001). *Postcolonialism: An Historical Introduction*. Oxford: Blackwell.
Yükleyen, A. (2007). *The European Market for Islam: Turkish Islamic Communities and Organizations in Germany and the Netherlands*. Unpublished PhD thesis for

the Doctor of Philosophy degree, Boston University, Graduate School of Arts and Sciences.
Yves, L. (1999). 'Religion in Modernity as a New Axial Age: Secularisation or New Religious Forms?' *Sociology of Religion*, 60(3), pp. 303–333.
Zeidan, D. (2003). *The Resurgence of Religion: A Comparative Study of Selected Themes in Christian and Islamic Fundamentalist Discourses*. Leiden: Brill Academic Publishers.
Zemni, S. (2002). 'Islam, European Identity and the Limits of Multiculturalism', in W. Shadid & P.S. van Koningsveld (eds.), *Religious Freedom and the Neutrality of the State: The Position of the European Union*. Leuven: Peeters, pp. 158–173.
Zerubavel, E. (2003). *Time Maps: Collective Memory and the Social Shape of the Past*. Chicago: The University of Chicago Press.
Ziani, A. (1997). *Jubelzang voor de bruidegom*. Amsterdam: El Hizjra.
Zondervan, T. (2008). 'Bricolage en bezieling: Hybride religieuze identiteit bij jongeren', in C. Doude van Troostwijk, E. Van Den Berg & L. Oosterveen (eds.), *Buigzame gelovigen. Essays over religieuze flexibiliteit*. Amsterdam: Uitgeverij Boom, pp. 95–107.
Zulehner, P. M. (2005). 'Religion in Austria', in G. Bischof, A. Pelinka & H. Denz (eds.), *Religion in Austria: Contemporary Austrian Studies*. Vol. 13. New Brunswick: Studien Verlag, pp. 37–63.
——— (2010). *Wie geht's Herr Pfarrer? Ergebnisse einer kreuz und quer-Umfrage: Priester wollen Reformen*. Styria: ORF.
Zulehner, P. M. & Naletova, I. (2009). 'Crkve na Balkanu' [Churches on the Balkans], in I. Džinić & I. Raguž (eds.), *Iščekivati i požurivati dolazak dana Božjega. Zbornik radova u čast prof. dr. sc. Peri Aračiću prigodom 65. Obljetnice života*. Đakovo: Katolički bogoslovni fakultet u Đakovu, pp. 39–63.
Zulehner, P. M. & Tomka, M. (2008). *Religionen und Kirchen in Ost (Mittel) Europa. Entwicklungen seit der Wender. Aufbruch 2007. Tabellenband*. Wien/Budapest: Loiris.
Zulehner, P. M., Tomka, M. & Naletova, I. (2008). *Religionen und Kirchen in Ost (Mittel) Europa: Entwicklungen nach der Wender*. Schwabenverlag, pp. 186–195.

Index

9/11 1, 24–5, 35, 114, 219

Aarab, Mustapha 122
Abttoy 127, 131
Abu Lughod, L. 232
African-Initiated Churches (AICs) 183, 187
Agadjanian, Alexander 82–3, 94
Agourides, Savvas 87
Akan 156–7, 246–66; chief 246, 249–50, 252–7, 265–6; diaspora 252
akathist 87, 95
Alberoni, F. 228
al-Hamarneh, A. 213
Allès, Elisabeth 98, 105, 111
Allievi, S. 197, 216
al-Qaeda 17, 25, 133, 139–40, 142, 144–6
al-Qaradawi, Yusuf 155, 210, 222–3, 229
Amicales 123, 128
Amiraux, V. 197–8
Amir-Moazami, S. 197, 211, 221
Ammerman, N. T. 232
AMREC (*Association Marocaine de la Recherche et de l'Echange Culturel*) 116
anarchists 134–5, 142, 146
Anderson, Allan 182
Anderson, Benedict 118, 130
Andreescu, Liviu 84, 95–6
Annan, Kofi 37, 40, 44
anti-globalist 85
anti-Western 16, 22, 24–5, 29, 59, 96, 112
anti-Westernism 25
Appadurai, A. 230
Appiah, K. A. 231, 248, 255, 266
Appleby, R. S. 160, 179
Arab spring 12, 29, 31–2, 36

Asad, Talal 121, 166, 205, 210–12, 221, 234, 244
Asante 247–8, 251–3, 262, 266
Ask, K. 202
Assassins 133
Assmann, Aleida 125, 129
Austen, R. A. 261
Australia 97, 190–1, 235–6
authentication 203–4
authenticity 145, 156, 173–4, 177, 182–3, 197, 238, 241–2
authority 3, 26, 70, 82–3, 94, 102, 106, 112, 121, 123, 146, 150–1, 154, 157–8, 163, 173, 177, 197–201, 205–10, 215–16, 219–21, 223–4, 252–3, 255–6
autocephalous 77, 83–4, 94
Avishai, O. 199, 209
Aynan, Asis 127

Baader, Andreas 136
Baba, Ali 223–4
Babb, L. A. 236–7
Babès, L. 197–8, 208
Bagader, A. A. 107
Bahá'í 12, 26, 42, 248
Bai, Shouyi 104
Bailey, Sydney 40–1, 234
Bainbridge, W. S. 78, 176
Barkin, J. S. 42–3, 47, 55
Barkun, Michael 143
Bartholomew I 86–7, 95
Basch, L. G. 222
base communities 180
Bastian, Jean-Pierre 181
Bauman, Z. 225, 230
Bayat, A. 223
Baylis, John 81
Bayly, C. A. 11
Beaman, Lori 79, 81, 230

Index

Beck, Ulrich 43, 45, 231, 244
Beckford, James A. 79
Beittinger-Lee, Verena 54–5
Belgium 126, 131, 196–8, 208
Belguendouz, Abdelkrim 124
belief 1–3, 10, 12, 21, 24, 27, 33–4, 58, 60, 63, 71, 73, 75, 78, 89, 98, 102–5, 110–11, 135, 142, 144–5, 158, 196–7, 199, 201, 211, 221, 235–6, 242, 244, 248–9, 257, 259–62, 264
Bell, Duncan S. 124
belonging 14, 27, 59, 61–2, 64–5, 75, 92, 96–7, 103–4, 129, 157, 177, 189, 197, 199–201, 206, 209, 212, 215, 219, 224–6, 255–6, 261, 264–5
Ben-Rafael, Eliezer 81
Berber 10, 16, 114–31; activism 118, 128; Amazigh 16, 114, 116–18, 121, 123–31; Berberism 16; Cultural Movement (Mouvement Culturel Amazigh) 10, 114, 116–19, 124, 129–30; Imazighen 117, 124, 131; Timazighin (Berber women) 127
Berger, Julia 38–41
Berger, Peter L. 27, 73–4, 79, 89, 144–5, 149, 159, 230–1
Bergunder, Michael 182
Berlin 1, 57, 97, 155, 157, 160, 172, 194, 211–18, 222, 224–8, 236
Berzano, Luigi 91
Bhabha, H. (Bhabha, Homi K.) 124, 201
Biggs, M. 141
Bijlmer 246, 248–51, 255–9, 261, 264–6
Bin Laden, Osama 31
Binns, John 85, 87, 94
Bloom, M. M. 132, 137, 139
Boafo-Arthur, K. 253
Bob-Milliar, G. M. 250
Bobrinskoy, Boris 91
Bogomilova, Nonka 85
Borowik, Irena 78, 83
Bouras, Nadia 117, 123
Bourdieu, P. 226, 232, 243
Boutros Boutros-Ghali 39
Bowen, John 154, 158, 205
Brand, Laurie A. 123, 128
Brettell, Caroline B. 97
Bria, Ion 84, 86–7, 90
bricolage 174, 201

Brock, Peggy 190
Brouwer, L. 251
Brubaker, Rogers 118, 124
Bruce, Steve 2, 27, 73, 158
Bruinessen, Martin van 154, 197, 216
Brusco, Elizabeth 153, 183
Buddhism 24, 100, 108, 174, 191
Buddhist 100, 143, 171, 189, 194, 201, 248
Burawoy, Michael 85
Burdick, John 181
Burke III, Edmund 119
Bush, Evelyn L. 38–9, 54
Buswell Jr., Robert E. 182
Byrd, R. O. 40, 42–3, 55

Calhoun, Craig 151, 158
Camus, Albert 135
Candle 250
Cao, Nanlai 189
Cardoso, Fernando Henrique 37
Carp, Radu 91
Casanova, José 2, 79, 82, 145, 149, 151, 158, 173, 220, 230
Cassinasco, Andrea 91
catallaxy 49–56
Catholic Church 12, 74, 78, 96, 167, 173; Roman 61, 166, 173; Greek 89, 95
Cesari, Jocelyne 3, 198, 209, 219, 228
Chandler, David 51–2
Chang, Ha-Joon 48
charismatic 181–2, 184, 188–9, 192–3, 222, 235–6, 239, 248–51, 258–9, 261; movement 188, 235; religious movement 233
Chatterjee, P. 167
Chechnya 17, 133, 143
Chérif-Chebbi, L. 100
chief 157, 246, 249–50, 252–7, 263–6
chieftaincy 249–50, 252–3, 255–7
China 4, 15, 18, 98–113, 149–50, 152, 161, 168–9, 172, 176, 187–9, 192
Chinese 10, 15–16, 18, 94, 98–9, 101–13, 153, 168–9, 188–9, 193; model 168; nation 10, 15, 98–9, 104, 106, 112
Christianity 10, 23–5, 35–6, 57, 59–60, 72, 76, 80–2, 85, 92–3, 101, 120, 149, 151–2, 154, 156–7, 165, 169, 173, 178, 180, 183, 187–91, 193, 221, 239, 248,

254–5, 258–9, 261; Protestant 182; *see also* Protestant (New) Christian Right 160
church 4, 12, 14, 32, 48, 57–63, 65, 67–8, 70–8, 80, 82–96, 150, 152–4, 157, 162–3, 166–7, 172–4, 176, 180–94, 248, 250–1, 259–61, 263; national 58, 77, 84; *see also* Catholic Church (Roman, Greek); Romanian Orthodox 10, 77, 79–80, 93, 97; *see also* Eastern Orthodox Church
church-state relations 58, 83, 90, 96
Ciobotea, Daniel 87–8
civil society 9, 12, 36–9, 43–5, 47–8, 50–2, 54–5, 74, 79, 86, 88, 128, 149, 220, 231
civility 153, 233–4
clash of civilisations 11, 22–3, 145, 232
Clément, Olivier 89, 91, 94
CMA (*Congrès Mondial Amazigh*) 118
codification 238, 240–1
Cold War 1, 11, 19–23, 29, 39, 43, 80, 83, 87, 145, 149
colonialism 25, 35, 119, 121, 149
communism 14, 23, 26, 29, 34, 78, 82–4, 88, 172
Communist Party of China (CPC) 101
Confino, Michael 83
Confucian 100, 168
Confucianism 24, 100, 168–9
Conovici, Iuliana 84
constituency costs 137
consumption 103, 221–2, 224–6, 240, 251, 256, 259
Cook, D. 138
Cook, M. 156
Cooke, M. 221
Cooper, Fredrick 118
cooperation 19, 47, 58, 64, 67, 100, 107–8, 133, 192, 254
cosmopolitanism 156, 231, 233–4, 239, 244
Cottaar, Annemarie 117, 123
Crawford, David 116
Csordas, T. 243
cultural 1–4, 10–12, 20, 24–7, 30, 33, 35, 56–7, 59, 61, 64–5, 67, 75, 81, 87, 89, 91, 95, 104, 106, 108, 110–11, 113–18, 120–1, 123–7, 129–31, 150, 152, 156–9, 161, 164–5, 178, 180–3, 187–91, 195, 197, 200–1, 208–10, 213, 216, 219–22, 226, 228, 230–4,

236–8, 240–3, 246–8, 250, 255, 258–9, 261, 266; revolution 15, 100–1, 188–9; translation 156, 230, 233–5, 237–8, 240, 244–5

Dahir 120–1
Daoism 100
Dassetto, F. 198
Davie, Grace 2, 63, 67–8, 73–4, 79, 145, 149, 157, 159, 172, 185
De Haas, Hein 117, 123, 131
death 61, 68, 130, 132, 136–9, 143, 146, 185, 235
Della Cava, Ralph 79
democracy 12, 21–2, 28–9, 31–6, 43, 50–3, 74, 86, 93, 115, 128, 220, 231; liberal 2, 21–4, 89
democratisation 22, 24, 28, 30–1, 35, 89, 96, 128, 158, 198, 215, 230
Dempster, Murray W. 180
desecularisation 159, 170
Diamond, L. 35–6
diaspora 9, 11, 14, 16, 80, 84, 90–2, 96–7, 117–18, 120, 123–4, 128–31, 146, 177, 189, 194, 196–7, 209, 236, 252; activism 118
Diderot, Denis 132
differentiation 2, 48–51, 73, 80, 145, 150, 152, 158, 162–3, 166, 197, 247
Dijk, Rijk van 194
Dingley, J. 136, 142
discourse 3, 16, 18, 22–3, 26, 36, 52, 84, 99, 101, 115–16, 118, 121, 124–5, 129–30, 143, 158–9, 196–8, 204–8, 210, 212, 220–1, 224, 226, 230–1, 233–4, 236, 239–40
discursive 196, 205–8, 210–12, 221
disembedded 45, 54, 241
diversity 3, 93, 159, 161, 171–2, 207
divine economy 86
Duffield, M. 47
Duffy-Toft, M. 230
Dungaciu, Dan 73
Durkheim, Émile 80, 165

Eastern 33, 58, 75, 94, 104, 107, 115, 223; approach 58; Europe 10, 14, 26, 31, 57–63, 68–77, 83–5, 89–90, 93, 96–7, 161, 165, 186; Orthodox 58, 68, 75–6, 82–3, 93; Orthodox Church 10, 83, 93
Eck, D. 232

Economic and Social Council (ECOSOC) 37
ecumenical dialogue 89–90
Eickelman, D. (D. F.) 111, 197, 215, 219–20, 222
Eisenstadt, S. N. 170, 232
El Ayoubi, Mohamed 127
elites 9–10, 31, 52, 86, 99, 104, 119–20, 128, 150, 152, 167–8, 182–3, 187, 192, 195, 208
Elster, Jon 144
Enev, Tihomir Nedelchev 87, 89
Ergil, D. 139
Erickson, John H. 85, 88
Esposito, J. L. 171
Essadki, Ahmed 127
ethnicity 59, 76, 99, 101, 103, 154, 156, 185–6, 189, 191, 250
ethno-religious 10, 16, 78, 98–9, 103–5, 111
European secularity 10, 57
European 1–2, 4, 10, 12, 14, 16, 22–5, 57–61, 68–74, 76–8, 81, 84–5, 89, 91, 93, 96, 112, 117, 120, 123, 126, 128–30, 133, 145, 150–1, 153–5, 157, 161–7, 169, 171–3, 178, 188, 196–8, 208, 211, 213–15, 221–2, 224, 226, 228, 245, 249–50; Union 25, 29, 96
evangelist 176, 223

Faas, D. 213
Fadil, Nadia 196–7, 208–9
faith 4, 15, 26, 31, 34, 36, 39, 56, 60, 83, 103, 114, 120, 138, 145, 151–7, 171, 180–1, 185–7, 189–90, 194, 196, 202–5, 207, 215, 233, 237, 244, 248, 258, 261, 264–5; faith community 205, 207, 215
Falk, Richard 86
Fantini, Paola 86
Färber, A. 213, 227
Fatah 139
Fattah, M. A. 30, 32–3, 36
Feldman, J. K. 138–40
Ferguson, N. 26
Finke, Roger 78, 159, 175
Fitzgerald, T. 55, 159
Flanagan, K. 174
Flora, Gavril 87–8
Foblets, Marie-Claire 128

focus groups 198, 204, 266
Fokkema, Tineke 117, 123
Fosztó, László 96
Foucault, M. 52, 134
Fox, George 40
Fox, Jonathan 40, 145
France 58, 69, 78, 117–21, 126, 131, 155, 159, 165–6, 169, 172, 191, 210–12, 214–15, 227, 249
Freston, P. 151–2
Friedman, J. 225–6
Friedman, T. 231
Friends Service Committee (Friend's Service Committee) 40, 41, 43
Friends World Consultation Committee 38
Frijhoff, Willem 125
Fukuyama, Francis 24, 231
fundamentalism 10, 23–4, 27, 143, 145–6, 160–1, 171, 173, 183, 233

Gallagher, Nancy 41
Gambetta, D. 132–3, 139
Garritano, C. 257–8
Gay y Blasco, Paloma 191
Geertz, C. 235
Gellner, Ernest 122
Ghana 156, 246–50, 252–7, 260–1, 264–6
Ghanaian films 156, 246, 256–262, 264, 266
Ghazal, M. 108
Giddens, Anthony 9, 45, 47, 50, 86, 209, 230
Gijsberts, Mérove 129
Gill, Anthony 181
Gillet, Olivier 82, 93
Gilson Miller, Susan 116, 129
Giscard d'Estaing, Valéry 24
Gitanos 191–2
Gladney, Dru C. 98, 100, 103–4, 106
Glick Schiller, N. 222
global 1–4, 9–16, 19–21, 23–4, 26–7, 29, 33, 35, 37–8, 41–55, 58, 75, 79–82, 84, 86, 88–9, 91–4, 99, 101, 106, 109, 112, 114, 116, 118, 121, 124, 127, 129–30, 133, 145–6, 149, 151–3, 155, 157–8, 161, 173–5, 177, 180–5, 189–90, 193, 195–6, 200, 212, 221–2, 224, 226, 230–3, 235–40, 243–4, 250–1; governance 10,

12–13, 38, 46–7, 53; Islam 174, 196, 251; religious system 80–2, 89, 92–3
globalisation 1–4, 9–12, 14, 18–22, 25–8, 33–5, 37–8, 43–54, 57, 79–82, 84–8, 91–5, 98–9, 149–51, 153, 156, 158, 160–2, 167, 170, 173, 175, 180, 200, 203, 219, 226, 230–5, 237, 241; cultural 231–2; negative 21; paradox of 10, 13, 37–8, 43–6, 48, 52–4; positive 21
globalism 20–1
glocalisation 200
Goldblatt, David 81
Göle, Nilüfer 103, 207, 218
Goodman, Jane E. 120
Goossaert, V. 99–100
Gorbachev, Mikhail 26
Gordenker, Leon 39
Gorski, P. S. 2, 158
Grever, Maria 125
Gross, Joan E. 119, 131
grounded theory 199
Guibernau, M. 9

Habermas, J. 160
Haddad, Y. Y. 171
hadith/ḥadīth 178, 205, 216
Hafez, M. M. 133, 139–40, 143, 146
ḥalāl 108–9, 113, 204, 228, 260, 264
Hall, D. D. 174
Hall, S. 201, 209
Halliday, Fred 41
Hamas 13, 32, 139
Hamid el-Zein, A. 227–8
Hammarskjöld, Dag 40
Hammoudi, Abdellah 115
Hannerz, U. 231
Hansen, Thomas Blom 149–50
ḥarām 204, 223
Harmsen, Carel 117, 123
Harries, Patrick 183
Hart, David 126
Harvey, D. 230, 240
Hastings, A. 15
Hayek, Friedrich 49, 55
headscarf 103, 109–10, 155, 219, 222
Heelas, Paul 75, 160, 179, 233, 236
Heelsum, Anja van 122, 128
Hegel, G. W. F. 208
hegemony 30, 48, 54–5, 153, 181; paradox of 38, 46, 51–2

Held, David 46, 81
Hellemans, S. 73–4
Henkel, H. 228
Hervieu-Léger, Danièle 73–4, 172, 201, 243
Hezbollah 133, 138
Hill Fletcher, J. 200–1
hip hop 222–5
histoire croisée 10, 114, 116, 130–1
Hoffman, Bruce 141
Hoffman, Katherine E. 116–17, 129
Hoisington, William A. 120
holiness 180, 182
Holmes, Stephen 133, 135
Holy See 12, 42
homeland 9, 16, 91, 96–7, 115, 118, 122, 124–5, 151, 157, 193
Horowitz, M. C. 133
Hu, J. 102
Hui 3, 10, 15–16, 98–113
Hülya Kandemir 225
hunger strikes 17, 136, 142
Huntington, Samuel P. 23–5, 28, 145, 172, 230–1
hybrid 118, 153, 200–5, 207–9, 233, 243
hybridisation 178, 196, 200–3, 205–7
hybridity 2, 116, 153, 196, 200–1, 207–8

Iannaccone, L. R. 78
identification 13, 15, 39, 104, 111, 115, 157, 166, 185, 218–9, 221, 224
identity 14, 16, 27, 34, 39, 49, 55, 57, 60, 65, 75, 83–4, 89–90, 95, 97–8, 105, 115–21, 124–5, 127–9, 142, 144, 150, 161, 163–5, 168, 172, 175, 185–6, 189–91, 200–1, 203, 205, 207, 209, 218, 222, 225, 232, 241, 244, 246–8, 250–1, 255–7, 260–1, 264–6; ethno-religious 104–5, 111; Muslim 16, 99, 103, 111, 131, 251
ʾijtihād 196, 199–200, 205–6, 208, 210
imagined communities 118, 125, 195
immigrant 3, 65, 92, 134, 153–5, 157, 171, 198, 202, 213, 215, 219, 222, 227–8, 249, 251
immigration 65, 114, 123, 161, 171, 197–9, 207, 209, 218
inculturation 182
indigenous 115, 117, 124, 153, 156–7, 181, 232, 237, 240, 248–9,

252–4, 260, 262–5; religion 248–9, 251–2, 254–7, 259–60, 262, 264–5
Indonesia 12, 28–9, 36, 169, 188–9
Inglehart, Ronald 94, 160
INLA (Irish National Liberation Army) 136
intercultural transitions 200
interdependence 19–20, 47
international 1, 4, 9, 13, 19–21, 23–6, 31, 34–44, 47–8, 51, 55, 90, 93, 98, 101, 107–8, 123, 134, 137, 145–6, 185, 187, 192, 209, 230–1, 235–6, 259, 265; institutions 13, 19, 37, 42, 47–8, 50, 52–54; relations 25–6, 34–5, 40–3, 47, 51, 53, 55, 101, 145, 159
internationalist model 43
Introvigne, M. 80
Iranian Revolution 11
Iran-Iraq war 138
Iraq 17, 29, 35, 112, 133, 140, 143, 213
IRCAM (*Institut de la Culture Amazigh au Maroc*) 129–31
Islam 3, 10, 12, 15–16, 19–20, 22–5, 28, 30–1, 33, 35–6, 74, 98–107, 109–13, 115, 120–1, 129, 131, 138–9, 142, 144, 154–5, 157, 161, 169, 171–4, 177–9, 191, 196–8, 202–28, 233, 239, 248, 251, 254–5, 258–9, 261–2, 264; political 35–6, 178, 228
Islamic 2–3, 10–11, 15–16, 25, 28, 32–4, 36, 39, 99–100, 102–4, 106–11, 114–17, 119–21, 124–30, 133, 137–40, 145, 149, 154–6, 160, 172, 185, 187, 192, 194, 198, 202, 204–6, 208–13, 215–16, 218, 220–5, 227–8, 240, 248, 250–1, 254, 260–5; fundamentalism 23–4, 27; resurgence 102–3, 106, 111; revival 15, 102–3, 221, 228–9
Islamism 16, 27, 112, 130, 224–5
Islamist 13, 22, 25, 32–3, 35–6, 102, 114, 127, 129, 133, 143, 187; traditionalist 32–3
Ismail, S. 215, 224–5
Israeli-Palestinian conflict 41, 133, 143
Issawi, Charles 122
Istiqlal 120–1
Iyall-Smith, K. 200
izran 127

Jacobson, J. 215
James, Paul 45
Japan 100, 150, 168–9, 188, 235–6
Japanese 94, 99, 146, 169, 185
jihād 36, 138–9, 223; Islamic 139
John Paul II 26
Jones, Ben 195
Jonker, G. 197
Jouili, Jeanette 197
Juergensmeyer, M. 11, 17, 26, 144–5, 161, 239
Jupp, P. C. 174
jurisdiction 83, 92–4, 164, 253, 255

Kabki, M. 249–50, 255, 266
kairos 91
Kalyayev/Kaliayev, Ivan 135
Kalyvas, S. N. 135, 137, 144
Katzenstein, P. J. 91
Kennett, Patricia 46
Kent, A. 236–7
Keohane, Robert 20, 47
Kepel, G. 140, 160
Kesich, V. 91
Khalid/Khaled, Amr 206, 222–3
Khosrokhavar, F. 138, 145, 228
Kille, K. J. 40
Kirill 58, 61, 77–8, 85–6, 95
Klass, M. 236
Klaus, Byron D. 180
Kleist, N. 250
Klinkhammer, G. 208
Komitee Marokkaanse Arbeiders in Nederland (KMAN) 131
Koran 138, 205; *see also* Qu'ran, Qur'an
Kratochwil, Gabriele 116, 118, 120
Kruijf, J. G. de 217–19, 226
Kumasi 246, 248–9, 251–7, 261–2, 264–6
Kurien, P. A. 171
Kurtz, L. 27–8, 82

laïcité 115, 166, 168
Lakatos, P. 88, 90
Lancaster, Roger N. 181
Landman, N. 251
Lantos, Tom 24–5
Lashkar-e-Taiba 25
latching 238, 241–2
Latin America 24, 151–2, 157, 165, 180–1, 186–8, 194
Lawrence, Babb 237
Lebanon 29–30, 133, 138–9, 142–3, 213

Index 315

Lee, R. L. M. 237
Lee, Timothy S. 182
Lehmann, David 183
Lemopoulos, G. 97
Leustean, L. N. 84
Levitt, Peggy 79, 232
Lewis, Jeffrey W. 141, 143
liberalism 12, 22, 156
liberation theology 12, 180–1
Lindhardt, Martin 184
Lipman, Jonathan N. 112–13
localisation 150, 197, 200, 212, 216–19, 221, 226
longue durée 116, 118, 150
Lorenz, Chris 118, 121, 125
LTTE (*Liberation Tigers of Tamil Eelam*) 139
Lubbers, Marcel 129
Luckmann, Thomas 74, 174
Luhmann, N. 164
Lyotard, J.-F. 160, 170

Macar, E. 94
MacInnis, D. E. 101, 112
Maddy-Weitzman, Bruce 124, 130
Madeley, John T. S. 185
Mahmood, S. 210, 215, 229
Makrides, V. N. 83, 85, 91
Maliepaard, Marieke 129
Māliki 199, 261
Māliki school of law 199
Mandaville, Peter 151, 154, 196–7, 215, 222
marketplace 27, 155
Marshall, Ruth 183
Martin, Bernice 153, 180, 184
Marty, M. E. 160
martyrdom 10, 17, 132–8, 140–6; offensive 134, 137–41; passive 134, 140
martyrologists 143
Massey, D. 221–2
Maxwell, David 153, 194
Mazzucato, V. 249–50, 255, 266
Mbiti, J. S. 257
McCarthy, S. 113
McCutcheon, R. T. 159
McDougall, James 115
McGres, Anthony 81
McGuire, M. 162, 174
McKinley, Blaine 134, 146
McLeod, H. 158
McMurray, David A. 119, 131
mediation 40, 106, 176, 243, 252

mediator 13, 252
megachurch 182, 185, 188–9, 194
Meinhof, Ulrike 136
memory 10, 59, 75, 97, 114, 116, 118, 124–5, 129–30, 140, 172; memory work 124
Merari, A. 132–3, 142, 146
Merdjanova, I. 89
metanoia 87
Methodism 190
Methodist 180, 182, 248, 261–2; Pentecostal Church 96, 182–4, 190, 194
Metropolitan 77, 86
Meulen, M. van der 250
Meyendorff, J. 83
Meyer, B. 152, 156, 256–7, 259
Mezran, Karim 121
Micklethwait, John 180
Middle East and North Africa (MENA) 21, 28–9, 35, 130
migrant 10, 14, 16, 115–18, 127, 129, 131, 213, 226–7, 255
migration 1, 3, 9–10, 16, 57, 59, 80, 84, 90–3, 97, 116–17, 121–5, 127–8, 131, 157, 159, 161, 171, 173, 177, 189, 193–4, 209, 213, 215, 218–19, 221, 231, 246, 264
military 12, 17, 30, 42, 47, 119, 132–4, 137–8, 143, 158
Millward, J. A. 112
minzu 104–6, 112–13
missionary 83, 90, 108, 166, 180, 182, 190, 194, 201, 246–7
Mitchell, J. 256
MJD (*Muslimische Jugend in Deutschland*) 212, 214–18, 220, 222–8
Moberg, D. O. 82
modernity 10–11, 18, 47, 57–60, 73–9, 85, 88, 99, 116, 132, 145–6, 149, 155, 158, 187, 189, 191–2, 195, 220, 224–5, 229, 233, 244–5; models of 58; religious 10, 57, 149, 153; Western 15, 57–8, 75–6; multiple modernities 14, 18, 57, 170, 232, 245
Moghadam, A. 132–3, 140, 143
Moors, A. 222
Morocco 16, 28, 31, 114–17, 119–21, 123–4, 126, 128–31, 213
Mouvement Populaire 121

MRE (*Marocains résidents à l'étranger*) 123–4, 128, 131
multiculturalism 157, 161, 184, 200, 234
Mungiu-Pippidi, A. 96
Muntean, A. 88, 90, 95
Murphet, H. 236
Muslim 3, 11, 15–16, 23, 25–6, 28–33, 35–6, 94, 98–113, 115, 131, 133, 140, 144, 149, 151, 153–5, 157, 168, 177–8, 189, 194, 196–7, 199, 202–3, 206, 208–15, 217–28, 236, 251–2, 264, 266; Brotherhood 100; women 4, 155, 196–9, 202, 205–8, 210, 212, 221
Muslimahs 196, 199–200, 202–3, 206, 208
Muslims 4, 10–11, 16, 22–4, 28, 32–3, 98, 101, 103, 105–13, 116, 140, 143–4, 154–5, 157–8, 168, 172, 177–8, 196, 198, 203, 206–23, 225–8, 248–51, 254, 256, 260–1, 264–5; European 154–5, 198
myth 10, 55, 114, 116, 118, 120–4, 130, 146, 247; Berber 119, 121, 124

Nadrani, Mohamed 126
Nagel, A. 236
nationalism 4, 9, 16, 29, 89, 91, 93–4, 115–16, 124, 130, 149–50, 160, 168, 172, 183, 187–8
nation building 98, 122
neoliberalism 11, 51, 149, 184
Netherlands, the 10, 16, 69, 78, 114–17, 122–31, 156–7, 172, 236, 246, 248–51, 255–6, 266
New Religions 185, 189
Niebuhr, Reinhold 43, 53, 55
Nieswald, B. 250
non-state actors 13, 19, 21, 41–2, 45–7
non-Western 2, 12, 18–19, 33, 58–60, 78, 130, 149, 230, 232–3, 244, 249
Nora, Pierre 125
normativity 196
Norris, Pippa 94
Northern Ireland 136–7, 142
Nussbaum, M. 231, 234
Nye, J. 21, 47
Nyman, M. 36

Oha, O. 257
Olick, Jeffrey 125
Olwig, K. F. 97

ontologies 235, 243
Orientalism 22–4
Orientalist 22–3, 167
Orthodox 14, 57–63, 65–6, 68–77, 80, 82–7, 89–97, 105, 202–4, 207–8, 248, 251; Christianity 10, 57, 59–60, 76, 80, 82, 85, 92–3; Church 14, 57–9, 77, 80, 83–96, 166, 172; products 62–3; religiosity 57, 60, 75; tradition 10, 79, 85, 91, 93, 96; values 57, 59, 65
Overmeyer, D. 99

Pacific Rim 187–8
Pacini, A. 80, 83, 85, 93–4
Padmanaban, R. 239
Palmer, N. 239
Pang, K.-F. 113
Pape, Robert A. 138–41, 143
Patriarch 58, 61, 77, 86–7, 95
Patterson, John 42
Paul, C. 137
Payne, D. P. 83–4, 89
Peace of Westphalia 163
Pedahzur, A. 139
Pedziwiatr, K. 196, 208
Pelkmans, Mathijs 194
Penn, William 40
Penninx, Rinus 127, 131
Pentecostal-Charismatic 248–51, 258–9, 261
Pentecostalism 248–51, 258–9, 261
Perraton, Jonathan 81
Peter, F. 3, 198, 210
Petersen, Douglas 180
Petito, F. 145
PFLP (Popular Front for the Liberation of Palestine) 139
Phalet, K. 209
Philippines 12, 188
Pietist 180
Pirenne, Henri 179
Piscatori, J. P. 215, 219–20
PKK (*Partîya Karkerén Kurdîstan*) 139
Platvoet, J. G. 247, 257
pluralisation 2–3, 76, 158, 198, 220
pluralism 10, 14, 22, 25–6, 35–6, 50, 80, 82, 89–90, 93, 156–7, 178, 183–4, 187, 200, 230, 232–4, 239–40, 244
plurality 38, 46, 48, 51–2, 54, 162–4, 171, 178, 233–5, 239, 244
Polak, R. 74

post-secular 160–1, 170–2
post-Westphalian 150–1, 170–3, 175, 177–9
post-Westphalianism 170, 172–3, 175, 179
post-World War II 161, 169
Pouessel, Stéphanie 116–18
PRC 99–102, 104
Protestant 17, 23, 39, 69, 81, 88, 90, 94, 96, 150, 152, 160, 163, 166–7, 171, 181–2, 185–6, 188–90, 261
Provisional IRA (Irish Republican Army) 136–7
privatisation 2–3, 60, 73–6, 96, 149, 157
proselytism 89–90
public sphere 14, 18, 62, 66, 76, 79, 84, 125, 211, 218, 220; religion into the/religion in the/religion to the/religion from the/religion and the 10, 13, 60, 77, 145, 224, 230–1

Quaker 38, 40–4, 48, 50, 55; movement 42
Quakers 10, 12–13, 37–8, 40–4, 47–50, 53, 55
Qu'ran/Qur'an 217–8/178, 208

RAF (*Rote Armee Fraktion*) 135–6, 142
Ralph, D. 264–5
Ramadan, Tariq 155, 206, 210, 222, 228
Ramet, Sabrina P. 85, 89
Ramji, R. 177
Ranstorp, M. 146
Rapoport, David C. 133–4, 142
rational choice 73, 75, 175
Reagan, Ronald 25–6, 49
Reid, M. A. 257
religiosity 3, 57, 60, 65, 74–5, 78, 101–2, 109, 127, 130, 155, 183, 186, 197–8, 210, 212, 217, 220–2, 224, 226; hybrid 200–1
religious; authority 3, 106, 158, 177, 197–200, 205–10, 215–16, 219–20, 223; change 151, 173, 246, 252, 256, 265–6; discourse 26, 158, 196–7, 220; diversity 161, 171–2; identity 39, 55, 65, 90, 163–5, 185, 189, 203, 207, 209, 246–8, 251, 255, 257, 260–1, 264–6; life 63, 73, 75, 82, 92, 258–60; market 3, 90, 151, 184, 187; movement 1–2, 79, 90, 101, 221, 233–4, 244, 248, 266; networks 10, 15, 98–9; NGOs 10, 13, 37–46, 48–56; organisation 12–13, 19, 26, 82, 94, 101, 152, 181, 185, 212, 226–7, 253; pluralism 10, 14, 80, 82, 89–90, 93, 156, 178, 230, 232–4; resurgence 18, 149–50, 158–9; *see also* charismatic religious movement, modernity
Renaerts, M. 199
resacralisation 160
resistance 1, 11, 14, 17, 26–7, 39, 49, 51, 53, 57, 76–7, 80–1, 101, 119–20, 132, 136
Reuter, C. 138
revivalism 10, 17, 152, 182, 191
revolutionaries 134–5, 142
Reychler, L. 26
Ricolfi, L. 138–9
Rif 16, 114, 117, 122–3, 125–7, 129, 131
Robbins, Joyce 125, 149
Robertson, Roland 25, 45, 93–4, 200
Roma 90, 191
Rosenau, J. N. 46
Roudometof, Victor 79, 83, 88, 93–4
Rousseau, J. J. 165–6
Roy, Olivier 3, 146, 151, 174, 208, 215, 219
Rudolph, S. H. 174
Russia 10, 14, 57–61, 63–4, 69, 74–7, 93, 159, 165, 172, 194

sacred canopy 27–8, 181, 186–7
Sahgal, S. 228
Sai Baba 156–7, 235–9
Sai devotees 234–5, 240–2, 245
Said, Edward 22–3, 25
Salafi 105, 133, 139–40, 142, 144–6
Salvatore, A. 211, 221–2
Sampson, Cynthia 41
Sánchez-Cuenca, I. 133, 135, 137, 142, 144
Sandler, S. 40
Sanktanber, A. 215, 225
Sater, James N. 128
Sathya Sai 156, 230, 233, 235–9, 244
sattvica 240–2
Schiffauer, W. 208
Schrover, Marlou 127, 131
Schwalgin, S. 97

secularisation 1–3, 34, 59–60, 73–6, 85, 87, 89, 96, 98, 100, 132, 145
secularism 2, 13, 127, 129, 131, 151, 166–8, 233
secularist 13–14, 32–3, 129, 149, 153, 172, 230
secularity 1, 10, 57, 129, 158, 168
Sedgwick, M. 144
self-sacrifice 10, 132–7, 140–3, 146
Shah, T. 230
sharia 33, 120
Shavit, U. 251
Sheffer, Gabriel 118
Sicarii 133
Sikhism 24, 167–8, 174
Silverstein, Paul 119, 121, 129, 131
Simmel, Georg 48–9, 165
Slyomovics, Susan 128
SMDN (*Stem Marokkaanse Democraten in Nederland*) 128, 130
Smith, Anthony D. 119, 124
Smith, Steve 81
social assistance 87–8, 95
socialisation 158, 199, 209
soft power 26
sovereignty 45, 51–2, 124, 144, 163
Soviet 11, 29, 77, 83, 104, 107, 112, 160, 186
Spain 24, 69–71, 126, 131, 191, 249
Spickard, James 25
Spielhaus, R. 213, 219, 227
spiritual revolution 160, 179
spirituality 14, 75, 85–7, 151, 153, 169, 174–5, 201, 233
Srinivas, S. 156–7, 230–2, 235–7, 240, 242
Staeheli, L. A. 264–5
Stark, Rodney 78, 159, 175–6
state modernisation 10, 98
Steger, Manfred 44
Stepan, A. 230
Stephens, Randall J. 180
Sternberg, Yitzhak 81
Stiglitz, J. E. 230–1
Stoica, Fr. Dr. I. 86
Stratton, A. 223
Sufi orders 100, 261
Suharto 12, 29, 169
suicide 17, 133–8, 140–6; attack 132–3, 135–41, 143, 146; attacker 143–4
Sweeney, G. 136

symphonia 14, 83, 94; symphonic 58, 76
Szanton Blanc, C. 222
Szilagyi, Georgina 87–8
Szonyi, M. 99
Sztompka, P. 85

Tablighi Jama'at 108–9
Tahtah, Mohamed 122
Tamazight 128, 130
Tambaih, S. J. 232
Tan, Z. 108
Tanasescu, A. I. 96
Tappe, E. 84
Tarifit 126, 130
ter Haar, G. 249–50, 265
terrorism 4, 9, 17, 101, 114, 132–7, 140–6; waves of modern 142
terrorist 24, 135–6, 141, 219; acts 114, 140; attacks 4; intent 17; organisations 132–3, 136–8, 141–3, 145–6; purposes 138, 145; violence 10, 132–3, 137, 145
Thatcher 49, 136
third space 124, 207
Thomas, Scott 40–1, 43, 51, 55
Thompson, D. 194
Thual, F. 83
Tifinagh 126, 128, 130
Tilly, C. 163, 230
Tjomsland, M. 202
Tomka, M. 60, 62, 70–1
Tomlinson, J. 230
Tonah, S. 250
transnational 9, 13–14, 17, 44, 80, 86, 92, 124, 177, 222; actors 13, 26, 79, 91–2; authority 12, 46; corporations 33, 86; faith 152; forces 212, 219, 222; Islam 222, 224; media organisations 9; migration 80, 84, 93, 161, 171, 173, 177, 222; networks 97, 106; NGOs 9, 37, 53, 86; religion 10, 35, 75, 79, 88, 91, 166, 173, 176, 180–195, 212, 235–6, 240, 250; religious authority 155, 166; terrorism 133, 139–40, 144–5; *see also* Roman Catholic Church, voluntarism
transnationalisation 84
transnationalism 91, 176
Triandafyllidou, A. 211
Trigeaud, Sophie-Hélène 50, 54–5

Troeltsch, E. 174
Turkey 29, 31, 36, 133, 212–13, 215, 228
Turner, Bryan S. 22, 79

Ukah, Asonzeh, F. K. 185
ummah 99, 112, 144, 146, 177, 218, 223–4, 227, 229
UN (United Nations) 9–10, 12–13, 37–56
Union national des Etudiants du Maroc 116
Universal Church of the Kingdom of God 181
universalisation 81, 197, 216, 238, 240
universalism 81, 232
universalist 12, 43, 55, 83
Urry, John 45
USA (United States of America) 11, 24–5, 29, 41, 75, 88–9, 91, 97, 149, 152, 155, 159–60, 166–7, 171, 176, 182, 185–6, 194, 223, 235–6, 241
Uyghur 15, 98, 102, 109, 111–12
Uyl, M. den 251

Van Amersfoort, Hans 122
Van der Valk, Ineke 128
Veer, Peter van der 150, 231, 244
Verdery, Katherine 85
Verkuyten, M. 200, 209
Vernooij, J. 251
Vertovec, S. 198, 209, 233
vicarious religion 63, 67–8, 74
Voicu, M. 95
Volkov, D. 83
voluntarism 152, 180, 185–7

Waardenburg, J. 199, 250
Wacker, Grant 182
Wanner, Catherine 194
Warburg, M. 20, 26
Ware, T. 91, 94
Warner, M. 151
Warner, S. 171
Weber, Max 15, 57, 83
Weiss, R. 236
Weiss, T. G. 39
Wendl, T. 257
Werner, Michael 116, 131
Westerlund, D. 159
Western 11, 204; academics (scholars), 23, 149, 167; capitalism 19; churches 58; civilisation 59, 85; colonialism 149; commitment to education 155; context 73, 130, 242; (Judeo-Christian) culture 23, 59, 74, 198, 224, 232, 239; democracy 33, 35, 74; directed 19; domination of Islam 21; Europe 14, 57, 60, 68, 70, 73, 75–6, 89, 96–7, 117, 150–1, 154–5, 162, 172, 185–6, 198, 211; European 57, 71, 74; (European) countries 2, 4, 12, 29, 78, 90, 149, 151, 171–2, 230; European Muslims 154, 208, 211–12; globalisation 22, 232; governments 29; history 129; (neo-)imperialism 11, 25, 33, 187, 232; import of religion 187; influence 59, 81, 87, 96; (neo-)liberalism 11, 156; model of social work 88; modernisation 77; (models/versions of) modernity 15, 57–8, 60, 75–8, 146, 149, 224–5; observers 159; politicians 23, 149; politics 150; power(s) 11–12, 59; principles 11; provenance 27; rationalism 57; (view of) religion 59, 63, 68, 73, 99, 150, 155, 168, 171; religious communities 58, 157; secularity 129, 149, 230, 232; security 31; social organisation 58; (European) society (societies) 3, 18, 58, 75, 153, 162, 197, 199, 225, 252; societal problems 199; thought 25; treatment of Muslims 112; values 21–4, 57, 59, 85, 93, 116, 130, 232; views of suicide attacks 146; world 3, 19, 258; *see also* anti-Western, anti-Westernism, church-state relations, non-Western
Western China 15, 104, 108
Western Mexico 190
Western Ukraine 186
Westerners 258
Westernisation 85
Westernising 19
Westphalia/Westphalian 41, 51, 145, 150–1, 162–79, 185–6; *see also* post-Westphalianism
Wijst, H. van der 255
Willetts, Peter 39

women; believing 153; Berber 120, 127; Moroccan 128, 155, 198–9; Muslim 4, 155–6, 197–209; and Pentecostalism 183, 189, 192; young 155–6, 190, 215, 219–21, 224, 227
women's; associations 127, 202; clothing 172; organisations in Morocco 128; rights 128, 30; spaces of Mosques 202; *see also* Timazighin
Woodhead, Linda 54, 75, 233, 236
Woods, Ngaire 47
Woodward, Kathryn 115
Wooldridge, Adrian 180
World Islamic Mission 251
World Value Study 70–1, 78, 94
World War I 20, 29, 97
World War II 20, 40–1, 97, 146, 173; *see also* post-World War II
Wright, M. 257
Wuthnow, R. 158

Yang, F. 171
Yang, M. M. 99
Yang, Z. 107–8

Yarrow, Mike 40–1
Yazigi, P. 86
Young, L. A. 175
Young, Marion 52
Young, Robert J. C. 124
youth 201, 214, 222; culture 212, 221, 223–6; Hui 102; employment 31; female 212, 214, 219–22, 225; migrant 227; Moroccan 16, 115–16, 127, 129, 223–4; Muslim 154–5, 212, 214–29, 251; in Flanders 155; organisations 128, 214, 253; (un)veiled 220, 225
youth's; socioprofessional reintegration 88; religiosity 212, 220, 222, 224–5

Zemni, S. 22
Zerubavel, Eviatar 125
Ziani, Ahmed 127
Zimmermann, Bénédicte 116, 131
Zionism/Zionist 13, 33, 150, 160, 167
Zondervan, T. 201, 209
Zulehner, Paul, M. 59–60, 62, 70–1, 73–4